How to Hike the North Country Trail
~~not quite~~ a Guide

by Joan H. Young
two-time end-to-end hiker of the NCT
30-year volunteer on the NCT

copyright © 2024 Joan H. Young

all rights reserved
booksleavingfootprints.com

ISBN 978-1-948910-10-1

The author of this book can not be held liable for incorrect or incomplete information. At time of publication, this information is believed to be correct. As the book ages, regulations may change, and businesses change hands or close. Always check critical information personally.

cover photo of South Lake on the Border Route Trail section of the NCT, by Joan H. Young

author photo provided by Rob Alway, Mason County Press

10 9 8 7 6 5 4 3 2

This book was suggested to me by Matt Rowbotham, the GIS Program Manager of the NCTA. I turned him down cold. But the next day, he convinced me that this would be a worthy and easy project. He was half right! It is noteworthy that Matt is still working for the NCTA after 20 years, and his skills have resulted in the excellent and easily available maps the NCTA now offers.

Thank you to the following people who helped with fact-checking and proofreading this text. These are almost all people who have been associated with the North Country Trail over significant periods of time, either in a professional capacity or as volunteers. Several have hiked significant portions of the trail, and many are present or former NCTA staff. All are volunteers who love the North Country Trail. I am proud to call each of them a friend.

Marie Altenau, Derek Blount, Nancy Brozek, Dave Brewer, Mary Coffin, Bill Courtois, Jean Davis, Matt Davis, Ruth Dorrough (end-to-ender), Marianne Duvendack, Paul Gagnon, Tom Gilbert, Joyce Hodgson, Lorana Jinkerson, Lauren Kennedy-Little, Andrea Ketchmark, Bobby Koepplin, Chris Loudenslager, Richard Lutz, Bill Menke, April Miller, Tom Moburg, Annie Nelson, Bob Papp, Randall Roberts, Matt Rowbotham, Kevin Schramm, Jerry Warner, Kenny Wawsczyk.

At the end of this immense project, of course, any remaining errors are mine alone.

How to use this book: Mark it up, tear it apart so you can carry sections, grumble about errors. But above all, camp legally! And please report errors/changes so the next edition will be better. See explorenct.info/explorenct.info/CorrectionsHHNCT.htm for live links of all web sites in appendix, and other links are being added.
Joan- jhyshark@gmail.com

Dedicated

to all the employees and volunteers who have spent countless hours working to make the North Country Trail the "premier trail of them all."

Psalm 18:36, "Broaden the path before me so that my ankles do not turn."

Table of Contents

Introduction 1

Foreword by Bill Menke 3

History and Info
    What is a National Scenic Trail? 5
    Can you name a National Scenic Trail? 5
    Authorization language 6
    History of the NCT 6
    National Trails Act of 1968 7
    Route of the NCT 8

List of National Scenic Trails and Brief Descriptions 10

Why is the NCT unique? 12

Who has responsibility for the NCT?
    National Park Service 15
    North Country Trail Association 16
        NCTA Staff and Headquarters 17
        Board of Directors 18
        Volunteers 18
            Chapters 19
            Affiliates 19
            Partners 19
    Partnership for the National Trails System 19
    Landowners 20
        Federal Agencies 20
            USDA Forest Service 20
            National Park Service 21
            Army Corps of Engineers 21
            US Fish and Wildlife Service 21
            Bureau of Reclamation 21
            McClusky Diversion Project 22
            A Note about Federal Wilderness 22
        Native Nation Lands 23
        State Ownership 23
            State Forests 23
            Adirondack Park 24
            State Wildlife Management Areas 24
            State Parks 24
            State Game Areas 25
            Other 25
        Local Governments 25

- Organizations ... 26
  - Private ... 26
- Management ... 27
- Land Protection ... 29
- Funding ... 31
- Early Hikers of the NCT ... 33
- Planning Your Hike Experience ... 35
  - What to Expect ... 35
    - General Information ... 35
      - History ... 35
      - Economy ... 36
      - Geology ... 36
      - Flora and Fauna ... 36
      - Terrain ... 37
      - Connections with Other Trails ... 37
    - North Dakota ... 38
    - Minnesota ... 41
    - Wisconsin ... 45
    - Michigan- general ... 48
    - Upper Peninsula ... 48
    - Lower Peninsula ... 51
    - Ohio ... 55
    - Pennsylvania ... 59
    - New York ... 62
    - Vermont ... 67
  - Trail Conditions ... 69
    - Maintenance ... 69
      - Who Does the Work? ... 70
      - What Can Go Wrong? ... 70
      - What You May Find ... 71
      - How You Can Help ... 71
    - Treadway ... 71
    - Drinking Water ... 72
    - Trail Structures ... 72
    - Safety and Safe Practices ... 74
      - Hazards ... 74
      - Safe Practices ... 75
    - Trail Closures ... 77
    - Permits ... 78
    - Dogs ... 79
    - Other Resources ... 80
  - How to Find Your Way ... 80
    - Blazes ... 80
      - NCT Blazes ... 81
      - Superior Hiking Trail ... 82
      - Buckeye Trail Blazes ... 82
      - Finger Lakes Trail Blazes ... 83
      - Long Trail ... 83
      - Turns and More ... 84

    More Confusion 84
    Purple Blazes 85
    Just for Fun 85
   Maps and Guides 86
    History of Maps and Guides 86
    Current Maps 87
    What Maps Do You Need? 88
     Interactive GIS Map 89
     Paper Maps 92
     Electronic Maps 93
    Current Guides and Data Books 96
    Bonus Section 97
     Pictured Rocks 97
     Adirondacks 97
     Vermont 97
    Websites 97
  When Should You Begin a Hike? 98
  Trail Angels and Support 99
   Chapters and Affiliates 99
   Shuttle Options 102
   Self Support 103
  Day Hikes vs. Backpacking 103
  How to Complete an E2E 104
   What is a Thru-Hike? 104
   What is a Section Hike? 104
   Planning for Supply Drops 105
   Planning for Overnights 105
   Weather 106
   Projecting Average Mileages 106
   The Mental Challenge 107
  Where to Camp/Stay 107
   Definitions 107
   Legend 112
   North Dakota 117
   Minnesota 141
   Wisconsin 212
   Michigan- Upper Peninsula 229
   Michigan- Lower Peninsula 263
   Ohio 299
   Pennsylvania 358
   New York 380
   Vermont 435

Appendix 439

Published Works by Joan H. Young 446

About the Author 447

Introduction

This book will serve as an aid in planning a long hike, but it is not a guide. A guide would include such things as water sources, nearby towns with possible re-supply options, public transportation options, all trail junctions, major turns, parking, etc.

It is impossible to understand why the management policies and regulations along the North Country Trail vary so much without understanding the history of how this trail came to be. Therefore, a large portion of this text seeks to clarity that history.

The primary objective of this book is to help potential long-distance hikers understand why it is so important to camp legally along the NCT, and to provide hikers with a list of known legal camping/lodging locations. Of course, this list must be qualified by saying that it is ever-changing, and no list will be 100% accurate for longer than, probably, ten minutes.

There have been several attempts to write a guidebook for the North Country Trail, with varying degrees of success.

One difficulty in collecting and printing a detailed list of junctions, waypoints, and resources is the sheer immensity of the trail. Michigan alone has more miles of the NCT than many "long" trails. A guide would need to be presented in volumes rather than a single book.

Alternatively, a guide might be created online. This would be easy to edit as changes were needed. However, this raises the question of who would do this maintenance. A couple of variations on this format have been tried over the years. The primary outcome has been to conclude that keeping such a document updated would be a full-time job. Crowd-sourcing (a wiki) was attempted, and was subject to a great deal of misinformation, requiring a full-time moderator.

Additionally, the NCT is as yet much too fluid to create a definitive guide to all the miles. It would be out of date before it ever came off the presses. New miles are continually being moved off road or to more sustainable or scenic locations.

This unsettled state of the trail is likely to be a reality for many years, perhaps forever, due to the pattern of land ownership and management along the trail. This will be more fully discussed in Land

Ownership and Management.

The early sections of this book cover some brief history and the administration and management of the trail. Reading this material will reveal the underlying reasons why this trail is so different from some others.

Again, this is NOT a guide. It does not include water sources, off-trail resources in towns, mileages between a variety of types of waypoints, elevations, access points, or lengthy descriptions of segments. However, the second section of this book is an attempt to compile information about legal camping and some info about other lodging opportunities in towns. Google and other web-based mapping resources are likely to have current information about motels and restaurants.

This is a trail to be sampled and savored. Those who are interested in genuinely experiencing the various ecosystems and cultural neighborhoods through which the trail passes might be advised to take on the trail as a section hike. This allows time to visit local museums, read interpretive signs, hunt for interesting trees or geological evidence, or rare plants. On the other hand, to thru-hike the trail is a challenge of a different kind. The sheer length of the trail is daunting. To hike 4800 miles with only some short breaks takes a type of mental stamina that is hard to grasp until it is attempted.

Foreword

Each of us has known influencers. Throughout my career, I have met many interesting and dedicated people, especially within my long involvement with the North Country National Scenic Trail and the North Country Trail Association.

One of these people is definitely Joan Young. Throughout the NCT community, Joan is known for her many years of involvement. She was the first woman to hike the entire North Country Trail, doing section hikes spanning two decades. In fact, my first awareness of Joan was following one of her earliest hikes, when she wrote to tell me about some of her findings (at that time, I was the NPS Trail Manager). We have been friends ever since.

You would think that completing the longest of all of the National Scenic Trails would be reward enough for anyone. Not for Joan. She knew that the trail had constantly evolved after her first hike, and she wanted to see those updates and experience the call of a long hike once again—this time as a continuous end-to-end hike, from Dec 2021- June 2023.

Joan has previously written and published *North Country Cache* and *North Country Quest*. These are informative and entertaining experience-based stories of her section hikes, not day-to-day journals. She is author of the Anastasia Raven cozy mysteries, Dubois Files children's mysteries, and more.

This book is a well-written and thorough offering for anyone who aspires to hike long distances on the trail. While not claiming to be a "guide book," *How to Hike the North Country Trail* is extremely comprehensive. It will help you understand the many complexities of hiking a 4,800-mile long trail and why uniform regulations along the entire length of the trail do not exist. In addition, it will thus help you understand that some time and effort is required to adequately plan a long hike.

Bill Menke

Former NPS Trail Manager and NCTA Regional Trail Coordinator

History and Info

What Is a National Scenic Trail?

National Scenic Trails are a special designation of long-distance trail, authorized by Congress under the National Trails Act of 1968, the purpose of which is to showcase locations of national significance. "Long-distance" is generally accepted to mean more than 100 miles in length. They are primarily for quiet recreational use, however, portions of the Continental Divide Trail are currently open to motorized vehicles, and portions of other trails, even non-certified sections of the NCT, are open for snowmobile or ATV use where the trail coincides with multi-use routes.

The Trails for America Report of 1966 stated, "Each National Scenic Trail should stand out in its own right as a recreation resource of superlative quality and of physical challenge."

The attempt to create a network of national trails was spearheaded by a US Senator from Wisconsin, Gaylord Nelson.

Can You Name a National Scenic Trail?

The first trail that pops into the minds of most people if you ask them to name a long trail would be the Appalachian Trail (AT). This is no surprise, since it was dreamed up in 1921, and literally thousands of people have hiked its entire length. Certainly tens of thousands have walked parts. Hundreds of books about the experience have been written by these hikers. Eastern mountains, green forests, and rocks are the dominant images.

The next two most familiar long trails are likely the Pacific Crest and Continental Divide Trails (PCT and CDT). As their names imply, these trails follow mountain ranges. More images of rocks and mountains appear in the mind's eye, although these western peaks are raw and brown.

These mental pictures have invaded our thinking to the point that it's tempting to think that rocks, mountains, cliffs, and waterfalls are what nationally important trails are all about.

This is a misconception that can lead to low-quality experiences on other trails. Many types of landscapes and experiences bring enjoyment, particularly if a hiker looks for unique local qualities rather than discounting anything that isn't rocky or filled with wild water.

Authorization Language

The National Trails Act of 1968 states, "National scenic trails are to be continuous, extended routes of outdoor recreation within protected corridors."

Section 3 (2) is worded: "National scenic trails, established as provided in section 5 of this Act, ...will be extended trails so located as to provide for maximum outdoor recreation potential and for the conservation and enjoyment of the nationally significant scenic, historic, natural, or cultural qualities of the areas through which such trails may pass. National scenic trails may be located so as to represent desert, marsh, grassland, mountain, canyon, river, forest, and other areas, as well as landforms which exhibit significant characteristics of the physiographic regions of the Nation."

History of the NCT

In 1966, the Department of the Interior, Bureau of Outdoor Recreation, prepared a document entitled "Trails for America." This report outlined the need for a system of pathways closed to motorized use for the enjoyment and health of people who desire to walk/hike, bicycle, and ride horses.

At the time of the report, many potential trails were identified. No labels such as Scenic, Historic, or Recreational were applied at the time. These designations came later.

The North Country Trail (NCT) is specifically mentioned in this report.

An east-west North Country Trail would provide millions of people with excellent opportunities for trail experiences: "opportunities now available chiefly to those living in the West and in the mountainous areas of the East. More than one-half of the Nation's population lives within half a day's drive of the projected trail route."

National Trails Act of 1968

The eventual outcome of that study was the National Trails Act, signed into existence by Lyndon B. Johnson on October 2, 1968. Established by that Act were National Scenic, National Historic and National Recreation Trails.

Generally speaking, National Scenic trails are designed for hiking and sometimes other non-motorized uses. Historic trails are collections of locations along transportation routes of the past. Recreation trails are shorter routes which meet certain qualifications but help to connect people with outdoor recreational opportunities; they may allow motorized uses.

The first two National Scenic Trails were designated at that time: the Appalachian and Pacific Crest Trails.

National Historic Trails are collections of locations associated with a specific transportation route of the past. Some are loosely connected by roads or pathways such that they can be walked or bicycled, but primarily the intention is that people will drive to the individual sites where interpretation is present, and some restored structures, replicas, or other evidence of the original journey is preserved. A familiar example is the Lewis and Clark Trail which includes places such as Fort Clatsop, Oregon; St. Louis, Missouri; and Fort Mandan, North Dakota. Readers familiar with the North Country Trail will be aware that the NCT intersects with the Lewis and Clark Trail very near the NCT's western terminus at Lake Sakakawea. Hikers can stand on the banks of the Missouri River just a few miles north of Fort Mandan and gaze on the same dark Black Hills as did Lewis and Clark in 1802.

The designation of National Recreation Trail may be given to an existing trail that provides connections to other trails for various kinds of recreation. They may be motorized. There are over 1300 such trails, and some are longer than some National Scenic or Historic Trails. For example, the Florida Circumnavigational Saltwater Paddling Trail is 1500 miles long, and the Hatfield-McCoy Trail System in West Virginia has 500 miles of trails for both motorized and non-motorized use on natural surfaces. At the other end of the length spectrum, the Anderson Road Fitness Trail in Tennessee is a paved trail, only a mile long. The Elk Creek Falls Trail in Idaho's Clearwater National Forest is an old two-mile-long wagon road where people may walk, bicycle, and ride horses. It provides access to the tallest waterfall in Idaho, and skiing and snowshoeing are popular in season.

A link to the Recreational Trails database is provided in the Appendix.

Route of the NCT

The North Country Trail was designed to maximize the off-road and scenic potential of roughly the eastern half of the northern United States. The projected map presented to Congress was literally on an 8 ½ " by 11" sheet of paper, was estimated to be 3200 miles, and would extend from the Appalachian Trail in Vermont to the Lewis and Clark Trail in North Dakota.

Soon after the original study, the NCT was denied the eastern extension into Vermont to connect with the Appalachian Trail. However, as time has passed the emphasis on making connections between trails has increased. The hope never died that the NCT would eventually meet the AT.

Also, early on, developers realized that a relatively straight route from Duluth to Grand Rapids, Minnesota, was impractical to build as it traversed 60 miles of cedar swamp. In the 1980s, the Superior Hiking Trail was being built to follow the north shore of Lake Superior. The Border Route Trail, extending from Grand Portage at the tip of Minnesota's Arrowhead westward to the Gunflint Trail (a road) was established in the 1970s by the Minnesota Rovers Outing Club. From the Gunflint Trail, the Kekekabic Trail, originally a fire trail, continues and ends a bit shy of Ely, Minnesota. Prior to 2000, these three trails and a potential route on the back side of the Arrowhead were agreed upon as a more scenic route than the straight line from Duluth to Grand Rapids. Since so many miles of these trails were established, the supporting organizations and agencies embraced this idea. However, a change of this magnitude required Congressional approval.

In 2019, with passage of the John D. Dingell, Jr. Conservation, Management, and Recreation Act, the Arrowhead Reroute and the Vermont Extension officially became part of the North Country Trail.

The trail is currently over 4800 miles long, and as more portions come off road, that total will only increase.

List of National Scenic Trails and Brief Descriptions

The national scenic trails, in order of establishment with approximate mileages are:

Appalachian Trail, 1968: extends from Georgia to Maine. This is the oldest (as proposed in 1921 by Benton MacKaye), best known, and most hiked of the NSTs. 2200 miles. Abbreviated AT.

Pacific Crest Trail, 1968: extends from Mexico to Canada across California, Oregon, and Washington. 2650 miles. Abbreviated PCT.

Continental Divide Trail, 1978: extends from Mexico to Canada along the primary Continental Divide. 3200 miles. Abbreviated CDT.

(The above three trails are often referred to as the Triple Crown.)

North Country Trail, 1980: extends from Vermont to North Dakota and is the subject of this book. 4800 miles. Abbreviated NCT.

Ice Age Trail, 1980: entirely within Wisconsin and traces the southernmost extent of the most recent glaciation. 1000 miles. Abbreviated IAT.

Florida Trail, 1980: entirely within Florida and extends from near Miami to the coast of the Florida panhandle. 1500 miles. Abbreviated FT.

Potomac Heritage Trail, 1983: generally follows the Potomac River through Pennsylvania to Virginia, with numerous branches. 700 miles. Abbreviated PHT.

Natchez Trace Trail, 1983: follows an historic native pathway through Mississippi and Tennessee. The hikeable portions are disconnected, and it is still primarily a vehicular parkway. 64 miles. Abbreviated NTT.

Pacific Northwest Trail, 2009: connects the Continental Divide to the Pacific Ocean, through Montana, Idaho, and Washington. 1200 miles. Abbreviated PNT.

Arizona Trail, 2009: crosses Arizona from south to North, from the Mexican border to Utah, traversing many of the state's varied ecosystems. 800 miles. Abbreviated AZT.

New England Trail, 2009: stretches from Long Island Sound to the New Hampshire border through Massachusetts and Connecticut. 200 miles. Abbreviated NET.

Although not a National Scenic Trail, the **American Discovery Trail** is worthy of note because of its length. It is a route that crosses the entire United States and incorporates portions of many other trails, including the North Country and Buckeye Trails. The western terminus is in Point Reyes National Seashore, California, and the eastern end is located at Cape Henlopen State Park on the Atlantic Ocean in Delaware. The route was conceived by the American Hiking Society with an event called HikeANation. In 1980 to 1981 people hiked from one coast to the other. Several people who also became involved with the NCT participated in this walk. It is under consideration as a National Scenic Trail, but currently many parts of the route are also open to vehicular traffic. Abbreviated ADT.

Why Is the NCT Unique?

Perhaps the most obvious difference between the North Country and the other National Scenic Trails is its length.

The trails commonly referred to as the big three, the AT, CDT, and PCT, roughly follow mountain ridges; each are between 2000 and 3500 miles in length. Four more of the eleven are under 1000 miles each: the Potomac Heritage, New England, Arizona, and Natchez Trace Trails. The Florida, Ice Age, and Pacific Northwest Trails are between 1000 and 1500 miles long. At 4800 miles and growing, the NCT is clearly the challenge in the mileage department. The NCT traverses terrain in four of the six major watersheds of North America.

Many of the NSTs have an identifying natural feature. The north-south mountain ranges have already been mentioned. The Arizona, Florida, and Ice Age Trails are each confined to a single state. Additionally, the IAT follows the southern extent of the Wisconsin glaciation.

The Natchez Trace Trail derives its identity from a Native American trail which was then used as a trade route by European settlers. It is often confused with the Natchez Trace Parkway, a vehicular road which also follows this historic route.

The Pacific Northwest and New England Trails clearly are associated with a particular region of the country. Even people who know little of geography have some mental images of New England and the Pacific Northwest.

One might wonder why the Natchez Trace and Potomac Heritage Trails were not established as National Historic Trails. This is a valid question, but the discussion is outside the scope of this book.

However, "north country" is a more ambiguous descriptor. The phrase may bring to mind such images as rivers, rocks, evergreen trees, snow, eagles, moose and bear. These perceptions would not be wrong, but there is much more to the NCT than these generalized ideas.

Small-town cultures are as much part of the NCT experience as

Pictured Rocks or the high cliffs of the Border Route segment. The trail passes through hundreds of small towns, even ghost towns. This is markedly different from the AT, where the norm is that you must leave the trail to find civilization and supplies. The large metropolitan areas of Duluth, MN; Battle Creek, MI; and Dayton, OH, host the NCT on urban pathways.

Partly due to the great length, varied ecosystems are encountered: prairies, coteaus, escarpments, glacial outwash plains, volcanically built mountains, the Great Lakes, edges of the Appalachian Mountain range, rivers, marshes, bogs, and fens. Historic uses of the land may be showcased: logging, mining, farming. Logging and farming are still actively observed in many locations along the trail, and in some instances limited mining is also a current activity. Dozens of historic transportation routes are part of the NCT: Native American trails, pioneer routes, stagecoach roads, the National Road (Cumberland Road), canals, numerous railways, and even aviation history are to be found along the NCT.

The varied ecosystems are often determined by the local geology. Was the area glaciated? What mountain building events or eras of erosion created the current topography? What is the underlying rock? How much erosion or shifting has occurred?

This is a trail with a prairie component; very few foot trails traverse so many miles of historic prairie grasslands. Maintaining treadways in tall grass is completely different from doing so in woodlands, involving serious mowing. Marking can also be a challenge.

Because of these many ecosystems, the NCT is rich in diverse plant life. Northeastern woodlands are the dominant habitats, but fens, bogs, prairies, and even alpine niches can be found.

The National Trails Act, as mentioned earlier, charges National Scenic Trails to conserve and showcase diverse national treasures. The vision statement of the North Country Trail Association echoes those words, stating, "Our vision for the North Country National Scenic Trail is that of a premier footpath of national significance, offering a superb experience for hikers and backpackers in a permanently protected corridor, traversing and interpreting the *richly diverse environmental, cultural, and historic features of the northern United States*." (emphasis mine)

In this author's opinion, no other National Scenic Trail fulfills the Act's mandate as well as the North Country Trail.

Precisely because the NCT passes through so many small towns, rural areas, cities, and diverse ecosystems, it brings hikers into contact with unfamiliar lifestyles, intriguing tales from history, diverse geology, and plants and animals unique to particular habitats.

The NCT is a trail to be explored at a pace which allows for taking in the diversity of possible experiences. If hiking fast is most important to a person, then a great deal of the scenic, cultural and historic value is going to be lost.

Who Has Responsibility for the NCT?

No one entity carries the complete burden of caring for the North Country Trail. The National Park Service is our federal manager. The mission of the NCTA is to "develop, maintain, protect and promote" the trail. But also within that same statement appear the words "through a coalition of volunteers and partners."

National Park Service

All National Scenic Trails are administered either by the USDA Forest Service (FS), the Bureau of Land Management (BLM) or the National Park Service (NPS). The NCT was assigned to the Park Service to be managed in the same manner as a National Park.

The NPS provides financial assistance (as appropriated by Congress) and coordinates with states, agencies, and partner organizations. It oversees planning, certification, and interpretation of the trail. It coordinates volunteer efforts at a national level and ensures that projects are done in accordance with regulations. The NPS provides safety training and equipment, offers protection for volunteers (liability), and awards individuals for volunteer service at levels from 100 to 10,000 hours. Each year, these hours are totaled, assigned a monetary value, and used to leverage funds for the trail.

Government policies lead to many difficulties for trails. National Parks encompass thousands to millions of acres. The smallest traditional National Park is the Gateway Arch of St. Louis with 90 acres. All but three have over 10,000 acres and 40 are over 100,000 acres. The NPS, on behalf of the NCT, now owns 281 acres. Any appropriations that are made to Parks based on how much land they must manage are going to leave the NCT out in the cold.

When asked how much infrastructure the NCT owns and must maintain, the answer is also revealing. There is not even a complete inventory of shelters, bridges, puncheon, benches, outhouses, stairways, stiles, or register boxes along the length of the trail. And who owns them? They were built with money from various sources which may include Congressional appropriations, grants, donations, and other private funds. Do they belong to the manager/owner of the land on which they are located, or do they belong to the NPS or the NCTA? Some were built by volunteers; larger structures might have been professionally contracted or built by volunteers working with a larger agency such as the Forest Service. This question has no clear answer.

Yet, as an estimate, 4800 miles of trail with a 10-foot right-of-way would mean that **at least** 5800 acres of land in eight states with eight different legal structures must be overseen in some capacity. This number is a bare minimum. The AT corridor is considered a half-mile wide, 528 times this 10-foot suggestion.

It's an immense task with few easy answers.

The first National Park Service Superintendent of the North Country Trail was Thomas Gilbert, who was also charged with superintending the Ice Age Trail and the Lewis and Clark Trail. Gilbert remained with the NCT for 30 years, until his retirement. This provided great stability as the organization grew and the trail was being planned and built.

The Trail Manager for the NPS was Bill Menke, hired in 1992, another familiar name in NCT circles. His job included route planning and setting standards for certification of trail.

Tom and Bill have left a legacy of excellence in leadership and trail standards to which we all still aspire. It is noteworthy that both men still volunteer for the NCT even in retirement.

Currently, the NPS has six staff members dedicated to the needs of the North Country Trail, and the Superintendent is Chris Loudenslager.

North Country Trail Association

The North Country Trail Association was founded one year after the NCT was authorized by Congress on March 5, 1980. It was established on March 28, 1981, as a 501(c)(3) non-profit organization. Its mission is and has always been to develop, maintain, protect, and promote the North Country National Scenic Trail.

NCTA Staff and Headquarters

Initially, the Association had no paid staff. All duties were accomplished by volunteers.

In 1981, Ginny Wunsch of White Cloud, MI, a board member, was able to purchase the former Birch Grove School near White Cloud, Michigan, for a dollar. The building was in poor shape, but Ginny and Peter Wolfe (see Early NCT Hikers) set to restoring the school to create a home for the NCTA.

All requests for information about the trail were answered by Ginny with hand-written letters. There were no maps. Indeed, the trail was still in the comprehensive planning stages.

The first issue of a newsletter was published in Winter 1981-82 under the name "North Country Trailblazer." John Hipps was the volunteer editor. The first national conference was in 1982, held in Yellow Springs, Ohio.

In 1992, the NCTA hired its first Executive Director, April Scholtz, and soon thereafter, part-time office help was added. Tiffany Halfmann came as a full-time mapping specialist in 2000, and the next position to be created was a Director of Trail Management in 2002. Matt Rowbotham was added in 2004 for IT and additional mapping. Gradually, Regional Trail Directors have been hired until, now, each state has someone who oversees and facilitates the planning and building of trail in that region. Development and marketing personnel were needed to raise funds and promote the trail. Most recently, a position dedicated to land protection has rounded out the staff. The Executive Director at the present time is Andrea Ketchmark. A current staff directory can be seen at northcountrytrail.org/about-us/staff.

Originally, Ginny Wunsch responded to requests for information, with the schoolhouse serving informally as a headquarters. In 1995, office space was acquired in Grand Rapids, first at 3777 Sparks Dr. SE, and then at 49 Pearl Street, right downtown. In 2001 the trail headquarters moved to Lowell, Michigan. The intent of the original founders of the Association was that the headquarters would be located somewhere near the geographic middle of the trail, which is in western Michigan. Also, the most members, both then and now, live in Michigan. This makes sense because Michigan also has the most miles of the Trail. The Lowell office is only a half-block off the trail, and many hikers stop by.

In 2009, responsibility for the NCT, Lewis and Clark, and Ice Age Trails was split. Our NPS staff no longer has to be shared. The NPS office for the NCT then also moved to Lowell. This facilitates much easier cooperation between the NPS and the NCTA.

Board of Directors

The Association is governed by a board of directors whose first president was Lance Feild. He was also member #1 to pay his dues and sign up. Feild came to the NCTA with a strong history of hiking experience. He had been associated with the International Backpackers Association which was absorbed into the American Hiking Society in 1982. Ginny Wunsch was Vice President, and Ken Gackler served as Treasurer.

Since that time, the NCTA has operated continuously under the board leadership of many capable presidents. The decisions of the board guide the staff. Since around 2000, this guidance has been aligned with a strategic plan which provides consistency through the natural turnover of board members and staff.

The structure and makeup of this body has changed greatly over the years, but currently the board uses a governance model. They hire and oversee the Executive Director of the NCTA. They develop and regularly assess progress against the strategic plan. The treasurer oversees the finances of the NCTA and keeps records which are audited as required by law.

The current Board President is Mike Chapple, an at-Large NCTA member.

Volunteers

Over 95% of the actual work of building and maintaining the North Country Trail is done by volunteers. Many years, the volunteers for the North Country Trail log more hours than any other National Scenic or Historic Trail.

A network of 39 Chapters, Affiliates, and Partners covers the length of the trail with only a few gaps remaining.

Chapters

There are thirty Chapters, which are subdivisions of the NCTA. These local groups receive funding through the Association, and individuals spend thousands of hours (over 64,000 hours reported in 2023, worth over $2 million) building, maintaining, and promoting the trail. See complete list later under Trail Angels and Support.

Affiliates

Affiliates are separate organizations that, in most cases, maintain their own trail system, which sometimes includes trail sections that are not part of the NCT. They have entered into a maintenance agreement with the NCTA.

Current affiliates are the Superior Hiking Trail Association, the Border Route Trail Association, the Northwestern Ohio Rails-to-Trails Association, the Buckeye Trail Association, the Rachel Carson Trails Conservancy, the Finger Lakes Trail Conference, the Adirondack Mountain Club, and the Middlebury Area Land Trust.

Partners

The Green Mountain Club of Vermont has chosen to align themselves with the NCTA as a Partner, currently without a maintenance agreement.

Partnership for the National Trails System

The PNTS was formed in 2001 to connect not-for-profit trail organizations that support National Scenic and Historic Trails. It advocates for land preservation and resource protection for the thirty member trails. They coordinate efforts during Hike the Hill, the week dedicated to lobbying in Washington, DC, concerning trail-related legislation. They present a collective voice on issues common to National Scenic and Historic Trails.

Although this organization is not directly responsible for decisions concerning the NCT, the actions of this group have implications for all the National Scenic and Historic Trails.

Landowners

This is not a complete list of landowners who host the trail. However, it will give you a sense of the scope and variety, and may help you understand why the rules vary so much from location to location.

Federal Agencies
USDA Forest Service

The Forest Service is the largest landowner along the North Country Trail. The trail passes through eleven areas managed by the Forest Service, and it hosts more miles of NCT than any other single owner.

- North Dakota: Sheyenne National Grassland
- Minnesota: Chippewa National Forest, Superior National Forest
- Wisconsin: Chequamenon National Forest
- Michigan: Ottawa National Forest, Hiawatha National Forest, Manistee National Forest
- Ohio: Wayne National Forest
- Pennsylvania: Allegheny National Forest
- New York and Vermont: Green Mountain/Finger Lakes National Forest (two units of the same Forest)

Rules for using the trail are mostly consistent in the National Forests. This is the closest you will come to finding corridor management along the NCT. That said, there are a few differences in permitted uses, and you should always check on the local interpretation of regulations.

National Park Service

Pictured Rocks National Lakeshore in Michigan is the most famous NPS property along the NCT. However, the St Crioix National Scenic Riverway in Wisconsin, Huffman Prairie Interpretive Center (Wright Brothers memorial) in Ohio, and Fort Stanwix and Crown Point State Historic sites in New York are also Park Service sites. If you like to collect stamps for your passport to the parks booklet, Pictured Rocks, Huffman Prairie, Fort Stanwix, and Crown Point have visitors' centers along the trail where you can find these. The Brule St-Croix Riverway interpretive center is miles off the trail in St. Croix Falls, Wisconsin.

The National Park Service, specifically on behalf of the North Country Trail, owns:

>Wisconsin: 200 acres near Solon Springs

>Michigan: 81 acres- Augusta Prairie

Army Corps of Engineers

The area surrounding Lakes Sakakawea and Ashtabula in North Dakota is managed by the US Army Corp of Engineers. Minnesota: Leech Lake, Pokegama Lake. Several reservoirs in Ohio: Harsha Dam at East Fork State Park, Caesar Creek State Park, Burr Oak Reservoir, Senecaville Lake, Salt Fork Lake, Clendening Lake, Tappan Lake, Leesville Lake, and Atwood Lake are also the purview of the USACE. In Pennsylvania, USACE lands include Tionesta Lake and the Allegheny Reservoir.

US Fish and Wildlife Service

The Audubon National Wildlife Refuge in North Dakota is a USFWS site.

The Tamarack National Wildlife Refuge in Minnesota has long been a friend of the NCT, and they now host 13 miles of trail through their property where access is not restricted during breeding seasons.

Bureau of Reclamation

There are a few pieces of land along the NCT owned by the Bureau of Reclamation. These are in the Chain of Lakes area along the McClusky Canal in North Dakota.

McClusky Diversion Project

About 90 miles of trail follow this federal irrigation canal in North Dakota along the McClusky and New Rockford Canals.

A Note About Federal Wilderness

There are five designated Federal Wilderness areas along the North Country Trail. All the ones on the NCT route are managed by the Forest Service. These have a specific definition and regulations. They are to have minimal impact from humans with few to no permanent improvements. Trails are generally not allowed to be blazed, although some have permitted minimal signage. Some bridges may exist, but the extent of trail amenities is usually regulated by the individual Wilderness. Nothing with wheels can be used, and no motors or mechanized vehicles (eg. bicycles, power boats, snowmobiles, or drones). Thus, all trail work, including heavy clearing of downed trees, must be done with hand tools. Even canoe or hunting dollies are not allowed. The Wilderness Act of 1964 calls a wilderness "an area of undeveloped Federal land retaining its primeval character and influence, without permanent improvements or human habitation, which is protected and managed so as to preserve its natural conditions" where humans are visitors.

A notable "treat" for hikers is the Agamok Bridge along the Kekakabic Trail in the BWCAW where the parts for the bridge were transported to the site in winter by dogsled, and the bridge assembled in warmer weather. This would be a seriously difficult river crossing without the bridge.

These are not to be confused with the two state parks in Michigan with the word "wilderness" in their names, or the "Wilderness Loop" of the Buckeye Trail/NCT through the Wayne National Forest in Ohio, or various other places with the word "wilderness" in their names.

To avoid confusion, it is perhaps more fitting to use the word "backcountry" to describe remote areas along the trail that are not designated wilderness.

Minnesota: Boundary Waters Canoe Area Wilderness within the Superior National Forest (power boats are allowed on a few designated lakes)

> Wisconsin: Rainbow Lake and Porcupine Lake Wildernesses within the Chequamegon National Forest
>
> Michigan: McCormick Wilderness within the Ottawa National Forest. Rock River Canyon Wilderness within the Hiawatha National Forest (currently the trail is mostly on road beside the Wilderness, but it has been approved for off-road trail to be built).

Additionally, within the Adirondack Park in New York, the trail officially passes through three designated Wilderness Areas: West Canada Lake, Siamese Ponds and Hoffman Notch. For now, the trail also uses the Blue Hill Trail in the Pharaoh Lake Wilderness. These are state rather than federal designations, however the Adirondack Park Agency has regulations virtually identical to Federal Wilderness.

Native Nation Lands

> Minnesota: White Earth Reservation
>
> Michigan: Little River Band of the Ottawa lands
>
> New York: Seneca and Oneida Nation Reservations

State Ownership

State Forests

State Forests are by far the largest landholders on a state level. Regulations vary by state.

> North Dakota: Sheyenne River, Fond du Lac
>
> Minnesota: White Earth, Paul Bunyan, Remer, Bear Island, Finland
>
> Wisconsin: Brule River
>
> Michigan: Copper Country, Gwinn, Shingleton, Newberry, Lake Superior, Mackinaw, Pere Marquette

Ohio: Maumee, Shawnee, Pike, Scioto Trail, Tar Hollow

Pennsylvania: Clear Creek

New York: Bucktooth, Elkdale, Rock City, McCarty Hill, Boyce Hill, Bear Creek, Bush Hill, Farmersville, Swift Hill, Slader Creek, Klipnocky, Bully Hill, Burt Hill, Birdseye Hollow, South Bradford, Goundry Hill, Sugar Hill, Texas Hollow, Danby, Shindagin Hollow, Potato Hill, Robinson Hollow, Hammond Hill, James Kennedy, Tuller Hill, Hoxie Gorge, Baker Schoolhouse, Taylor Valley, Cuyler Hill, Maxom Creek, Morgan Hill, DeRuyter, and soon Clark Hill

Adirondack Park

In New York, the Adirondack Park is essentially a state forest, although it has its own unique regulations. It is the largest park in the contiguous United States, 6 million acres. About half of that land is public. The NCT traverses six units of the park, three of them designated as Wilderness with rules similar to those of Federal Wilderness.

State Wildlife Management Areas

In general, State Wildlife Managment Areas do not allow camping with the exception of some in North Dakota, but they also host a great many miles of the NCT.

North Dakota: Wolf Creek, Lonetree, Clausen Springs, Fort Ransom

Minnesota: Fergus Falls, Hubbel Pond, Hill-Annex Mine, Lake Vermilion-Soudan Underground Mine

State Parks

In general, State Parks require a camper to stay in designated areas.

North Dakota: Lake Sakakawea, Fort Ransom

Minnesota: Maplewood, Itasca, Vermillion-Soudan, Judge C. R. Magney, Cascade River, Temperance River, George H. Crosby Manitou, Tettegouche, Split Rock Lighthouse, Gooseberry Falls, Jay Cooke

Wisconsin: Pattison, Copper Falls

Michigan: Porcupine Mountain Wilderness, Craig Lake, Muskallonge, Tahquamenon Falls, Straits, Wilderness, Petoskey

Ohio: Mary Jane Thurston, Independence Dam, Lake Loramie, East Fork, Pike Lake, Scioto Trail, Hocking Hills, Lake Logan, Burr Oak, Wolf Run, Salt Fork, Beaver Creek

Pennsylvania: McConnell's Mill, Moraine, Cook Forest

New York: Allegany, Watkins Glen, Robert H. Treman, Pixley Falls

In most states, the state forests and state parks are managed by one state agency. In Vermont and New York it's called the Department of Environmental Conservation (DEC), in Pennsylvania it's the Department of Conservation and Natural Resources (DCNR), Ohio, Michigan, Wisconsin, and Minnesota have a Department of Natural Resources (DNR), and North Dakota State Parks and Recreation Areas are under the Parks and Recreation Department while the Sheyenne River State Forest is managed by the North Dakota Forest Service.

State Game Areas

SGAs are primarily designated hunting lands. They are funded by hunting and fishing licenses and other fees. Most are found in Michigan and Pennsylvania. Hikers are guests. In Michigan, dispersed camping is allowed only from September 11 to May 16, and is otherwise restricted to a few designated areas. In Pennsylvania, no camping is allowed except in designated sites.

Other State Owned Lands

Examples of other designations of state-owned land:

    Scientific and Natural Areas

    Waterfowl Production Areas

Recreation Areas

Aquatic Management Areas

Natural Areas

Wildlife Management Areas

Historic Sites

other types of state ownership

Local Governments

Counties: Becker County, MN, and Douglas, Bayfield and Iron Counties, WI, have significant miles of trail.

Cities: Duluth city land hosts a number of miles of trail, as does Battle Creek, Michigan. The NCT passes through several Metroparks in Ohio, and other smaller cities and villages allow the trail passage through parks, forests, and other city properties.

Towns and townships also own property through which the trail passes.

Organizations

Land trusts

Nature preserves

Natural Areas

North Country Trail Association: A few permanent easements exist, but these may also come with various rules attached.

Private

Timber companies usually own large tracts of land, and therefore, when agreements can be reached, provide forested land through which the trail may pass. Commercial logging operations continue, and hikers need to accept that occasionally harvests will conflict with their ideal of untouched wild forest. Some allow camping and others do not.

A number of private camps with various affiliations allow the trail passage.

Various kinds of arrangements with individual landowners have been agreed upon for hosting trail miles.

Management

The dream condition for the NCT would be Corridor Management. This would mean that the rules would be the same almost everywhere along the entire trail.

However, there are over 160 landowners with differing management goals along the length of the NCT. For Corridor Management to become a reality, all of these entities would need to agree on goals, strategies, and regulations concerning the strip of land that hosts the trail at some agreed-upon width. A ten-foot wide right-of-way might carry the trail, but would not offer enough space for a campsite. A 200-foot-wide right-of-way might cover most of the possible needs of a trail user (sanitary considerations, water access, foraging, camping), but it's unlikely that every owner would agree to that plan. In areas where ecosystem/wildlife preservation and protection are the primary goal, the trail's priorities would be in direct conflict with this. The AT considers a half mile to be a standard width.

It will be a long, long time, if ever, before Corridor Management could happen for the NCT.

Because of the many land managers, some of which are private individuals or entities, the North Country Trail is managed differently from the familiar Appalachian Trail. This leads to a great deal of confusion about the rules along the length of the trail.

Understanding the differences requires a look at the establishment of the trails themselves.

When the Appalachian Trail was officially recognized as the first National Scenic Trail in 1968, it was given the power of eminent domain. This is sometimes referred to as condemnation authority. Private landowners whose properties were desirable to incorporate into the route of the trail could be forced to sell their land. This power was exercised, but even so, it took about thirty years for the AT trail corridor to be completed.

There was so much backlash from the use of eminent domain, that the North Country, Florida, and Ice Age Trails, when authorized in 1980, were denied even the right to purchase land. Not only could they not pursue any such purchases, they were not allowed to buy from a willing seller. If someone wanted to transfer land to the North Country Trail for a dollar, it was not legal.

It took until 2009, after a dozen years of intense lobbying, for Congress to pass the Public Lands Omnibus Bill. This act finally gave the NCT, and several other National Trails, the right to acquire and hold land. The pertinent part of this bill was commonly called "Willing Seller."

While the AT was already striving to protect an adjoining viewshed for the trail by this date, the NCT was at last allowed to have land they could call their own.

Implementing the administration of this privilege took additional years.

As of this date, the National Park Service has purchased several small key pieces of property which preserve critical places along the route of the NCT. More are sure to follow, as opportunities are identified and best practices for acquisition and management are defined.

However, a pattern of ownership and management along the NCT was solidly established in the preceding 30 years, and it worked well. The funds and staff certainly were not, and are not, available to acquire ownership of the entire route of the NCT.

Land Protection

Protection of a treadway, some width of trail corridor, a width loosely defined as creating an "ideal hiker experience," and even of (as the Appalachian Trail Conservancy is working on) the viewshed is a topic that is critical to the long-term stability of a trail. Right now, there are a good many portions of the NCT that are not protected as trail at all.

Early on, when the trail was trying to find any sort of way to wind through the landscape, a number of miles of trail were built with nothing more than handshake agreements. This is true particularly in New York where our Affiliate the Finger Lakes Trail predates the NCT by nearly 20 years. This was not necessarily a bad thing. Being able to have a continuous trail was the first priority. However, this has led to many instances of "loss of landowner permission." Those are sad words to see on any trail map alert since the trail is usually thrown off to a road.

Although some people are happy to host the trail on their property, when the land is sold or the next generation inherits, the new owner may not feel the same way.

Another unfortunate, but common, scenario is abuse of the privilege either by hikers or by locals who see a trail as easy access to a convenient location for partying, dumping, etc. Common hiker abuses are camping where the landowner has requested no camping, building fires, digging holes, and hiking during hunting closures.

Of course, before the trail can be protected, it must be planned. When trying to connect two pieces of public land, there may be more than one landowner option for the connection. In other places, there are key parcels of land where the right to cross must be obtained in order to preserve trail to some place of interest or perhaps where terrain forces the trail into a certain location.

Even finding the actual boundaries can be an adventure for those seeking to create legal agreements. Most of the information, even on seemingly modern digital apps, initially came from tax assessment records, sometimes a century or more old. Older boundaries were often described in terms of notable trees, ever-changing waterways, or long-rotted posts. "Fudging" the lines was always to the advantage of padding the tax rolls. It's unwise to treat a boundary line on a map as gospel truth unless the owners have had it recently surveyed.

There are a number of tools available to protect a trail of some agreed-upon width. Simple easements, conservation easements, donation, and purchase are the most often used. Keep in mind that until 2009, purchase was not even an option for the North Country Trail.

For years, a great portion of this task fell to volunteers, some of whom were good at talking with landowners. But for many people, initiating conversations that might easily lead to confrontation is a non-starter.

The National Park Service has always worked toward finding a suitable trail corridor.

A few years ago, the NCTA hired a summer intern to begin identifying key pieces of property that the association should be looking at, and in the fall of 2022, a Land Protection Specialist was hired, full-time, by the NCTA.

Volunteers will never be fully replaced by staff, but having one central person coordinating all efforts, and providing consistency and sound answers to the many questions is an important step toward protection of the North Country Trail for generations to come.

Funding

The North Country Trail is supported by Federal dollars, funding of specific projects by State Agencies, grants (private and corporate), member dues, and contributions. Each year, the NCTA publishes an annual report which lets people know the impact their support is making across the Trail.

Federal

Each year, the NPS receives a varying number of dollars for the North Country Trail. From this, they must fund their own offices and staff that are designated for the NCT and cover volunteer support services as mentioned above. Then, through what is called a "cooperative agreement," a certain portion of that money becomes available to the NCTA so that the organization can deliver services and products related to the trail. Additional supplemental federal money may be available in specific instances. Of interest is the fact that the NCTA has never received so much as a million dollars a year from the federal government. Think about this: I'm sure you've read news articles mentioning the cost of various trails of only two or three miles that cost over a million dollars, yet the NCTA is charged with building and promoting 4800 miles.

With the recent designation as a Unit of the National Park System, there is good hope that the NCT will receive more equitable funding. Now, the NCT is one of 428 Units of the National Park System. We are all waiting to see just how this will play out. Unit status will also increase federal promotion of the trail.

Other sources of federal funding might be for construction of specific projects such as bridges, interpretive materials, trailheads, etc within the borders of National Forests or on other federal lands. This money comes from the budgets of those entities.

Occasionally, other federal sources of money have been acquired for specific trail projects. Examples are the now defunct Transportaion Enhancement funds which could be used for projects such as pedestrian walkways on bridges, and Safe Routes to School which occasionally helped build urban portions of trail.

State Agencies

Where the trail goes through State Forests, State Parks, etc., specific projects may be covered through those budgets, but any monies used in this way are not funneled through the NCTA.

Some states have programs which can help protect land where trail can be built. The Clean Ohio Green Space Conservation Program is an example.

Grants

For a number of years, the NCTA has had a Development staff member This person's role is to develop financial stability for the Association. This is accomplished through individual giving, corporate support, and grants to raise funds. Grants are one way the NCTA receives dollars. These may come from corporations or private foundations created by individuals. As anyone who has had to "write grants" knows, this can be a daunting task.

Memberships

The dues paid by members help support the NCTA. Each member receives a subscription to the *North Star*, the quarterly magazine of the NCTA, and a Trail Shop discount. From time to time there are other small perks associated with membership. One-quarter of the value of a membership is designated as belonging to the chapter chosen by the member. The remainder of the membership dollars go to support the NCTA generally. The NCTA is a membership-based organization with several levels to choose from. Memberships play a significant role in NCTA's general operations budget.

Donors

Any individual or other entity can donate to the NCTA at any time. Gifts support the general operations budget or can be designated for a specific project or chapter. Individual gifts range from a few dollars to thousands of dollars. Growth in this area is increasingly important. To create a sustainable funding model for NCTA, a minimum of 80% of the organization's support is secured through membership and unrestricted individual contributions.

Early NCT Hikers

Before the trail was even authorized, before there was an actual route, a group of hikers started in New York with the goal of following the approximate corridor that the trail might use. This consisted of four men and two women. The men dropped out early, but Carolyn Hoffman and Lou Ann Fellows (Johnson) continued on. Lou Ann was seriously injured in Ohio and had to go home for a period of time. Carolyn switched to bicycling where roads were the only way to continue. Carolyn is credited as the first person to follow the trail.

The first person to hike the entire length of the North Country Trail was a man named Peter Wolfe. He was a reformed alcoholic who desired to do something which would help him remain sober. His quest lasted from 1974 to 1981.

Next, Ed Talone completed the NCT in a single season, in 1994. Sue Lockwood accompanied him for 2800 miles.

Chet Fromm was the next hiker to compete the NCT. He did this over the years 1991 to 1995. Alan Shoup hiked the trail in 2004.

Some of these hikers completed the trail before the Minnesota Arrowhead was even a consideration. Their hikes ranged from 3200 to 4000 miles. The trail was continually stretching as sections were moved off road. In 2000, with the agreement of the SHT to become concurrent with the NCT, the Arrowhead became the unofficial, but generally accepted route. This was officially recognized by Congress in 2019.

Andy Skurka followed the Sea to Sea Route (a collection of trails, including the NCT, which connect the Atlantic and Pacific Oceans) in 2004-2005, and his hike included the Arrowhead. All hikes since that time have included the Arrowhead which added about 400 official miles to the trail.

Don Beattie finished his End-to-End (E2E) in 2005, doing most of the trail twice as out and back hikes. Bart Smith was number seven. Bart is a photographer who has now hiked all the National Scenic and Historic Trails.

Eighth was Eb Eberhard (Nimblewill Nomad) who hiked the NCT in 2009, ninth was Joan Young who completed a 20-year section hike effort in 2010, and the tenth person was Luke Jordan (Strider) who hiked it in 2013. He went on to actually work for the trail as the NPS Planner.

One other person has done a combination muscle-powered trip (hiking and bicycling). This is Judy Geisler. She finished in 2009.

Now, the length of the trail has stretched to over 4800 miles, and the total number of people who have hiked the entire trail is more than 25. Some known end-to-enders have not requested recognition.

Many people have completed one or more states, and/or a thousand or more miles. Because of the length of this trail, all completions are recognized as E2E efforts (hikes or trips). Separating out "thru-hikers" (the definition of that term varies, and in most cases seems overly burdensome to impose on hikers of a trail of this length) is not recognized. See a list at explorenct.info/NoCoLo/index.htm.

Planning Your Hike Experience

What to expect

General Information

The NCT traverses a great swath of the northern United States. The following broad strokes describe the area the entire trail spans, followed by state-by-state descriptions.

History

Pre-historic mound builders who left traces throughout the Great Lakes were likely hunter-gatherers. Early native cultures across the northern part of North America with significant archeological traces are represented by the Hopewell culture which flourished from about 1000 BC to 500 AD (Early and Middle Woodland periods) and were probably small communities connected mostly by trade routes. Hopewell traces have been found from New York to the Mississippi River. In the Late Woodland period, the "three sisters," corn, maize, and beans were planted by many tribes, and the bow and arrow came into common use. The Iroquois Confederacy in the east came into being around 1500, with the historic Hiawatha helping in the peacemaking pact. The Iroquois Five Nations (becoming Six in 1722) dominated the native tribes during that time. The Iroquois aligned themselves with the British, and in 1779, the Sullivan Campaign marched through western New York, destroying villages and orchards, breaking the power of the Confederacy.

The Anishinaabe (Ojibwa, Odawa, Potawatomi, and others) occupied the Great Lakes region, particularly Michigan, Wisconsin, and Minnesota along the NCT.

Natives of the plains are generally of the Siouan language group. One subgroup is that of the Dakota tribes who were pushed west from the Lake Superior area through a series of inter-tribal wars. In the early 1700s, horses were brought from the south by the Spaniards.

As more and more European immigrants arrived on this side of the Atlantic, native tribes were continually pushed westward. Much has been written about the ethics of many historic conflicts, and it is not the intent of this book to comment on that topic. However, a great many of the stories of this westward expansion can be traced in the path of the North Country Trail. As the official ballad of the North Country Trail so eloquently states, you're "putting history's footsteps under your boot heels."

Two of the NCT states were in the original 13 colonies: Pennsylvania and New York, Vermont was admitted to the union in 1791. The remainder of the trail states were parts of various acquisitions of land from treaties with native peoples.

Economy

Along the entire length of the trail, the historic economy, in broad strokes, has been driven by agriculture, lumbering, and the mining of various minerals such as iron, copper, and fossil fuels. Transportation industries, notably historic roads and their accompanying structures, along with canals and railroads feature prominently in the route of the NCT.

Geology

Sedimentary prairies and the igneous formations of the Lake Superior basin and New York's Adirondacks define those areas. The uplifted limestone and sandstone formations of the Allegheny Escarpment stretch from southern Ohio continuously to the Finger Lakes of New York. The Wisconsin Ice Age eroded the landscape into much of the topography you will now find along the NCT, excluding only southeast Ohio, Pennsylvania, and a tiny triangle of New York. This glacial legacy affects the ecology. Near the eastern terminus, the Trail climbs to the ridge of the Green Mountains, part of the actual Appalachian Range.

As a result of various geological activites, waterfalls in most of the NCT states are numerous and varied.

Flora and Fauna

Wildlife common to all the "north country" includes bear, beaver, whitetail deer, turkeys, rabbits, squirrels, raccoons, turtles, salamanders, some snakes, eagles, herons, raptors, songbirds and woodpeckers. Most of the flora is typical of northeastern North America, including conifers and northern hardwood forests. However the prairies have distinctly different botany.

Terrain

The NCT is hillier than many people realize. With the exceptions of the ND/MN and MI/OH border areas which are the remains of glacial lakes, hills and eastern mountains are the norm. Western New York, portions of Vermont, and Bergland Hill in Michigan have climbs exceeding 500 feet, but generally, the elevation changes are in the 200-300 foot range. Some of these are gentle, and some are rocky and steep.

Connections with Other Trails

Connecting trails mentioned are almost all non-motorized (possible exceptions are for winter snowmobile use in some places, two driving tours, and US Bicycle Routes include roads). There are numerous connecting and interwoven trails within many state parks and wildlife areas, etc. Most of these are not listed. The criteria for inclusion are somewhat subjective, but generally if there are more than ten miles of side trail, and/or a possible connection for a multi-day or multi-activity adventure, it may be noted.

North Dakota

This is the prairie component of the trail. There are few long-distance trails in the Great Plains which makes the NCT very special. The North Dakota experience is that of big sky and tall grass. There are also wooded hills and lots more water than you might expect. This is the prairie pothole region. There are about 450 miles of NCT in North Dakota.

Name

The Dakota Territory was divided into north and south regions for statehood, and was named for the Dakota Sioux Nation. The word "dakota" means ally or friend. Its nickname is the Peace Garden State.

History

The Dakota Territory was established in 1861. Native American tribes: Mandan, Hidatsa, Arikara, Ojibwe, Cree, and several Sioux groups populated the area. The Homestead Act of 1862 brought many settlers of European descent to the area. Fort Abercrombie (where the trail crosses the Red River from ND to MN) was the gateway to the territory. Both North and South Dakota were admitted to the Union in 1889. Native American trade and travel routes, the military supply roads, the emigration and gold-seeking wagon train routes, river crossings and other opportunities and constraints related to the rivers, and in some places, the early railroad lines are related to agriculture. Those routes directly influenced the location of the NCT track across ND.

Unique Features

The Badlands can be seen across the Missouri River. Prairie potholes support many waterfowl, songbirds, and prairie plants not seen elsewhere along the NCT. The endangered western prairie fringed orchid is found in the Sheyenne National Grasslands. This NCT state is known for tallgrass prairie. Various evidences of Plains Indians including a teepee site and the Biesterfeldt village site lie along the trail. The Karnak and High-Line railroad bridges along Lake Ashtabula, and the lake itself, are stunning. Fort Abercrombie museum and reconstructed blockhouses are located on the Red River. You will encounter more cattle (beef, as they are called in ND) here than in any other NCT state.

Economy

Historically, business in North Dakota was focused on ranching and agriculture, and although methods change, this remains the primary focus, particularly along the NCT. The canals of ND were built for irrigation– to support agriculture. Some oil and coal resources exist, but except at Coal Mine Lake are not evident along the NCT

Weather

North Dakota dishes out extremes of weather. In the winter, temperatures plummet, the wind is brutal, and snow may be deep. In the summer, continuous days of temperatures over 100 degrees are likely, and there is little shade.

Geology

The Badlands begin just west of the Missouri River and the western terminus of the NCT. Proceeding east, the trail crosses the Missouri Coteau (plateau) to the Sheyenne River. The valley of the Sheyenne can be up to a mile broad and 330 feet deep. The Sheyenne River was formed when glacial Lake Souris suddenly released water which flowed into glacial Lake Agassiz. The remains of Lake Agassiz (on both sides of the Red River valley, in ND and MN) is one of only two areas along the trail that are truly flat.

Watersheds

The western terminus of the Trail on the Missouri River is in the Mississippi Watershed. Water there will flow to the Gulf of Mexico. At the eastern end of the McClusky Canal (the western end of Lonetree Wildlife Management Area), you cross into the drainage of the Sheyenne and Red Rivers, which ultimately flows north to Hudson Bay.

Flora and Fauna

At certain times of year, you will see a wealth of waterfowl. One-half of the migratory waterfowl of North America depend on this region. This is the eastern edge of western wildlife populations. The trail passes through the Audubon National Wildlife Refuge, a key location on the migratory Central Flyway. You may see, in addition to common eastern species, black-tailed jackrabbits, western meadowlarks, sharp-tailed grouse, prairie dogs, the flickertail ground squirrel, and possibly a prairie chicken. The only NCT state where you are almost guaranteed to see white pelicans is North Dakota. Take your prairie plant guidebooks, as very few of the wildflowers are the same as those along the rest of the trail. The rare white prairie fringed orchid can be found along the trail in the Sheyenne National Grasslands. You will likely encounter more ticks in North Dakota than any other trail state because they love grass.

The Trail

Most of the off-road trail in North Dakota must be maintained by mowing. If you are there in the spring or early summer before crews have been out, be prepared to find your way through tall grass with the use of electronic maps. Many miles of the trail in ND have been taken off road in the past ten years. Chapters are working hard to build relationships with landowners. Some campsites on private land are also available. About 95 miles of trail are on the service roads for the Garrison Diversion Project (McClusky and New Rockford Canals). While these are flat and monotonous, they do have the advantages of relatively easy access to treatable water, and very limited interaction with vehicles. Special note: The 4.2 miles in the Sheyenne River State Forest do not yet connect with the main trail, but they are worth doing for the terrain and to see the state's only waterfall. In the east, there are 31 miles of trail in the Sheyenne National Grasslands.

Connections with Other Trails

At the western terminus, the trail connects with the Lewis and Clark National Historic Trail.

The Audubon Wildlife Refuge has a driving tour route.

US Bicycle Route 30 passes through Cooperstown.

Biggest Challenges

The weather extremes can be brutal. The tall grass presents an unusual but real impediment. Sharing the land with "beef" (cattle) can be a challenge if you are timid because they can be curious, and the trail crosses a lot of land open to grazing. You must climb many stiles over fences, and there may be a lot of mud mixed with organics where the beef find access to water. Strong winds and storms uninhibited by hills can be dangerous. There are limited resupply options. Many of the towns near the trail are too small to have even a convenience store.

Minnesota

The 860 miles of NCT in Minnesota will take you from the eastern edge of the prairies, through rolling hills, to the Mesabi Iron Range, and finally to the volcanically built hills of the north shore of Lake Superior. Minnesota is true "north country," famed for lakes and forests. Here you will find the headwaters of the Mississippi River. The northernmost point on the NCT is located along the Border Route section (there are two places that are tenths of a second different) at about 48° 6' 2.2".

Name

The name is from the Dakota language. "Mni" is water. "sota" is clear blue, and "ssota" is cloudy. So whether the Dakota considered the area to have sky-blue waters or cloudy waters, Minnesota has lots of water.

History

The area was originally populated by Dakota and Anishinaabe (Ojibwe, Chippewa) peoples. The Dakotas were pushed westward as a result of many tribal wars. East of the Mississippi, the land became part of the United States at the end of the Revolutionary War, while west of the great river, the land was acquired through the Louisiana Purchase. The Minnesota Territory, in its approximate political form, was organized in 1849, becoming a state in 1858.

Unique Features

Minnesota is dotted with small lakes. You are never far from water. Villages in the western part seem to be in competition to erect the world's largest: loon, turkey, prairie chicken... The trail passes near the headwaters of the Mississippi River. Grand Rapids is home to the Forest History Center, a living history experience. The Mesabi Trail features interpretation of iron mining history including large-scale equipment, railroad artifacts, views of the huge, operating Hull-Rust-Mahoning Mine, and the fourth-longest bridge on the NCT, the Rouchleau mine lake bridge at 1132 feet. The small city of Ely is noted for being the gateway to northern recreation in the Boundary Waters Canoe Area Wilderness. The Kekekabic and Border Route Trails are the northernmost portion of the NCT with wilderness, cliffs, the amazing Magnetic Rock, and views into Canada. The SHT Is hilly and rocky with unusual volcanic geology. Duluth is one of the two largest cities on the NCT, and it includes a paved lakewalk which passes by the aerial lift bridge where you may see lake freighters. The trail goes by the SS William A. Irvin, now a floating museum.

Economy

The earliest industries were fur trapping, lumbering and agriculture. Although the urban areas now are home to a number of large companies, in the areas near the NCT, agriculture is still the primary source of income, including turkey processing as well raising crops. In the Arrowhead, iron mining was king and still has a presence. The eastern side of the Arrowhead is supported largely by tourism, and Duluth is a major shipping port on the Great Lakes.

Weather

Minnesota can serve up severe and snowy winters, and heat and humidity in the summer. The northern portions of the trail should not be attempted in the winter without proper gear and plenty of winter experience. Due to the steep terrain all along Lake Superior's north shore, the SHT portion of the trail is susceptible to dangerous flooding events.

Geology

Western Minnesota where the NCT enters the state is the flat land that once was glacial Lake Agassiz. As you approach Rothsay (at about mile MN 25) you will see the land begin to "bubble up" into low green hills. This is "knob and kettle" country. The area is characterized by eroded glacial landforms such as moraines, eskers, outwash plains and kettle lakes. The trail swings north up the back side of the Arrowhead, currently following the multi-use Mesabi Trail through the Iron Range. Iron deposits were laid down in Precambrian seas. Some of the oldest rocks on earth can be seen along the northern Arrowhead where volcanic gneisses appear in the Canadian shield. The north shore of Lake Superior has unique geology where older, lighter blocks of rock were uplifted when they floated on newer magma extrusions of the Midcontinent Rift. These became the hills of the Superior Hiking Trail.

Watersheds

When you enter Minnesota from the west you are still in the Hudson Bay Watershed. The trail enters the Mississippi Watershed near the Tamarac National Wildlife Refuge, until crossing back to the Hudson Bay Watershed near Biwabik. (If you want to see the Mississippi headwaters at Lake Itasca, you must take a six-mile spur trail, although some experts argue that DeSoto Lake is the actual head.) At the Swamp River, approximately at the junction of the Border Route and Superior Hiking Trail, you enter the Great Lakes Basin and the Laurentian Watershed which ultimately enters the Atlantic Ocean via the St. Lawrence River.

Flora and Fauna

Probably the most sought-after wildlife sightings in Minnesota are the moose and timber wolf, and you will have a good chance of spotting them in the northernmost sections. You may also see otters, loons, the Richardson's groundsquirrel (flickertail), eagles, and beaver. A tiger salamander would be a lovely find. In some of the chilly, rocky sections of the Arrowhead you may find alpine plants such as butterwort or Siberian yarrow. Wild rice grows freely in many of the lakes and rivers, and is a popular culinary specialty of the state. Prairie plants and oak savannahs predominate in the western section.

The Trail

From the ND border to Grand Rapids, the trail varies from flat to gently rolling hills and crosses the Chippewa National Forest. At the current time, from Grand Rapids to Ely, the trail mostly follows the paved Mesabi Trail. In most places, this is not a rail-trail, so there will be hills but nothing strenuous. However, once you reach the Snowbank Lake TH east of Ely, and join the Kekekabic Trail, the challenges and vista rewards begin. The "Kek" is rugged and rocky with poor footing. It doesn't receive quite enough use to keep the vegetation beaten down. The Border Route section is hilly and remote. However, the trail there does get used more and is easier to follow. Magnetic Rock monolith is unique. Views across the border lakes into Canada are spectacular. Much of the northern portion is in the Superior National Forest and the Boundary Waters Canoe Area Wilderness. The Superior Hiking Trail section is extremely rocky and hilly. This gets significant use, and is well-marked, but it continually goes up and down with rocky scrambles. Most of the summits will provide great vistas.

Connections with Other Trails

Maplewood State Park has about 30 miles of hiking trails that interconnect with the NCT.

At the north edge of Maplewood State Park, the NCT and the Heart of the Lakes Trail (total length 32 miles, multi-use) are concurrent for 5.5 miles.

The NCT crosses the Heartland (45 miles) and Paul Bunyan (123 miles) State Trails (multi-use) just south of Walker.

There are various loop trail connections from the Kekekabic and Border Route Trails- Snowbank being the longest, but there is a nice loop including the BRT, the South and Moss Lake Trails.

The Trail passes many lakes in the Boundary Waters Canoe Area Wilderness (BWCAW) which would allow for the possibility of hike/paddle loops.

The NCT is concurrent with most of the Mesabi Trail, and all of the Kekekabic, Border Route, and Superior Hiking Trails at this point in time.

The Gitchi-Gami state bicycle trail will connect Two Harbors to Grand Marais, MN. (not complete but several segments exist).

The Willard Munger State Trail (multi-use) connects Hinkley and Duluth.

Biggest Challenges

The serious winters are a challenge for planning a multi-state hike that starts at one terminus or the other. The Kek and Border Route Trails are remote and difficult and must be backpacked, due to lack of road access points. Although the Kek has been hiked in one day by an extreme hiker, most people take at least four days to do it, and the Border Route requires about six days. However, there are road access point that can shorten the non-accessible distance of the BRT to 45 miles. There are few re-supply points and phone reception is spotty at best. Mosquitoes, blackflies, and ticks can be problematic. A permit is required in the BWCAW, and the authorities are not always flexible about picking up the permit more than 24 hours in advance of entering the Wilderness. This can be problematic for a thru-hiker. The SHT is rocky and hilly, but has enough road access points that shorter treks are possible.

Wisconsin

With just over 200 miles of trail across the northern portion of the state, Wisconsin can be quickly hiked. Wisconsin is a mild and pleasant change from the rugged terrain in its flanking states, Minnesota and Michigan's Upper Peninsula. Northern woodlands, rivers, and glacial landforms define the trail. Most of the trail in the western portion of the state is in Douglas County, which entity has granted permission to build trail. Planning is in progress to add many off-road miles.

Name

The name possibly comes from the Algonquian "meskonsing," meaning "it lies red" referring to the red sandstone along the Bad River. The French spelled it "ouisconsin," which was anglicized to Wisconsin. It's nickname is the Badger State.

Geology

From the St. Louis River near the very eastern edge of Minnesota through most of Wisconsin, there is volcanic rock overlain with sedimentary layers. However, the erosion of the glaciers and glacial melt exposed the volcanic rock in many places. The trail lies entirely within the region geologically known as Northern Highland. At Copper Falls State Park you will see stunning evidence of the Midcontinent Rift, with jumbled geologic layers and the line of the rift fault.

Watersheds

The western portion of the trail in Wisconsin is in the Mississippi Watershed, but just east of Solon Springs, at the Brule- St. Croix Portage, you cross into the Great Lakes/ St. Lawrence Watershed.

Flora and Fauna

The most likely-to-see but unusual flora in Wisconsin will be a variety of native orchids including twayblades and coralroots. Fungi and parasitic plants abound in the rich soil. Birding is excellent, and a variety of frogs and turtles may be seen. It's unusual to see a yellow-headed blackbird east of Wisconsin. Although it is possible to see a badger in the Badger State, the nickname refers to miners working underground. The only states where the author has seen a wild badger are North Dakota and Michigan.

History

Algonquian and Sioux native peoples occupied the area. Immigrants, mostly German and Scandinavian, populated the state beginning in the 18th Century. Like many states in the upper Midwest, fur trading was a large part of the early economy. The Wisconsin

Territory was created in 1836, and it became a state in 1848.

Unique Features

The "Bird Sanctuary" in the Douglas County Wildlife Area west of Solon Springs is a unique glacial outwash ecosystem including pine barrens. The Brule-St. Croix portage, located in the Brule River State Forest, is a primary historic transportation connection. The Gaylord Nelson portal features a trailhead monument to honor the man who was the founder of Earth Day, and whose efforts resulted in the creation of the National Trails System. Geologic evidence of the Midcontinent Rift can be seen at Copper Falls State Park. In the eastern portion of the state jumbled boulders of limestone and the broken core of the iron range have resulted in hills and waterfalls. There is even an old gold mine along the trail.

Economy

In the northern counties through which the NCT passes, the economy was forged on lumbering, mining of iron ore, commercial fishing in Lake Superior, and subsistence farming. Today the economy is still driven by logging, but recreation and tourism also play an important role. Dairy farming is important to the state, but most large farms are south of the trail.

Weather

The winters in Wisconsin can have heavy snow or be mild. The terrain is suitable for snowshoeing and possibly skiing the trail. Summers are generally pleasant.

The Trail

In the western part of Wisconsin, the trail goes through Pattison State Park where you hike between Big and Little Manitou Falls. Big Manitou is the highest waterfall in the state. The St. Croix National Scenic Riverway hosts two miles of trail (although the visitor's center where you can get a National Park passport stamp is 90 miles away in St Croix Falls). As you approach Solon Springs, glacial outwash plain is preserved as the Douglas County Wildlife Area, popularly known as "The Bird Sanctuary." Several ecologically unique miles of trail traverse the plain. One special piece of trail is the Brule- St. Croix Portage. This three-mile section is the historic connection between the St. Croix River which flows to the Mississippi and the (Bois) Brule River which flows north to Lake Superior and the Atlantic Ocean. Markers line this trail commemorating historic users of the portage. The Chequamegon National Forest hosts 63 miles of pleasant forested trail which include the Rainbow Lake and Porcupine Lake Wildernesses. Copper Falls State Park showcases the past violent geological upheaval of the Mid-continent Rift. Most recently, off-road trail in the eastern section of the state has been built. Included here are the Potato River, Wren's Falls, and a large bridge at the eastern crossing of Tyler Forks. The foundations of a wooden three-legged fire tower predating the usual four-legged metal ones can be visited at Porcupine Hill. Many large rock outcroppings can be seen in the Trap Ridge at the northern edge of historic iron and gold mines.

Connections with Other Trails

There is no direct connection with the Ice Age National Scenic Trail, but their closest approach is about 50 miles apart between Solon Springs and Grassy Lake, via US 53.

The Saunders/Soo Line Trail is concurrent with the NCT for a half mile about four miles from the WI/MN border. There are 120 miles of gravel rail-trail.

The Gandy Dancer, multi-use State Trail crosses the NCT at Dedham (49 miles).

The St. Croix National Scenic Riverway includes 200 miles of navigable water.

The Tour de Chequamegon 108-mile bicycle route circles the National Forest, mostly on back roads and crossing the NCT near Drummond by Lake Owen.

Biggest Challenges

The trail in Wisconsin is a pleasant hike with moderate terrain. However, winters can have heavy snowfall and mosquitoes can be thick in the summer. Until the DNR completes a bridge across Tyler Forks east of Copper Falls State Park (potentially in 2025) there is a deep ford which may require a hiker to walk around on roads. Check waterdata.usgs.gov/monitoring-location/04026561. Stricker Road is about two miles downstream from the crossing, so if the water is 5 feet deep at the gage, it will be about the same or a little less (a tributary flows in between the points) at the crossing.

Michigan

Michigan has more miles of North Country Trail than any other state, almost 1200 of them, about equally divided between the peninsulas. Because of this, and because the two peninsulas are quite different, the descriptions will be separated for most of the topics. The terrain varies from rugged hills to flat farmland. The NCT touches three of the five Great Lakes; Lake Superior is seen from the NCT in Michigan, Wisconsin, and Minnesota, but views of Lakes Huron and Michigan from the trail are unique to Michigan. The trail includes the five-mile long Mackinac suspension bridge (the longest bridge on the NCT) connecting the Upper and Lower Peninsulas. There is only one NCT crossing of the 45th Parallel, and that is in Michigan.

Name

Michigan comes from the Ojibwe word "mishigami" which means large water. The nickname is the Great Lake State because it touches four of the five Great Lakes.

History

Various tribes of the Anishinaabe Nation: Ojibwe (Chippewa), Odawa (Ottawa), and Potawatomi inhabited the state at the time of European settlement. The first permanent village was at Sault St. Marie, established 1688. Detroit (Fort Pontchartrain du Détroit, 1701) and the Straits of Mackinac (Fort Michilimackinac, 1715) were also important militarily and for trade routes. Originally French, the territory came into British possession at the end of the French and Indian War (1763). The Territory was organized in 1805 without the Upper Peninsula. In 1835, Michigan and Ohio came to blows over the "Toledo Strip" which included the Great Black Swamp. Ohio wanted control of the mouth of the Maumee River and the agricultural lands, but Michigan had included the area in its petition for statehood. Michigan agreed to give up the Toledo Strip in exchange for the entire Upper Peninsula, and statehood was achieved in 1837.

Upper Peninsula

Unique Features

The UP has more waterfalls than anywhere else along the trail; some days you will pass several. Lake of the Clouds on the Escarpment Trail in Porcupine Mountain Wilderness State Park looks like a piece of the Adirondacks dropped into Michigan. Norwich Bluff, a 350-foot, nearly-sheer cliff is visible in the Trap Hills. The landscape around Marquette features black igneous rocks. Pictured Rocks National Lakeshore and Tahquamenon Falls are two of the most famous natural features of the Midwest. The Mackinac Bridge, one of the longest suspension bridges in the world, spans the Straits of Mackinac. You will see all three of the Great Lakes that the NCT touches in the UP. The only place on the trail where you can see Lake Huron is at the Straits.

Economy

Copper and iron mining, along with fishing and lumbering, drove the early economy of the UP. The trail passes through copper country, while most of the iron was farther south. Today, tourism is the most significant source of income in the UP.

Weather

Winters in the UP can be severe with heavy snowfall, some locations regularly receive over 200 inches per season. It is not unusual for over three feet of snow to cover the ground until May. Temperatures often drop below zero. By contrast, summers can be hot and humid, peppered with mosquitoes and black flies in season.

Geology

The western Upper Peninsula displays some of the oldest rocks on earth at the surface. A long basalt escarpment extends from Wisconsin out along the Keweenaw Peninsula, and a similar ridge to the south of that is the Trap Hills, so named because the volcanic rock trapped minerals, such as copper, during formation. The familiar, red, often striped, stone of the Lake Superior shore is red Jacobsville sandstone. East of there, the area was scoured and flattened by glaciers, leaving outwash plains in the Baraga area. Around Marquette, volcanic rocks are much in evidence, with many hills and rugged terrain. Pictured rocks, on the shore of Lake Superior, is the edge of the Michigan Basin (see Lower Peninsula Geology), which protrudes from the ground like the rim of a shallow bowl that is filled with sand. Continuing southeast to the straits, sedimentary rock predominates and the trail crosses the Niagara Escarpment which arcs from the southern shore of Lake Ontario, creating Niagara Falls, then bends northward, separating Lake Huron from the Georgian Bay, through the UP and ends in Door County, Wisconsin. Waterfalls abound in this geologic mish-mash. The largest falls, Tahquamenon, is the result of different rates of erosion in layers of sedimentary rock.

Watersheds

All of the UP is in the Great Lakes Watershed, with most streams along the NCT running to Lake Superior. Streams between the Pine River in Chippewa County and the Carp River in Mackinac County flow to Lake Huron, but the Brevort River flows to Lake Michigan.

Flora and Fauna

It is possible to see moose and wolves in the Upper Peninsula. In the winter, you'll certainly see tracks. Mountain lions have been spotted, and their tracks seen by many. Bobcats, beaver, and pine martens may be found. Whitefish point is considered a key migration point highly valued by birdwatchers. Clintonia and ladyslipper orchids carpet the forests in the spring. Northern conifers such as balsam, hemlock, black spruce, and white pine scent the forests. The western UP is considered the largest stand of old growth hardwoods west of the Appalachians. Ravens are more often seen than crows, sandhill cranes are somewhat common, and you may see a spruce grouse. In late summer, blueberries and thimbleberries are plentiful. Big Lake is known for rare plants if you manage to be there at the right time.

The Trail

The trail in the western UP is rugged and challenging. However, as a result of the geology there are numerous waterfalls and vistas. In Porcupine Mountain Wilderness State Park, the trail now skirts Lake of the Clouds, one of the scenic wonders of Michigan. The Ottawa National Forest hosts 90 miles of trail. The longest single climb/descent in Michigan is 600 feet, on Bergland Hill at the west end of the Trap Hills. The McCormick Wilderness, Craig Lake State Park and Silver Lake Basin are slightly less hilly, but still challenging. Volcanically-built hills surround Marquette where there are several miles of relatively easy urban and semi-urban trail. One of the best-known geologic features of the NCT is Pictured Rocks (an NPS site), between Munising and Grand Marais. Close to 150 miles of trail are located in the two units of the Hiawatha National Forest. There, the terrain becomes even less hilly with sandy soil, passing world-renowned Tahquemenon Falls. Sandy hills dot the landscape until reaching St. Ignace.

Connections with Other Trails

There are about 90 miles of loop trails within Porcupine Mountain Wilderness State Park.

The Bay de Noc/Grand Island Trail connects with the NCT near AuTrain Lake and extends south for about 40 miles to near Rapid River.

The Fox River Pathway tees into the NCT within Pictured Rocks. Its southern end is 27 miles south, near Seney.

Within Tahquamenon Falls State Park is the Wilderness Loop, about 8 miles.

US Bike Route 10 converges with the NCT at St. Ignace.

Biggest Challenges

The weather presents a challenge for long-distance hiking. Porcupine Mountain Wilderness State Park, The Trap Hills, McCormick Wilderness and Silver Lake Basin have limited to no vehicular access in the winter, and deep snow is almost always an issue. The PMW State Park requires advance reservations to stay overnight. Phone reception is spotty at best, and there are very few resupply options that can be reached on foot anywhere in the UP. The UP is definitely in the running (with Minnesota and the NY Adirondacks) for the worst mosquitoes along the NCT. Biting stable flies along Lake Superior have been known to drive people off the trail, but their presence is largely a local weather phenomenon and is unpredictable. At Victoria Dam, the river is not fordable if water is being released. There is a phone number to call to get information about releases, but calls may go unanswered, leaving a hiker wondering if he or she should take the long road detour. Instead, check the website uppco.com/hydro-water-levels/ , and if the total flow for Victoria is above 800 cfs, water is being released. Pictured Rocks requires a permit for overnight stays, but a way to hike through with day hikes is described later in this book. If you want to hike the five miles of the Mackinac Bridge, you can only do so on Labor Day. The Bridge Authority will shuttle hikers across for a fee at other times.

Lower Peninsula

Unique Features

The Mackinac Bridge, one of the longest suspension bridges in the world, spans the Straits of Mackinac. You will see two of the three Great Lakes the NCT touches in the LP. Reconstructed Fort Michilimacinac, at the northern tip of the LP is the oldest fort along the trail, established in 1715. The Headlands Dark Sky Park is only a mile off the trail, and although camping is not allowed, you can choose to visit at night to watch the sky. You will certainly see more sand than in any other state, studded with glacial features. The Geology section explains why. The only crossing of the 45th parallel is here. The NCTA Headquarters and NPS office for the NCT are located in Lowell, just a half-block from the trail near the Lowell Showboat. Battle Creek, the Cereal City, has several miles of pleasant urban trail and the largest statue commemorating the Underground Railroad in the United States, by Tina Allen. Historic Bridge Park gives the hiker a look at the progression of bridge engineering through time. The Rose Hartwick Thorpe bell in Litchfield honors the author of the poem "Curfew Must Not Ring Tonight," so famous in the early 1900s it was even quoted in *Ann of Green Gables*.

Economy

Although most people think of the auto industry in the same breath as Michigan, that is largely centered in the southeast corner of the state, although some small industries outstate supply parts. The western LP is noted for lumber, Christmas tree farms, fruit growing and tourism. Southern Michigan is dotted with farms.

Weather

Although the LP can have snowy winters, the temperatures usually do not get as low as in the UP, as Lake Michigan has a buffering effect on the west side of the state. This same meteorological phenomenon can produce heavy lake effect snow. Summers are generally pleasant with perhaps a week or two of hot and humid days.

Geology

Michigan's Lower Peninsula is defined by the Great Basin. Think of Michigan as a shallow bowl centered around the city of Gladwin. The bedrock there is about three miles below the surface, and the bowl is filled with sedimentary rock and sand. As mentioned above, the edge of the bowl surfaces at Pictured Rocks. The basin may have been created when the Appalachian Mountains were formed. All hills in the LP are remains from the erosion of the Wisconsin Glacier's terminal moraine, or are sand dunes. You may be lucky enough to find a Petoskey stone, or even more rare, a Charlevoix stone, both fossilized corals found only in Michigan. The northern Lower Peninsula is hilly while southern Michigan is nearly flat.

Watersheds

All of the LP is in the Great Lakes Watershed, with most streams running to Lake Michigan. However, water in Crooked Lake at Conway, north of Petoskey, actually ends up in Lake Huron. Just east of Hillsdale, the trail enters the Lake Erie Watershed.

Flora and Fauna

The northern LP offers the conditions necessary for several rare orchids: calypso, and rams-head ladyslipper have been found growing beside the trail. Showy orchid and strawberry-blite are common in the Jordan Valley. Almost all the Michigan woodlands have a shrub layer of blueberry. Shadbush and dogwood brighten the early spring woodlands. Whitetail deer and black bear are the most numerous large mammals. You will commonly encounter skunks, porcupines, opossums, raccoons, squirrels and chipmunks. These smaller animals are a much greater menace to your food bags than bear. There are populations of Blanding's and spiny softshell turtles. Although lower Michigan has populations of elk and Kirtland's warblers, the trail does not pass through those regions. There is a good eagle population.

The Trail

If you want to hike the five miles of the Mackinac Bridge, you can only do this on Labor Day. The Bridge Authority will shuttle hikers across for a fee at other times. From the Straits is the only place on the trail you will see Lake Huron. The trail south of the Bridge is quite flat through Wilderness State Park, and then begins a roller-coaster of low glacial hills and dunes. The Jordan River Pathway is hillier, with trail in a deep valley of the Jordan River where the trail crosses the 45th parallel. There are many near-contiguous, off-road miles through state forests and the Manistee National Forest. The terrain features gentle hills most of the way south (trail east) to Grand Rapids, south of which the land is much more level. Petoskey is a good-sized city with urban trail, and ten trail miles east of there at the Skyline viewing platform, you will get your last glimpse of Lake Michigan (or first if westbound). In Battle Creek there are considerable miles of paved urban trail, and much of the trail south (trail east) of there is still road walk, with the notable exception of Lost Nation State Game Area.

Connections with Other Trails

At Mackinaw City, several trails converge including US Bike Route 35 (also connects at Harbor Springs/Petoskey), the multi-use North Western State rail-trail forming a loop with the NCT at Petoskey, and the Midland to Mackinac hiking trail.

The NCT uses part of the 26-mile Little Traverse Wheelway in Petoskey which also connects with the North Western State Trail.

Near Traverse City, the NCT intersects at several places with the Shore-to-Shore Trail network. Although this can be hiked, it is primarily an equestrian trail and the treadway is often deeply rutted.

In the Udell Hills within the Manistee NF, there is a network of ski/cycling/hiking trails. Its outer loop is 26 miles long.

The White Pine Trail is a 92-mile multi-use trail which extends from Cadillac to Grand Rapids, and the NCT is concurrent with it for eight miles near Cedar Springs.

The Iron Belle Trail has been conceived as a huge figure-eight trail encircling Michigan. It plans to piggyback on the NCT on much of the western leg in the LP. You will see signage for it on the Linear Pathway in Battle Creek, also shared by the NCT.

There are three popular loop trails of about 20 miles each which include the NCT. They are the Jordan Valley Pathway, the Fife Lake Loop, and the Manistee River Loop; these have been nicknamed the Michigan Triple Crown.

US Bike Route 20 intersects with the NCT at 5-Mile Road in Lake County.

Biggest Challenges

You may want snowshoes for winter hiking in the northern LP, and although some roads are seasonal, there is generally good access to the trail, year-round. Resupply through the Manistee National Forest is difficult. The many miles of roadwalk in the southern section can be a mental challenge, and there are still few places to camp legally in those areas, although this is improving.

Ohio

Ohio has almost 1110 NCT miles; 960 of them are concurrent with the Buckeye Trail. The state offers treasures of botany, history, and culture not found in any other NCT state. Historic transportation routes criss-cross and even define the trail in many places. Old roads, canals and rail corridors tell the stories of earlier times. The western portion is flat, but the south and east are hilly and can be challenging.

Name

Ohio is a Seneca word, ohi;yo', meaning good river. Its nickname is the Buckeye State, from the buckeye tree which grows there in abundance.

History

Pre-historic native groups who lived in the area of the NCT include the Hopewell and Fort Ancient cultures. In the early 1800s, the Shawnee people became the predominant tribe interacting with early settlers. The famous chief Tecumseh rallied the various indigenous peoples and nearly succeeded in pushing back the Europeans to east of the Appalachians. Many battles of the French and Indian War were fought in Ohio. As part of the 1787 Northwest Territory, land in Ohio was granted to veterans of the Revolutionary War, and settlers flocked to the state, clashing with the native peoples. Statehood was granted in 1803, although an interesting side note is that Congress did not pass a resolution to this effect. When the error was discovered in 1953, Ohio was formally admitted, retroactive to 1803.

Unique Features

Ohio has more covered bridges along the trail than any other state. There are miles of historic transportation canals with locks and associated structures. Grand Rapids, Ohio, features a recreated canal ride ending at the historic, operating Ludwig Mill powered by canal overflow. At two places in Ohio, the NCT crosses the National Road. A wealth of railroad history is found along the trail. Dayton is the largest city on the NCT, and the trail passes such unique places as the Wright Brothers Memorial (an NPS site) and the Wright Patterson Air Force Museum. Ohio has the southernmost point of the NCT, and the Ohio River is visible. The limestone and sandstone cliffs and shelf caves of the Arc of Appalachia are well represented. Serpent Mound is one of the largest remaining North American Effigy Mounds. The trail passes one of the three crash sites of the dirigible USS Shenandoah. At Zoar, a closed community of German Separatists lasted for 81 years. The village survives as a living-history museum.

Economy

In its early days, Ohio's European population largely depended on trapping and farming. In the 19th and 20th Centuries, industry was important, although most of that was centered in the northeast (on Lake Erie) and the southwest (on the Ohio River). Transporting of goods, as evidenced by the many canals and rail lines was important, including shipping on the Great Lakes. The processing of metal ores shipped from Minnesota, Wisconsin, and the Upper Peninsula was big business. Mostly, NCT hikers will see small farms and small-town industries. The edge of Appalachia has few economic resources, and many people struggle to make a living. In the southeast portion of the state, glass and pottery industries were important, and still retain a small presence.

Weather

Ohio is the mildest of any of the NCT states. Although it is likely to be hot and humid in the summer, the gentler winters make it a popular state in which to start a "flip-flop" hike during the months that the northern NCT states are socked in. There is generally not deep snow, but temperatures can fall below zero on occasion, and the wind can be a factor in the flatter sections.

Geology

The northwest portion of Ohio is one of only two truly flat areas along the trail. This is the remains of the Great Black Swamp, finally drained in the late 19th Century, and which is now rich farmland. From Ohio's lowest point on the Maumee River, there is a rise of only 300 feet to the Loramie Summit, the high point of the Miami-Erie Canal, 120 trail miles south (NCT east). In southern Ohio, the trail intersects the Allegheny Escarpment, and roughly follows it all the way to New York. Once reaching southern Ohio, the trail becomes hilly with many rock outcrops of limestone and sandstone. Hills are the result of the eroded Allegheny Plateau. The area is noted for hanging shelf caves, perhaps best seen in Hocking Hills. The Ohio River is geologically young, drains almost 200,000 square miles, and is the largest tributary of the Mississippi. The entire southeast portion of Ohio was not glaciated in the most recent Ice Age.

Watersheds

The northern portion of Ohio drains to the Great Lakes. At Loramie Summit, near Lake Loramie, the land begins to fall to the south, and all of the remainder of the NCT in Ohio is within the Mississippi Watershed via the Ohio River.

Flora and Fauna

Beaver, muskrats, whitetail deer, several kinds of turtles and salamanders are common to Ohio. Surprisingly, you will probably not see any porcupines, although they may be returning to the northeast part of the state. Copperhead snakes may be encountered in the southeastern portion of the state. Timber rattlers are endangered and may only be found in seven of the southern counties. Massasaugas may be encountered in the northern region, but they prefer wetlands and are extremely shy. The state tree is the buckeye, and to see this tree in flower is spectacular. Ohio has the greatest diversity of native flowering plants of any NCT state, with over 1800 species. Of course, these are spread through many ecosystems, but the trail in Ohio traverses a good selection of these. Butterflies and moths are also well-represented in the state. Black buzzards can be seen in the southern portions.

The Trail

The northernmost portion of the trail in Ohio bends east and then west on lines of the Wabash Cannonball rail trail, connecting the north and south legs through Oak Openings Metropark with natural surface. The NCT joins the Buckeye Trail at Waterville, Ohio and continues with it (BT counter-clockwise) until Zoar. There is one section of 14 NCT miles at Caeser Creek State Park where the NCT and BT differ, the NCT taking the bike path farther from the lake. In the western portion of the state, the trail is mostly on Wabash-Erie and Miami-Erie canal towpaths. Once Loramie Summit is crossed, there is some towpath as the trail begins to descend toward the Ohio River, but the canal there primarily was routed in the rivers, so the trail mostly follows the Miami Valley Trail system on the Great Miami River Trail, passing through Dayton on urban trail, and then on the bed of the Little Miami RR from Yellow Springs to Milford. Eastward from there is a mix of road and off-road walking. In Adams County, new trail through the Arc of Appalachia Nature Preserve runs beside the Allegheny Escarpment. From here eastward, off-road trail predominates through state forests and state parks, with some back roads. The southernmost point on the trail is within Shawnee State Forest at the crossing of Little Twin Creek, 38°41'13.9", -83°15'39.3". The NCT leaves the main BT to loop through the Wayne National Forest. Now the BT has enveloped that route as well, and it is known as the Wilderness Loop. The original BT route closes the narrow mouth approximately between Stockport and Belle Valley, but NCT hikers will need to take the long loop through the Wayne. Coming up the eastern side of Ohio, there are roadwalks combined with trail around several large reservoirs, and a small portion of the Ohio-Erie Canal. At Zoar, the NCT leaves the BT (the BT continuing north, counter-clockwise), crossing the Zoarville Station Bridge, and working east, mostly along the route of the Sandy & Beaver Canal.

Connections with Other Trails

There are over 25 miles of loops that can be hiked in Oak

Openings Metropark.

At Waterville, the Buckeye Trail (clockwise) heads east.

US Bicycle Route 25 is concurrent with the NCT in Piqua and roughly runs parallel or concurrent until they separate at Deed's Point Metropark in Dayton.

In Milford, the NCT connects with the American Discovery Trail (a coast-to-coast route which includes many roads).

The Ohio-Erie multi-use trail (326 miles) connecting Cincinnati to Cleveland includes the Buckeye Trail spur into Cincinnati.

Also at Milford, the trail intersects the Underground Railroad Cycling Route, part of the 52,000-mile Adventure Cycling Association system.

There is a backpacking loop trail and side trails totaling about 55 miles in Shawnee State Forest.

Within the Wayne National Forest there are connections with the Scenic River, Archer's Fork, and Lamping Homestead Trails.

The Ohio-Erie Towpath Trail stretches from Zanesville to Cleveland, intersecting and sometimes concurrent with the NCT/BT, particularly around Zoar.

And at Zoar, the BT continues north (still counter-clockwise) while the NCT turns east.

Near Salt Fork State Park, at the crossing of Birmingham Road North, the NCT crosses US Bicycle Route 50.

Biggest Challenges

There are still a lot of road miles in Ohio, however, these often showcase scenic and cultural features that would not be seen if the trail was in the woods. Ohio clay has been described as "the slipperiest in the world," and when the trails are wet, hiking is messy and difficult. There are many fords, including a number that are simply unsafe if the water is high or moving fast; alternate roadwalks are not always easy. It is still difficult, but not impossible, to backpack through Ohio and find legal places to camp. In recent years, the uptick in BT thru-hikers has resulted in an increase in shelters and campsites. Technically, around Caesar Creek, the NCT diverges from the BT. The NCT stays on a bike path, and the BT takes a trail by the lake.

Pennsylvania

Pennsylvania hosts about 280 miles of trail in the northwestern corner of the state, and most of these are now off-road. Where the trail passes, the state was not glaciated in the most recent Ice Age. The westernmost 90 miles are moderately hilly, and include the beautiful Slippery Rock Gorge, followed by 50 miles of rail-trail along the Allegheny River and Sandy Creek. Through Cook Forest State Park and the Allegheny National Forest, the trail is fairly rugged and hilly, featuring rocky scenery of the Allegheny Escarpment.

Name

Sylvan means "woods," and William Penn founded the colonial Province in 1681. The name of the province became Penn's woods... Pennsylvania. It's nickname is the Keystone State. A keystone is the trapezoidal central stone in an arch which keeps the entire arch from collapsing. Pennsylvania had a central and critical role in the formation of the United States, politically, agriculturally, and economically.

History

Pennsylvania was one of the original thirteen colonies, and in fact, Philadelphia was the capital of the United States until 1800. Many Civil War battles, notably Gettysburg, were fought here. However, most of this densely packed history is found east of the Appalachian Mountains. Western Pennsylvania was, and remains, largely wooded with scattered population centers. The colony of Pennsylvania was founded by a royal land grant to William Penn in 1681. Pennsylvania became the second state to ratify the Constitution in 1787. The native Susquehannock and Iroquoian people inhabited the western part of the state until they were driven out by the Five Nations (Iroquois) Confederacy. The route George Washington took on his first military campaign in 1753 (a delaying tactic wherein he was sent by the British to tell the French to vacate Fort LeBoeuf, predicting they would refuse) is incorporated into the trail for short stretches.

Unique Features

Slippery Rock Gorge is noted for its rocky beauty. The NCT follows a portion of one of George Washington's military routes. There are two fairly long railroad tunnels on the NCT in Pennsylvania. Cook Forest State Park contains the largest remaining stand of several varieties of old-growth hardwoods and conifers. The trail continues to follow the Allegheny Escarpment where large blocks of rock calve from the bluff. The Allegheny Reservoir formed by the Kinzua Dam is the second largest reservoir on the NCT (Lake Sakakawea is much larger).

Economy

Early commerce in Pennsylvania depended on trapping, hunting and subsistence farming. Coal mining became important to the region, and oil for commercial use was first drilled in Pennsylvania, just 20 miles west of the NCT, at Titusville. Forestry and tourism remain important in western Pennsylvania. Lawrence County is known for its Vanport limestone deposits, which served the cement and steel industries. Cemex, a cement and concrete producer, hosts about five miles of NCT in the area.

Weather

Winters in Pennsylvania may be serious, but perhaps less dangerous than other NCT states because the trail is not so remote. Summers can have hot and muggy weeks, but are generally pleasant.

Geology

The Appalachian Mountains are found in the central portion of Pennsylvania. However, the NCT is west of this range, and east of the small northwest corner of the state that was covered with the Wisconsin glacier. Beaver, Butler and Clarion Counties are part of this Low Plateau section, known for coal deposits, including cannel coal (a bright-burning soft coal that was economically important in the 1850s). Cannelton, Pennsylvania, near the Ohio border takes its name from that industry. Venango and Warren Counties are part of the High Plateau section, where, as in Ohio, the hills are the result of plateau erosion rather than mountain building. Rocks are sedimentary limestone and sandstone. Typical scenes along the trail include huge blocky boulders calved from the Allegheny Escarpment which have slid or tumbled down the escarpment's incline.

Watersheds

All NCT in Pennsylvania is within the Mississippi Watershed, with most of the water draining to the Allegheny River, which joins with the Monongahela at Pittsburgh (south of the NCT) to form the Ohio River.

Flora and Fauna

The flora is that of eastern woodlands with a wealth of wildflowers. You will find more native rhododendron and mountain laurel than in any other NCT state. Northern hardwood forests cover the majority of the hills, and a large stand of virgin trees can be seen at Forest Cathedral in Cook Forest State Park with over ten species of trees older than 150 years. No other such stand of old-growth remains in the eastern United States. Black bears, whitetail deer, beaver and fox may be seen. The red eft (technically a newt) is a common sight. Hellbenders, the largest salamander in North America, are present, although you are unlikely to see one without hunting, and they are considered vulnerable.

The Trail

A great many miles in Pennsylvania are through State Game Lands. These properties have made possible many off-road miles of trail, but finding legal places to stay can be a test because PA SGAs do not allow camping. Slippery Rock Gorge is challenging but spectacular, especially in the spring when water is high. The trail crosses the Allegheny River at Parker, on a long, blue Pratt truss bridge, 1140 feet long, making it the third longest bridge on the NCT. Directly east of Parker, the trail joins a rail-trail on the bed of the Allegheny Valley RR and turns north. The trail passes through two long brick tunnels, a unique experience. At East Sandy, the NCT turns east on the Sandy Creek Trail, the route of the Franklin-Clearfield RR. At the junction, a 1385-foot-long bridge built in 1907 spans the Allegheny River, and is now part of the Sandy Creek Trail, although the NCT does not cross to the west side of the river. After fifty miles of rail-trails there is another SGA and another short rail-trail segment. North of the Clarion River, private land, SGAs, Cook Forest State Park, and 96 miles within the Allegheny National Forest provide the hiker with nearly unbroken off-road and hilly miles to the New York border.

Connections with Other Trails

Two other National Scenic Trails are partially located in Pennsylvania, the Appalachian and Potomac Heritage Trails, but the NCT has no connections with these.

Washington's Trail is actually a driving route, but a more accurate portion of the military route is followed by the NCT through Moraine State Park.

The Allegheny Valley rail-trail continues north from East Sandy for an additional 12 miles to Oil City.

At Cook Forest, the NCT crosses the 134-mile hiking and backpacking Baker Trail and is concurrent with it for about 15 miles.

There are several medium-length spurs and loops within the Allegheny NF that connect with the NCT. Tracy Ridge is 33 miles.

Just east of Sheffield, US Bicycle Route 36 follows US 6.

Biggest Challenges

The trail in Pennsylvania can be difficult in the spring with mud and steep climbs. Some creeks still must be forded. Winters can be snowy and cold. No camping is allowed in State Game Areas, and a hiker needs to pay attention to find legal camping. Resupply through the Allegheny NF can be an issue.

New York

New York is the most populous NCT state, with the fourth-highest population in the nation. However, you would never know this by traveling through on the NCT, since most of that urban area is concentrated nearer New York City. The NCT is concurrent with the Finger Lakes Trail, and its Onondaga Branch, for over 400 miles. Three hundred additional miles cover central NY and the Adirondacks. Most of the state varies from rural farm country to forested slopes. The western portion of the state is defined primarily by glacial landforms including the spectacular Finger Lakes, but in the northeast corner, the ancient, igneous rocks of the Adirondack Mountains dominate the landscape.

Name

New York was named for James Stewart, the second son of King Charles I of Great Britain (and thus the younger brother of Charles II). His title was Duke of Albany and York. Charles II granted land between the Delaware and Connecticut Rivers to James. Its nickname is the Empire State, although it is interesting that the exact origin of this moniker is unknown. It was in use before 1820, and may refer to the riches and commerce in the state.

History

Native peoples include the Algonquins and Iroquois. Some of the earliest continental settlements were in New York; New York City and Albany were founded in the 1620s. As explorations moved farther into the interior, the portage between Rome and Oneida Creek became important as the only reasonable way to connect the Atlantic Ocean with the Great Lakes without going far north along the seacoast to reach the mouth of the St. Lawrence. Fort Stanwix at Rome was built in 1758 to protect that portage. In time, the Five Nation Confederacy of the Iroquois pushed the Algonquins north and west. New York was one of the original colonies and became the eleventh state in 1788.

Unique Features

Western New York has the highest climbs and descents along the trail. The Finger Lakes are geologically unique, where glaciers created such wonders as Watkins Glen through which the trail passes. The trail follows a portion of the NYS Barge Canal and the Old Erie Canal into Rome, where Fort Stanwix (an NPS site) has been reconstructed. At the Quarry Art Park you will walk among the sculptures. The Adirondack experience is wild, rocky, and includes more designated Wilderness miles than anywhere else along the trail. Crown Point Fort (an NPS site) is considered the best-preserved colonial era fort anywhere. Lake Champlain is the lowest elevation on the NCT, and the Lake Champlain bridge is the only fixed-link crossing of Lake Champlain within 120 miles.

Economy

There are no large economically developed areas near the trail in New York State. Industry and big business are centered in the New York City region, spreading up the Hudson River to Albany, with some in the Buffalo/Rochester and Syracuse areas. Historically, with the Hudson and the Erie Canal, transportation of goods from the seacoast to the interior of the country has been economically significant. Small farms have been the norm "upstate" since the days of the earliest settlements. Dairy production is still important. The climate is right for prosperous fruit growing and maple syruping, and more recently, small wineries have become big business. The Finger Lakes and the Adirondacks have counted tourism as economically important for well over a century, the onset coinciding with the development of passenger trains. Active timber harvesting is common in the state forests.

Weather

New York State weather is consistent with other northern states. Cold winters with significant snow are the norm. Summers will usually have a hot and muggy period. Spring rains coupled with the hills and gorges create muddy spring conditions with high water.

Geology

There are five geologic areas in New York through which the trail passes. Allegany State Park at the Pennsylvania border is a triangle of land that was not covered by the most recent glacier. The geography and ecology is slightly different in this area, and the water there still flows south to the Ohio River. The Finger Lakes region is defined by strong north-south ridges, between which are found the Finger Lakes, long, narrow water-filled valleys gouged by glaciers. To travel east-west in New York is a challenge for hikers or vehicles, except in the fairly level Mohawk River/Erie Canal valley (former shores of glacial Lake Iroquois) which is the third region hosting the NCT. The Adirondack Mountains are geologically new mountains built from ancient rock. There may yet be a volcanic hot spot beneath the circular dome of rock, causing the Adirondacks to rise. Finally, the Champlain Valley is the northernmost section of the Appalachian Valley which reaches south to Alabama. Lake Champlain is the lowest elevation on the entire NCT at only 100 feet above sea level.

Watersheds

The unglaciated triangle of the western Southern Tier is in the Mississippi Watershed. In Bush Hill State Forest, the trail passes into the Great Lakes Watershed. The other major North American watershed along the trail, the Atlantic Watershed is entered at Slader Creek State Forest, with water flowing to the Susquehanna River and thus to Chesapeake Bay. Crossing the state, the trail wanders several times across the zig-zagging Laurentian/Atlantic Divide. The Black and Moose Rivers in the western Adirondacks both flow to the Great Lakes, but then the trail passes into the Hudson basin (the headwaters are in the High Peaks), but on Stony Lonesome Road, east of the Adirondacks, the trail again enters the St. Lawrence Watershed, where waters flow to Lake Champlain and via the Richelieu River to the St. Lawrence.

Flora and Fauna

New York is also rich in eastern wildflowers. Several varieties of trillium are common, including the pink-and-white painted trillium. An occasional blight-resistant American chestnut is seen in the woods. Black bears and whitetail deer are found throughout the state, and moose may be seen in the Adirondacks. Red efts (newts) are common on the damp forest floor. Eastern painted turtles (vs. Midlands painted turtles) are found in New York. Birds, from bald eagles, hawks and herons to golden-crowned kinglets attract attention.

The Trail

From the NY/PA border to Cuyler Hill, the NCT is concurrent with the Finger Lakes Trail. Allegany State Park is the only unglaciated portion of New York State. Just northeast, one of the best examples of the Allegheny Escarpment geology is seen at Rock City where the blocks are actively (although slowly) calving from the scarp face. The southern strip of New York from Lake Erie to the Catskill Mountains is known as the Southern Tier. This area is noted for hills and is part of the Allegheny Plateau. Near Bath, the trail begins to head into the Finger Lakes Region, although only Keuka and Seneca Lakes are seen from the trail. At the south end of Seneca Lake, the trail passes through Watkins Glen, a spectacular shale gorge. The official trail is on the south rim because the gorge trail is not open in winter months; however, NCT hikers are encouraged to take the gorge route in summer. The Finger Lakes are deep north-south glacial valleys, and crossing the state west/east means hilly hiking. The trail continually rises and drops from 500-1200 feet at a time. Cattaraugus County boasts the FLT nickname of the "Western Wall." At Cuyler Hill, the NCT turns off the FLT main trail and heads north on the Onondaga Branch of the FLT. From Canastota east, the trail follows the NYS Barge Canal and the Erie Canal to Rome and Fort Stanwix where it again turns north. Just east of Forestport, the Adirondack Park begins, and a route through the Adirondacks for the NCT has only recently been defined. Portions are still being determined, but the interactive map roughly shows the route, and hopefully in 2025, better maps will be available.

The trail mostly follows pre-existing trails, but some miles near Speculator, and the Wakely Brook and Jones Hill Trails have been built specifically for the NCT. East of the mountains, the trail follows roads to Crown Point, an historic site of significance. The new (2011) Crown Point Bridge to Vermont is the second-longest bridge on the NCT at just over a half mile in length. Throughout the state, there are many stone foundations and low walls/fences serving as memorials to the long history of settlement.

Connections with Other Trails

The Finger Lakes Trail has six major branch trails. The Conservation Trail is concurrent with maps M1-M4 of the FLT and then goes north to Niagara Falls where it connects with the Bruce Trail in Ontario (150 miles, 100 of which are not NCT).

The Letchworth Branch goes north at Portageville through Letchworth State Park (27 miles).

The Bristol Hills Branch goes north from M12 and terminates at the Ontario County Park (56 miles).

The Crystal Hills Branch goes south from M13 at South Bradford State Forest (50 miles). This "branch" ends at the Pennsylvania border, but it is part of the Mid-State and Great Eastern Trail which continues all the way to Alabama.

US Bicycle Route 11 (118 miles) crosses the NCT at Watkins Glen.

The Interloken Branch goes north from Hector to the north edge of the Finger Lakes National Forest (11 miles).

In Mariposa State Forest, a connection can be made (via road at this time) to the Link Trail, which continues north to again meet the NCT at the north end of Tioughnioga Wildlife Management Area (40 miles).

At Cuyler Hill, the NCT takes the Onondaga Branch, and the main FLT continues east for an additional 200+ miles to terminate at Slide Mountain in the Catskills where it connects with the Long Path.

The 750-mile, multi-use Empire State Trail is a recently collected group of routes which form a T from Buffalo to Albany, and from New York City to the Canadian border, and on to Montreal via La Route Verte. The NCT is concurrent with it for about nine miles west of Rome.

Once in the Adirondack Park, there is a vast network of hiking trails best understood by studying the National Geographic maps of the area.

Biggest Challenges

All FLT miles on private land are closed for one day each year, on the first Monday of February, to meet legal requirements dealing with private landowners. There are numerous hunting season closures on the FLT. These are clearly indicated on the FLT maps. Many agreements with individual landowners are unofficial "handshake" agreements. This means that the trail is not protected for long-term use, and rights-of-passage are rescinded fairly often due to user abuse of the privilege. The FLT maps are brought up to date quickly, but you should always check the web site for changes and updates. The biggest climbs and descents on the entire trail are found in western New York. Black flies and mosquitoes can be a serious issue in the Adirondacks. In the spring, mud and fast-flowing, high streams can be issues. Some streams have posted high-water routes. The Adirondacks can be dangerous in winter, and many roads are closed until Memorial Day. The route through the Adirondacks is still in development, and extra care must still be taken to understand the current selection of trails to make your way through.

Vermont

Vermont is the newest addition to the NCT states, and it has the shortest number of miles. However, it also boasts the lowest and highest elevations along the trail, and includes everything from farmland to small city to mountains. At the eastern terminus the NCT connects with the Appalachian Trail.

Name

When Samuel de Champlain saw the area in 1609, he called the area the Green Mountains. "Green mountain" in French is *vert mont,* which became Vermont. The nickname is the Green Mountain State.

History

The natives in the region encountered by the first explorers were Abenaki, of the Algonquin language group. In the colonial era, the land was part of the New Hampshire Grants, but New York also laid claim to the area. Ethan Allen's famous Green Mountain Boys formed partly to fight against New York settlers and speculators. In 1777, Vermont declared itself independent from New Hampshire, calling itself the Republic of New Connecticut. After New York finally gave up any claim to the land, it became the 14th state in 1791. Vermont was the first state to ban slavery.

Unique Features

The lowest elevation of the NCT is at Lake Champlain, and the highest at Gillespie Peak on the ridge of the Green Mountains, the only portion of the NCT that is in the true Appalachian range. The eastern terminus connects with the Appalachian Trail.

Economy

Vermont's number one product has always been maple syrup. Dairy farming and forestry remain important sources of income, as is tourism.

Weather

The climate is typical of other northern states along the NCT with summers that can have hot, muggy days, but winters can be severe. In the Green Mountains it is not unusual to have 120" of snow.

Geology

The Green Mountains are a subrange of the famous Appalachian Mountains which stretch from Quebec to Alabama. Just to the west of the mountains is the parallel Champlain Valley which also reaches south as far as Alabama. This ridge and valley account for the low and high points along the North Country Trail. Lake Champlain has the lowest elevation at 100 feet, and Gillespie Peak is 3366 feet high, only 49 trail miles apart (24 straight-line miles). Because of the steep topography, areas are subject to flooding in times of heavy precipitaton.

Flora and Fauna

Most of the plants and animals in Vermont are typical of the northern forests along the trail. You are more likely to see a fisher than in any other NCT state. The Great/Horrid Cliffs near Brandon Gap along the Long Trail is a nesting site for peregrine falcons. The side trail is closed to hikers usually from early spring until August 1, but these dates are dependent upon when the falcons arrive. The Green mountains are covered with conifers and northern hardwoods. Although there are alpine plants on some of the highest peaks in the Green Mountains, it's unlikely that any will be found along the NCT portion.

The Trail

The new (2011) Crown Point Bridge over Lake Champlain is a half-mile long with a pedestrian walkway. From there until joining the Trail Around Middlebury (TAM), the trail currently follows roads. The TAM is a loop with a spur to connect to the NCT, totally encircling Middlebury and mostly off-road. The NCT follows the east side of the loop. This gives easier access to services. Note that this trail was built to maximize the recreational opportunities for local people. There are lots of meanders and extra ups and downs. A highlight is the double suspension bridge over Otter Creek and Beldens Falls. The trail continues on roads through East Middlebury. After crossing the Middlebury River, the trail enters the Moosalamoo Recreation Area within the Green Mountain National Forest. After crossing Mount Mossalamoo, the trail drops again to roughly follow Sucker Brook. A long climb rises to the ridge of the Green Mountains where the NCT turns south on the Long Trail for about 24 miles to the NCT's eastern terminus at Maine Junction. Maine Junction is basically a signpost in the woods where the AT turns east off the Long Trail and heads for Maine. NCT hikers must continue south for another mile to reach the trailhead on VT route 4, eight miles east of Rutland.

Connections with Other Trails

US Bicycle Route 7 (227 miles), along with the NCT, is on VT route 125 just south of Chimney Point.

The Trail Around Middlebury is an 18-mile loop encircling the outer edge of the city, and includes a four-mile spur to the west for the NCT. The NCT follows the eastern side of the loop.

There are over 70 miles of trails within the Moosalamoo Recreation Area having various connections with the NCT. At the Sucker Brook Shelter, the NCT joins the Long Trail, a north-south trail

(200 miles) that spans the state of Vermont.

The Appalachian Trail joins the Long Trail at the southern border of the state, and continues with it until Maine Junction where it veers to the northeast.

Biggest Challenges

The topography is the most serious challenge. The final climb to the Long Trail is a steep 400 feet, with 900 more feet of rise, south of there, to reach the top of Gillespie Peak, the high point of the trail at 3366 feet. There are many ups and downs on the LT. Trail construction in the east favors steep climbs and large rock steps, and blazes are few and far between. The Long Trail is closed during spring mud season, usually until Memorial Day.

Trail Conditions

One way of distinguishing trail miles is as certified and non-certified. The National Park Service certifies trail and defines such as "optimally located, built to the prescribed standard, permanently protected, and considered complete."

Ideally, any category of trail would always be clear, dry, properly graded, well marked, and easy to find. In reality, there are going to be sections with maintenance issues.

Maintenance

There are standards set for the North Country National Scenic Trail which are meant to create a trail that is a joy to hike. As volunteer *extraordinaire* Irene Szabo used to say, "A trail should be a trail, not a trial."

In 1996, the National Park Service produced a book, authored by Bill Menke, entitled *A Handbook for Trail Design, Construction, and Maintenance,* to provide instructions to standardize the work done by all trail partners and create what Bill described as the "thread of continuity." With revisions, this work remains the core document describing what a hiker should find to be true of the trail.

Good design results in trail that will be less affected by erosion and less damaged with use. It will also be easier to maintain.

Generally speaking, the trail opening is to be four feet wide and eight feet in height. The treadway on natural surfaces should be 18 inches wide. Grades should not exceed ten percent unless in short stretches where such construction is not possible. Trail should neither be at the exact top of a ridge or in the bottom of a valley, because these present drainage problems. Trail is best located benched into the side of a hill for changes in elevation, switchbacked with long runs (rather than short-legged "zippers"). Trail benched into hillsides should have 5° outslope to allow water to drain off. Other drainage aids such as Coweeta dips can channel water off the trail.

Trail structures such as puncheon, boardwalks and small bridges should be constructed properly. In most cases, structures should conform to ADA standards in case someone with mobility issues manages to get to the trail, they should not be hampered by an inability to cross a bridge or use a latrine. However, there remains a great deal of local interpretation on this point since exclusions for backcountry trail are allowed.

The reality has yet to reach these many goals, but they are still worth striving toward. Also, certified sections may fall into disrepair while retaining their certification because there isn't adequate means to track trail conditions over time.

Who Does the Work?

For one thing, the trail is maintained almost exclusively by volunteers. The NCT reports more volunteer hours most years than any other national trail. Of couse, it also has more miles.

Paid groups such as Youth Conservation Corps may sometimes take on large maintenance or construction projects.

Where the trail passes through federal or state land, sometimes maintenance, usually involving heavy mowing, chain saw work, large construction projects, etc. may be done by professionals.

Large bridges, which are beyond the capabilities and liability constraints of volunteers are usually contracted out.

What Can Go Wrong?

Particularly, in the late winter into early spring, hikers are often out seeking a welcome outdoor experience before volunteers have had a chance to do spring cleanup. Be patient.

But many issues can affect areas of trail that need work. For one thing, in some of the remote locations, volunteers may live several hours from their sections of trail. Often, work weeks are scheduled for groups to travel together and collectively clean an area. A volunteer may sign up for a trail segment and then fail to follow through. It may take a while for other volunteers to realize there is a problem. Wind, wet snow, or ice can cause a lot of damage to a trail corridor in a short amount of time, and volunteers may not be able to get to the trail immediately to do cleanup. If there is a serious blowdown—straight line winds or a tornado, sometimes it can take months for the damage and danger to be assessed and dealt with. Road walks should be expected around such problem areas.

What You May Find

A lot of what kind of trail conditions you will encounter may depend on the time of year you are hiking. If you are attempting a single-year thru hike, it just goes without saying that you are going to encounter some bad trail conditions. Snow, ice, mud, flooding, and wind are going to happen, and you are likely to be out there walking before crews of any kind can get to the trail.

There are a number of waterways on the NCT that must be forded, or bridges may be damaged. Always be prepared on a long hike. A good solution is mesh-reinforced plastic feed sacks which can be put on right over your footwear and pulled up to the knees. Tie or simply hold in place as you wade. Some streams and rivers may be too dangerous to ford in high water. Particularly in New York and along the SHT, ankle-deep rivulets become raging thigh-deep torrents in spring, and high-water detours may be posted.

Specific areas that often present problems are the Kekekabic Trail which can be overgrown because it is cleared only about twice a year, and as yet, does not receive enough traffic to keep things beaten down. It is also extremely rocky and the walking is difficult. The Superior Hiking Trail and the Long Trail are known for rocky climbs and descents. North Dakota mowing often does not happen early enough in the season for west-to-east thru-hikers. The Adirondack mud is black, peaty and loose and can be a serious obstacle.

How You Can Help

Report trail condition problems to the local chapter, or at northcountrytrail.org/the-trail/report-trail-conditions/ where the information will be sent to the correct group.

Consider volunteering to help with trail work before and/or after your hike.

Treadway

The treadway can vary from roadwalks or hardened trails to narrow single-track pathways. There are about 1500 miles still on roads, however, many of these are pleasant country by-ways. If a lane is not gated or otherwise closed to the public, it must be labeled as a road walk. On the other hand, for example, the 95 miles of service road for the McClusky Canal in North Dakota are clearly a dirt road, but they are not open to the public, so are considered off road.

There are currently over 1000 miles of the NCT that are on closed roads or shared with hardened multi-use trails. Everyone recognizes that this is not the ideal for a National Scenic Trail, but in many cases these can serve as an acceptable way to provide the safety of being off a road until better options are identified.

Officially, an off-road trail corridor is supposed to have at least a four-foot wide and eight-foot high clearance, with an 18-inch treadway. Natural surface treadway is ideally benched into a hillside to be nearly level (a 5° outslope is the standard to drain water) with no more than ten percent grade. However, rocky terrain may make this impossible.

Where concurrent trails pre-existed the NCT, the host trail may have differing standards. Even where there is an active chapter and willing volunteers, it can take a significant number of years to correct poor trail design and construction done by eager but un-trained builders. In many cases, good trail might have been constructed, but there was a lack of volunteers to maintain the treadway.

Drinking Water

The NCTA is attempting to mark reliable natural water sources suitable for filtering with small blue diamonds on the Interactive Map, but as of yet, this is certainly incomplete. You can also use the topographic background layer on that map to find most of the reliable streams. What you often cannot tell from that map is how accessible the water surface may be, especially in areas of significant topography. There is adequate water along most of the NCT. Filtering or treating is highly recommended.

In eastern North Dakota, the Dakota Prairie Chapter has placed caches of bottled water, clearly marked, in wildlife-proof containers, at appropriate intervals. There is one near Robinson Road in the Harbor Springs Chapter area of the northern LP. There are water caches at the two NORTA campsites in northern Ohio.

Trail Structures

Structures can be anything from large, commercially-built bridges installed just for the NCT to simple puncheon—boards laid on the ground, usually supported on low sills, and put down to lift the trail above wet ground. Of course, in many places, the trail crosses waterways on vehicular bridges, and this is likely to remain the case forever in some locations. Any man-made addition, from fire rings to benches and register boxes is a trail structure.

Puncheon

Puncheon is boards, usually lengthwise to the trail, raised on low sills. They provide dry footing where the trail crosses wet meadows or consistently muddy areas.

The surface of puncheon may be smooth milled wood or rough-cut wood. Traction surfacing may be added because these structures are usually slippery when wet. Asphalt roofing singles provide a short-term solution, however these are not long-lasting and they leach petroleum products into the soil or water. Chicken wire is somewhat better, but it tears and creates a hazard within a few years. Hardware cloth is better yet, but expanded metal mesh is being used more, and this provides a stable and fairly durable walking surface. Even more durable traction surfacing may be available.

Boardwalks

Higher, raised walkways, usually with the decking placed crosswise, are called boardwalks. These carry the trail across wetter areas which may occasionally have standing water. They are usually built to ADA standards, wide enough for wheelchairs or trail mowers to cross. They may be footed into the ground, or in recent years "floated" on swamp pans which can respond to frost heave with less damage to the boardwalk.

Bridges

Bridges are much like boardwalks, but they span features like streams or deep, narrow gullies. If more than three feet above the waterline, they require a railing. Similar to boardwalks, they should be built to ADA standards, however in practice, there are still many, many narrow or log bridges on the trail, in addition to quite a few fords, some of which can be serious. The ultimate goal is that the NCT would be a "dry boots" trail.

Shelters

A few of the NCT affiliates consider shelters a high priority. There are many of them along the FLT in New York. Some are found in the Adirondacks, on the Long Trail, and in Pennsylvania. A few have been built in the UP of Michigan, and a couple also exist in Lower Michigan. The Buckeye Trail Association has been attempting to increase the number of legal camping spots, including shelters, although most of the Ohio ones built, to date, are simple plywood boxes, whereas most of the other shelters are Adirondack-style open-fronted log cabins. As yet, the NCT has only a few hostel-type places to stay along the route. All these are listed in the final section of this book.

Other

Benches, tables, and outhouses are nice treats to encounter, but are not priorities, except that many backcountry campsites will include them. Register boxes are provided in some areas, but not in others. Except in the Adirondacks, these are primarily for the hikers' and maintainers' enjoyment. In the Adirondacks, signing in is a safety issue.

Safety and Safe Practices

Hazards

The only places where you are likely to encounter venomous snakes are in southern Ohio where you may see a copperhead, and in Pennsylvania and southern New York it is possible you could come across a timber rattlesnake. Although present in Minnesota and Wisconsin, their range does not overlap the NCT route. Michigan and northern Ohio have a small population of massasauga rattlers, but these are fairly non-aggressive and prefer wetland habitats. The massasauga is federally protected as threatened, and timber rattlers are protected in Vermont, New York, Ohio, Minnesota, and several other non-NCT states.

Black bears could be encountered in any of the trail states. Note that black bears are not nearly as aggressive as brown bears, but food should be protected from them (and more likely from squirrels, raccoons, and chipmunks). It is highly unlikely you would be attacked by a black bear unless you manage to get between a mother and cub. Make yourself look large, make noise, and don't run. The Superior National Forest and the Adirondacks REQUIRE "all food, food containers and scented items be safely stored to help prevent bear-human interactions." At the present time, this includes bear-resistant containers and appropriate hanging techniques.

Moose may be a bigger threat than bears. Do not approach them, do not run.

Ticks are much more prevalent in the northern states than they used to be. Use repellants, and check yourself daily as they carry many diseases as well as Lyme. Mosquitoes and blackflies can be problematic depending on the time of year and weather. Plan on needing repellants, headnets, and full skin coverings at certain times of year.

Hazards from plant material comes under three headings: those you touch which can cause a skin reaction, those which are unpleasant to touch, and plants which are poisonous to ingest. The plants listed affect most people, however, any one person might have an allergy to something not listed.

You can find poison ivy in any of the eight states. Poison sumac does grow in some wetlands, but it is unlikely to be contacted if you stay on the trail. Two plants are known for causing burn-like skin reactions if you get the sap on your skin and are exposed to sunlight. These are giant hogweed and wild parsnip. Encountering these is possible, but if you familiarize yourself with their basic looks and avoid breaking any plants that look similar, you should be fine.

Some plants cause mechanical irritation. If you like to hike in shorts, just accept that you will probably get pricked and scratched. Nettles has stinging hairs. Although the itching doesn't last long, there is lots of this plant along the trail. Common plants with briars that intrude into the treadway include various types of berry canes, greenbriar, and the alien multi-flora rose.

Unless you are certain of the identity, you are much safer to not ingest wild plants or fungi. That said, with a little study, you can enjoy treats such as blueberries, raspberries, thimbleberries, wintergreen, wild cranberry, puffball, apples, haw apples, and various greens. Two deadly plants of note are poison hemlock (not the tree, but a carrot relative) and foxglove. Don't break these plants and then get the sap in your mouth.

Safe Practices

There is a certain amount of risk inherent in hiking a backcountry trail. Slippery rocks, cliff edges, fast-moving water, and various kinds of poor footing all pose hazards. Hikers are expected to be able to judge their own abilities and to avoid rash decisions. Proper footwear is essential–whatever that means for your own feet.

Many people and/or their families feel more comfortable and safe if a hiker carries a satellite tracking devise. Examples are the

Spot or Garmin Inreach. Apple and Android satellite SOS systems are now available on smartphones as well. If you do think you are lost, stop and consider your location and situation. If you are truly lost, staying in one place will assist in your rescue.

Portions of the NCT are still on roads. In most places there is shoulder to walk on, but that is not guaranteed. Walk on the left side, facing traffic. Wearing bright colors such as blaze orange is suggested.

Various hunting seasons are legal throughout most of the fall, winter, and spring months of the year, and much of the forested areas through which the NCT passes are open for hunting. The one season which offers a higher risk to hikers is gun deer season. The exact dates vary from state to state, but it is generally in the fall. Plan to wear blaze orange (at least a hat which provides 360° visibility) during these weeks. Some hikers even choose to stay out of the woods at this time. Wearing orange during any of the hunting seasons is an excellent way to increase your personal safety. If you hike with a dog, don't forget to provide your pet with an orange vest.

Where the trail crosses private land, the owners may request that the trail be closed during hunting seasons, and an alternate road walk is specified. This is the case on many sections along the Finger Lakes Trail in New York. FLT maps clearly indicate these and the dates of the closures. Please abide by these rules. Intrusion by hikers during closures usually results in the loss of trail passage.

Trail registers are found in many places along the trail, although certainly not all. In most cases, these are optional for trail users to sign, mainly allowing hikers to enjoy reading about who else has passed that way or providing a way for the maintainers to receive feedback on user experience. However, they can be a safety net, if a date is entered and a person goes missing, that notation can show a known location. In particular, in the Adirondacks, large register kiosks are located at entry points to various units of the Park. Hikers are expected to sign in and out (or in the case of the NCT, to indicate they are hiking thru and will not return to that location). Because of the rugged and primitive conditions in the Adirondacks, signing in and out at register boxes is one facet of safe hiking practice.

It's always recommended that you have someone who knows your approximate itinerary, and with whom you have set specific check-in times. Pre-arrangements such as, "If I do not contact you by [time] on [day], contact authorities." If you have an extra meal with you, you can push the emergency contact day and time about 24 hours after your expected arrival at a certain point. This way, your contact person can assume that something is wrong and you need help if you don't check in.

Trail Closures

Some portions of the trail are closed to hikers on a regular basis. The Mackinac Bridge (connecting Michigan's Upper and Lower Peninsulas) is closed to pedestrians for all but one day of the year. A hiker who arrives there at other times with no vehicular support can request transport from the Bridge Authority for a fee. Anyone can participate in the Labor Day Bridge Walk. The number of people who make this trek each year is usually 30,000 or more.

Both the SHT in Duluth and the Long Trail in Vermont close the trail in the spring during mud season. In Vermont, this usually lasts until Memorial Day. The SHT within the city limits of Duluth is closed for 24 hours after every rain event.

In New York, all private land through which the FLT passes is closed for 24 hours on the first Monday of February each year. Also, there are numerous hunting season closures of the trail in New York with alternate road walks mapped around these sections. These closures are usually the entire month of May, and October 1 through January 1 of the following year. The FLT is attempting to align all of these dates to be the same, but individual maps should still be consulted.

One unusual, potential closure is at Victoria Dam in the UP. The trail fords the West Branch of the Ontonagon River below the dam. When water is being released below the dam, fording is impossible. The website at uppco.com/hydro-water-levels updates every ten minutes. Scroll down to Victoria Dam and check the number labeled Total Flow. If that is over 800 cfs (cubic feet per second) it is guaranteed that water is being released. Upper Peninsula Power Company states that there might occasionally be a scenario when the Total Flow is under 800 cfs, but they might be releasing some water anyway. But this information is accurate most of the time. They are in the process of creating a web page that clearly indicates in real time if water is being released. Do not use the imagery base layer on the Interactive Map or Google to attempt to see what is happening as that imagery is generally one to three years old.

Additionally, sections may be temporarily closed for logging operations, uncleared serious blowdowns, damaged or destroyed bridges, etc. A long-distance hiker needs to be flexible enough to adapt to these types of disturbances. In many cases, checking the Interactive Map for alerts, and the websites of affiliate trails where appropriate will provide advance information. It's not much fun to arrive at a bridge that is out and the waterway unfordable, requiring a long, unexpected road detour.

Permits

The Boundary Waters Canoe Area Wilderness of Minnesota, which includes portions of the Kekakabic and Border Route Trails, requires an entry permit. Permits for canoeing are snapped up early in the season and the vast majority of users are paddlers. Usually, you won't have much trouble getting a permit for hiking. However, occasionally there are difficulties for a person on foot because you are supposed to pick up the permit within 24 hours of entering the BWCAW. In the author's experience, the enforcement of this depends somewhat on who you deal with. It is suggested that you acquire the permit at the Forest Service office in Grand Marais, MN, where they have more experience in dealing with hikers. See bwca.com for complete information on various kinds of permits.

Douglas County, Wisconsin, hosts 37 miles of NCT, and you must have a permit to camp on that property. This costs $40, and would cover 10 nights per year. The permit is available on line at douglascountywi.gov/DocumentCenter/View/14431

You need to have a permit to disperse camp in the Brule River State Forest of Wisconsin, and you are supposed to get this at the Brule River State Forest station 6250 S Ranger Rd., Brule, WI 54820, 715-372-5678. The several designated sites also technically require the permit.

Most state parks do not allow dispersed camping, and you must stay in designated campsites for a fee.

Two Michigan State Parks should be noted because of the amount of use they receive. You should reserve early. In Porcupine Mountain Wilderness State Park you must have a reserved campsite. Dispersed camping is not allowed. Long-distance NCT backpackers should call Park Headquarters at 906-885-5275 prior to their hike. Craig Lake State Park is now requiring advance campsite reservations. Dispersed camping is not allowed. Long-distance NCT backpackers should call the Van Riper State Park Campground Office at 906-339-4461 prior to their hike.

If you plan to stay overnight in Pictured Rocks National Lakeshore, you must have a permit. Apply for this as early as possible. You must stay at designated campsites and keep to your submitted itinerary. See recreation.gov/camping/campgrounds/256367 Later in this book is a plan to hike through Pictured Rocks using day hikes.

In Michigan, you can disperse camp in State Forests, however, you must have a free permit for each location. This permit can be acquired on line at michigan.gov/-/media/Project/Websites/dnr/Documents/Forms/folder2/PR4134_CampRegCard.pdf?rev=33fb7ab70add4249a4344613a6a3e186.

Note that you are supposed to fill out one of these cards for every night you camp, and leave it where you camped. This seems counterintuitive to Leave No Trace principles, but nevertheless, that is the regulation.

If you are overnight hiking in larger groups (sometimes 8 or more, sometimes 10 or more), there are many areas which require a permit or some sort of use notification. If you plan to hike and camp with a group of that size, check with local land managers.

A few other places require permits. See Campground Section.

Dogs

Dogs are welcome, if leashed, most places on the NCT. However, the following areas prohibit them. Most of these are short sections, but without prior arrangements, arriving at one side or the other of these segments might result in a long road detour.

Greenwater Lake State Scientific and Natural Area, just east of Tamarac Wildlife Refuge in Minnesota, hosts approximately two miles of trail, and dogs are not allowed.

In Wisconsin's Copper Falls State Park, dogs are not allowed where the NCT is concurrent with the Doughboy's Trail (from the concession stand for about a mile until approximately at Devil's Gate on the Bad River). However, a dog-friendly route on the accessible and Brownstone Loop Trails will take a hiker with a dog around this section without adding miles.

Pictured Rocks National Lakeshore in Michigan's UP–all North Country Scenic Trail segments that pass through the length of the park (sometimes referred to as the Lakeshore Trail) are closed to pets

Dogs are not permitted on the Mackinac Bridge walk.

Pets are prohibited in Ohio Nature Preserves. Along the NCT, this includes Davis Memorial, Boch Hollow, Little Rocky Hollow, Scheick Hollow, and Sheepkin Hollow Nature Preserves.

Dogs are prohibited on the Watkins Glen Gorge Trail. Technically, the NCT/FLT stays on the Rim Trail because the Gorge Trail is closed in winter. But summer hikers may prefer to take the Gorge route.

It is possible that various pieces of private property could be signed to exclude pets.

Please note that hiking with a dog in southern Ohio can be problematic due to the number of loose dogs along that portion of the trail.

Dogs ARE allowed on the trail through Fort Custer National Cemetery near Battle Creek, Michigan, if leashed. However, they are not allowed in the actual cemetery. This has been confirmed in writing as a lot of questions arise concerning this property.

The NCT does not go through the Adirondack High Peaks, but if you are planning an adventure that includes that area, dogs are not allowed.

Other Resources

Always visit Affiliate web sites for trail alerts.

NCT: look for yellow ! diamonds on the Interactive Map https://nct.maps.arcgis.com/apps/View/index.html?appid=247bfb7befd64180a4471533b937ec25

SHT: superiorhiking.org/trail-conditions/

BT: buckeyetrail.org/alerts.php

FLT: fingerlakestrail.org/plan-hikes-finger-lakes-trail/trail-conditions/

Long Trail: greenmountainclub.org/hiking/trail-updates/

Several non-trail websites exist that can give a hiker valuable information.

For snow cover: www.nohrsc.noaa.gov/nsa/

For climate near any significant city: usclimatedata.com/climate/united-states/us

For wildfires: arcgis.com/home/webmap/viewer.html?webmap=df8bcc10430f48878b01c96e907a1fc3#!

How to Find Your Way

Blazes

Blazes are what trail people call the (usually) color-coded markings that indicate the correct pathway. The origin of the word comes initially from the idea of a blazing fire, a light shining on the path to show the way. A trail blaze should clearly indicate the way a hiker should travel.

NCT Blazes

It is curious but true, that until 1996, there was no standard for blazing of the NCT. In fact, there was not even agreement that the trail should be marked on the road segments, or marked as NCT on affiliate sections. Blazes were variously gray diamonds, blue diamonds, rectangular or diamond-shaped paint blazes in almost any shade of blue–usually what someone had in their garage. Where the trail was concurrent with other trails, their blazing system needed to be understood. It might have been red or yellow discs, squares, diamonds... almost anything. The Ohio Buckeye Trail and the New York Finger Lakes Trail had agreed to allow the NCT to also follow their pathways, and these blazes were (and still are) painted rectangles in light blue and white, respectively.

Now, everyone agrees that standard blazing along the entire length is the goal. That said, there are still various blazing schemes used by the different affiliates, and some landowners require their own blazing style.

Blue

The official blaze of the North Country Trail is a painted 2"x6" rectangle in Nelson Boundary Blue. Bill Menke has always pointed out that this is about the size of a dollar bill. Boundary paint is formulated to resist weathering and repel the growth of lichen and moss. In some places, nail-up plastic blazes may be substituted where the landowner has requested this. To see this color on a computer (allowing for differences in monitor display) open any graphics program and choose color by the hex code 5CA8D8. Stick-on reflective blazes are usually a darker blue, because of the lack of availability of the brighter blue.

White

Officially, white 2"x6" blazes should be found on spurs and side trails.

Emblems

Additionally, the triangular emblem of the NCT with a central compass rose may be found at road crossings and occasionally at other locations.

used with permission of the NPS

Superior Hiking Trail

The NCT is concurrent with the Superior Hiking Trail in Minnesota for its entire length of about 300 miles. This is marked with a combination of NCT blue blazes and the SHT lozenge-shaped logo with curled ends.

Buckeye Trail Blazes

Light Blue

The NCT is concurrent with the Buckeye Trail in Ohio for about 900 miles. Buckeye Blue is a much lighter blue than the NCT blue, but it is blue. The official shade is Sherwin Williams Sweeping Blue. You can see this at myperfectcolor.com/paint/27939-sherwin-williams-sw2408-sweeping-blue, but allow for the fact that not all monitors display exactly the same.

Emblems

The BT usually has its logo only at road crossings or on other signage.

Finger Lakes Trail Blazes

White

The NCT is concurrent with the Finger Lakes Trail in New York for more than 400 miles. The FLT is older than the NCT, and has traditionally used white 2"x6" blazes for the main trail.

Blue

The FLT has the exact opposite color codes from the NCT. Its spur trails are blazed in blue.

Emblems

The FLT usually has large yellow square signs at road crossings and trailheads.

Long Trail

The NCT is concurrent with the Long Trail in Vermont for about 24 miles. This is marked occasionally with white blazes.

Turns and more

There is a standard format for marking changes in direction on trails. If there are two blazes, one above the other, the top one is offset in the direction of the turn.

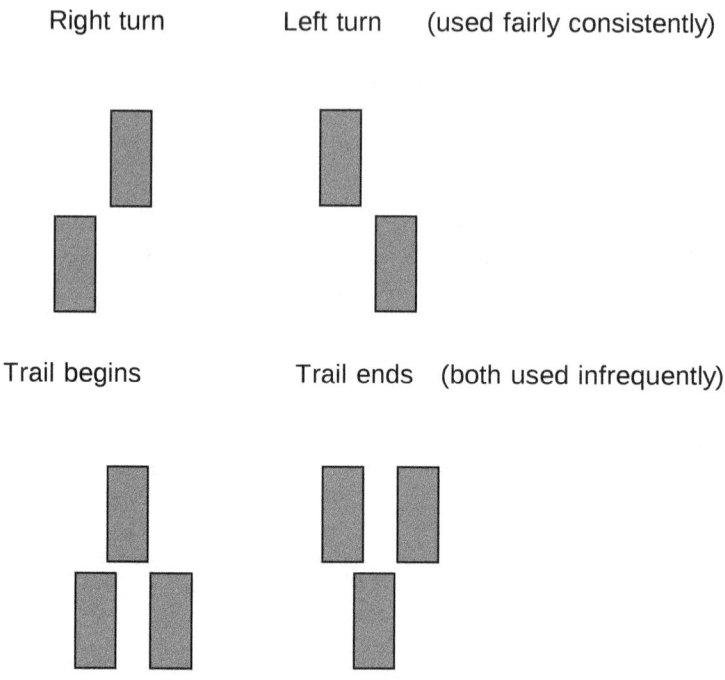

Additionally, you may see two blazes, one above the other with no directionality. This has been used to mean "pay attention," a change is coming up. You will see this used most often in New York.

More confusion

There are going to be marks made by people who don't know the standard "code." You will see arrows, < and > marks, slashes, diamonds, and also in New York, upside-down L-shaped blazes where the short leg of the L points in the direction of the turn. Some agencies still prefer the nail-up plastic diamonds.

There are going to be actual logging or boundary marks which may be single or multiple slashes, or dots. These are often in Boundary Blue which is particularly confusing, but in some cases where the marking entity is aware of the trail, a turquoise color will be used for the logging marks.

When the NCT is concurrent with other, shorter trails such as in parks or nature preserves, the landowner may not agree to having NCT blue blazes. In these cases, you need to follow whatever the local trail blazes are whether yellow diamonds, posts at junctions, red dots, etc. Road walks often have fewer blazes, if any.

Beware of forks in the trail with one blaze in the middle between the two forks. This is the author's personal pet peeve. Pay attention to your maps, and look for a confirmation blaze farther down one of the forks. Nail-up diamonds may or may not be angled in a direction you should turn.

One particular place to pay attention is when hiking on an old woods road. It's easy to keep walking down the wide clearing and miss even a well-marked turn.

Purple Blazes

In recent years, purple has become the standard color to mark private property. If you see a line of trees marked neatly or not-so-neatly with purple, you can be sure there is private property beyond those trees.

Just for Fun

There are two types of nail-up blazes of an historic nature that can still be found in only a few locations along the NCT.

Early on, a gray diamond blaze with NCT on it was designed by Keith Myrmel, the artist who now offers the "romance style" maps of the trail. You might still see one or two of these in the Chequamgon National Forest, WI, where they built trail for the NCT before it was even authorized and also in the Chippewa NF, MN.

Also, the Michigan Trail Finders Club was called upon to build trail in the Manistee National Forest, MI, from Croton Dam to McCarthy Lake. This was called the Manistee Trail, and it basically became the NCT. There is at least one of their emblems still along the trail.

Maps and Guides

History of maps/guides

Maps for the trail were few and poor for many years. Most National Forests printed a brochure which had a blue line wandering across a tan or gray background with almost no waypoints and no topographic information. But at least these helped make people aware that a trail existed.

In Michigan, Arden Johnson created some maps for the northern Lower Peninsula which were hand-drawn political maps with the trail superimposed on them. In 1989, Rod MacRae wrote a guidebook to the NCT in Minnesota's Chippewa National Forest. Glenn Oster wrote an abbreviated guide/data book for the NCT in Pennsylvania. Olive Anderson created a guide to Pictured Rocks in the Upper Peninsula of Michigan.

In 1991, a couple, Byron and Margaret Hutchins, produced guidebooks to the certified sections of NCT through each of the National Forests and all of Michigan's Lower Peninsula. These included hand-sketched maps with accompanying text. They measured distances with a wheel and, interestingly, always noted how many minutes it took them to hike between waypoints. Although primitive, these were invaluable to hikers.

The Manistee National Forest produced a mapset that was better than the tan brochures.

Of course, there weren't many long-distance hikers. Most of the people using the trail were the volunteers who were dedicated to their own local section, and so they knew where the trail went. Some chapters did create brochures with additional information about the trail.

The most encompassing effort to create a trail guide was put forth by Wes Boyd in the 1990s. Wes was not really a hiker. But he was on the board, was the editor of the *North Star* magazine, and had a passion for the trail. He drove through the then seven states of the trail, taking excellent notes and creating better maps. He completed all but New York. As we have now learned about this trail, most trailwide projects collapse under their own weight because of its great length. However, Wes' guide was useful in some places well into the 2000s. He also wrote a book, *Following the North Country National Scenic Trail*, which gave an overview of progress in each state (1989, revised 1991, 1999).

In 2003, the NCTA produced a book called *Hikeable Segments of the North Country National Scenic Trail*, This was a bare bones guide to off-road segments.

The final effort to create a bound paper trail-wide guide was in 2013. *The North Country Trail: The Best Walks, Hikes, and Backpacking Trips on America's Longest National Scenic Trail* was produced by the NCTA and credited to Ron Strickland. Again, this book covered the longest of the off-road segments of trail.

Perhaps the best idea was, in the 2000s, the creation of a Wiki Guide to the trail which could be updated by anyone. However, this was also its downfall. A great deal of incorrect information was entered, and it needed a full-time administrator to oversee the data. It was eventually taken down.

Current Maps

Before beginning the discussion on available maps, it needs to be explained that the NCTA does not compete with the Superior Hiking Trail Association, the Buckeye Trail Association, the Finger Lakes Trail Conference, or the Green Mountain Club (Long Trail) regarding their maps. Each of these organizations (all affiliates or partners of the NCTA) produces its own maps and sells them. The NCTA has chosen to make maps free, which is in conflict with the goal of these other trail organizations, to generate income. Therefore, for the best resource on the four trails mentioned above, a total of over 1700 miles, you will need to purchase their maps. There is more information below.

The official NCT maps are updated twice a year in March and September. Changes will appear on the Interactive Map and be populated through the paper maps and Avenza and FarOut apps.

It is highly recommended that you use maps to find your way on the North Country Trail. Although it would be great to say that you can just hop on the trail and follow the blue blazes, in reality, this is not always true. Roadwalks may be sporadically blazed, turns may not be adequately marked, older blazes may have faded or disappeared. Both paper and electronic maps have their own values.

What Maps Do You Need?

Personal note: I like having as many map resources as possible. On my recent end-to-end hike (Dec 2021 to Jun 2023), I spent over $300 on maps, and even with that, there were additional guides I could have purchased. You may decide you don't need that many options. At the present time, I would say that you'd be minimally covered with the electronic map options everywhere except in the Adirondacks. However, those miles should have correctly GPSed tracks and maps in 2025. That said, it's a really good idea to always have a paper map backup and a compass; I always carried these.

Of course, the risk with using only electronic maps is that your phone might become unusable. Most of the mapping options do not require that you have a cell signal, but the phone has to be charged and not broken or lost. You'll certainly need a power pack to keep the phone battery healthy, and these can be heavy, a lot heavier than several sheets of paper. You might also drop electronics in water, on a rock, or off a cliff. We all say, "that won't happen," But it often does. I've lost paper maps on too many occasions. I've even lost my phone, but always found it.

You have to decide what level of map security you are comfortable with. Keep in mind that place names are not always consistent. Back when paper maps were the only option, I quickly learned that I wanted to have maps from three sources (topographic and two political) on any hike to be able to assess the terrain, see the surrounding area, and perhaps clarify things if the road name at a corner is different from the road name shown on a map which is the case all too often.

A personal example of where a larger paper map "saved" me was long ago when the trail disappeared in a logging clearcut. I finally found a road (with no sign), and then a survey marker on a tree. With the paper map showing survey section numbers, I was able to determine my location.

Interactive GIS Map

The first place to begin your investigation into the trail is the

Interactive GIS map at northcountrytrail.org/The Trail/Trail Maps and Downloads. I recommend doing this on a computer because it's much easier to navigate, but it will work on a smart phone/tablet.

You can scroll out (or click the - sign) far enough to view the entire trail, or scroll in (or click the + sign) to ever-tightening levels of detail. The first things to notice are:

1. Road walks are marked with a dotted line, and off-road treadways (including paved multi-use trails and gated roads) are a solid line. The key issue being if the "road" is open to public use.

2. Each state is marked with mileage numbers at half-mile intervals. These can be very useful when communicating with others about locations. However, see a warning below under Updates

3. The background map (base layer) has information about the surrounding area. There are many base layers to choose from. See more below.

4. There are yellow diamonds with an exclamation point which indicate trail alerts. Click on these, and a box will open for more info.

Using the vertical tool box

You will see a +, a house, a -, and a circle with four tabs

1. The + can be used to scroll in (make the map view closer)

2. The - can be used to scroll out (make the map view more broad)

3. The house will return you to the default level of zoom

4. The circle will allow you to use this map for navigation- if you have this open in your car, and have enabled it, you will see a blue dot for your location, just like you would on Google maps or other navigational apps.

Using the menu bar

1. Click on the three lines to open the legend. It will explain the things mentioned in the above paragraph and more.

2. Click on the "stack of papers" to open the layer dialog. You will see that most of these features are already checked if you are zoomed in far enough. But you might want to scroll down and find "US Protected Areas" These are things like National Forests (green) and State Forests (medium purple). You can click on the legend (see point 1) for a key to all these colored areas, or click on the colored areas for a pop-up box with the specific information (if the pop-up box shows the NCT map number, notice that it says "1 of 2" at the top and you can click the triangle to get the landowner info). Note that using this layer may slow scrolling the map. Also available in layers is the NOHRSC (National Operational Hydrologic Remote Sensing Center) snow cover map. When this is clicked to show, the legend will give you the snow depths corresponding to the colors, basically shading from gray through light blue to deep purple. Recently, the NCT paper map numbers have been added as a layer. Default is "on," but it can be turned off.

3. Click on the "window pane" to find different base layer maps. Particularly helpful are the Open Streets map, the USGS topographic map (note that you can not zoom in indefinitely on this map or it will disappear), and the satellite imagery maps. The default layer is not one of the choices. If you want the default background you must reload the page. Other basemaps can be interesting and/or helpful for other reasons.

4. Click the triangle for measuring lines and areas. The area tool looks like a sheet of paper with a folded corner and a pen. Choose your units (square miles to square feet) and click on the map at one corner of the area you want to measure. Keep clicking on corners until you have arrived back where you started. Double click to end, and the area will show in the box below the tool. Note that you cannot undo a click. If you make a mistake, you'll have to start over.

To measure distances, select the line and pen. Chose your units. Click where you want to begin measuring; double click to end. The distance will show in the space below the tool. Note that you cannot undo a click. If you make a mistake, you'll have to start over.

To find a location's coordinates, click on the circle with crosshairs. You can choose to see coordinates in Degrees (decimal) or Degrees/Minutes/Seconds. Move the mouse across the screen and you will see the numbers change. When you click, a green marker will appear on the map, and the bottom line will note that location.

5. Click the small circle with three arrows to share a map. You can share the default view, or click the box "Share the Current Map View" to share a particular section centered where you are currently working.

6. Printing- using this icon to print maps is not recommended unless you want something for an overview. To get the high-quality, detailed free maps that are good to take to the trail, see the heading below for paper maps.

Using the search feature

You can search for cities, streets, and political features like state parks, but usually not for topographic features like the names of mountains or rivers unless they have some sort of facility or community associated with them. You can put in the coordinates for a particular location, but you may have to enter them "backwards," with the longitude first. For example -84.94624 45.353151 or -84°56'46.3" 45°21'11.2", (either format should take you to the North Central Michigan College Nature Area). If you enter them in the normal order, the map may take you to somewhere in Antarctica. If it's being wonky, switch the order and try again.

Other features of the Interactive Map

1. The first thing you might notice is that there are numbers beside small red diamonds along the way. These are half-mile markers which begin at the (trail) western edge of the state. These are useful to help coordinate locations. THE CAVEAT: Twice a year, any updates to the trail are added to the interactive map. Almost without exception, this will cause these numbers to shift, and it is why those half-mile reference numbers are not used in this book. They would be outdated before it ever got to print. If you are using these numbers to plan a hike with other people, make sure that everyone is using the most recent update. Misadventures with one person using the interactive map (most recent) and another person using an older set of printed maps are common.

2. Trail that is off-road (think closed to vehicles rather than a particular type of treadway) will be indicated by a solid red line. This will include off-road but paved, such as most multi-use trails. Dotted lines indicate road walks.

3. Some trail shelters and camping areas are located on the map with familiar symbols, however, there is a more complete list of options in the second half of this book

4. Small blue diamonds indicate reliable water sources, most of which provide water which will need to be treated. This feature is a work in progress, and not all water sources are marked yet.

5. You will notice yellow diamonds with an exclamation point in them. Click on these and a box will open showing you a current trail alert for that location. For example, a bridge that is out, or place where changes on the ground have occurred, but the map is not updated yet.

6. Click on any trail line segment, and a box will open and the segment glows light blue. This will show you the length of that piece (determined by a unique set of facts associated with that piece, thus the lengths vary). The box will contain information such as the owner and managing authority, what uses are permitted, what types of camping are allowed– if any, the name of the maintaining chapter/affiliate, and what the surface is.

Paper Maps

From the NCTA

Go to northcountrytrail.org/The Trail/Trail Maps and Downloads. Scroll down or click on Printable Maps. There you will find map bundles that the NCT offers listed by state. These are PDFs that you can download and print for free. Again, remember that the BRT, SHT, BT, FLT, and LT sell their own maps. However, the Border Route maps can be purchased through the NCTA Trail Shop. Note: printing maps directly from the Interactive Map is usually disappointing.

From Keith Myrmel

Keith Myrmel of Minnesota is known for his "romance maps" of many trails or natural areas. He has created two that cover the entire NCT. They are printed front and back of one single large poster (25" x 39"). Thus, if you want to display the entire trail at one time, you need two copies.

myrmelmaps.com

From Affiliates/Partners

The Superior Hiking Trail Association sells a set of paper maps of their entire trail, and the NCT uses all of these.

The Buckeye Trail Association sells a set of paper maps of their entire trail. To buy just the miles concurrent with the NCT you should buy: Defiance, Delphos, St Marys, Troy, Caesar Creek, Loveland, Williamsburg, West Union, Shawnee, Sinking Spring, Scioto Trail, Old Man's Cave, New Straitsville, Stockport, Whipple, Road Fork, Belle Valley, and Bowerston maps. These include the text of a guide which is written in a clockwise (of the entire BT loop) direction. This can be confusing if hiking counter-clockwise, which is NCT west to east. However, mileages from both directions are given. The political basemaps are light blue and difficult to read. It may be less expensive to buy the entire set of maps and just use the ones you need.

The Finger Lakes Trail Conference sells paper maps. These are updated often, which is good, but if you buy too far in advance, you may find that things have changed by the time you hike. On the back of each paper map is a guide to the section which is written in a west to east format. Individual maps are inexpensive, but buying the entire set can add up. The NCT uses maps M1-M21 and O1,O2 (Main Trail 1-21, and Onondaga Trail 1,2).

In the Adirondacks, at the current time, it is recommended to purchase National Geographic Adirondack Park maps (west to east) 745- Old Forge/Oswegatchie, 744-Northville/Raquette Lake, and 743- Lake George/Great Sacandaga.

In Vermont, the Green Mountain Club sells a paper map of the Long Trail. store.greenmountainclub.org

Note: most state parks have good pdf maps you can download and print online which will show locations of camping areas, water, toilet facilites, etc. Some nature preserves or other kinds of parks through which the trail passes may also offer paper maps. Increasingly, these are being georeferenced, so they can be loaded into Avenza. Links to some of these are provided in the Appendix.

Electronic Maps

Note: Both Avenza and FarOut have arrangements with the NCTA so that when you use these, you have the most recent and accurate updates of the official maps (again, keep in mind that this does not include the SHT, BT, FLT, or LT). When using other trail apps, many of them popular, you can not be sure that the trail line is totally accurate. This should be seriously considered when planning a long hike, particularly since Avenza is free.

Official GPX or KML files can be downloaded free at northcountrytrail.org/The Trail/Trail Maps and Downloads.

Avenza

Avenza is one of the two electronic mapping apps where you can find official NCT maps which are updated regularly. It offers a large selection of features. You should probably make sure that maps are downloaded to your phone before you get to the woods, but once there, you do not need cell service for the app to work. In fact, it's often a good idea to put it on airplane mode while in the woods to minimize battery drain.

The maps can be downloaded for free through the Avenza store (the shopping cart icon). You will need to search for the bundle of maps you want. This can sometimes be frustrating, but if you enter "north country trail [state name]" and search, you should get the desired results. You can have an unlimited number of free maps in Avenza provided that you download them through their store. If you add maps by using the orange + symbol, you can only have three at a time without paying for a plan. Their Avenza Plus plan is about $35 a year, and allows you to add unlimited maps from other sources. This may be important if you are doing a long NCT hike. The Finger Lakes Trail digital maps are geospatially referenced, and can be loaded into Avenza. They can also be purchased through the Avenza store, but the cost is considerably higher than buying the 23 FLT maps you'll need as a paper and digital package, and then adding them to Avenza under the Plus plan.

A blue dot locater will show you your exact position in real time. The maps with half-mile waypoints correspond to the paper maps you can print as to their name/number. One difference to note is that in Avenza off-road trail appears as rounded dots (instead of a solid line), and roadwalks are dashed lines. These can look very similar if you don't look carefully. With some degree of accuracy, a green background indicates public land and white is private.

You can track your hike. You can mark waypoints. You can take pictures with your phone and pin them to coordinates on the maps. These tracks and waypoints can be downloaded to separate KML files, which can be sent to other people or saved on your computer.

Downloading updates: If you have tracks and waypoints marked that you want to be sure not to lose, it is a good idea to export the KML files to yourself before updating. Occasionally, I have had that information not be retained through the update. Click the icon that looks like a stack of paper, click the three dots beside the layer(s), and choose export. Select the kml layer and name it something meaningful. Click the orange circle with a box and an arrow. Wait a minute and you can select whether to email it to yourself or someone, send to Dropbox, etc.

Extra notes about Avenza:

The DeLorme (now Garmin) state atlas maps are available, usually at about $25 per state, on Avenza. Search for [state name] Atlas and Gazateer. These can be extremely helpful in finding your way to trailheads and locating nearby towns.

Avenza also has added an OSM (Open Street Maps) Baselayer (still beta version as of June 2024) which provides a free basemap layer for anywhere in the world, although the author has little experience with its accuracy in other places, it has been extremely helpful in the Central United States.

FarOut

The NCT maps on FarOut are official, but they are not free.

Some people prefer the FarOut (formerly GutHook) app, primarily for two reasons. You can generate an elevation profile that includes waypoints, and it contains crowd-sourced information at a level more-or less related to how much use the trail gets and how interested people are at making entries.

FarOut also includes automatically showing the distance to the next map feature in each direction. Also, you can change the base layer to show either topography or a political map.

One thing to be aware of is that the guts of the app for Apple and Android are totally different. Some features do not work well on Android. For one thing, you can't get coordinates for a location on Android, or put in a location and find it. It's true that there are many apps that will do this, but it seems awkward not to be able to do this on such a popular trail app just because you have an Android phone.

Other Mapping Apps

Other popular mapping apps include Gaia and AllTrails. Some people pay for services such as OnX Hunt because it will show private property lines fairly accurately. What you need to know about any apps except Avenza and FarOut is that they are guaranteed not to be 100% accurate for the line of the North Country Trail. Some trail sections are crowd sourced. Some of the lines may be taken from Google or outdated files, such as old DNR tracks. On a trail that is still fairly fluid, such as the NCT, you want to have up-to-date information.

GPX files. You can download the centerline of the NCT as a GPX file at northcountrytrail.org/the-trail/trail-map-and-downloads/

FLT digital maps come with GPX files.

Electronic Maps from Affiliates

SHT: At superiorhiking.org you can purchase a full set of maps for Avenza, or find them through the Avenza store, as a full set or by sections.

BT: The Buckeye Trail maps can be purchased on FarOut. There is a lot of detailed information on these.

FLT: If you purchase the digital maps from fingerlakestrail.org, they are georeferenced and can be individually loaded into Avenza. Or you can purchase the FLT maps through the Avenza store, but they are considerably more expensive there.

LT: The entire Long Trail is available through Avenza or FarOut. However, it has the exact same level of detail as the paper map, and it may not be of much additional help except that you can locate yourself relative to the trail.

Current Guides and Data Books

A guide to North Dakota, by Rennae Gruchalla, will be available in 2025.

There is a *Guide to the North Country Trail in Minnesota*. shop.northcountrytrail.org/collections/books

The Kekekabic Trail Guide was revised in 2023. shop.northcountrytrail.org/collections/books

SHT: There is the official SHT guidebook, and another by Annie Nelson. Additionally, there is an actual SHT data book. All are available at superiorhiking.org.

MI UP: The Hiawatha Shore-to-Shore Chapter has a guide drive.google.com/file/d/11cte3PY7m67NxmtswvSGsf8r22OKzYWS/view?usp=drivesdk

MI LP: The author has created a data book for several counties in the Lower Peninsula of Michigan. Although the level of detail is what hikers would like, it would be more than a full time job to keep such a resource up to date. Portions are already outdated. This can be found at explorenct.info/MILP under the individual counties.

BT: The Buckeye Trail maps include text (which needs some revision, but can be useful), written in a clockwise (of the entire BT loop) direction. This can be confusing if hiking counter-clockwise, which is NCT west to east. However, mileages from both directions are given. buckeyetrail.org

FLT: The reverse side of every FLT map includes detailed information between various waypoints. This is organized west to east, but isn't too difficult to interpret if hiking east to west. fingelakestrail.org

LT: the Long Trail does sell guides which include the entire 200 miles. store.greenmountainclub.org

Various other files posted by hikers can be found on Facebook/North Country Trail Community in the Files section.

Bonus Section

Pictured Rocks can be completed by day hiking, thus needing no permit. Text is west to east.

Day 1- Munising Falls Creek parking to the Chapel Road TH

At Mosquito Campsites turn inland on the Mosquito River Trail. 11.7 NCT miles with an additional 1.8 miles on the spur for a total of 13.5 miles. (Note that this day can be split into two shorter ones, by stopping and starting at Miners Beach parking.)

Day 2- Chapel Road TH to Little Beaver Boat Launch

1.8 miles to the NCT on Mosquito River Trail, then 8.5 NCT miles to the junction of the Lake Superior Trail- turn inland to the Little Beaver Boat Launch. 1.5 miles on the spur for a total of 11.8 miles for the day. The road to Little Beaver Boat Launch is steep and large vehicles are restricted.

Day 3- Little Beaver Boat Launch to Hurricane River parking.

1.5 miles on the spur from Little Beaver Boat Launch, then 12.7 miles on the NCT for a total of 14.2 miles.

Day 4- Hurricane River to Grand Sable Visitor Center. 9.5 miles.

Note that days 3 & 4 can be evened out more by ending day 3 at Twelvemile Beach (10.2 plus the 1.5 miles on the spur) and making day 4 from Twelvemile Beach to the Visitor Center with 12.0 miles).

Adirondacks: This author has written some tips for finding the route through the Adirondacks:

docs.google.com/document/d/1x0fIxygUf3P03fKoq2No9y5Jw6Q4EpN-DgU4Rs7Gldg/edit?usp=sharing

Vermont: This author has written some tips for finding the route through Vermont:
docs.google.com/document/d/1pPOJZ4aoMqNkVmn0R3SRNo_FiDH6f5tbbycJNIZbQh8/edit?usp=sharing

Websites

The NCTA chapters, in many cases, have detailed maps and descriptions of their sections on their websites. See a complete list of chapters under Support/Trail Angels.

When Should You Begin a Hike?

It's simple math. The trail is just over 4800 miles long. To hike the entire length in ten months, to avoid January and February, you have to hike 4800/306 = 16 miles a day with no days off. More sensibly, you'd need to take some zero days. This would leave 66 days in the 10 months for resting. It sounds like a lot, but everyone needs an extra day here and there to deal with repairs, real-world needs, unpleasant or dangerous weather conditions, illness/injury, and more. If you hiked 20 miles per day (mpd) that's 240 days on trail.

That many miles per day is unrealistic for a lot of people. You need to assess your own abilities, willingness to be in pain for long periods of time, stamina, and mental fortitude.

Beginning in either North Dakota or Vermont in March may not even be possible. Both are known for heavy snow cover. North Dakota temperatures and wind can be brutal and potentially deadly. More than one hiker has attempted to begin a thru-hike at one terminus or the other in early spring, only to have to alter plans due to weather.

Many people prefer a flip-flop so they don't get caught in the upper latitudes in winter. ND, MN, the UP, upper NY and VT can all present life-threatening winter conditions.

An NCT flip-flop can by done by starting anywhere from lower Michigan to southern Ohio. Hike trail east or west, then find transportation to the other terminus and hike back to your starting location. Several end-to-end hikers have used this general plan.

The miles can be broken into many configurations depending on how much time you want to spend dealing with transport and logistics.

It's easy to set up a spreadsheet and create approximate mileages and daily goals. Yes, it's a big trail, but this is probably the easiest way to plan a hike of any length. Explaining spreadsheet use is beyond the scope of this book, but general suggestions would be to create columns with date, starting location, ending location, daily mileage, cumulative mileage, and potential camping/lodging. After row 1, have the spreadsheet pull the next day's starting location from the cell with the previous day's stop. That way, if you change your end point, the next row gets updated automatically. Similarly, have the spreadsheet add your cumulative mileages.

A spreadsheet will allow you to see if you can reach some goal before snow is likely to hit. You can make changes much more easily than on paper.

Trail Angels and Support

The external (not provided by the hiker) support system on the NCT is different from on the AT, but there are willing helpers available. Because there is not yet a constant population of long-distance hikers on the trail, support needs to be requested. For a hiker who does not have friends and relatives to call upon, contacting the local chapters is the best thing to do. Offering gas money for shuttles is considered good etiquette, although in many cases, payment will be declined.

You can also request advance help through the Facebook groups: North Country Trail Community, and Trail Angels of the NCNST. Note that some chapters and affiliates have their own Facebook pages as well, but each chapter has a website, and an official email which will reach key leaders.

Chapters and Affiliates

Complete list, west to east, of chapters and the range covered by each. See the map at northcountrytrail.org/contact/chapters-affiliates for additional clarity. Note that each chapter has a three-character code to identify their website and email. For example, the Central Flyway Chapter's code is fly.

Their website is at northcountrytrail.org/trail/north-dakota/fly and their email is fly@northcountrytrail.org. So, the website address is northcountrytrail.org/trail/*state-name*/*code*. Single-word state names in the URL are obvious; hyphenate north-dakota and new-york.

Central Flyway, code fly: covers from the western terminus to the eastern end of the Lonetree Wildlife Management Area.

No coverage: from the eastern end of the Lonetree Wildlife Management Area to the north boundary of Lake Ashtabula.

Sheyenne River Valley, code srv: covers from the north end of Lake Ashtabula to the east boundary of the Sheyenne River State Forest.

Dakota Prairie, code dpc: covers from the east boundary of the Sheyenne River State Forest to the North Dakota/Minnesota state line at Fort Abercrombie State Park.

Minnesota Waters and Prairie, code mwp: covers from the North Dakota/Minnesota state line at Fort Abercrombie State Park to the Otter Tail/Becker county line southwest of Frazee.

Laurentian Lakes, code llc: covers from the Otter Tail/Becker county line southwest of Frazee to the intersection of the Eagle Scout and Nicollet Trails in Itasca State Park.

Itasca Moraine, code itm: covers from the intersection of the Eagle Scout and Nicollet Trails in Itasca State Park MN-84.

Star of the North, code stn: covers from MN-84 to Highway 6, northeast of Remer.

Arrowhead, code arw: covers from Highway 6, northeast of Remer to the Bear Head SP Road at Mesabi Trail.

Ely Northwoods, code ely: covers from Bear Head SP Road at Mesabi Trail to Kawishiwi Falls.

Kekekabic Trail, code kek: covers from Kawishiwi Falls to the Gunflint Trail.

The Border Route and Superior Hiking Trails are covered by Affiliates. Both have Facebook Pages (Border Route Trail and Superior Hiking Trail) where you are likely to find information and assistance from fellow hikers.

Brule St Croix, code bsc: covers from the Minnesota/Wisconsin state line to Bayfield County Road A.

Chequamegon, code che: covers from Bayfield County Road A to the Sandstone Ledges Spur in Copper Falls State Park.

Heritage, code htg: covers from the Sandstone Ledges Spur in Copper Falls State Park to the Wisconsin/Michigan state line.

Ni-Miikanaake, code nmk: covers from the Wisconsin/Michigan state line to M-64 in the Ottawa National Forest.

Peter Wolfe, code pwc: covers from M-64 in the Ottawa National Forest to Long Lake west of Craig Lake State Park.

Marquette Area, code mac: covers from Long Lake west of Craig Lake State Park to Rock River Road (H01) in Alger County.

Superior Shoreline, code ssc: covers from Rock River Road (H01) in Alger County to the mouth of the Two Hearted River.

Hiawatha Shore-to-Shore, code hss: covers from the mouth of the Two Hearted River to the south end of the Mackinac Bridge.

Harbor Springs, code hbr: covers from the south end of the Mackinac Bridge to Kipp Road, east of Harbor Springs.

Jordan Valley 45°, code j45: covers from Kipp Road east of Harbor Springs to Starvation Lake Road southeast of Mancelona.

Grand Traverse, code gtc: covers from Starvation Lake Road southeast of Mancelona to the Wexford/Manistee county line at Hodenpyl Dam Pond.

Spirit of the Woods, code spw: covers from the Wexford/Manistee county line at Hodenpyl Dam Pond to the Lake/Newaygo county line (approximately 96th Street).

Western Michigan, code wmi: covers from the Lake/Newaygo county line (approximately 96th Street) to the Kent/Barry county line on County Line Road.

Chief Noonday, code cnd: covers from the Kent/Barry county line on County Line Road to the Calhoun/Hillsdale county line on South County Line Road.

Chief Baw Beese, code baw: covers from the Calhoun/Hillsdale county line on South County Line Road to the Wabash Cannonball Trail in Ohio at West Unity, Ohio.

Northern Ohio is covered by the Affiliate **NORTA**, the Northwest Ohio Rails-to-Trails Association. Although not a chapter, there a several volunteers who actively assist NCT hikers. Contact mbduvendack@gmail.com

The Buckeye Trail Association is an Affiliate. The Facebook group Buckeye Trail Association is a good way to communicate with other hikers.

Wampum, code wam: covers from Zoar, Ohio to the Lawrence/Butler county line east of McConnells Mill State Park, Pennsylvania.

Butler, code but: covers from the Lawrence/Butler county line east of McConnells Mill State Park to the Armstrong/Clarion County line at the Allegheny River.

Clarion, code cla: covers from the Armstrong/Clarion County line at the Allegheny River to the southern border of the Allegheny National Forest.

The Rachel Carson Trails Conservancy is a Affiliate which maintains 15 miles of trail, but contact the Clarion Chapter for trail angels.

Allegheny National Forest, code anf: covers from the southern border of the Allegheny National Forest to the New York State boundary.

The Finger Lakes Trail Conference is an Affiliate. The NCT and Finger Lakes Trail are concurrent for more than 400 miles. The Facebook group The Finger Lakes Trail: Hikers & Friends is a good way to communicate with other hikers.

Central New York, code cny: covers from the northern terminus of the Link Trail, west of Tuscarora Lake, to the Oneida/Herkimer county line east of Forestport where the trail crosses the "blue line" and enters the Adirondack Park.

The Adirondack Mountain Club, Onondaga Chapter is an Affiliate. Their website is info@adk.org, but for assistance it is recommended that you contact the Central New York Chapter.

The Middlebury Area Land Trust is an Affiliate, which covers a spur that connects the NCT to the Trail Around Middlebury and the TAM. Their email is info@maltvt.org.

The Green Mountain Club is a Partner. This relationship is in its infancy, and finding trail angels through that group is not an established practice.

Shuttle Options

Public Transportation and/or commercial shuttle services is difficult to find In most places along the trail.

There are a few established shuttle services- Along the length of the SHT, a current list of these are found at superiorhiking.org/shuttles/

In Michigan's UP, shuttles in the Pictured Rocks area exist. Current info is at nps.gov/piro/planyourvisit/shuttle-service.htm

Sometimes, canoe liveries will shuttle hikers for a fee.

Uber or Lyft is occasionally available, but there is no guarantee that they will cover rural areas.

Two People, One Car

One person with one support person can complete a series of day hikes if the person with the vehicle does not want to hike and will drop off and pick up the hiker. The driver can even walk part way in and then back out and/or walk in to meet the hiker in the afternoon.

Two Hikers, One Car

If both people want to complete a section A to B the puzzle is still manageable if they don't hike together. The driver drops off the other person at point A where that person starts hiking toward point B. The driver goes to point B, parks and starts hiking toward point A. When the hikers pass each other, the keys are handed to the person headed for the car (or if you have two sets of keys, this handoff is not needed). When the hiker who now has the keys reaches point B and the car, he or she drives back to point A and picks up the other hiker.

Self Support

Ways to support yourself: hike in and out, stash a bicycle at one end and ride back on trail where it is allowed, or otherwise, via roads.

Some sections have a parallel waterway where a hike/paddle loop is possible. See the July 2020 issue of *North Star* at northcountrytrail.org/files/north%20star/39-3.pdf for suggestions.

Dayhikes vs. Backpacking

One of the biggest advantages to doing the trail in sections is that you can choose the time of year you'll be in a particular location more so than on a thru-hike. You can avoid the blazing sun of the plains, or perhaps choose the stunning colors of autumn on the SHT, or the riot of spring wildflowers in southern Ohio. If you do a thru-hike, you can only mitigate the extremes of weather to some degree (for example, by doing the coldest months in Ohio). Other than that, you have to take whatever comes your way.

However, you can complete all of the NCT, with some sort of support, as day hikes, with the following exceptions (most hikers do not want to walk this many miles in a day). Keep in mind that the minimum backpacking distances in these examples presume that the roads are open. This is not guaranteed in mud, snow, or ice.

Kek

The Kekekabic Trail in Minnesota has 39 miles where there is no vehicular access, and no reasonable side trail options which would allow you to shorten the distance on foot. However, it might be possible to create loops which include paddling to allow for shorter walks, but would still require camping.

BRT

The Border Route Trail in Minnesota is 65 miles long and remote, however, it is possible to take some miles off the ends with day hikes. By hiking the spur from Mucker Lake (one extra mile) and leaving a car at McFarland Lake, the distance with no access can be shortened to 34 miles. Again, there are some possible paddling options which could be imagined to plan trips which would still involve camping, but allow for limited back-to-back hiking days.

Adirondacks

There are two sections in the Adirondacks which are too long for most people to cover in one day. From Otter Brook to Pillsbury Mountain parking is 17 miles, and from Cisco Brook to the Raymond Brook TH is 23 miles.

Except in the winter, there are road access points at reasonable trail distances apart almost everywhere else. Using one of the road atlas base layers on the Interactive Map can help you identify these. From about December 1 (when many remote and/or seasonal roads close to vehicles and become snowmobile routes) to Memorial Day, you will have to check with local sources to find out if any particular back road is passable.

How to complete an E2E

What is a Thru-hike?

Pop culture says that a thru-hike should be completed in 12 months to be valid. The NCTA rejects this notion due to the immense length of this trail and its east-west orientation in northern latitudes. What if a person completes the trail in 366 or even 367 days? How long is one allowed to take a break? A week? Three months for winter? What if someone hiked ten miles a day for 480 days, never taking a day off (a rather ridiculous scenario), and completed the NCT. Would anyone suggest they hadn't done a thru-hike?

Therefore, the NCTA only recognizes end-to-end completions. This can be done in sections or as a continuous hike. A set of a central patch and rockers for various accomplishments is awarded on the honor system. When completed on foot, an outer rocker is provided that says End-to End Hike.

In addition, the NCTA provides a set of patches for what is called an End-to-End Trip. This recognizes those who complete the entire trail under muscle power but perhaps bicycled portions.

See explorenct.info/NoCoLo/

What is a Section Hike?

A section hike is simply an end-to-end hike that isn't done in one fairly continuous outing. The qualifier refers to the fact that there is no hard-and-fast rule about how much time someone is allowed to take off before a "thru" becomes a "section."

Do the trail at a pace that makes sense for you. Hiking 4800 unique miles across eight states is an accomplishment, no matter how you organize it.

Planning for Supply Drops

Keep in mind that a great many of the NCT miles are far from any potential resupply at stores. If you are doing a long backpacking trek, you'll need to make prior arrangements by finding nearby towns that have post offices where you can have packages sent to you, or by arranging supply drops through chapters or individuals. DO NOT assume that every town on the map will at least have a convenience store or even a post office.

This can be particularly true in North Dakota, the northern Arrowhead of Minnesota, and the Upper Peninsula of Michigan. It's potentially dangerous to "wing it" through these areas.

To mail packages to yourself, send them to [your name] at General Delivery, [PO, address, state zip]. Add the line "Hold for pickup until [date about two weeks beyond when you expect to be there], then return to sender."

While some people have taken long NCT hikes and foraged for food by hunting, fishing, and gathering herbs and mushrooms, such plans are beyond the scope of this book.

Planning for Overnights

Ideally, a long trail would have dispersed camping everywhere, or a campsite every five or six miles. This provides options for those who want a leisurely trip, an average day length (about 10 miles), and those who can hike longer daily mileages. The NCT is not there yet, but the options are so much better than they were even a few years ago that things are looking hopeful. Increased use by long-distance hikers is driving the need to create legal campsites.

This problem is compounded by the fact that the NCT does not have, and probably never will have, "corridor management." This would mean that the rules would be the same almost everywhere. Planning an NCT hike can be daunting.

The second section of this book attempts to list all known legal camping and lodging options along the Trail. It can not be emphasized enough that barring true emergencies, it's important to camp legally. Your choices can affect the future hikeability of the Trail.

It's a fact that there are not yet quite enough legal camping options along the entire length of the NCT. You will probably need to occasionally be picked up by a "trail angel," or base camp somewhere and be shuttled to the trail for a few days. However, with careful planning, it's much more possible to backpack the whole trail than it used to be.

Weather

The NCT is an unforgiving trail in winter. North Dakota, Minnesota, Michigan's Upper Peninsula, the Adirondacks of New York, and Vermont are difficult at the very best, and are likely out of contention for most hikers from November through May.

Conditions can be severe and even dangerous without four-season equipment.

An additional consideration is that many of the back roads in these areas are totally closed in the winter, but if not, even trucks can be unable to access many of the popular trailheads once the snow begins in earnest.. Roads may be open for snowmobiles. In fact, some roads are specifically changed to snowmobile use in winter.

One way of lessening the chance of needing to hike in deep snow is to do what has become known as a North Country flip-flop. To accomplish this, a hiker would start in lower Michigan, or perhaps Ohio, in the winter. These areas are not immune to winter conditions, but they are usually milder. There is almost never 20-30 inches of snow on the ground in Ohio. Hike to one end of the trail, then travel to the other end of the trail and hike back to the starting point.

Projecting Average Mileages

In order to complete an E2E in one year a hiker must average close to 15 miles a day, allowing for a certain number of days off. Taking no rest/ maintenance/ weather/ personal days in a year is unrealistic for most hikers. As mentioned earlier, At 10 miles per day, with no days off, it would take 480 days to complete the NCT. Simply divide 4800 miles by the number of miles you think you can hike per day, and add in a reasonable number of rest days.

Some hikers can sustain 20-35 mile days, but 10-15 mile days are more in the comfortable range for most people.

These are some of the reasons that the North Country Trail Association's Long Distance Hiker Recognition program makes no distinction between a thru hike and an section hike. Anyone who hikes the 4800+ unique miles of the NCT, in any time frame, has accomplished a monumental goal.

What is a reasonable number of miles you can hike in a day on the NCT? This is a question that is difficult for anyone else to answer for you. Most anyone of reasonable health and fitness with long-distance hiking goals can do ten miles a day, even in the difficult sections. The flatter areas, or long road walks make 12-15 miles fairly attainable, perhaps even 20 miles. A few young hikers have averaged as much as 35-40 miles a day, but this is a stretch for most of us.

The best plan is to look at the terrain, the local treadway conditions at the time you plan to hike (ice, mud?), the predicted weather, and then chose a number of miles that you are confident to complete. If you have a plan that spans multiple days or even multiple weeks, you can possibly predict some parts of that equation, but a long-distance hiker must remain flexible to find success.

The Mental Challenge

Some hopeful thru-hikers have underestimated the difficulty of the NCT because it does not seem to have the mountainous terrain of the "Big Three." However, in all states except North Dakota/ western Minnesota and southern Michigan/ western Ohio there is plenty of topography. Climbing and descending 500-600 feet over and over in one day can present a serious physical challenge. Most of the hills on the NCT are more in the range of 200-300 feet elevation change, but don't ever assume that the NCT is easy.

On the other hand, in the portions of North Dakota that are quite level, there are also few trees. Summer temperatures often exceed 90°. This can be as deadly as an early November blizzard. And prairie thunderstorms offer more excitement than most hikers desire.

The solitude either can present a challenge or be a gift.

There are always going to be days that don't go as planned. There are going to be extra-long days because you took a wrong turn and had to backtrack several miles. There are going to be days of total discomfort and even pain. There are going to be days you have to huddle in your tent while an unexpected thunderstorm passes through. You have to just roll with the "punches," and rework the plan.

For almost everyone who has thru-hiked the NCT, even experienced hikers, there is a moment somewhere near halfway when you realize you've been hiking "forever" and you still have over 2000 miles to go.

Where to Camp/ Stay

Definitions

Commercial Campground: a campground, usually with multiple sites and amenities, owned by an individual or a corporation for profit. There will be a fee.

Public Campground: a campground, usually with multiple sites and amenities, owned by a governmental agency or a non-profit organization. These may or may not have a fee attached.

Public Campsite: an established and sanctioned site with room for only one or a few tents, hammocks, etc. It may or may not have amenities such as a picnic table, fire ring, or latrine. These are usually created by agencies or organizations due to need for a site along the trail (such as one backpacker site that might be located along the NCT in a State Park where camping is not otherwise allowed), but it is possible that they might be created by a commercial enterprise.

Dispersed Campsite: a campsite established for one or two nights only, in a location not designated as a campsite, nor one that is obviously used regularly even if not recognized by the managing agency. Leave No Trace practices are expected. Different managers have various rules about choosing a dispersed site. If you select a location that is at least one mile from a campground, one-quarter mile from a road, 200 feet from the trail, and 200 feet from any waterway, you will meet even the most stringent regulations.

Social Campsite: This term is being used in the sense that a "social/volunteer/herd path" is an unofficial pathway, but has been established to the point of being obvious because of popular use whether authorized or unauthorized. Social campsties are often-used but not officially recognized campsites. These are often found in illegal locations and it may be impossible to discern whether the managing agency doesn't know about the site or if they are unofficially ignoring it because it's such a popular site that it keeps being re-established even when broken up. This can often be true of open, flat areas near waterways. Some people refer to these as dispersed campsites, however, this author finds that term misleading in this case because then people begin to think that dispersed camping means you have to find one of these herd campsites to stay at.

Hosted Campsite: A campsite on private property where the owner allows hikers only to camp for free or for a small fee.

Stealth Camping: In this book, stealth camping is defined as illegally tucking yourself for the night into a fencerow, woodlot, field, forest, lawn, shed, or ANYWHERE on public or private property where it is not explicitly allowed. Some people equate dispersed camping with stealth camping. But I am specifically defining it as spending the night where it is illegal to do so.

Stealth camping can adversely affect the future of the trail. Where trail crosses private property, the landowners often place stipulations on use, such as no overnight camping, no fires, or perhaps even no straying from the trail. Particularly, but not exclusively, along the FLT and the SHT the trail has lost all rights to cross certain properties because hikers think the rules don't apply to them, or that the rules are silly, or even that they must be in error because "it's a trail and everyone knows you can camp anywhere along a trail." Inevitably, this forces the trail back onto roads until an alternate route can be identified, permission obtained, and trail built.

Your Responsibility

Keep in mind the earlier section about how recently the NCT was given the right to own land. It is a reality of this trail that having one set of rules for the entire trail (corridor management) is far in the future, and it might never be a reality, given the established management structure that had to exist for the first 29 years of the trail's existence.

Your personal choices as you traverse the trail can have a lasting effect on the future route. Be respectful of private landowners and adhere to their rules.

Planning ahead can help you choose legal campsites. Simply walking until you are ready to drop, only to discover that you are four or five miles from any legal place to stay is an invitation to disaster. Most hikers who do this just camp wherever they want, because they are too tired to go on, with no thoughts as to the consequences. How many times must a farmer find someone camped in his woodlot, or how much trash will the owner of a private nature preserve tolerate before withdrawing permission for the trail to cross? Although the NCTA and NPS are continually striving to create permanent easements or find other ways of protecting the trail, there are still many "handshake agreements" which depend on the good will of all parties.

Suitability

An indication that dispersed camping is allowed does not imply that all locations are appropriate or suitable. Land may have too much slope, be soggy, or covered with thick brush. Keep in mind that there are always regulations as to how far you must be from the trail, a road, water sources, and established campgrounds/campsites.

Where there are developed (although primitive) campsites, for example throughout Wisconsin, these have been chosen for good locations with level, dry land with space for one or two tents, and access to treatable water. Of course, if dispersed camping is allowed, you are not constrained to use these sites, however, designated sites are likely to be much better in many ways. Particularly in the Adirondacks and Vermont's Green Mountains, just because dispersed camping is legal does not in any way imply there is suitable terrain or even a large enough opening between trees.

Leave No Trace principles should always apply. Some land managers specifically prohibit building fires or digging holes. This may not always be included in the text if information was unavailable. Dispersed campsites should have a small footprint and preferably be fireless. Cut no trees or live branches. Hang hammocks so as not to damage bark. Except for perhaps some temporarily flattened grass or scuffed leaves, no one should be able to tell a camper was there a few hours later. There are many excellent resources about LNT Camping. Start at lnt.org

Boundaries

Boundaries are located in this text with both latitude/longitude in a format recognized by the NCT Interactive Map and also What3Words. If you are not familiar with W3W, you can download the app or check what3words.com. Basically, the entire globe is divided into 57 trillion ten-foot squares, and each is assigned a three-word "code." This is easier for many people to deal with than a long string of numbers. W3W addresses begin with three slash marks, and the words are separated by periods. The front door of the Lowell NCTA HQ is ///admits.boxing.glitz. If you install W3W on your phone, Avenza will include it in the list of options for coordinate display.

Boundary coordinates given in the following pages are taken from maps, not recorded in the field. Thus they are guaranteed to be inaccurate at some level. A signpost in the woods should always be considered more accurate than this book. No trespassing or no camping signs should be honored in all cases. In general, a good practice would be to stay well inside a boundary of public land where camping is allowed.

You can always ask permission of landowners to camp for a night. Many people are willing to accommodate hikers if they are asked in person. Occasionally, churches or town (township) halls will let a hiker camp for one night. If you are turned down, don't argue. Just move on. Trail angels may offer to take you to a campground, or even to their homes.

Legal Campsites and Lodging

The list is presented from west to east. That seems to be the preferred direction traveled so far by the known thru hikers. However, one of my pet peeves is guides that are impossible to use from the opposite direction. This one is slightly less smooth from east to west, but it mostly works. Distances between places to stay are presented just below the next place west, so if you are traveling from the east, you'll need to glance up if there is intervening text. Also, notes about types of use allowed, etc are listed just below a boundary (so if you are reading east to west, you'll need to look at the western end of a section to find the note).

Also, there are places where the trail crosses a tiny bit of public land that are not noted in this list. If places to camp are numerous, there's a good chance that an extra 0.1 mile of intermittent state or national forest is not included. However, if there are few places to camp, every effort has been made to meticulously include any possible legal camping locations.

Please keep in mind that:

1. this is the first time anyone has tried to collect all this information in one place

2. this is a first edition- there are bound to be errors.

3. information like this changes all the time- there are bound to be errors.

4. feel free to email me with corrections jhyshark@gmail.com.

Abbreviations

NWR: National Wildlife Refuge
NF: National Forest
ROW: right-of-way

SF: State Forest
SP: State Park
WMA: Wildlife Management Area
DNR: Department of Natural Resources
DEC: Department of Environmental Conservation
DCNR: Department of Conservation and Natural Resources
BWCAW: Boundary Waters Canoe Area Wilderness
PIRO: Pictured Rocks National Lakeshore
USACE: US Army Corps of Engineers

Legend

$CCg: Commercial Campground, fee
$L: Commercial Lodging such as hotel, motel, AirBnB, fee
$PCg: Public (owned by government or agency) Campground, fee
$PCs: Public (owned by government or agency) Campsite, fee
PCs: Public (owned by government or agency) Campsite, no fee
D: Dispersed Camping
p (lower case) added to a code means a permit is required
pD: Dispersed Camping, free permit required
$pD: Dispersed Camping, paid permit required

H: Hosted by private landowner or other entity such that the site is only for trail hikers' use- may be combined such as HCs for hosted campsite

E: added to another code, such as PE, or HE indicates a shelter enclosed on three or four sides. One side may be screening

+ spur: additional mileage on a trail
+ road: additional mileage on a road or street
bold is actual trail miles

↔ land ownership (or other) boundary

$▲ camping option with multiple sites, fee

$△ camping option generally with 1-3 sites, fee

△ camping option generally with 1-3 sites or dispersed, no fee

p△ camping option generally with 1-3 sites or dispersed, free permit required

$p△ camping option generally with 1-3 sites or dispersed, paid permit required

∠ three-sided shelter, no fee

⌂ enclosed shelter, although 4th side may only be screened, no fee

$ ⌂ enclosed shelter, although 4th side may only be screened, fee

$ ■ motel or other commercial lodging with multiple rooms/ units

$ □ motel or other commercial lodging with few rooms/units

✲ village center

Y junction with a major hiking trail where the NCT and that trail separate or join

Locations one mile or under from the trail are left justified. Locations more than one mile from the trail are right justified.

In an attempt to make the listings sensible while traveling in either direction, between every place to stay overnight are several lines of text. As an example, the very first such entry is

$PCg
+0.7 road
4.2 miles
+0.3 spur
$CCg

this means that trail west (the "upper" entry) is a publicly owned campground (in this case a state park) which charges a fee. There is 0.7 extra mile on a road between it and the main North Country Trail. There are 4.2 trail miles between the two full entries listing places to sleep. There are 0.3 extra miles on a trail between the NCT and the next listed lodging option to trail east ("lower" entry), which is a commercially owned campground where there is a fee.

Locations are noted with latitude/longitude, because trail state mileage markers may change twice a year as the maps are updated. What3Words locations are also given. Also, as the trail changes over time, mileages between camping/lodging options may change.

Campgrounds which are more than 1 mile off the trail (and thus right justified in the text) may be listed, but they are not included in the "coded" centered sections. The camping/lodging options which are right justified are more than 1 mile off trail, but potentially within walking distance if a hiker is looking for certain amenities. Campgrounds/sites more than 3 miles from the trail are usually not included, although these (and others not listed) could be used for base camping and hiking.

No dispersed camping is allowed anywhere on roadwalks unless specifically noted and then it probably involves getting as much as 1/4 mile off the road (sometimes less).

Where dispersed camping is allowed, each management area will have its own regulations, but generally camp more than 1/8 mile from a road, more than 1 mile from an established campground or building (such as a headquarters or visitor center), and more than 200 feet from water, the trail, or any structure (except trail shelters). Note that these rules will mean that some miles marked as allowing dispersed camping will be too close to other features to use. You MUST keep this in mind when planning campsites.

Water means potable water (unless noted as dry, sites have a natural water source, but you will need to treat the water). Seasonal water means either a hand pump or where winter temperatures dictate that the water is turned off. If it says dry, there is no potable or treatable water in the immediate vicinity.

Fire ring means any kind of containment designed for a fire. This could be a metal ring, a stone lined pit, a grill, or in a couple of cases a fireplace.

Latrine may be a vault toilet, porta potty, enclosed latrine, or wilderness pit (a hole with an open wood or fiberglass seat over it).

Bathhouse means toilets and showers. Restroom means toilets and sinks only. If one of these are listed then water is implied.

If it says seasonal, then that is definite information. Anything in the North Country may be seasonal by implication. Always check to see if developed campgrounds are open. Oct 15- May 1 are average dates of closure, but should not be used as accurate dates for all sites. Almost all public and commercial campgrounds are seasonal along the North Country Trail.

Some campgrounds may not allow pets. Campgrounds with a fee may have a drop box (so you'd need cash or check), or you may need to make reservations.

Commercial options go out of business or change hands; new ones open. Use this as a planning guide, but check with the campgrounds/hosts you wish to use before starting a trip.

Local NCTA chapters are usually more than willing to help hikers. Trail Angel-ing is a specialty! While it is always good not to abuse people's generosity with multiple requests, finding help to get through one or two difficult sections of trail is almost always possible.

This information is current as of date of publication, but be aware that data of this nature can change at any time. Probably there are several things that have changed between my final edit and the date of printing. Any change in a portion of the trail will change mileages in this book between noted locations.

You will need to use this information in conjunction with the Interactive Map for it to make the most sense.

Again, descriptions and the campsite section of this book are written from west to east, however, an attempt has been made to keep the information fairly easy to decipher for east to west hikers.

Geographical W-E Listing of Current Legal Campsites and Lodging Options

North Dakota

See legend and general info for help in interpreting the listings

↔ Chapter boundary
Western terminus of the NCT
47.519731 -101.453548   ///cuminate.combining.interactive
Central Flyway Chapter
northcountrytrail.org/trail/north-dakota/fly

$▲ *Lake Sakakawea SP Campground*
0.7 mile off trail
47.529733 -101.443672   ///bikes.shallow.jigging
public campground
149 electric sites, 42 primitive sites, cabins
tables, fire rings, restroom
fee
managed by North Dakota Parks and Recreation
parkrec.nd.gov
701-487-3315

Note: no dispersed camping within Lake Sakakawea SP

$PCg
+0.7 road
4.2 miles
+0.3 spur
$CCg

↔ boundary Lake Sakakawea SP
47.505396 -101.437935   ///score.luminosity.revealing
↔ boundary National Fish Hatchery
managed by US Fish and Wildlife Service

Note: no camping on hatchery property

Y approximate location of three nearby places the NCT crosses the Lewis & Clark Historic Trail (not a hiking trail, and as such not a visible path on the ground). There is an interpretive kiosk on the shore of the Missouri River.
47.494505 -101.41941   ///flights.avocado.freezers
nps.gov/lecl

$▲ *Downstream Campground*
0.3 mile off trail
47.480715 -101.429445   ///shouted.assorted.impressions
commercial campsite
114 vehicular sites
98 electric, 16 primitive sites
tables, fire rings, restroom
fee
managed by US Army Corps of Engineers
recreation.gov
701-654-7440

$CCg
+0.3 spur
3.5 miles
$L

↔ boundary National Fish Hatchery
47.491365 -101.394327   ///windshield.dererring.begin
↔ boundary private land

✻ city of Riverdale
47.493281 -101.364463   ///technically.nest.cases
limited services

$ ■ *Sakakawea Sunset Lodge*
47.48895 -101.378081   ///dish.collections.slip
commercial lodging
13 rooms
fee
garrisondam.weebly.com
701-654-7600

$L
0.5 mile
PCs

△ *Riverdale City Park*
47.495719 -101.377322   ///unions.matchup.deriving
public land
NCT hikers only, with permission
primitive, no amenities, dry
riverdalecity.com/parks.html
701-654-7636

PCs
10.3 miles
+0.5 road
$PCg

$▲ *Wolf Creek Campground*
1.2 miles off trail
47.547906 -101.308811   ///flicked.scenic.roaming
67 rustic sites, latrine
only one tent allowed per site
fee
managed by US Army Corps of Engineers
recreation.gov

✻ village of Coleharbor
47.542184 -101.222042   ///overflowed.cleaned.extreme
limited servies

$▲ Coleharbor City Park
0.5 mile off trail
47.542184 -101.222042   ///overflowed.cleaned.extreme
public campground
RV sites, tent sites,
fee
ndtourism.com
701-430-9986

$PCg
+0.5 spur
15.3 miles
D

$▲ East Totten Trail Campground
4.6 miles off trail
47.617925 -101.26231   ///reef.rangers.trifle
commercial campground
40 vehicular sites
30 electric, 10 primitive
tables, fire rings, latrine, seasonal water
fee
managed by US Army Corps of Engineers
701-654-7411
recreation.gov

↔ boundary private land
47.574782 -101.249266   ///heave.turnaround.positions
↔ boundary Audubon NWR
managed by US Fish and Wildlife Service

Note: no camping within the refuge

↔ boundary Audubon NWR
managed by US Fish and Wildlife Service
47.568287 -101.095358   ///projection.exhaled.hips
↔ boundary McClusky Canal
managed by Garrison Diversion Project

△ *dispersed camping* allowed
10.7 miles in ROW
garrisondiversion.org

↔ boundary McClusky Canal
47.534114 -100.907818   ///forgotten.goals.worldly
↔ boundary private land

D
2.9 miles
+0.1 road
$PCg

$▲ *Lake Brekken Campground*
0.1 mile off trail
47.547049 -100.853445   ///goodbyes.duplicates.rings
public campground
RV and tent sites
tables, fire rings, latrine, seasonal water
fee
managed by city of Turtle Lake
turtlelakend.org
701-448-2596

$PCg
+0.1 road
3.9 miles
D

↔ boundary private land ND 51.3
47.516393 -100.872242   ///palace.electricity.busy
↔ boundary McClusky Canal

△ *dispersed camping* allowed
7.1 miles in ROW
garrisondiversion.org

↔ boundary McClusky Canal
47.435813 -100.90254   ///starred.notary.inhibition
↔ boundary private land

Note: temporary road walk due to ongoing repairs on the canal

D
5.7 miles
D

↔ boundary private land
47.400677 -100.843746   ///catty.quickly.loosen
↔ boundary McClusky Canal

△ *dispersed camping* allowed
4.0 miles in ROW
garrisondiversion.org

↔ boundary McClusky Canal
47.360936 -100.794912   ///densely.gracing.overworked
↔ boundary Chain of Lakes Recreation Area

Note: managed by US Bureau of Reclamation, camp only in designated sites. There are a total of 55 free, primitive sites. Latrines are at intervals convenient for people with vehicles, not hikers. 701-250-4242 ndtourism.com

D
0.1 mile
+0.3 road
PCs

△ *Chain of Lakes Recreation Area site M01*
0.3 mile off trail
47.36041 -100.7917   ///throat.lagoon.almost
public campsite
primitive, fire ring, latrine is 0.6 mile west and south
ndtourism.com
701-250-4242

        PCs
        +0.3 road
        0.5 mile
        PCs

△ *Chain of Lakes Recreation Area site M19*
47.363346 -100.788514   ///chickens.nasal.chapter
public campsite
primitive, fire ring, latrine is 0.8 mile west & south of lake
ndtourism.com
701-250-4242

        PCs
        0.2 mile
        PCs

△ *Chain of Lakes Recreation Area site M18*
47.363863 -100.782976   ///methods.fluent.tourist
public campsite
primitive, fire ring, latrine is 1.0 mile west & south of lake
ndtourism.com
701-250-4242

        PCs
        0.8 mile
        +0.1 spur
        PCs

△ *Chain of Lakes Recreation Area site M15*
0.1 mile off trail
47.364297 -100.776688   ///powerful.rulings.richer
public campsite
primitive, fire ring, latrine is 1.4 miles west & south of lake
ndtourism.com
701-250-4242

        PCs
        +0.1 spur
        0.1 mile
        PCs

△ *Chain of Lakes Recreation Area site M17*
47.365811 -100.765215   ///coiling.fall.vocalists
public campsite
primitive, fire ring, latrine is 1.9 miles west & south of lake
ndtourism.com
701-250-4242

OR

△ Chain of Lakes Recreation Area site M16
47.365838 -100.763919   ///shorthand.booster.inaccurate
public campsite
primitive, fire ring, latrine is 1.9 miles west & south of lake
ndtourism.com
701-250-4242

      PCs
      1.5 miles
      +0.1 spur
      PCs

△ Chain of Lakes Recreation Area site M14
0.1 mile off trail
47.361849 -100.734612   ///targets.bends.waxers
public campsite
primitive, fire ring, latrine is 1.3 mile east
ndtourism.com
701-250-4242

      PCs
      +0.1 spur
      0.6 mile
      +0.1 spur
      PCs

△ Chain of Lakes Recreation Area site M13
0.1 mile off trail
47.360948 -100.727832   ///caskets.panthers.periods
public campsite
primitive, fire ring, latrine is 0.8 mile east
ndtourism.com
701-250-4242

      PCs
      +0.1 spur
      0.6 mile
      +0.1 spur
      PCs

△ Chain of Lakes Recreation Area site M12
0.1 mile off trail
47.358623 -100.72324   ///worktable.straw.icebergs
public campsite
primitive, fire ring, latrine is 0.1 mile east
ndtourism.com
701-250-4242

      PCs
      +0.1 spur
      0.3 mile
      +0.1 spur
      PCs

latrine at
47.356035 -100.717789   ///sediment.mindset.contest

△ Chain of Lakes Recreation Area site M04
0.1 mile off trail
47.356035 -100.717789   ///sediment.mindset.contest
public campsite
primitive, fire ring, latrine is 0.3 mile west
ndtourism.com
701-250-4242

                    PCs
                    +0.1 spur
                    0.1 mile
                    PCs

△ Chain of Lakes Recreation Area site M05
47.355744 -100.715171   ///otter.fillets.nights
public campsite
primitive, fire ring, latrine is 0.4 mile west
ndtourism.com
701-250-4242

                    PCs
                    1.6 miles
                    PCs

△ Chain of Lakes Recreation Area site M06A
47.34708 -100.688435   ///shudders.funky.silvery
public campsite
primitive, fire ring, latrine is 0.8 mile east
ndtourism.com
701-250-4242

                    PCs
                    0.2 mile
                    PCs

△ Chain of Lakes Recreation Area site M06B
47.345364 -100.686375   ///automobiles.blanked.required
public campsite
primitive, fire ring, latrine is 0.5 mile east
ndtourism.com
701-250-4242

                    PCs
                    0.6 mile
                    PCs

△ Chain of Lakes Recreation Area site M07
47.340857 -100.675346   ///overshadow.gaps.participate
public campsite
primitive, fire ring, latrine
ndtourism.com
701-250-4242

                    PCs
                    0.1 mile
                    PCs

△ *Chain of Lakes Recreation Area site M08*
47.338967 -100.674445   ///bubble.respecting.poster
public campsite
primitive, fire ring, latrine is 0.1 mile west
ndtourism.com
701-250-4242

        PCs
        0.1 mile
        PCs

△ *Chain of Lakes Recreation Area site M09*
47.337687 -100.673973   ///speculates.discussions.gift
public campsite
primitive, fire ring, latrine
ndtourism.com
701-250-4242

        PCs
        0.1 mile
        PCs

△ *Chain of Lakes Recreation Area site S01*
47.337542 -100.671355   ///moguls.gravity.eggshells
public campsite
primitive, fire ring, latrine is 0.4 mile west
ndtourism.com
701-250-4242

        PCs
        0.5 mile
        PCs

△ *Chain of Lakes Recreation Area site S02*
47.331552 -100.669372   ///alienated.jeering.fiesta
public campsite
primitive, fire ring, latrine is 0.8 mile east
no fee
ndtourism.com
701-250-4242

        PCs
        0.3 mile
        PCs

△ *Chain of Lakes Recreation Area site S03*
47.328498 -100.670574   ///operate.worlds.composts
public campsite
primitive, fire ring, latrine is 0.5 mile east
ndtourism.com
701-250-4242

        PCs
        0.5 mile
        PCs

△ *Chain of Lakes Recreation Area site B01*
47.323931 -100.662206   ///evolving.irrational.fallen
public campsite
primitive, fire ring, latrine
ndtourism.com
701-250-4242

                    PCs
                    0.3 mile
                    PCs

△ *Chain of Lakes Recreation Area site B02*
47.321808 -100.659159   ///closely.distinction.correct
public campsite
primitive, fire ring, latrine is 0.3 mile west
ndtourism.com
701-250-4242

                    PCs
                    0.2 mile
                    PCs

△ *Chain of Lakes Recreation Area site B03*
47.320295 -100.655468   ///straighter.tarnished.hostels
public campsite
primitive, fire ring, latrine is 0.3 mile west
ndtourism.com
701-250-4242

                    PCs
                    0.4 mile
                    PCs

△ *Chain of Lakes Recreation Area site B04*
47.317356 -100.647271   ///uptown.account.perhaps
public campsite
primitive, fire ring, latrine is 0.3 mile east
ndtourism.com
701-250-4242

                    PCs
                    0.1 mile
                    +0.1 spur
                    PCs

△ *Chain of Lakes Recreation Area site B05*
0.1 mile off trail
 47.315844 -100.643623   ///modify.temptation.share
public campsite
primitive, fire ring, latrine is 0.2 mile east
ndtourism.com
701-250-4242

                    PCs
                    +0.1 spur
                    0.2 mile
                    PCs

△ Chain of Lakes Recreation Area site B06
47.31564 -100.643537   ///befriended.digits.interactive
public campsite
primitive, fire ring, latrine
ndtourism.com
701-250-4242

        PCs
        0.5 mile
        +0.1 spur
        PCs

△ Chain of Lakes Recreation Area sites B07A & B07B
0.1 mile off trail
47.315465 -100.634053   ///spaceships.extremely.pets
public campsite
primitive, fire ring, latrine is 0.5 mile west
ndtourism.com
701-250-4242

        PCs
        +0.1 spur
        0.6 mile
        PCs

△ Chain of Lakes Recreation Area site B08
47.312003 -100.622766   ///takeovers.answers.credentials
public campsite
primitive, fire ring, latrine is 1.1 miles west
ndtourism.com
701-250-4242

        PCs
        0.5 mile
        +0.15 spur
        PCs

△ Chain of Lakes Recreation Area site B09
0.15 mile off trail
47.313196 -100.615042   ///spawned.gaps.geek
public campsite
primitive, fire ring, latrine is 1.6 miles west
ndtourism.com
701-250-4242

        PCs
        +0.15 spur
        0.3 mile
        D

↔ boundary Chain of Lakes Recreation Area
47.313853 -100.601489   ///intervened.evenly.beanbag
↔ boundary McClusky Canal

       △ *dispersed camping* allowed
       19.8 miles in ROW
       garrisondiversion.org

$▲ *McClusky Heart Park*
3 miles off trail
city of McClusky
47.48285 -100.439773   ///blanket.sensing.blueberry
public campground
RV sites, electric, water
tables/grills in park- not at sites
fee
701-363-2345
mccluskynd.com

↔ boundary McClusky Canal
47.508353 -100.468606   ///warthog.tilts.calculator
↔ boundary Hoffer Lake area

D
0.7 mile
+0.15 or 0.6 road
$PCg

$▲ *Hoffer Lake Recreation Area*
0.15 mile off trail
managed by Sheridan County
47.513889 -100.463113   ///queens.belief.hips
public campground
primitive campsites, latrine
fee
managed by Sheridan County
co.sheridan.nd.us/departments/parks-and-recreation

OR

$▲ *Hoffer Lake Recreation Area*
0.6 mile off trail
managed by Sheridan County
47.516179 -100.454101   ///stylist.arbitrator.encloses
public campground
electric, tables, fire rings, seasonal bathhouse
fee
managed by Sheridan County
co.sheridan.nd.us/departments/parks-and-recreation
701-363-2205

$PCg
+0.15 or 0.6 road
1.5 miles
D

↔ boundary Hoffer Lake area
47.525338 -100.446891   ///camels.diamonds.loafing
↔ boundary McClusky Canal

△ *dispersed camping* allowed
13.6 miles in canal ROW
garrisondiversion.org

Drop Chute
↔ boundary McClusky Canal
managed by Garrison Diversion Project
47.698693 -100.336384   ///tolerating.turtle.homing
↔ boundary Lonetree Wildlife Management Area
managed by North Dakota Game and Fish

△ *dispersed camping* allowed
6.2 miles in Lonetree WMA
gf.nd.gov

△ *Jensen Campground*
47.695516 -100.23961   ///wrestle.skinny.feelers
public campsite
primitive, tables, fire rings, latrine, seasonal water
managed by North Dakota Game and Fish
gf.nd.gov
701-328-6300

△ *dispersed camping* allowed
5.5 miles in Lonetree WMA
gf.nd.gov

△ *Coal Mine Lake Campground*
47.678442 -100.13803   ///persuasive.encroach.flopping
public campground
primitive, tables, fire rings, latrine, seasonal water
managed by North Dakota Game and Fish
gf.nd.gov
701-328-6300

△ *dispersed camping* allowed
5.4 miles in Lonetree WMA
gf.nd.gov

△ *Faul Campground*
47.652171 -100.071039   ///rots.shutter.shells
primitive, tables, fire rings, latrine, seasonal water
managed by North Dakota Game and Fish
gf.nd.gov
701-328-6300

△ *dispersed camping* allowed
10.6 miles in Lonetree WMA
gf.nd.gov

↔ boundary Lonetree Wildlife Management Area
Eastern edge of Lonetree WMA
47.690172 -99.938487   ///photographs.tumblers.blaze
Central Flyway Chapter
northcountrytrail.org/north-dakota/fly
↔ **Chapter boundary**

↔ **Chapter boundary**
East end Lonetree Wildlife Management Area
47.690172   -99.938487   ///photographs.tumblers.blaze
No designated chapter
northcountrytrail.org

↔ boundary New Rockford Canal

chapter boundary
△ *dispersed camping* allowed
5.4 miles in ROW
garrisondiversion.org

$▲ *Harvey West Side Park*
6.5 miles off trail
managed by city of Harvey
47.771156   -99.94302   ///remit.digit.ashes
public campground
17 electric sites
tables, bathhouse
fee
harveynd.com
701-324-2628

△ *Designated campsite*
0.6 mile down W side of the canal
47.720669   -99.844274   ///adamant.miracle.rectangular
public land
primitive campsite with shade
no amenities, possibly dry
managed by Garrison Diversion Project
garrisondiversion.org

△ *dispersed camping* allowed
34.4 miles in ROW
garrisondiversion.org

↔ boundary New Rockford Canal
47.723441   -99.147543   ///obeyed.blatant.parading
↔ boundary private land

D
3.0 miles
+0.5 road
$PCg

$▲ *Eddy County Fairgrounds*
0.5 miles off trail
47.673483   -99.147943   ///alteration.vibrations.validated
public land
vehicular sites
tables, fire rings, bathhouse
fee
managed by Eddy County
cityofnewrockford.com
701-947-2084

$PCg
+0.5 road
1.0 mile
+0.5 road
$PCg

⁂ city of New Rockford
47.680147 -99.136931 ///playfully.functioning.text
services

$▲ *North Riverside Park*

0.5 mile off trail
47.686792 -99.128232 ///mercifully.reshape.minutes
public campground
RV and tent sites with electric
tables, fire rings, bathhouse
fee
managed by city of New Rockford
cityofnewrockford.com
701-947-2461

$PCg
+0.5 road
0.1 mile
$L

$ ■ *Rock Inn*

47.680423 -99.12501 ///powerhouse.couples.reclaiming
commercial lodging
rooms
fee
rockinnnewrockford.com
701-947-2152

$L
32.3 miles
+0.1
$PCg

△ *Juanita Lake*

2.25 miles off trail
47.540764 -98.75512 ///transformed.raven.zeal
amenities uncertain
management unknown
freecampsites.net

⁂ village of McHenry
47.576309 -98.59188 ///rides.attainable.coursework
limited services

$▲ *McHenry City Campground*
0.1 mile off trail
47.573978 -98.583687 ///panicking.stepping.fractional
public campground
5 RV and tent sites, electric
tables, fire rings, bathhouse
fee
managed by city of McHenry
701- 785-2112

$PCg
+0.1 road
11.0 miles
+0.3 road
$PCg

$▲ *Binford Park Campground*
0.3 mile off trail
47.563385 -98.350207 ///bleaching.sticky.cooling
public campground
4 RV and tent sites, 3 furnished cabins
tables, fire rings, electric, bathhouse
fee
managed by city of Binford
ndtourism.com
218-205-8422

$PCg
+0.3 road
18.7 miles
+0.2 road
PCg

✲ village of Binford
47.561919 -98.345031 ///deliver.photon.anthems
limited services

$▲ *Cooperstown City Park Campground*
0.2 mile off trail
47.448523 -98.12129 ///furious.scarcely.token
public campground
12 vehicular sites, tent sites
tables, bathhouse
no fee for tents
ndtourism.com
701-797-3613

$PCg
+0.2 road
0.1 mile
$L

✲ city of Cooperstown
47.444519 -98.123821 ///disapprove.cubist.signs
services

$ ■ *Coachman Inn*
47.443916 98.124106 ///bobbing.departure.navigate
commercial lodging
21 rooms
fee
701-797-2181

OR

$ ☐ *other Air BnBs* in town
various off trail
fee

           $PCg
           9.5 miles
           HCs

△ *Cooperstown Bible Camp*
47.369343 -98.033976 ///patrolling.disengage.transistor
private hosted site
hikers may camp with advance permission
mail@cbcnd.com
701-581-6921

           HCs
           4.8 miles
           D
           chapter boundary

North end of Lake Ashtabula
47.340212 -97.977585 ///token.corrections.hesitate
No designated chapter
northcountrytrail.org
↔ **Chapter boundary**

↔ **Chapter boundary**
North end of Lake Ashtabula
47.340212 -97.977585   ///token.corrections.hesitate
Sheyenne River Valley Chapter
northcountrytrail.org/trail/north-dakota/srv

↔ boundary Lake Ashtabula property
managed by Army Corps of Engineers

△ *dispersed camping* allowed
9.4 miles on USACE property
mvp.usace.army.mil

△ *Sibley Remote Campsite*
47.233434 -97.980589   ///chaotic.comfortable.outstanding
public land
primitive, table, fire pit, latrine
maintained by Sheyenne River Valley Chapter
srv@northcountrytrail.org
701-845-2970

△ *dispersed camping* allowed
7.4 miles on USACE property
mvp.usace.army.mil

$▲ *Sibley Campground*
47.215622 -97.964985   ///sung.excited.clouds
commercial campground
tables, fire rings, bathhouse
primarily an RV park, but they allow hikers to tent
fee
701-733-2221

△ *dispersed camping* allowed
5.8 miles on USACE property
mvp.usace.army.mil

$▲ *East Ashtabula Crossing Campground*
0.3 mile off trail
47.157731 -98.00453   ///rotations.stunningly.hobble
public campground
vehicular sites, 32 electric, 6 walk in
tables, fire rings, bathhouse
fee
managed by Army Corps of Engineers
www.recreation.gov
701-845-2970

△ *dispersed camping* allowed
6.9 miles on USACE property
mvp.usace.army.mil

△ *Clyde Anderson Baldhill Creek Campsite*
47.132209 -98.045346   ///cadets.pointed.trump
public land
primitive, table, fire ring, latrine
maintained by Sheyenne River Valley Chapter
in Baldhill creek WMA
northcountrytrail.org/trail/north-dakota/srv

△ *dispersed camping* allowed
9.3 miles on USACE property
mvp.usace.army.mil

↔ internal boundary USACE
47.038145   -98.078754   ///mended.craft.orbits
↔ mixed ownership

D
1.0 mile
+1.0 road
$PCg

$▲ *Mel Rieman Recreation Area*

1.0 mile off trail
47.033436   -98.071868   ///distracts.cloth.shrubs
public camground
15 electric campsites, 12 primitive sites
tables, fire rings, bathhouse
fee
managed by Army Corps of Engineers
www.recreation.gov
701-845-2970

$PCg
+1.0 road
3.1 miles
+0.3 road
PCs

△ *Faust Park*

0.3 mile off trail
46.985269   -98.087575   ///honeycomb.chooses.luckier
public land
primitive, table, fire ring, latrine
managed by Barnes County
maintained by Barnes County Wildlife Federation
freecampsites.net
barnescountywildlifeclub.org
701-762-4450

PCs
+0.3 road
7.3 miles
+0.5 road
$PCg

$▲ *Valley City Tourist Park*

0.5 mile off trail
46.923841   -97.99226   ///education.rigorously.jobless
public campground
27 RV and tent sites
tables, bathhouse
fee
vcparks.com
701-845-3294

$PCg
+0.5 road
2.1 miles
+ various short
$L

✷ city of Valley City
46.923516 -98.003261   ///digits.recipes.riding
services

$ ■ *Motels*
various off trail
most near Interstate 94
46.912859 -98.01138   ///full.thermal.sued
commercial lodging
fee

                    $L
                    + various
                    20.4 miles
                    +0.15 spur
                    $PCg

$▲ *Clausen Springs Campground*
0.15 mile minimum off trail
46.683706 -98.048427   ///extracted.spuds.curricula
public campground
21 electric sites, 32 primitive
tables, fire rings, seasonal bathhouse
fee, online reservation required for some sites
managed by Barnes County
ndtourism.com
701-762-4450

                    $PCg
                    +0.15 spur
                    4.2 miles
                    +0.15 road
                    $PCg

$▲ *Kathryn Campground*
0.15 mile off trail
46.679937 -97.971222   ///soldiers.dwarves.progressive
public campground
6 RV sites, tent sites
restroom
fee
managed by city of Kathryn
ndtourism.com
208-589-6554

                    $PCg
                    +0.15 road
                    4.4 miles
                    +1.0 road
                    $PCg

✷ village of Kathryn
46.67938 -97.968783   ///unsure.bottled.drills
limited services

$▲ Little Yellowstone Park
1.0 mile off trail
46.632351 -97.951438   ///pigeons.calculate.scars
public campground
16 electric sites, 18 primitive
tables, fire rings, latrine, seasonal water
fee, online reservation only
managed by Barnes County
ndtourism.com
701-762-4450
    $PCg
    +1.0 road
    10.1 miles
    +0.1 spur
    $PCg

↔ boundary private land
46.565847 -97.929578   ///populate.nightmares.poet
↔ boundary Fort Ransom State Park

Note: Camp only at designated locations in Fort Ransom State Park

$▲ Fort Ransom SP Sunne Farm Campground
0.1 mile off trail
46.558038 -97.924294   ///anybody.bleach.weekday
public campground
5 primitive sites
tables, fire rings, latrine
fee
managed by North Dakota Parks and Recreation
parkrec.nd.gov
701-973-4331
    $PCg
    +0.1 spur
    1.4 miles
    +0.1 road minimum
    $PCg

$▲ Fort Ransom SP West Side Campground
0.1 mile minimum off trail- various sites on both sides of river
46.544019 -97.934787   ///chilled.unfortunate.stardom
public campground
14 electric sites
tables, fire rings, bathhouse
fee
managed by North Dakota Parks and Recreation
parkrec.nd.gov
701-973-4331
    $PCg
    +0.1 road minimum
    2.0 miles
    $L

↔ boundary Fort Ransom State Park
46.543285 -97.935886   ///swallowing.frenzy.printouts
↔ boundary private land

$ ☐ *Rockstad's River Inn*
46.520425 -97.926879 ///storing.departures.disclaimer
commercial lodging
6 rooms
fee
rockstadsriverinn.com
701-973-2103

$L
2.8 miles
+0.5 minimum, mixed
D

✲ village of Fort Ransom
46.520477 -97.925973 ///luckily.founding.viewfinder
limited services

△ *Sheyenne River State Forest*
0.5+ mile off trail minimum
46.502669 -97.878109 ///hoping.tripling.cooling

Note: dispersed camping is allowed in the SF. There are two designated primitive campsites. (When ROW is secured, the SF will be connected off road from Fort Ransom to some point east.)
managed by North Dakota State Forest Service
ag.ndsu.edu/ndfs/documents/state-forests-rules-2020.pdf
701-228-3700

△ *Sheyenne River State Forest Campsite*
2 miles off current trail route
46.503113 -97.894282 ///defers.revolting.slowed
public land
primitive, table, fire ring
maintained by Sheyenne River Valley Chapter
northcountrytrail.org/trail/north-dakota/srv

△ *Sheyenne River State Forest Waterfall Campsite*
2.7 miles off current trail route
46.50327 -97.901681 ///compress.owns.farmers
public land
primitive, table, fire ring
maintained by Sheyenne River Valley Chapter
northcountrytrail.org/trail/north-dakota/srv

D
0.5 mile
chapter boundary

Eastern boundary of the Sheyenne River State Forest
46.510359 -97.867951 ///limitations.animal.offhand
Sheyenne River Valley Chapter
northcountrytrail.org/trail/north-dakota/srv
↔ **Chapter boundary**

↔ **Chapter boundary**
East boundary of the Sheyenne River State Forest
46.510291   -97.868182   ///mallets.panther.embedding
Dakota Prairie Chapter
northcountrytrail.org/trail/north-dakota/dpc

                        chapter boundary
                        12.9 miles
                        $PCg

$▲ *Sandager Park*
0.4 mile off trail
46.448156   -97.68774   ///spark.recent.sand
public campground
10 RV sites, additional primitive sites, bathhouse
fee
managed by city of Lisbon
cityoflisbon.net/parks
701-683-2158

                        $PCg
                        0.6 mile
                        $L

✻ city of Lisbon
46.441438   -97.681522   ///member.feared.punt
services, Airbnbs, possible hipcamp

$ ■ *Lisbon Inn*
46.438569   -97.681693   ///error.danger.flap
commercial lodging
fee
lisbon-inn.com
701–683-9076

                        $L
                        18.7 miles
                        D

                        $▲ *Dead Colt Creek Recreation Area*
                        2.5 miles off trail (future route of trail)
        46.373484   -97.615583   ///arrange.morphing.invisibly
                        public campground
                        RV and primitive sites, bathhouse
                        fee
                        managed by village of Milnor
                        milnornd.com/dead_colt
                        701-683-5766

↔ boundary private land
46.398956   -97.469394   ///denim.payback.dunks
↔ boundary Sheyenne National Grasslands
managed by USDA Forest Service
fs.usda.gov

               △ *dispersed camping* allowed
               28. 4 miles in Sheyenne NG

△ *Jorgen 's Hollow Campground*
46.524357 -97.201259 ///promises.coins.warrant
public land
7 horse sites, 7 tent sites
tables, fire rings, latrine, seasonal water
fee
managed by USDA Forest Service
fs.usda.gov
701-683-4342

△ *dispersed camping* allowed
2.6 miles in Sheyenne NG

↔ boundary Sheyenne National Grassland
46.528856 -97.155796 ///shave.pasted.resemble
↔ boundary mixed ownership

D
3.0 miles
+0.1 spur
H

△ *Ekre Campsite*
0.1 mile off trail
46.548222 -97.140732 ///turtles.fattest.celery
hosted campsite
primitive, latrine
managed by NDSU School of Natural Resource Sciences
contact northcountrytrail.org/trail/north-dakota/dpc

H
+0.1 spur
3.9 miles
H

△ *Berg Campsite*
46.571651 -97.095199 ///prompts.soothing.spatula
hosted campsite
primitive, latrine
maintained by Dakota Prairie Chapter
northcountrytrail.org/trail/north-dakota/dpc

H
11.8 miles
+0.15 road
PCs

✲ village of Walcott
46.548368 -96.938122 ///amp.unheard.collarbone
limited services

△ *Walcott City Park*
0.15 mile off trail
46.548015 -96.936498 ///troubles.insecurity.receptions
public land
primitive, table, restroom
cityofwalcott.org
check at Brewzer's Bar
701-469-2271

PCs
+0.15 road
4.8 miles
H

△ *FFA Campsite*
46.4841 -96.886717   ///fatherhood.police.crunches
hosted campsite
primitive, no fire ring, latrine, dry
maintained by Dakota Prairie Chapter
northcountrytrail.org/trail/north-dakota/dpc

H
1.2 miles
PCg

✣ village of Colfax
46.47091 -96.876881   ///debut.pursuing.knocked
limited services

△ *Colfax Park*
46.470535 -96.872512   ///largest.spots.secret
public land
primitive, no fire ring, latrine
owned by Richland County
maintained by Dakota Prairie Chapter
northcountrytrail.org/trail/north-dakota/dpc

PCg
8.6 miles
$PCg

✣ village of Abercrombie
46.447774 -96.730186   ///gravity.strongman.slides
limited services

$▲ *Fort Abercrombie Pavilion Park*
46.447092 -96.724368   ///sensing.zest.flights
public campground
RV and tent sites
electric, seasonal water, seasonal bathroom
fee
managed by City of Fort Abercrombie
701-730-0093

$PCg
0.7 mile in ND
chapter boundary
state line

North Dakota/Minnesota state line
46.444223 -96.716386   ///drive.benefit.scatters
Dakota Prairie Chapter
https://northcountrytrail.org/trail/north-dakota/dpc
↔ **Chapter boundary**

Minnesota

See legend and general info at the beginning of this section for help in interpreting the listings. One regulation unique to Minnesota State Forests is that you must be one full mile from developed campsites to disperse camp. Minnesota remote camping regulations do not state any specific distance you must be off road to camp. Some road walks are bounded by state land where one could go off-road to camp. A good practice is to be at least 200 feet away, and 1/8 mile (660 feet) would be even better.

A great deal of the land noted as Becker, Clearwater, and Hubbard County Forests is Minnesota tax-forfeit land, which is not quite the same as a county forest. However, full regulations can be seen at revisor.mn.gov/rules/6100.1350

↔ **Chapter boundary**
Minnesota/North Dakota state line
46.444233 -96.716346   ///dodges.crank.pulling
Minnesota Waters and Prairie Chapter
northcountrytrail.org/trail/minnesota/mwp

↔ mixed ownership

✲ city of Kent
46.437357 -96.684945   ///pepper.labs.elbow
no services

> state and chapter boundary
> **23.5 miles**
> +0.5 road
> $L

$ ■ *Comfort Zone Inn*
46.47833 -96.279542   ///spectators.grossly.plankton
commercial lodging
12 rooms, laundry
fee
218-867-2777

✲ city of Rothsay
46.471673 -96.280682   ///tapestries.track.feelers
limited services

> $L
> +0.5 road
> **22.5 miles**
> $PCg

✲ city of Fergus Falls
46.283527 -96.077975   ///finely.left.skips
services

> $ ■ *Motels*
> near west I-94 interchange
> approximately 2 miles off trail

$▲ Delagoon Park
managed by city of Fergus Falls
46.258617 -96.038486   ///hunched.communal.exporters
public campground
14 electric sites, 22 primitive
tables, fire rings, latrine, seasonal water
fee
ci.fergus-falls.mn.us
218-332-5400

Fergus Falls YMCA
0.3 mile off trail
46.295298 -96.056943   ///disjointed.myself.fussed
may waive fee for showers
no overnight accommodations
fergusfallsymca.org
218-739-4489

$PCg
23.1 miles
+0.0 or 0.1 spur
$PCs

↔ private land
46.486576 -95.962773   ///gatekeeper.kennels.seatbelt
↔ boundary Maplewood State Park
managed by Minnesota DNR

$∠ Grass Lake Campsite
46.509802 -95.954269   ///assemble.archive.mashed
public land
shelter, latrine
fee, online registration only
managed by Maplewood State Park
reservemn.usedirect.com
218 863-8383

OR

$∠ Cow Campsite
0.1 mile off trail
46.507557 -95.951437   ///thumbs.structure.bookcases
shelter, latrine
fee, online registration only
managed by Maplewood State Park
reservemn.usedirect.com
218 863-8383

$PCs
+0.0 or 0.1 spur
1.3 miles
+0.15 spur
$PCg

$▲ Knoll Loop
0.15 mile off trail
46.522914   -95.948261   ///workshops.switch.piracy
12 tent sites
tables, fire rings, latrine
fee, online registration only
managed by Maplewood State Park
reservemn.usedirect.com
218 863-8383

          $PCg
          +0.15 spur
          0.3 mile
          +0.4 or 1.0 spur
          $PCg

$▲ Hollow Loop
0.4 mile off trail
46.526753   -95.946888   ///tulip.rainforest.aims
13 tent sites
tables, fire rings, latrine, water
fee, online registration only
managed by Maplewood SP
reservemn.usedirect.com
218 863-8383

OR

$▲ Main Campground
1.0 mile off trail
46.525276   -95.941137   ///spells.hotter.stung
32 electric and tent sites
tables, fire rings, bathhouse
fee, online registration only
managed by Maplewood SP
reservemn.usedirect.com
218 863-8383

          $PCg
          +0.4 or 1.0 spur
          12.3 miles
          $L

↔ boundary Maplewood State Park
46.549769   -95.948728   ///oblige.grounds.prominently
↔ boundary mixed ownership

$ ■ Resorts
several near 46.624527   -95.849812   ///someday.cuff.donates
fee

          $L
          3.3 miles
          $L

✹ city of Vergas
46.657279 -95.804152   ///beard.melt.subjecting
limited services

$ ☐ *Homestead Inn*
46.661812 -95.801057   ///news.disorderly.tarred
commercial lodging
3 rooms, 1 cabin
fee
218-342-2141

$L
8.7 miles
chapter boundary

Otter Tail/Becker county line
46.717588 -95.720273   ///soil.rushes.thousands
Minnesota Waters and Prairie Chapter
northcountrytrail.org/trail/minnesota/mwp
↔ **Chapter boundary**

↔ **Chapter boundary**
Otter Tail/Becker county line
46.717588 -95.720273   ///soil.rushes.thousands
Laurentian Lakes Chapter
northcountrytrail.org/trail/minnesota/llc

      chapter boundary
      $L
      1.1 miles
      +0.25 road
      $PCg

$▲ *Frazee South River Campground*
0.25 mile off trail
46.72419 -95.697807   ///thus.mannerisms.goodnight
public campground
RV and tent sites, all electric, latrine
fee
managed by city of Frazee
frazeecity.com
218-334-4991

      $PCg
      +0.25 road
      0.5 mile
      $PCs

$△ *Frazee Wildflower Park*
46.733058 -95.700789   ///exceptional.weeds.centrally
public campsite
2 primitive sites, seasonal latrine
fee
managed by city of Frazee
frazeecity.com
218-334-4991

      $PCs
      9.6 miles
      HCs

△ *Primitive Campsite*
46.825259 -95.646743   ///errand.furniture.pleased
hosted site
primitive, fire ring, latrine, dry
maintained by Laurentian Lakes Chapter
llc@northcountrytrail.org

      H
      21.6 miles
      D

↔ boundary mixed ownership
46.825016 -95.648177   ///bared.triumphant.unframed
↔ boundary Hubbel Pond Wildlife Management Area
managed by MN DNR

Note: no camping in Hubbel Pond WMA

↔ boundary Hubbel Pond WMA
46.890343   -95.646606   ///credits.matrons.destroyer
↔ boundary Tamarac National Wildlife Refuge
managed by USFWS

Note: no camping in Tamarac NWF

↔ boundary Tamarac National Wildlife Refuge
46.944151   -95.546272   ///fell.pedestrian.declines
↔ boundary state land

△ *dispersed camping* allowed
0.3 mile on state land
888-646-6367

↔ boundary state land
46.947491   -95.542152   ///resounding.boxes.elders
↔ boundary Becker County Forest

△ *dispersed camping* allowed
3.6 miles in Becker County Forest
no fires

↔ boundary Becker County Forest
46.969635   -95.497692   ///nests.racetrack.catchy
↔ boundary state land

△ *dispersed camping* allowed
0.7 mile on state land
888-646-6367

↔ boundary state land
46.976897   -95.494946   ///terminally.spawned.pelt
↔ boundary Greenwater Lake State Scientific and Natural Area

Note: no camping in state SNAs

D
1.9 miles
D

↔ boundary Greenwater Lake State Scientific and Natural Area
46.991321   -95.492903   ///blamed.firming.crate
↔ boundary Becker County Forest

△ *dispersed camping* allowed
5.6 miles in Becker County Forest
no fires

△ *Flooded Woods Campsite*
47.048452   -95.470267   ///description.salmon.thrones
public campsite
primitive, bench, fire ring, latrine
no fee
managed by Becker County
maintained by Laurentian Lakes Chapter
co.becker.mn.us
218-847-0099

△ *dispersed camping* allowed
2.6 miles in Becker County Forest
no fires
co.becker.mn.us

↔ boundary Becker County Forest
47.088089 -95.449946   ///rooks.dogs.objects
↔ boundary White Earth State Forest

Note: dispersed camping is allowed in White Earth State Forest

△ *dispersed camping* allowed
0.3 mile in White Earth SF
888-646-6367

↔ boundary White Earth State Forest
47.075249 -95.452631   ///vitamins.tapping.motivating
↔ boundary Becker County Forest

△ *dispersed camping* allowed
1.0 mile in Becker County Forest
no fires, LNT
co.becker.mn.us

↔ boundary Becker County Forest
47.087918 -95.450653   ///provocative.done.stack
↔ *boundary White Earth State Forest*

△ *dispersed camping* allowed
0.5 mile in White Earth SF
888-646-6367

↔ boundary White Earth State Forest
47.093337 -95.447996   ///touchy.cross.sensitivity
↔ boundary Becker County Forest

△ *dispersed camping* allowed
0.8 mile in Becker County Forest
no fires, LNT
co.becker.mn.us

↔ boundary Becker County Forest
47.093308 -95.44791   ///swelling.collars.nuance
↔ boundary White Earth State Forest

△ *dispersed camping* allowed
0.2 mile in White Earth SF
888-646-6367

↔ boundary White Earth State Forest
47.107872 -95.452198   ///mumbled.clearly.sneezed
↔ boundary Becker County Forest

△ *dispersed camping* allowed
0.5 mile in Becker County Forest
no fires, LNT
co.becker.mn.us

△ *Horseshoe Lake Campsite*
0.1 mile off trail
47.113534 -95.445633   ///transfixed.tanned.translated
public campsite
primitive, fire ring, bench, latrine
managed by Becker County
co.becker.mn.us

△ *dispersed camping* allowed
1.6 miles in Becker County Forest
no fires, LNT
co.becker.mn.us

↔ boundary Becker County Forest
47.133252 -95.441362   ///vortex.misted.advises
↔ boundary White Earth State Forest

△ *dispersed camping* allowed
0.3 mile in White Earth SF
888-646-6367

↔ boundary White Earth State Forest
47.13696 -95.444494   ///waffle.functions.permits
↔ boundary Becker County Forest

△ *dispersed camping* allowed
0.4 mile in Becker County Forest
no fires
co.becker.mn.us

↔ boundary Becker County Forest
47.140551 -95.439903   ///glass.hooking.flicks
↔ boundary White Earth State Forest

△ *dispersed camping* allowed
0.6 mile in White Earth SF
888-646-6367

↔ boundary White Earth State Forest
47.147769 -95.439384   ///glass.hooking.flicks
↔ boundary Becker County Forest

△ *dispersed camping* allowed
0.2 mile in Becker County Forest
no fires
co.becker.mn.us

△ *Pine Island Lake Campsite*
47.148817 -95.439432   ///jaguar.searing.battled
public campsite
primitive, fire ring, bench, latrine
managed by Becker County
co.becker.mn.us

△ *dispersed camping* allowed
0.2 mile in Becker County Forest
no fires, LNT
co.becker.mn.us

↔ boundary Becker County Forest
47.151207 -95.438335   ///revisit.milked.grin
↔ boundary Clearwater County Forest

△ *dispersed camping* allowed
3.4 miles in Clearwater County Forest
218-694-6227

△ *Old Headquarters Campsite*
47.166166 -95.412317   ///avenge.spent.calculating
public campsite
primitive, fire ring, latrine
managed by Clearwater County
218-694-6227

△ *dispersed camping* allowed
5.2 miles in Clearwater County Forest
218-694-6227

△ *Gardner Lake Campsite*
47.157944 -95.336666   ///promoting.removers.moderately
public campsite
primitive, fire ring, latrine
managed by Clearwater County
218-694-6227

△ *dispersed camping* allowed
2.9 miles in Clearwater County Forest
218-694-6227

↔ boundary Clearwater County Forest
47.173758 -95.297242   ///neater.resign.business
↔ boundary Itasca State Park

west boundary Itasca State Park
47.173758 -95.297242   ///neater.resign.business
Laurentian Lakes Chapter
northcountrytrail.org/trail/minnesota/llc
↔ **Chapter boundary**

↔ **Chapter boundary**
west boundary Itasca State Park
47.173758 -95.297242   ///neater.resign.business
Itasca Moraine Chapter
northcountrytrail.org/trail/minnesota/itm

Note: camp in designated sites only in Itasca SP

       chapter boundary
       0.8 mile
       PCs

△ *Itasca SP NCT Campsite*
47.170826 -95.28381   ///walks.after.potentially
public campsite
primitive, fire ring, latrine
no reservation required
managed by Itasca SP
dnr.state.mn.us
       PCs
       5.0 miles
       $PCs

$△ *Itasca SP Backpaker Sites 3,4*
47.14878 -95.219422   ///register.cheat.trapped
public campsite
primitive, fire ring, table, latrine
fee
reservation required
managed by Itasca SP
reserve at dnr.state.mn.us
866-857-2757
       $PCs
       2.8 miles
       $PCs

$△ *Itasca SP Backpaker Site 6*
47.152093 -95.170799   ///nurses.catches.motorist
public campsite
primitive, fire ring, table, latrine
managed by Itasca SP
fee
reserve at dnr.state.mn.us
866-857-2757
       $PCs
       1.6 miles
       D

↔ boundary Itasca State Park
47.152227 -95.146209   ///applies.ignore.discarding
↔ boundary Hubbard County Forest
managed by Hubbard County
co.hubbard.mn.us
218-732-2300

Note: dispersed camping is allowed in Hubbard County Forest

     △ *dispersed camping* allowed
     3.2 miles in Hubbard County Forest
     co.hubbard.mn.us

△ *Zingwak Campsite*
47.14532 -95.088212   ///fondest.cascade.geographer
public land
primitive, fire ring, latrine
managed by Hubbard County
maintained by Itasca Moraine Chapter
northcountrytrail.org/trail/minnesota/itm/

△ *dispersed camping* allowed
10.2 miles in Hubbard County Forest
co.hubbard.mn.us

∠ *Amikwik Shelter*
47.155225 -94.958666   ///falling.locating.note
public land
open shelter, fire ring, latrine
managed by Hubbard County
co.hubbard.mn.us

△ *dispersed camping* allowed
0.9 mile in Hubbard County Forest
co.hubbard.mn.us

↔ boundary Hubbard County Forest
47.147873 -94.944831   ///zest.shoestring.shadows
↔ boundary Paul Bunyan State Forest
managed by MN DNR
dnr.state.mn.us
651-296-6157

Note: dispersed camping is allowed in Paul Bunyan State Forest

△ *dispersed camping* allowed
7.1 miles in Paul Bunyan State Forest
dnr.state.mn.us

△ *Nelson Lake Campsites*
0.35 mile off trail
47.156045 -94.841405   ///canoe.smacked.deform
public land
primitive, fire ring, latrine
managed by Paul Bunyan State Forest
dnr.state.mn.us

OR

$▲ *Gulch Lake Campsites*
1.0 mile off trail
47.160247 -94.836513   ///mashing.backer.jogged
public campsite
14 primitive sites
tables, fire rings, latrine, seasonal water
fee
managed by Lake Bemidji State Park
dnr.state.mn.us
866-857-2757

△ *dispersed camping* allowed
9.1 miles in Paul Bunyan State Forest
dnr.state.mn.us

△ *Waboose Lake Campsite*
0.2 mile off trail
47.059363   -94.822437   ///helpers.restoration.marine
public land
primitive, fire ring, latrine
managed by Paul Bunyan State Forest
maintained by Itasca Moraine Chapter
itm@northcountrytrail.org

△ *dispersed camping* allowed
7.8 miles in Paul Bunyan State Forest
dnr.state.mn.us

△ *Sprinkle Trail Campsite*
47.077556   -94.701664   ///haggis.rushing.dragons
public land
primitive, fire ring, latrine
managed by Paul Bunyan State Forest
maintained by Itasca Moraine Chapter
itm@northcountrytrail.org

△ *dispersed camping* allowed
2.4 miles in Paul Bunyan State Forest
dnr.state.mn.us

↔ boundary Paul Bunyan State Forest MN 211.5
47.074108   -94.663534   ///clash.socialists.issues
↔ boundary Chippewa National Forest

Note: dispersed camping is allowed in Chippewa National Forest

△ *dispersed camping* allowed
4.0 miles in Chippewa NF
fs.usda.gov/chippewa

△ *Shingobee Campsite*
47.038175   -94.62903   ///expressions.reaction.bribing
public land
primitive, fire ring, no latrine
managed by the Chippewa NF
fs.usda.gov/chippewa
218-547-1044

△ *dispersed camping* allowed
0.8 mile in Chippewa NF
fs.usda.gov/chippewa

↔ boundary Chippewa National Forest
47.034182   -94.618473   ///hunched.calculate.founders
↔ boundary MN state land

△ *dispersed camping* allowed
1.2 miles on MN state land
dnr.state.mn.us

↔ boundary MN state land
47.032808   -94.597187   ///sundial.moods.cartridges
↔ boundary Chippewa National Forest

△ *dispersed camping* allowed
3.5 miles in Chippewa NF
fs.usda.gov/chippewa

Cyphers Lake Warming Shelter
47.030704   -94.546126   ///earl.wriggling.think
no camping

△ *dispersed camping* allowed
4.7 miles in Chippewa NF
fs.usda.gov/chippewa

△ *Campsite W90*
46.994192   -94.514008   ///amazed.enabled.lyricism
public land
primitive, fire ring, latrine
managed by Chippewa NF
fs.usda.gov/chippewa

△ *dispersed camping* allowed
3.3 miles in Chippewa NF
fs.usda.gov/chippewa

△ *Diamond Lake Campsite W71*
1.0 mile off trail
46.997412   -94.456158   ///socialists.spray.lilac
public land
primitive, fire ring, latrine
managed by Chippewa NF
fs.usda.gov/chippewa

△ *dispersed camping* allowed
3.3 miles in Chippewa NF
fs.usda.gov/chippewa

△ *Hovde Lake Campsite*
47.006836   -94.447833   ///litmus.radio.above
public land
primitive, fire ring, latrine
managed by Chippewa NF
fs.usda.gov/chippewa

△ *dispersed camping* allowed
1.4 miles in Chippewa NF
fs.usda.gov/chippewa

△ *Gut Lake Campsite W53*
47.004612   -94.427362   ///sapping.doghouse.fractional
public land
primitive, fire ring, latrine
managed by Chippewa NF
fs.usda.gov/chippewa

△ *dispersed camping* allowed
3.9 miles in Chippewa NF
fs.usda.gov/chippewa

△ *Moccasin Lake Campsite*
0.1 mile off trail
47.002124 -94.360371   ///laying.selfish.clarifies
public land
primitive, fire ring, latrine
managed by Chippewa NF
fs.usda.gov/chippewa

    △ *dispersed camping* allowed
    1.4 miles in Chippewa NF
    fs.usda.gov/chippewa

△ *Hazel Lake Campsite W57*
0.1 mile off trail
46.998701 -94.28745   ///clashing.swigs.activating
public land
primitive, no latrine
managed by the Chippewa NF
fs.usda.gov/chippewa
218-547-1044

    △ *dispersed camping* allowed
    3.1 miles in Chippewa NF
    fs.usda.gov/chippewa

↔ boundary Chippewa NF
47.022555 -94.2475   ///fostering.tidy.tripped
↔ boundary Leech Lake Reservation

Note: no camping on Leech Lake Reservation

    D
    0.4 mile
    D

↔ boundary Leech Lake Reservation
47.022496 -94.242092   ///jeep.merit.posters
↔ boundary Chippewa NF

    △ *dispersed camping* allowed
    1.2 miles in Chippewa NF
    fs.usda.gov/chippewa

↔ boundary Chippewa NF
47.034022 -94.235569   ///duty.publisher.perceptual
↔ boundary Leech Lake Reservation

    D
    0.2 mile
    D

↔ boundary Leech Lake Reservation
47.037795 -94.236299   ///doped.astounding.pampering
↔ boundary Chippewa NF

    △ *dispersed camping* allowed
    0.5 mile in Chippewa NF
    fs.usda.gov/chippewa

↔ boundary Chippewa NF
47.041509 -94.231235   ///thorns.aside.thud
↔ boundary Leech Lake Reservation

D
0.3 mile
D

↔ boundary Leech Lake Reservation
47.041363 -94.225742   ///scavengers.pigment.houseboat
↔ boundary Chippewa NF

△ *dispersed camping* allowed
0.7 mile in Chippewa NF
fs.usda.gov/chippewa
chapter boundary

MN Hwy 84
47.043655 -94.214902   ///service.digits.search
Itasca Moraine Chapter
northcountrytrail.org/trail/minnesota/itm
↔ **Chapter boundary**

↔ **Chapter boundary**
MN Hwy 84
47.043655 -94.214902   ///service.digits.search
Star of the North Chapter
northcountrytrail.org/trail/minnesota/stn

↔ boundary Leech Lake Reservation

Note: no camping on Leech Lake Reservation

D
0.7 mile
D

↔ boundary Leech Lake Reservation
47.041509 -94.204198   ///perspective.beyond.steroids
↔ boundary Chippewa NF

Note: dispersed camping is allowed in Chippewa National Forest

chapter boundary
△ *dispersed camping* allowed
1.5 miles in Chippewa NF
fs.usda.gov/chippewa

△ *Crown Lake Campsite*
47.045193 -94.184334   ///insulation.formations.senior
public land
primitive, table, fire ring, latrine
maintained by the Star of the North Chapter
stn@northcountrytrail.org

△ *dispersed camping* allowed
0.4 mile in Chippewa NF
fs.usda.gov/chippewa

↔ boundary Chippewa NF
47.04439 -94.176496   ///clingy.draw.basis
↔ boundary Leech Lake Reservation

D
0.5 mile
D

↔ boundary Leech Lake Reservation
47.039944 -94.170853   ///restriction.revisiting.pampering
↔ boundary Chippewa NF

△ *dispersed camping* allowed
3.1 miles in Chippewa NF
fs.usda.gov/chippewa

↔ boundary Chippewa NF
47.043987 -94.115534   ///hurricanes.informants.watchdogs
↔ boundary state land

△ *dispersed camping* allowed
0.6 mile on state land
note: very marshy

↔ boundary state land
47.0448 -94.104818   ///chat.overdue.ramming
↔ boundary Chippewa NF

△ *dispersed camping* allowed
0.2 mile in Chippewa NF
fs.usda.gov/chippewa

$▲ *Mabel Lake Campground*
2.0 miles off trail
47.048885 -94.072062   ///fleets.shipwreck.schooling
public campground
19 vehicular sites
tables, fire rings, latrine, water
fee
managed by the Chippewa NF
fs.usda.gov
218-335-8600

↔ boundary Chippewa NF
47.04711 -94.102157   ///nightclubs.pupils.income
↔ boundary state land

△ *dispersed camping* allowed
0.3 mile on state land

↔ boundary state land
47.050678 -94.101041   ///diminishes.spenders.decently
↔ boundary private land

D
0.1 mile
D

↔ boundary private land
47.051906 -94.099668   ///remodels.hourglass.perceptive
↔ boundary Chippewa NF

△ *dispersed camping* allowed
4.4 miles in Chippewa NF
fs.usda.gov/chippewa

△ *Old Pines Campsite W47*
47.090332 -94.046599   ///factories.insults.harmony
public land
primitive, table, fire ring, latrine
maintained by the Star of the North Chapter
stn@northcountrytrail.org

△ *dispersed camping* allowed
8.1 miles in Chippewa NF
fs.usda.gov/chippewa

↔ boundary Chippewa NF
47.132692 -93.938821   ///ridge.pleasing.covered
↔ boundary private land

D
0.2 mile
PCs

↔ boundary private land
47.134327   -93.934529   ///avoids.sometimes.leaders
↔ boundary Chippewa NF

△ *Milton Lake Campsite*
47.133472   -93.934133   ///baked.parents.modern
primitive, bench, fire ring, latrine
managed by the Chippewa NF
primitive, fire ring, latrine

△ *dispersed camping* allowed
6.5 miles in Chippewa NF
fs.usda.gov/chippewa

↔ boundary Chippewa NF
47.097011   -93.854894   ///reassures.funded.fidgeted
↔ chapter boundary

MN Hwy 6
47.097011   -93.854894   ///reassures.funded.fidgeted
Star of the North Chapter
northcountrytrail.org/trail/minnesota/stn/
↔ **Chapter boundary**

↔ **Chapter boundary**
MN Hwy 6
47.097011   -93.854894   ///reassures.funded.fidgeted
Arrowhead Chapter
northcountrytrail.org/trail/minnesota/arw

                    chapter boundary
                    6.3 miles
                    +0.3 spur
                    HCs

Note: the next 10+ miles of trail are moving off road in 2024-25. Two backcountry campsites are being built along the new route.

△ *Forgotten Lake Campsite*
0.3 mile off trail
47.167613   -93.768547   ///parcel.decoded.according
hosted by Itasca County Forest
primitive, fire ring, latrine
maintained by Arrowhead Chapter
arw@northcountrytrail.org

                    HCs
                    +0.3 spur
                    17.7 miles
                    +0.2 road
                    $L

                                            $ ☐ *Green Heron BnB*
                                                        1.1 miles off trail
                  47.217878   -93.578542   ///fragrances.streetcar.chromatic
                                                         commercial lodging
                                                                       2 rooms
                                                                            fee
                                                           greenheronbandb.com
                                                              218-999-5795

                                                     $▲ *Pokegama Dam Campground*
                                                               2 miles off trail
                  47.249485   -93.583705   ///replays.childcare.undertaken
                                                            public campground
                              19 electric sites, 2 primitive sites, bathhouse
                                                                        fee
                                        managed by Army Corp of Engineers
                                                           recreation.gov
                                                           218-326-6128

✻ south part city of Grand Rapids
various +-1.0 mile off trail
47.220142   -93.528706   ///follow.force.bliss
services

$ ■ *Itascan Motel*
0.15 mile off trail
47.225558 -93.5284 ///senses.erase.hired
commercial lodging
fee
218-326-3489

$ ■ *Motels*
1.0+ mile off trail
47.212361 -93.528851 ///bands.simply.crowds
commercial lodging
fee

$L
+0.15 road
0.9 mile
+0.4 road
$L

Itasca County YMCA
47.229585 -93.5212 no overnight accommodations
hikers may shower during regular hours of operation for a fee
ymcaitasca.org
218-327-1161

$ ■ *Hotel Rapids*
0.4 mile off trail
47.234875 -93.517679 ///layers.above.glass
commercial lodging
5 rooms/suites
hotelrapids.com
218-326-3458

$L
+0.4 road
0.5 mile
$PCg

✲ north part city of Grand Rapids
various off trail
47.236042 -93.528264 ///jokes.grow.forced
services

$▲ *Itasca County Fairgrounds*
47.247239 -93.519074 ///grape.using.fear
public campground
57 electric and primitive sites
tables, fire rings, bathhouse, laundry
fee
online reservation required
managed by Itasca County
co.itasca.mn.us/284/Itasca-County-Fairgrounds-Park
218-327-2855

$PCg
7.8 miles
D

Y southern terminus of Mesabi Trail (paved multi-use trail)
47.248166 -93.523934   ///taped.audio.follow
Note: The NCT is no longer concurrent with the paved Mesabi Trail from this point to near the Greenway Mine tailings pond. (about 3.1 miles of Mesabi Trail, but the NCT is now about 4.5 miles between these points, most of it off-pavement)

Y junction NCT at Mesabi Trail
47.275746 -93.496297   ///skinny.bared.sanitation
NCT and Mesabi Trails are concurrent from this point north almost to Hibbing.

Note: No effort has been made to secure camping sites along the Mesabi Trail and road walks into Ely since this is a temporary route for the NCT. All efforts are being made to take this section off the paved trail. A hiker may need to have daily spotters.

However, the Mesabi Trail wanders intermittently through state land where dispersed camping is allowed. You must have access to a map that shows the boundaries (Avenza does, OnX with a subscription does) or find clear signage that you are on county/state land. The best practice is to stay well inside the boundaries as mapped lines are somewhat inaccurate. The suitability of these public lands for camping is uncertain. They may be swamp, too brushy, etc.

↔ boundary mixed ownership
47.289245 -93.469832   ///farming.super.barefoot
↔ boundary state land

△ *dispersed camping* allowed
1.2 miles on MN state land
1/8 mile off trail
dnr.state.mn.us

↔ boundary state land
47.28974 -93.448246   ///waltz.drills.perspective
↔ boundary mixed ownership

D
14.1 miles
D

✲ city of Coleraine
47.289863 -93.427649   ///inviting.pogo.craziest
limited services

✲ city of Bovey
0.2 mile off trail
47.295554 -93.417779   ///nursing.dimes.marching
limited services

✲ city of Taconite
0.1 mile off trail
47.312753 -93.382223   ///handsets.encoded.vinegar
limited services

✲ city of Marble
0.3 mile off trail
47.316841 -93.304589   ///hazards.repeating.alternate
limited services

✲ city of Calumet
47.323008   -93.277124   ///elephant.rehearsing.calms
limited services

↔ boundary mixed ownership
47.332607   -93.220475   ///departure.imprint.bedroom
↔ boundary state land

△ *dispersed camping* allowed
0.3 mile on MN state land
out of sight of the trail
dnr.state.mn.us

↔ boundary state land
47.334163   -93.215154   ///flagpole.mend.imagination
↔ boundary mixed ownership

D
4.2 miles
+0.2 road
$PCg

$▲ *Swan Lake Campground and Resort*
3.0 miles off trail
47.311116   -93.17107   ///ulterior.witness.attends
commercial campground
electric and non-electric sites, cabins
tables, fire rings, bathhouse
fee
grandrapidsmnresort.com
218-256-4573

✲ city of Nashwauk
47.376639   -93.167046   ///idealist.longest.smiling
limited services

$▲ *Nashwauk Campground*
0.2 mile off trail
47.383985   -93.167984   ///hurry.habitation.decades
public campground
15 vehicular sites
tables, fire rings, bathhouse
fee
reserve online
nashwaukmn.gov
218-885-1210 or Police Department at 218-885-1000

$PCg
+0.2 road
10.4 miles
D

✲ city of Keewatin
47.398845   -93.075551   ///doctor.ignore.imagination
limited services

↔ boundary mixed ownership
47.414968 -93.009619   ///ounce.pursuing.unsuitable
↔ boundary state land

△ *dispersed camping* allowed
0.7 mile on MN state land
out of sight of the trail
dnr.state.mn.us

↔ boundary state land
47.424463 -93.006057   ///futuristic.similar.windmill
↔ boundary mixed ownership

D
1.5 miles
D

↔ boundary mixed ownership
47.427033 -92.984774   ///resettle.caters.horses
↔ boundary state land

△ *dispersed camping* allowed
0.9 mile on MN state land
out of sight of the trail
dnr.state.mn.us

↔ boundary state land
47.429094 -92.969668   ///enjoyment.door.raced
↔ boundary mixed ownership

D
1.5 miles
D

$ ■ *Hampton Inn*
and services
2.5 miles off trail
47.398134 -92.952997   ///sentimental.oldest.demand
commercial lodging
fee
hilton.com
218-262-0000

↔ boundary mixed ownership
47.428634 -92.948104   ///picking.autographs.script
↔ boundary state land

△ *dispersed camping* allowed
0.4 mile on MN state land
out of sight of the trail
dnr.state.mn.us

↔ boundary state land
47.432858 -92.947632   ///veto.scarcely.tycoon
↔ boundary mixed ownership

D
0.9 mile
+0.3 road
$PCg

✲ city of Hibbing
various off trail
47.435906   -92.938809   ///point.oceans.directly
services
better services and motels near Hampton Inn (see above)
47.398134   -92.952997   ///sentimental.oldest.demand
but farther off trail

$▲ North Hibbing Campground
0.3 mile off trail
47.445252   -92.941127   ///pancake.competitive.restoration
public campground
10 vehicular sites
8 electric, 2 non-electric
tables, fire rings, bathhouse
fee
hibbingmn.gov

$PCg
+0.3 road
5.4 miles
D

↔ boundary mixed ownership
47.468433   -92.846002   ///question.corner.diagonally
↔ boundary state land

△ *dispersed camping* allowed
0.3 mile on MN state land
out of sight of the trail
dnr.state.mn.us

↔ boundary state land
47.471711   -92.849521   ///examine.salsa.freezer
↔ boundary mixed ownership

D
5.9 miles
$PCg

✲ city of Chisholm
various off trail
47.489362   -92.883865   ///cheerful.spills.plan
services

$ ■ Chisholm Inn and Suites
1.1 miles off trail
47.481467   -92.889873   ///homecoming.purse.prune
commercial lodging
43 rooms/suites
fee
chisholminn.com
218-254-2000

▲ *Chisholm Iron Trail Campground*
47.489783   -92.89004
1.6 miles off trail
///reserving.steered.exhibitions
public campground
51 vehicular sites
46 electric, 5 non-electric
tables, fire rings, bathhouse
fee
managed by city of Chisholm
ci.chisholm.mn.us
218-421-7158

$▲ *Stubler Beach Campground*
47.490585   -92.787716   ///variances.informers.unsuitable
public campground
8 primitive sites
tables, fire rings, latrine
fee
managed by city of Buhl
mesabitrail.com/trail-towns/buhl
218-258-3226

$PCg
1.0 mile
D

✻ city of Buhl MN
47.493688   -92.778457   ///restrictive.honesty.stretches
limited services

↔ boundary mixed ownership
47.498008   -92.77187   ///elbowing.guide.applause
↔ boundary state land

△ *dispersed camping* allowed
0.3 mile on MN state land
out of sight of the trail
dnr.state.mn.us

↔ boundary state land
47.499168   -92.766248   ///clued.cashew.generals
↔ boundary mixed ownership

D
0.5 mile
D

↔ boundary mixed ownership
47.500886   -92.75671   ///defined.granny.heights
↔ boundary state land

△ *dispersed camping* allowed
0.3 mile on MN state land
out of sight of the trail
dnr.state.mn.us

↔ boundary state land
47.502292 -92.749575   ///crumble.frowned.leaders
↔ boundary mixed ownership

>D
>**3.0 miles**
>D

↔ boundary mixed ownership
47.495401 -92.692739   ///wreck.nests.lighthouse
↔ boundary state land

>△ *dispersed camping* allowed
>**0.4 mile** on MN state land
>out of sight of the trail
>dnr.state.mn.us

↔ boundary state land
47.49672 -92.687997   ///meaty.asteroid.socialists
↔ boundary mixed ownership

>D
>**2.3 miles**
>D

>$▲ *West Two Rivers Campground*
>1.8 miles off trail
>47.479364 -92.66352   ///ears.decorate.underlined
>public campground
>45 electric sites
>tables, fire rings, bathhouse
>fee
>managed by City of Mountain Iron
>218-735-8831
>mtniron.com

↔ boundary mixed ownership
47.513143 -92.645768   ///kettle.aced.items
↔ boundary state land

>△ *dispersed camping* allowed
>**0.2 mile** on MN state land
>out of sight of the trail
>dnr.state.mn.us

↔ boundary state land
47.514883 -92.640511   ///discontent.ordered.shaving
↔ boundary mixed ownership

>D
>**1.5 miles**
>D

↔ boundary mixed ownership
47.532426 -92.629396   ///spotlights.overdone.minority
↔ boundary state land

>△ *dispersed camping* allowed
>**0.4 mile** on MN state land
>out of sight of the trail
>dnr.state.mn.us

↔ boundary state land
47.533882 -92.624086   ///aura.camps.belts
↔ boundary mixed ownership

          D
          0.3 mile
          D

✻ city of Mountain Iron
47.532484 -92.622154   ///mixer.gates.lime
no services

↔ boundary mixed ownership
47.532469 -92.618893   ///scans.rated.voter
↔ boundary state land

△ *dispersed camping* allowed
0.2 mile on MN state land
out of sight of the trail
dnr.state.mn.us

↔ boundary state land
47.531419 -92.616479   ///weep.entry.freed
↔ boundary mixed ownership

          D
          0.8 mile
          D

↔ boundary mixed ownership
47.527702 -92.60428   ///target.lock.exile
↔ boundary state land

△ *dispersed camping* allowed
0.3 mile on MN state land
out of sight of the trail
dnr.state.mn.us

↔ boundary state land
47.528166 -92.598701   ///flat.serve.patrol
↔ boundary mixed ownership

          D
          0.5 mile
          D

↔ boundary mixed ownership
47.528412 -92.587479   ///runner.price.once
↔ boundary state land

△ *dispersed camping* allowed
0.5 mile on MN state land
out of sight of the trail
dnr.state.mn.us

↔ boundary state land
47.531238 -92.582157   ///most.homing.steely
↔ boundary mixed ownership

          D
          2.2 miles
          $L

✳ city of Virginia
0.3 mile off trail
47.523128 -92.538656   ///pouch.becomes.idealist
services

$ ■ *Lakeshor Motor Inn*
47.526594 -92.541323   ///factory.pint.sharpening
commercial lodging
7 rooms
fee
lakeshor.com
218-741-3360

$ ■ *Quality Inn and Suites*
0.3 mile off trail
47.523128 -92.538656   ///pouch.becomes.idealist
commercial lodging
fee
218-749-1000

$L
2.1 miles
D

↔ boundary mixed ownership
47.515437 -92.516579   ///forgive.matters.worried
↔ boundary state land

△ *dispersed camping* allowed
0.6 mile on MN state land
out of sight of the trail
dnr.state.mn.us

↔ boundary state land
47.509118 -92.508167   ///motionless.galloped.goals
↔ boundary mixed ownership

D
3.1 miles
+0.6 road
$PCg

$▲ *Sherwood Forest Campground*
0.6 mile off trail
47.483969 -92.464364   ///confirm.melons.spoons
public campground
57 vehicular sites, electric and primitive
tables, fire rings, bathhouse
fee
managed by City of Gilbert
gilbertmn.org
218-748-2221

$PCg
+0.6 road
9.1 miles
$PCg

⁑ city of Gilbert
47.491118 -92.46243 ///imported.bedspread.contraband
limited services

⁑ city of Biwabik
47.533219 -92.345485 ///confiding.joking.sonic
limited services

$▲ *Vermillion Trail Park Campground*
47.531685 -92.32579 ///famous.progressive.vibrations
public campground
40 vehicular sites
electric and non-electric sites
tables, fire rings, bathhouse
fee
City of Biwabik
irontrail.org/lodging/campgrounds/vermilion-trail
218-865-6705

$PCg
4.5 miles
+0.3 road
$L

$ ■ *Giant 's Ridge Recreation Area*
0.3 mile off trail
47.579028 -92.304996 ///headlight.cracker.waitresses
commercial lodging
67 condos, guest houses, villas
fee
giantsridge.com
800-688-7669

$L
+0.3 road
3.9 miles
D

↔ boundary mixed ownership
47.602988 -92.261176 ///gull.watercress.replaying
↔ boundary state land

△ *dispersed camping* allowed
1.0 mile on MN state land
out of sight of the trail
south side of trail only
dnr.state.mn.us

↔ boundary state land
47.602294 -92.240405 ///splits.quickening.prowl
↔ boundary mixed ownership

D
15.2 miles
+0.3 road
$L

Y junction NCT at Mesabi Trail (paved multi-use trail). NCT is concurrent with Mesabi Trail southwest of this point. The NCT turn northwest toward Tower; Mesabi Trail is not yet complete
47.60202 -92.236355   ///dividing.disown.hammer

$▲ *Heritage Park*
3.0 miles off trail
47.664221   -92.195155   ///empty.automobiles.snap
public campground
10 electric sites, 7 tent sites
tables, fire rings, bathhouse
fee
managed by city of Embarrass
embarrass.org/heritage-park--campground.html
218-410-7743

$ ■ *Marjo Motel*
0.3 mile off trail
47.803433 -92.28369   ///orbits.philosopher.reheat
commercial lodging
8 rooms
fee
marjo-motel.com
218-753-4851

$L
+0.3 road
0.3 mile
D

✲ city of Tower
0.2 mile off trail
47.805314 -92.275316   ///embellish.proved.arrange
services

↔ boundary mixed ownership
47.802763 -92.276325   ///decreasing.pastime.dynamics
↔ boundary state land

△ *dispersed camping* allowed
0.5 mile on MN state land
out of sight of the trail
dnr.state.mn.us

↔ boundary state land
47.805393 -92.265789   ///burning.straying.window
↔ boundary mixed ownership

D
1.4 miles
$L

$▲ *Hoodoo Point Campground*
1.6 miles off trail
47.819488   -92.299199   ///forgives.thankfully.carpets
public campground
70 vehicular sites, electric and non-electric
tables, fire rings, bathhouse
fee
managed by city of Tower
cityoftower.com/campgrounds
218-753-4070

$▲ *McKinley Campground*
2.0 miles off trail
47.827912   -92.273892   ///beetles.temperature.angers
70 vehicular sites
tables, fire rings, bathhouse
fee
managed by city of Tower
mckinleyparkcampground.com
218-753-4070

✻ village of Soudan
47.815921   -92.245574   ///boosted.overlook.dismissive
limited services

$ ■ *Vermillion Park Inn*
47.816108   -92.245348   ///uppers.sweetened.dishing
commercial lodging
10 rooms
fee
vermilionparkinn.com
218-753-2333

$L
2.9 miles
+0.4 spur
$PCs

$△ *Lake Vermillion Backpacker Campsites 1-5*
0.4 mile off trail
47.824627   -92.201873   ///activation.parading.presuming
public land
5 primitive sites
table, fire rings, latrine, dry, bear box
fee
reserve online
managed by Lake Vermillion SP
dnr.state.mn.us/state_parks/park.html?id=spk00285#reservations
218-300-7000

$PCs
+0.4 spur
3.8 miles
D

$▲ *Lake Vermilion-Soudan Underground Mine State Park*
1.3 miles off trail
47.847133   -92.187963   ///examine.whimpered.planets
public campground
31 electric sites, cabins
tables, fire rings, bathhouse
fee
managed by Minnesota DNR
218-300-7000
dnr.state.mn.us

↔ boundary mixed ownership
47.846132 -92.137393   ///spout.straddled.reveals
↔ boundary state land

△ *dispersed camping* allowed
1.0 mile on MN state land
out of sight of the trail
dnr.state.mn.us

↔ boundary state land
47.848033 -92.115506   ///series.lolly.drops
↔ boundary mixed ownership

D
1.5 miles
D

↔ boundary mixed ownership
47.841063 -92.096237   ///skillet.seasick.spills
↔ boundary state land

△ *dispersed camping* allowed
0.3 mile on MN state land
out of sight of the trail
dnr.state.mn.us

↔ boundary state land
47.837779 -92.094477   ///radical.pushing.extra
↔ boundary mixed ownership

D
0.3 mile
chapter boundary

Y junction with Mesabi Trail which the NCT follows to the east

Jct Bear Head SP Road at Mesabi Trail
47.833803 -92.095293   ///briefed.briefing.majority
Arrowhead Chapter
northcountrytrail.org/trail/minnesota/arw
↔ **Chapter boundary**

↔ **Chapter boundary**
Jct Bear Head SP Road at Mesabi Trail
47.833803 -92.095293   ///briefed.briefing.majority
Ely Northwoods Chapter
northcountrytrail.org/trail/minnesota/ely

Y junction with completed portion of the Mesabi Trail. The NCT follows it to the east

                                 chapter boundary
                                 8.1 miles
                                 D

↔ boundary mixed ownership
47.881454 -91.977911   ///futuristic.similar.windmill
↔ boundary Superior National Forest

Note: dispersed camping is allowed in the Superior NF

                             △ *dispersed camping* allowed
                             0.3 mile in Superior NF
                             out of sight of the trail
                             fs.usda.gov/superior

↔ boundary Superior National Forest
47.8818 -91.971345   ///breakaway.providing.parents
↔ boundary private land
                             D
                             5.5 miles
                             + various
                             $L

✻ city of Ely
0.2 mile off trail
47.903252 -91.866868   ///love.drive.ending
services
Ely is known for providing services specific to outdoor recreation

$ ■ *Motels*
various off trail
47.903252 -91.866868   ///love.drive.ending
commercial lodging at many levels
fee
                             $L
                             + various
                             5.6 miles
                             D

↔ boundary private land
47.907745 -91.832834   ///anymore.incurring.ambition
↔ boundary Superior National Forest

Note: no camping in this area of Superior NF; too close to the ranger station.

Y junction Mesabi Trail. NCT is concurrent with it west of this point.
47.905641 -91.829849   ///driveways.fences.hatter

↔ boundary Superior National Forest
47.907874   -91.825474   ///displayed.compromised.tonic
↔ boundary mixed ownership

✲ city of Winton
0.2 mile off trail
47.92735   -91.80131   ///silks.buzzed.degrees
limited services

↔ boundary mixed ownership
47.927019   -91.774402   ///much.rulers.factory
↔ boundary Superior National Forest

△ *dispersed camping* allowed
0.2 mile in Superior NF
off road on north side
fs.usda.gov/superior

↔ boundary Superior National Forest
47.927985   -91.771541   ///crinkled.streamers.contenders
↔ boundary mixed ownership

D
0.2 mile
$CCg

$▲ ■ *Cliff Wold's Outfitter*
47.928181   -91.766705   ///visits.verses.styled
commercial outfitter
bunkrooms and campsites
tables, fire rings, bathhouse
fee
cliffwolds.com
218-365-3267

$CCg
0.6 mile
chapter boundary

Kawishiwi Falls Parking
47.931819   -91.755505   ///primal.girder.hoops
Ely Northwoods Chapter
northcountrytrail.org/trail/minnesota/ely
↔ **Chapter boundary**

↔ **Chapter boundary**
Kawishiwi Falls Parking
47.931819 -91.755505   ///primal.girder.hoops
Kekakabic Chapter
northcountrytrail.org/trail/minnesota/kek

                          chapter boundary
                          3.8 miles
                          D

                                            $▲ *Fall Lake Campground*
                                                    1.3 miles off trail
                      47.948421 -91.724863   ///usually.circle.mapped
                                                       public campground
                                        tables, fire rings, bathhouse
                                                                           fee
                                                             fs.usda.gov/superior
                                                                    recreation.gov
                                                                    218-365-7600

↔ boundary mixed ownership
47.938302 -91.679888   ///stacked.bypassed.shins
↔ boundary Superior National Forest

                          △ *dispersed camping* allowed
                          5.6 miles in Superior NF
                          fs.usda.gov/superior

↔ boundary Superior National Forest
47.9617 -91.566763   ///sunk.eggplants.screenings
↔ boundary mixed ownership

△ *Tofte Lake Campsites*
0.2 mile off trail
47.962203 -91.570368   ///increased.scorched.cheekbone
public campsite
4 primitive campsites
fire rings, amenities uncertain
fs.usda.gov/recarea/superior/recarea/?recid=37083

                          PCs
                          1.0 mile
                          D

↔ boundary mixed ownership
47.959199 -91.549673   ///useful.clutches.musts
↔ boundary Superior National Forest

                          △ *dispersed camping* allowed
                          0.8 mile in Superior NF
                          off road
                          fs.usda.gov/superior

↔ boundary Superior National Forest
47.961412 -91.534095   ///retraining.trucks.pebble
↔ boundary mixed ownership

D
0.2 miles
D

↔ boundary mixed ownership
47.96078   -91.528945   ///collapsing.unsure.doses
↔ boundary Superior National Forest

△ *dispersed camping* allowed
0.4 mile in Superior NF
off road
fs.usda.gov/superior

↔ boundary Superior National Forest
47.960062   -91.520405   ///winner.twisted.capers
↔ boundary mixed ownership

D
1.0 mile
D

↔ boundary mixed ownership
47.956728   -91.501565   ///period.eating.meadows
↔ boundary Superior National Forest

△ *dispersed camping* allowed
0.5 mile in Superior NF
off road
fs.usda.gov/superior

↔ boundary Superior National Forest
47.955952   -91.490836   ///advertising.custom.selection
↔ boundary mixed ownership

D
0.3 mile
D

↔ boundary mixed ownership
47.954917   -91.485214   ///reuniting.braced.roadway
↔ boundary Superior National Forest

△ *dispersed camping* allowed
2.7 miles in Superior NF
off road
fs.usda.gov/superior

Y junction west end Kekekabic Trail; all 46 miles are concurrent with the NCT
47.967742   -91.465884   ///lifesaving.trusts.every

Note: dispersed camping is allowed on public land all along the Kekekabic Trail, and is so indicated in this list. However, perhaps more than in any other section of NCT, there are few good camping spots other than the designated sites. Use of these established campsites is recommended.

↔ boundary Superior National Forest
47.952956   -91.456794   ///caters.researched.mobile
↔ boundary private land

                D
                0.8 mile
                D

↔ boundary private land
47.949506 -91.442889 ///replica.servants.shameless
↔ boundary Superior National Forest/ MN state land

        △ *dispersed camping* allowed
        1.0 mile in Superior NF
        off road
        fs.usda.gov/superior

↔ boundary Superior National Forest/ MN state land
47.951978 -91.426367 ///chairing.patient.closely
↔ boundary mixed ownership

        D
        1.2 miles
        D

↔ boundary mixed ownership
47.953186 -91.405038 ///dramas.sofa.sprinter
↔ internal boundary Superior NF/ BWCAW

Note: obtain overnight permit well in advance for BWCAW. Day use permits are available free at entry kiosks. See usfs-public.app.box.com/v/BWCAW-TripPlanner to see where you can pick up your overnight permit in Ely or Grand Marais at a Forest Service office or cooperating business. Link to Federal Wilderness regulations

        $p△ *dispersed camping* allowed
        0.3 mile in BWCAW with permit
        fs.usda.gov/superior

$p△ *Becosin Lake Campsites*
0.3 mile off trail
47.950688 -91.394731 ///cabinet.countering.elimination
public campsites
2 primitive sites, fire ring, latrine
permit fee
maintained by the Kekekabic Chapter
kek@northcountrytrail.org

        $p△ *dispersed camping* allowed
        0.3 mile in BWCAW with permit
        fs.usda.gov/superior

$p△ *Parent Lake Campsites*
0.4 mile off trail on Snowbank Trail
47.961437 -91.389152 ///nominal.supersonic.speedily
public campsites
3 primitive sites, fire ring, latrine
permit fee
maintained by the Kekekabic Chapter
kek@northcountrytrail.org

$p△ *dispersed camping* allowed
0.8 mile in BWCAW with permit
fs.usda.gov/superior

$p△ *Benezie Lake Campsites*
0.4 mile off trail
47.955114   -91.374732   ///lightened.herself.royals
public campsites
2 primitive sites, fire ring, latrine
permit fee
maintained by the Kekekabic Chapter
kek@northcountrytrail.org

$p△ *dispersed camping* allowed
2.7 miles in BWCAW with permit
fs.usda.gov/superior

$p△ *Drumstick Lake Campsite*
47.9751   -91.32834   ///pester.dialects.renting
primitive, fire ring, latrine
public campsite
permit fee
maintained by the Kekekabic Chapter
kek@northcountrytrail.org

$p△ *dispersed camping* allowed
2.5 miles in BWCAW with permit
fs.usda.gov/superior

$p△ *Moiyaka Lake Campsite*
47.986705   -91.284223   ///renovation.testy.entertainer
public campsite
primitive, fire ring, latrine
permit fee
maintained by the Kekekabic Chapter
kek@northcountrytrail.org

$p△ *dispersed camping* allowed
0.1 mile in BWCAW with permit
fs.usda.gov/superior

$p△ *Medas Lake Campsite*
0.1 mile off trail
47.985298   -91.283279   ///commenced.rosette.cushioned
public campsite
primitive, fire ring, latrine
permit fee
maintained by the Kekekabic Chapter
kek@northcountrytrail.org

$p△ *dispersed camping* allowed
2.1 miles in BWCAW with permit
fs.usda.gov/superior

$p△ *Thomas Lake Campsite*
48.005047 -91.252515   ///calculates.picked.albatross
public campsite
primitive, fire ring, latrine
permit fee
maintained by the Kekekabic Chapter
kek@northcountrytrail.org

$p△ *dispersed camping* allowed
5.0 miles in BWCAW with permit
fs.usda.gov/superior

$p△ *Strup Lake Campsite*
48.046556 -91.183447   ///responders.waltz.ruffling
public campsite
primitive, fire ring, latrine
permit fee
maintained by the Kekekabic Chapter
kek@northcountrytrail.org

$p△ *dispersed camping* allowed
4.2 miles in BWCAW with permit
fs.usda.gov/superior

$p△ *Harness Lake Campsite*
48.062735 -91.112636   ///sour.connects.triangular
public campsite
primitive, fire ring, latrine
permit fee
maintained by the Kekekabic Chapter
kek@northcountrytrail.org

$p△ *dispersed camping* allowed
4.0 miles in BWCAW with permit
fs.usda.gov/superior

$p△ *Agamok Bridge Campsite*
48.078158 -91.05019   ///sincere.conqueror.broker
public campsite
primitive, fire ring, latrine
permit fee
maintained by the Kekekabic Chapter
kek@northcountrytrail.org

$p△ *dispersed camping* allowed
2.4 miles in BWCAW with permit
fs.usda.gov/superior

$p△ *Gabimichigami Lake Campsite*
48.082201 -91.007318   ///punctuate.hurricane.wordy
public campsite
primitive, fire ring, latrine
permit fee
maintained by the Kekekabic Chapter
kek@northcountrytrail.org

$p△ *dispersed camping* allowed
1.0 mile in BWCAW with permit
fs.usda.gov/superior

$p△ *Howard Lake Campsite*
48.081857 -90.980839   ///clapped.thyroid.scavengers
public campsite
primitive, fire ring, latrine
permit fee
maintained by the Kekekabic Chapter
kek@northcountrytrail.org

$p△ *dispersed camping* allowed
5.6 miles in BWCAW with permit
fs.usda.gov/superior

$p△ *Bingshick Lake Campsite*
48.085297 -90.894622   ///obligated.imagination.pythons
public campsite
primitive, fire ring, latrine
permit fee
maintained by the Kekekabic Chapter
kek@northcountrytrail.org

$p△ *dispersed camping* allowed
0.6 miles in BWCAW with permit
fs.usda.gov/superior

↔ internal boundary BWCAW MN 491.3
48.084795 -90.879244   ///burger.emotional.sunflowers
↔ boundary Superior NF

△ *dispersed camping* allowed
2.7 miles in Superior NF
fs.usda.gov/superior
chapter boundary

Y junction east end of Kekekabic Trail; all 46 miles are concurrent with the NCT
48.089354 -90.824098   ///thigh.fateful.laws

Gunflint Trail
48.089354 -90.824098   ///thigh.fateful.laws
Kekakabic Chapter
northcountrytrail.org/trail/minnesota/kek
↔ **Chapter/Affiliate boundary**

D
0.2 mile
D

↔ **Chapter/Affiliate boundary**
Border Route Trail
48.09175 -90.825368   ///fluttering.award.landing
Border Route Trail Association
borderroutetrail.org

Y junction west end Border Route Trail; all 65 miles are concurrent with the NCT
48.09175 -90.825368   ///fluttering.award.landing

　　　　　　　　　affiliate boundary
　　　　　　　　　△ *dispersed camping* allowed
　　　　　　　　　6.5 miles in Superior NF
　　　　　　　　　watch for boundaries near trail
　　　　　　　　　fs.usda.gov/superior

Notes on camping along the BRT: Canoeists are required to stay at designated campsites and have priority at these. Dispersed camping is allowed for backpackers following standard guidelines, but staying at the designated sites is recommended.
borderroutetrail.org/backpacking

$ ■ *Gunflint Lodge*
0.7 mile off trail
48.085068 -90.749697   ///feasting.shuffle.crinkle
commercial outfitter
lodge, cabins, bunkhouse, bathhouse
fee
gunflint.com
800-328-3325

　　　　　　　　　△ *dispersed camping* allowed
　　　　　　　　　1.4 miles in Superior NF
　　　　　　　　　fs.usda.gov/superior

△ *Loon Lake Campsite*
0.7 mile off trail
48.074796 -90.729363   ///jokes.hollow.weedy
public campsite
primitive, latrine
managed by Superior NF
www.fs.usda.gov
218-626-4300

　　　　　　　　　△ *dispersed camping* allowed
　　　　　　　　　2.9 miles in Superior NF
　　　　　　　　　fs.usda.gov/superior

$ ■ *Heston's Lodge*
0.6 mile off trail
48.091017 -90.70328   ///stylist.blares.fractional
commercial lodging
cabins, no camping, but they will hold supplies for hikers
fee
hestons.com
218-388-2243

　　　　　　　　　△ *dispersed camping* allowed
　　　　　　　　　4.4 miles in Superior NF
　　　　　　　　　fs.usda.gov/superior

↔ internal boundary Superior NF
48.090393   -90.620573   ///revived.jockey.both
↔ boundary BWCAW

*Note: obtain permit well in advance for BWCAW (required for overnight or day use)
see usfs-public.app.box.com/v/BWCAW-TripPlanner
and select where you will pick up your permit in Ely or Grand Marais at a Forest
Service office or cooperating business. See Appendix for link to Federal Wilderness
regulations*

$p△ *dispersed camping* allowed
2.6 miles in BWCAW with permit
fs.usda.gov/superior

$p△ *Topper Lake Campsite*

48.087463   -90.568354   ///denser.molten.shutting
public campsite
primitive, fire ring, latrine
permit fee
maintained by BRTA
borderroutetrail.org

$p△ *dispersed camping* allowed
1.4 miles in BWCAW with permit
fs.usda.gov/superior

$p△ *Sock Lake Campsite*

0.3 mile off trail
48.08299   -90.540374   ///vortex.decoded.volunteered
public campsite
primitive, fire ring, latrine
permit fee
maintained by BRTA
borderroutetrail.org

$p△ *dispersed camping* allowed
2.2 miles in BWCAW with permit
fs.usda.gov/superior

$p△ *South Lake Campsite*

0.3 mile off trail
48.096635   -90.507415   ///robe.paddle.unlike
public campsite
primitive, fire ring, latrine
permit fee
maintained by BRTA
borderroutetrail.org

$p△ *dispersed camping* allowed
1.2 miles in BWCAW with permit
fs.usda.gov/superior

$p△ *Partridge Lake East Campsite*
0.3 mile off trail
48.090215 -90.479091   ///decamp.brushing.prospects
public campsite
primitive, fire ring, latrine
permit fee
maintained by BRTA
borderroutetrail.org

$p△ *dispersed camping* allowed
4.4 miles in BWCAW with permit
fs.usda.gov/superior

$p△ *Rose Lake West Campsite*
48.09675 -90.417121   ///theatrical.laptop.doors
public campsite
primitive, fire ring, latrine
permit fee
maintained by BRTA
borderroutetrail.org

$p△ *dispersed camping* allowed
0.6 miles in BWCAW with permit
fs.usda.gov/superior

$p△ *Rose Lake East Campsite*
48.102024 -90.406478   ///homecare.administer.criminally
public campsite
primitive, fire ring, latrine
permit fee
maintained by BRTA
borderroutetrail.org

$p△ *dispersed camping* allowed
1.9 miles in BWCAW with permit
fs.usda.gov/superior

$p△ *Daniels Lake North Campsite*
0.6 mile off trail
48.082646 -90.384333   ///ritual.migrations.groom
public campsite
primitive, fire ring, latrine
permit fee
maintained by BRTA
borderroutetrail.org

$p△ *dispersed camping* allowed
2.1 miles in BWCAW with permit
fs.usda.gov/superior

$p△ *Clearwater Lake West Campsite*
0.3 mile off trail
48.085743 -90.345538   ///lifelong.bloodshot.clearances
public campsite
primitive, fire ring, latrine
permit fee
maintained by BRTA
borderroutetrail.org

$p△ *dispersed camping* allowed
5.9 miles in BWCAW with permit
fs.usda.gov/superior

$p△ *Clearwater Lake East Campsite*
48.085513 -90.263655   ///vacates.chairs.tone
public campsite
primitive, fire ring, latrine
permit fee
maintained by BRTA
borderroutetrail.org

$p△ *dispersed camping* allowed
1.6 miles in BWCAW with permit
fs.usda.gov/superior

$p△ *Gogebic Lake Campsite*
48.079435 -90.248549   ///haircuts.laundry.goats
public campsite
primitive, fire ring, latrine
permit fee
maintained by BRTA
borderroutetrail.org

$p△ *dispersed camping* allowed
5.7 miles in BWCAW with permit
fs.usda.govuperior

$p△ *Pine Lake Campsite*
0.5 mile off trail
48.067162 -90.169928   ///fingernails.refused.deflection
public campsite
primitive, fire ring, latrine
permit fee
maintained by BRTA
borderroutetrail.org

$p△ *dispersed camping* allowed
3.5 miles in BWCAW with permit
fs.usda.gov/superior

$p△ *Pine Ridge Campsite*
48.070489 -90.108302   ///sentimental.fitness.assemble
public campsite
primitive, fire ring, latrine
permit fee
maintained by BRTA
borderroutetrail.org

$p△ *dispersed camping* allowed
3.2 miles in BWCAW with permit
fs.usda.gov/superior

↔ boundary BWCAW
48.062344 -90.056289   ///odds.inactivity.pelt
↔ internal boundary Superior NF

△ *dispersed camping* allowed
0.3 mile in Superior NF
fs.usda.gov/superior

↔ boundary Superior NF
48.059388 -90.057158   ///sulky.unrest.overstated
↔ boundary Grand Portage State Forest

Note: dispersed camping is allowed in Grand Portage SF

△ *dispersed camping* allowed
0.5 mile in Grand Portage SF

△ *McFarland Lake SF Campground*
48.053739 -90.057147   ///rental.seafood.brains
public campground
primitive, tables, fire rings, latrine
managed by Judge Magney State Park
dnr.state.mn.us
218-387-6300

↔ boundary Grand Portage State Forest
48.05562 -90.051566   ///kazoo.perceptions.storyline
↔ boundary mixed ownership

△ *dispersed camping* allowed
7.5 mile in Superior NF/ Grand Portage SF

△ *Portage Brook Campsite*
48.004835 -89.985907   ///strictly.mocked.originated
public land
primitive, fire ring
maintained by BRTA
borderroutetrail.org

△ *dispersed camping* allowed
0.5 mile in Superior NF/ Grand Portage SF

△ *Otter Lake Campsite*
0.9 mile off trail
47.990706   -89.997752   ///supply.soliciting.ghostly
public land
primitive, fire ring, latrine
maintained by BRTA
borderroutetrail.org

△ *dispersed camping* allowed
4.2 miles in Superior NF/ Grand Portage SF

△ former *Swamp River Campground*
47.987105   -89.935452   ///query.indirectly.kiosk
public land
amenities uncertain

△ *dispersed camping* allowed
0.2 mile in Superior NF/ Grand Portage SF
affiliate boundary

Y junction east end BRT; all 65 miles are concurrent with the NCT
47.986461   -89.933521   ///fevered.bypassed.horizon

Otter Lake Rd Parking   MN 558.9
47.986461   -89.933521   ///fevered.bypassed.horizon
Border Route Trail Association
borderroutetrail.org
↔ **Affiliate boundary**

↔ **Affiliate boundary**
Otter Lake Rd Parking
47.986461 -89.933521   ///fevered.bypassed.horizon
Superior Hiking Trail Association
superiorhiking.org

Notes: The 300 miles of the Superior Hiking Trail are probably the most heavily used of any section of the NCT. As a result, there are a number of specific regulations, but there are also abundant campsites, except through the city of Duluth. Because the trail crosses a mix of public and private lands, and you must camp only at designated sites, the landowner boundaries are not indicated for this section.

Dispersed camping along the SHT is not allowed. You must camp at designated sites. No reservations needed at SHT-maintained sites. Leave group sites open if possible unless you are a group. You must share any campsite with other hikers who wish to use the location. info@superiorhiking.org 218-834-2700

Reservations may be needed for State Park Campgrounds. The state parks along the SHT are required to find space for a backpacker in an emergency situation. Hikers must still pay the fee, but can find safe haven in the event that weather, injury, etc. prevents further travel for the day.

affiliate boundary
1.7 miles
PCs

△ *Andy Creek Campsite*

47.968298 -89.918616   ///mindset.shock.autofocus
public land
primitive, benches, fire ring, latrine
maintained by volunteers of the SHTA

PCs
5.1 miles
PCs

△ *Jackson Creek Campsite*

47.923915 -89.91338   ///refined.quote.processes
public land
primitive, benches, fire ring, latrine
maintained by volunteers of the SHTA

PCs
3.3 miles
PCs

△ *Woodland Caribou Pond Campsite*

47.900385 -89.91484   ///wedges.introduce.delved
public land
primitive, benches, fire ring, latrine
maintained by volunteers of the SHTA

PCs
3.7 miles
PCs

△ North Carlson Pond Campsite
47.89454 -89.952554 ///sneezing.temptation.pipeline
public land
primitive, benches, fire ring, latrine
maintained by volunteers of the SHTA

        PCs
        2.1 miles
        PCs

△ South Carlson Pond Campsite
47.891738 -89.983791 ///balcony.florists.smaller
public land
primitive, benches, fire ring, latrine
maintained by volunteers of the SHTA

        PCs
        2.8 miles
        PCs

△ Hazel Campsite
47.895501 -90.027661 ///elect.volley.boils
public land
primitive, benches, fire ring, latrine
maintained by volunteers of the SHTA
Note: Hazel is often very busy- avoid if possible

        PCs
        8.3 miles
        +0.15 spur
        $PCg

$▲ Judge Magney State Park
0.15 mile off trail
47.818243 -90.052807 ///evolution.charity.parkway
public campground
27 vehicular sites
tables, fire rings, bathhouse
fee
dnr.state.mn.us
651-296-6157

        $PCg
        +0.15 spur
        3.4 miles
        PCs

△ Northwest and North Little Brule River Campsites
47.821106 -90.090617 ///amazing.commodities.rejoins
public land
primitive, benches, fire ring, latrine
maintained by volunteers of the SHTA

PCs
0.4 miles
PCs

△ *South Little Brule River Campsite*

47.816372 -90.087913   ///rules.educations.removers
public land
primitive, benches, fire ring, latrine
maintained by volunteers of the SHTA

PCs
2.5 miles
PCs

△ *Mule Kicker Beach Water Trail Campsite*

47.796412 -90.11421   ///uplifting.refrained.decorative
public land
primitive, no amenities
Note: this campsite is part of the Lake Superior State Water Trail. Paddlers have priority
mndnr.gov

PCs
0.5 mile
PCs

△ *Lake Walk South Water Trail Campsite*

47.795668 -90.12361   ///volunteered.answers.simulating
public land
primitive, no amenities
Note: this campsite is part of the Lake Superior State Water Trail. Paddlers have priority
mndnr.gov

PCs
2.3 mile
PCs

△ *Kadunce River Campsite*

47.804356 -90.15585   ///handyman.positioning.admires
public land
primitive, benches, fire ring, latrine
maintained by volunteers of the SHTA

PCs
0.4 mile
PCs

△ *West Fork Kadunce River Campsite*

47.800371 -90.160743   ///environment.heap.process
public land
primitive, benches, fire ring, latrine
maintained by volunteers of the SHTA

PCs
0.3 mile
PCs

△ *Crow Creek Campsite*

47.799708 -90.164337   ///incomplete.engravings.windows
public land
primitive, benches, fire ring, latrine
maintained by volunteers of the SHTA

PCs
1.2 miles
PCs

△ *Kimball Creek Campsite*

47.793438 -90.183692   ///writings.cringes.magnifying
public land
primitive, benches, fire ring, latrine
maintained by volunteers of the SHTA

PCs
2.5 miles
PCs

△ *Cliff Creek Campsite*

47.79787 -90.221403   ///pathfinder.middle.wriggle
public land
primitive, benches, fire ring, latrine
maintained by volunteers of the SHTA

PCs
1.1 miles
PCs

△ *Durfee Creek Campsite*

47.793901 -90.239629   ///roundabout.grabs.just
public land
primitive, benches, fire ring, latrine
maintained by volunteers of the SHTA

PCs
2.4 miles
PCs

△ *Wood's Creek Campsite*

47.783305 -90.266097   ///tree.kettle.immediate
public land
primitive, benches, fire ring, latrine
maintained by volunteers of the SHTA

PCs
2.5 miles
PCs

△ *East Devil Track Campsite*
47.780947   -90.297339   ///cheese.heater.deprive
public land
primitive, benches, fire ring, latrine
maintained by volunteers of the SHTA

    PCs
    0.1 mile
    PCs

△ *West Devil Track Campsite*
47.781401   -90.294893   ///survived.durations.citizenship
public land
primitive, benches, fire ring, latrine
maintained by volunteers of the SHTA

    PCs
    10.6 miles
    PCs

$ □ △ *Hungry Hippie Hostel*
1.3 miles off trail
47.812275   -90.179068   ///concept.complains.seesaw
commercial hostel
bunks, rooms, tent sites
fee
hungryhippie.com
218-387-2256

✻ city of Grand Marais
1.5 miles off trail
47.749281 -90.336054
///acid.pledge.reader
✻ city of Grand Marais
services
$ ■ *Commercial Lodging*
many commercial options
fee

△ *North Bally Creek Pond Campsite*
47.769094   -90.431515   ///squint.tolerable.deciding
public land
primitive, benches, fire ring, latrine
maintained by volunteers of the SHTA

    PCs
    0.2 mile
    +0.1 spur
    PCs

△ *South Bally Creek Pond Campsite*
0.1 mile off trail
47.76794 -90.433188   ///sapped.disorderly.tabloid
public land
primitive, benches, fire ring, latrine
maintained by volunteers of the SHTA

                        PCs
                        +0.1 spur
                        1.3 mile
                        +0.5 spur
                        PCs

△ *Sundling Creek Campsite*
0.5 mile off trail
47.771754 -90.452801   ///believe.firmly.surface
public land
primitive, benches, fire ring, latrine
maintained by volunteers of the SHTA

                        PCs
                        +0.5 spur
                        3.7 mile
                        PCs

△ *North Cascade River Campsite*
47.754532 -90.518912   ///moments.flashed.awestruck
public land
primitive, benches, fire ring, latrine
maintained by volunteers of the SHTA

                        PCs
                        +0.5 spur
                        2.4 mile
                        PCs

△ *Cut Log Campsite*
47.73125 -90.538857   ///outpost.mutant.shopkeeper
public land
primitive, benches, fire ring, latrine
maintained by volunteers of the SHTA

                        PCs
                        1.5 miles
                        PCs

△ *Big White Pine Campsite*
47.725848 -90.538012   ///milked.jugs.coefficient
public land
primitive, benches, fire ring, latrine
maintained by volunteers of the SHTA

                        PCs
                        1.3 miles
                        +0.6 spur
                        $PCg

$▲ Cascade River SP Campground
0.6 mile off trail
47.709413 -90.51961   ///rides.hindering.fairer
public campground
40 vehicular sites
electric, non-electric
tables, fire rings, bathhouse
fee
reservation required
managed by Cascade River SP
dnr.state.mn.us
651-296-6157

$PCg
+0.6 spur
0.9 mile
$PCs

$∠ Lookout Mountain Campsite
47.713503 -90.54068   ///sitting.traditional.sample
public land
open shelter, table, fire ring, latrine
fee
reservation required
managed by Cascade River SP
dnr.state.mn.us
651-296-6157

$PCs
0.8 mile
PCs

△ Camp Creek Campsite
47.707457 -90.558265   ///strut.declaring.revealing
public land
primitive, benches, fire ring, latrine
maintained by volunteers of the SHTA

PCs
3.2 miles
PCs

△ Spruce Creek Campsite
47.695009 -90.607966   ///futile.inventors.intervened
public land
primitive, benches, fire ring, latrine
maintained by volunteers of the SHTA

PCs
2.2 miles
PCs

△ Jonvik Creek Campsite
47.689029 -90.644901   ///superficial.crunching.composers
public land
primitive, benches, fire ring, latrine
maintained by volunteers of the SHTA

PCs
2.3 miles
PCs

△ *East Lake Agnes Campsite*
47.700323   -90.679615   ///lorry.mildly.rulers
public land
primitive, benches, fire ring, latrine
maintained by volunteers of the SHTA
Note: East Lake Agnes is often very busy- avoid if possible

PCs
0.4 mile
PCs

△ *West Lake Agnes Campsite*
47.699565   -90.686755   ///recipes.massage.stems
public land
primitive, benches, fire ring, latrine
maintained by volunteers of the SHTA

PCs
2.9 miles
PCs

△ *East Poplar River Campsite*
47.682189   -90.701056   ///devours.applicable.hypocrite
public land
primitive, benches, fire ring, latrine
maintained by volunteers of the SHTA

PCs
0.4 mile
PCs

△ *West Poplar River Campsite*
47.67878   -90.705412   ///myth.winced.super
public land
primitive, benches, fire ring, latrine
maintained by volunteers of the SHTA

PCs
2.1 miles
PCs

△ *Mystery Mountain Campsite*
47.669402   -90.728222   ///division.reassuring.probable
public land
primitive, benches, fire ring, latrine
maintained by volunteers of the SHTA

PCs
4.4 miles
PCs

△ *East & West Rollins Creek Campsites*
47.63182 -90.760805   ///idea.solicitor.illustrates
public land
primitive, benches, fire ring, latrine
maintained by volunteers of the SHTA

                PCs
                2.0 miles
                PCs

△ *Onion River Campsite*
47.625305 -90.78944   ///disclaimer.misled.necklace
public land
primitive, benches, fire ring, latrine
maintained by volunteers of the SHTA

                PCs
                1.1 miles
                PCs

△ *East Leveaux Pond Campsite*
47.61764 -90.805061   ///revive.tangling.brings
public land
primitive, benches, fire ring, latrine
maintained by volunteers of the SHTA

                PCs
                0.1 mile
                PCs

△ *West Leveaux Pond Campsite*
47.617242 -90.805823   ///vortex.thinker.tasty
public land
primitive, benches, fire ring, latrine
maintained by volunteers of the SHTA

                PCs
                2.2 miles
                PCs

△ *Springdale Creek Campsite*
47.6033 -90.834568   ///shrewd.reporting.butter
public land
primitive, benches, fire ring, latrine
maintained by volunteers of the SHTA

                PCs
                5.9 miles
                +0.2 spur
                $PCg

$▲ Temperance River SP Campground
0.2 mile off trail
47.554875   -90.871223   ///underwrite.thrashed.oppose
public campground
52 vehicular sites
18 electric, 34 non-electric
tables, fire rings, bathhouse
managed by Temperance River SP
dnr.state,mn.us
651-296-6157

$PCg
+0.2 spur
3.0 miles
PCs

△ South Cross River Campsite
47.557721   -90.916123   ///drooling.brought.ditches
public land
primitive, benches, fire ring, latrine
maintained by volunteers of the SHTA

PCs
0.1 mile
PCs

△ North Cross River Campsite
47.558988   -90.916671   ///kinds.spectacle.unattached
public land
primitive, benches, fire ring, latrine
maintained by volunteers of the SHTA

PCs
0.6 mile
PCs

△ Ledge Campsite
47.565923   -90.913495   ///minimalist.aimless.devoured
public land
primitive, benches, fire ring, latrine
maintained by volunteers of the SHTA

PCs
0.8 mile
PCs

△ Falls Campsite
47.565141   -90.927314   ///nursery.clipboard.orchestras
public land
primitive, benches, fire ring, latrine
maintained by volunteers of the SHTA

PCs
1.8 mile
PCs

△ Fredenberg Creek Campsite
47.551327 -90.948621   ///forgive.walked.innocently
public land
primitive, benches, fire ring, latrine
maintained by volunteers of the SHTA

> PCs
> **2.9 miles**
> PCs

△ Dyer's Creek Campsite
47.53254 -90.970422   ///ferried.unassuming.take
public land
primitive, benches, fire ring, latrine
maintained by volunteers of the SHTA

> PCs
> **3.4 miles**
> PCs

△ Sugarloaf Pond Campsite
47.506811 -90.988264   ///football.bead.description
public land
primitive, benches, fire ring, latrine
maintained by volunteers of the SHTA

> PCs
> **2.6 miles**
> +0.1 spur
> PCs

△ Crystal Creek Campsite
0.1 mile off trail
47.483128 -91.013681   ///crosses.headrest.imperious
public land
primitive, benches, fire ring, latrine
maintained by volunteers of the SHTA

> PCs
> **1.4 miles**
> PCs

△ East Caribou River Campsite
47.471091 -91.032328   ///professes.rarely.trademark
public land
primitive, benches, fire ring, latrine
maintained by volunteers of the SHTA

> PCs
> **0.1 mile**
> PCs

△ West Caribou River Campsite
47.470293 -91.035321   ///bombard.cocktail.closest
public land
primitive, benches, fire ring, latrine
maintained by volunteers of the SHTA

        PCs
        2.8 miles
        PCs

△ Horseshoe Ridge Campsite
47.483513 -91.077882   ///millionaire.buck.dressings
public land
primitive, benches, fire ring, latrine
maintained by volunteers of the SHTA

        PCs
        2.5 miles
        $PCs

$△ Crosby Manitou Backpacker Site #5
47.478928 -91.097561   ///royals.required.epidemics
public campsite
primitive, table, fire ring, latrine
fee
reservation required
managed by Crosby Manitou SP
dnr.state,mn.us
651-296-6157

        $PCs
        0.5 mile
        $PCs

$△ Crosby Manitou Backpacker Site #4
47.483359 -91.102206   ///smudges.slugs.intrusions
public campsite
primitive, table, fire ring, latrine
fee
reservation required
managed by Crosby Manitou SP
dnr.state,mn.us
651-296-6157

        $PCs
        0.1 mile
        $PCs

$△ Crosby Manitou Backpacker Site #3
47.484468 -91.104148   ///betrayed.archduke.sleeveless
public campsite
primitive, table, fire ring, latrine
fee
reservation required
managed by Crosby Manitou SP
dnr.state,mn.us
651-296-6157

$PCs
1.0 mile
+0.2 spur
$PCs

$△ *Crosby Manitou Backpacker Sites #20,21,22*
0.2 mile off trail
47.47573   -91.111433   ///moderation.stars.imported
public campsite
primitive, table, fire ring, latrine
fee
reservation required
managed by Crosby Manitou SP
dnr.state,mn.us
651-296-6157

$PCs
+0.2 spur
0.9 mile
PCs

△ *Aspen Knob Campsite*
47.479102   -91.128696   ///noses.follows.roof
public land
primitive, benches, fire ring, latrine
maintained by volunteers of the SHTA

PCs
2.0 miles
PCs

△ *Blesner Creek Campsite*
47.473432   -91.160298   ///ignores.ideal.organic
public land
primitive, benches, fire ring, latrine
maintained by volunteers of the SHTA

PCs
0.6 mile
PCs

△ *East Branch Baptism River Campsite*
47.47821   -91.169423   ///refuse.relaxation.kennel
public land
primitive, benches, fire ring, latrine
maintained by volunteers of the SHTA

PCs
1.8 miles
PCs

△ *North Sonju Lake Campsite*
47.482489   -91.201958   ///unveil.joining.glades
public land
primitive, benches, fire ring, latrine
maintained by volunteers of the SHTA

PCs
0.3 mile
PCs

△ *South Sonju Lake Campsite*

47.481785 -91.205616   ///nutcracker.register.certainly
public land
primitive, benches, fire ring, latrine
maintained by volunteers of the SHTA

PCs
3.0 miles
PCs

△ *North Egge Lake Campsite*

47.457431 -91.215819   ///hurtles.unsettled.volleyball
public land
primitive, benches, fire ring, latrine
maintained by volunteers of the SHTA

PCs
0.2 mile
PCs

△ *South Egge Lake Campsite*

47.455277 -91.21554   ///zapped.view.farmers
public land
primitive, benches, fire ring, latrine
maintained by volunteers of the SHTA

PCs
4.6 miles
PCs

△ *Leskinen Creek Campsite*

47.424222 -91.192495   ///worthy.indulgence.routines
public land
primitive, benches, fire ring, latrine
maintained by volunteers of the SHTA

PCs
3.7 miles
PCs

△ *Section 13 Campsite*

47.424121 -91.152423   ///staging.warps.surnames
public land
primitive, benches, fire ring, latrine
maintained by volunteers of the SHTA

PCs
6.1 miles
HCs

△ East & West Kennedy Creek Campsites
47.376514 -91.183939   ///fatherhood.intrigues.irony
hosted sites
primitive, benches, fire ring, latrine
maintained by volunteers of the SHTA

        HCs
        3.3 miles
        junction SHT/spur

Y junction with SHT spur trail that leads to MN 61.
47.349404   -91.205198
///exploration.tenure.occur
Note: the swinging bridge above the High Falls on the Baptism River is out, so at the present time, you must walk down to the road to cross the river.

- - - - - - - - - - -

If you must walk down to MN 61, the Tettegouche Campground is near the trail. When the bridge is replaced, this campground will be 1.3 miles off trail.

        when the bridge is replaced
        there is **0.6 mile**
        between the spur junctions

        junction SHT/spur
        1.0 mile
        +0.3 spur
        $PCg

$▲ Lake Superior Cart-In Campground
0.3 mile off trail
47.334448 -91.201142   ///risking.squares.divergence
public campground
13 walk-in sites
tables, fire rings, latrine, bear lockers
managed by Tettegouche SP
dnr.state,mn.us
651-296-6157

        $PCg
        +0.3 spur
        1.6 miles
        junction SHT/spur

- - - - - - - - - - -

Y junction with SHT spur trail that leads to MN 61.
47.348276 -91.216334   ///treaties.goodbye.paella
Note: the swinging bridge above the High Falls on the Baptism River is out, so at the present time, you must walk down to the road to cross the river.

        junction SHT/spur
        4.1 miles
        PCs

△ *East Palisade Creek Campsite*
47.325502 -91.266852   ///intent.booked.speedily
public land
primitive, benches, fire ring, latrine
maintained by volunteers of the SHTA

        PCs
        0.1 mile
        +0.15 spur
        PCs

△ *West Palisade Creek Campsite*
0.15 mile off trail
47.32316 -91.270961   ///jiffy.citizen.sheep
public land
primitive, benches, fire ring, latrine
maintained by volunteers of the SHTA

        PCs
        +0.15 spur
        0.5 mile
        PCs

△ *Round Mountain Beaver Pond Campsite*
47.31916 -91.272205   ///school.slushy.bands
public land
primitive, benches, fire ring, latrine
maintained by volunteers of the SHTA

        PCs
        1.2 miles
        +0.1 spur
        PCs

△ *Bear Lake Campsite*
0.1 mile off trail
47.313683 -91.28862   ///justify.demoted.smallest
public land
primitive, benches, fire ring, latrine
maintained by volunteers of the SHTA
Note: Bear Lake is often very busy- avoid if possible

        PCs
        +0.1 spur
        1.2 miles
        PCs

△ *Penn Creek Campsite*
47.302625 -91.296098   ///conductor.detonated.toothpaste
public land
primitive, benches, fire ring, latrine
maintained by volunteers of the SHTA

PCs
5.3 miles
HCs

✲ city of Silver Bay
1.5 miles off trail via Red Dot Trail or CR 5
47.29478 -91.271388 ///narrating.bathtubs.deductions
services

$ ■ *Mariner Motel*
1.6 miles off trail
47.295274 -91.258917 ///cups.enormous.ploys
commercial lodging
218-226-4488

△ ***East Beaver River Campsite***
47.267553 -91.300744 ///repairs.yarn.stilted
hosted site
primitive, benches, fire ring, latrine
maintained by volunteers of the SHTA

HCs
0.3 mile
HCs

△ ***West Beaver River Campsite***
47.267538 -91.305872 ///mosaic.complains.steep
hosted site
primitive, benches, fire ring, latrine
maintained by volunteers of the SHTA

HCs
4.4 miles
PCs

✲ city of Beaver Bay
1.0 mile off trail
47.258208 -91.301416 ///flexibly.envisioned.produce
limited services

△ ***Fault Line Creek Campsite***
47.244779 -91.347872 ///artists.spite.ending
public land
primitive, benches, fire ring, latrine
maintained by volunteers of the SHTA

PCs
1.4 miles
PCs

△ ***Beaver Pond Campsite***
47.236126 -91.366497 ///touchy.blotches.carries
public land
primitive, benches, fire ring, latrine
maintained by volunteers of the SHTA

PCs
1.7 miles
PCs

△ Chapins Ridge Campsite
47.222217   -91.380767   ///configure.cult.undertaken
public land
primitive, benches, fire ring, latrine
maintained by volunteers of the SHTA

PCs
4.6 miles
PCs

△ Southeast Split Rock Campsite
47.199363   -91.42096   ///senator.justifying.cage
public land
primitive, benches, fire ring, latrine
maintained by volunteers of the SHTA

PCs
0.2 mile
PCs

△ Northeast Split Rock Campsite
47.20114   -91.422926   ///stunner.employ.noticeable
public land
primitive, benches, fire ring, latrine
maintained by volunteers of the SHTA

PCs
0.3 mile
PCs

△ Northwest Split Rock Campsite
47.201552   -91.428862   ///waggled.oath.wishful
public land
primitive, benches, fire ring, latrine
maintained by volunteers of the SHTA

PCs
0.3 mile
PCs

△ Southwest Split Rock Campsite
47.198822   -91.421054   ///dotted.hike.recoil
public land
primitive, benches, fire ring, latrine
maintained by volunteers of the SHTA

PCs
3.9 miles
PCs

△ Blueberry Hill Campsite
47.173756 -91.443947   ///tonsils.turtles.wages
public land
primitive, benches, fire ring, latrine
maintained by volunteers of the SHTA

                          PCs
                          3.6 miles
                          +1.0 spur
                          $PCg

$▲ Gooseberry State Park Campground
1.0 mile off trail
47.140348 -91.45993   ///rigorously.discusses.speeds
public campground
69 vehicular sites
tables, fire rings, seasonal bathhouse
fee
managed by Gooseberry SP
dnr.state.mn.us
651-296-6157 $PCg
                          +1.0 spur
                          2.6 miles
                          PCs

△ Gooseberry River Campsite
47.15136 -91.498297   ///digress.angular.breakdowns
public land
primitive, benches, fire ring, latrine
maintained by volunteers of the SHTA

                          PCs
                          0.8 mile
                          PCs

△ Middle Gooseberry Campsite
47.151695 -91.509176   ///signs.upshot.third
public land
primitive, benches, fire ring, latrine
maintained by volunteers of the SHTA

                          PCs
                          0.1 mile
                          PCs

△ East Gooseberry Campsite
47.150772 -91.510667   ///cookers.saved.tulips
public land
primitive, benches, fire ring, latrine
maintained by volunteers of the SHTA

                          PCs
                          0.9 mile
                          PCs

△ **West Gooseberry Campsite**
47.148817 -91.518725   ///consented.graphic.hotline
public land
primitive, benches, fire ring, latrine
maintained by volunteers of the SHTA

>PCs
>**3.2 miles**
>PCs

△ **Crow Valley Campsite**
47.1252 -91.558013   ///mosaic.hacker.scout
public land
primitive, benches, fire ring, latrine
maintained by volunteers of the SHTA

>PCs
>**8.4 miles**
>PCs

△ **Silver Creek Campsite**
47.076057 -91.64387   ///jetted.opening.invest
public land
primitive, benches, fire ring, latrine
maintained by volunteers of the SHTA

>PCs
>**5.7 miles**
>PCs

△ **Reeves Falls Campsite**
47.112609 -91.691489   ///futile.minute.launcher
public land
primitive, benches, fire ring, latrine, dry
maintained by volunteers of the SHTA

>PCs
>**4.0 miles**
>PCs

△ **Stewart River Campsite**
47.140634 -91.709852   ///fusion.ruffle.jaguars
public land
primitive, benches, fire ring, latrine
maintained by volunteers of the SHTA

>PCs
>**5.5 miles**
>PCs

△ **Ferguson Campsite**
47.113943 -91.765041   ///unites.protagonist.thorns
public land
primitive, benches, fire ring, latrine
maintained by volunteers of the SHTA

PCs
1.1 miles
PCs

△ McCarthy Creek Campsite
47.111406   -91.78424   ///scares.expectancy.cones
public land
primitive, benches, fire ring, latrine
maintained by volunteers of the SHTA

PCs
6.1 miles
PCs

△ Big Bend Campsite
47.073452   -91.847648   ///doodle.overpower.vertical
public land
primitive, benches, fire ring, latrine
maintained by volunteers of the SHTA

PCs
7.3 miles
PCs

△ Fox Farm Pond Campsite
47.033058   -91.913453   ///congregate.weeps.worries
public land
primitive, benches, fire ring, latrine
maintained by volunteers of the SHTA

PCs
2.7 miles
PCs

△ Sucker River Campsite
47.014277   -91.93755   ///cushioned.catchy.rapidly
public land
primitive, benches, fire ring, latrine
maintained by volunteers of the SHTA

PCs
4.0 miles
PCs

△ Heron Pond Campsite
46.989231   -91.972258   ///creeps.weeds.rangers
public land
primitive, benches, fire ring, latrine
maintained by volunteers of the SHTA

PCs
3.8 miles
PCs

△ Lone Tree Campsite
46.963683 -92.013692 ///mallets.stints.afflicted
public land
primitive, benches, fire ring, latrine
maintained by volunteers of the SHTA

      PCs
      5.5 miles
      PCs

△ White Pine Campsite
46.930878 -92.066929 ///curling.storing.gaps
public land
primitive, benches, fire ring, latrine
maintained by volunteers of the SHTA

      PCs
      1.2 miles
      PCs

△ Bald Eagle Campsite
46.917007 -92.071145 ///butlers.vented.premium
public land
primitive, benches, fire ring, latrine
maintained by volunteers of the SHTA

      PCs
      9.7 miles
      +0.4 spur
      $HCs

↔ boundary mixed ownership
46.87651 -92.055966 ///masters.speeded.toothpaste
↔ city limit Duluth

Note: Natural surface trails in Duluth are closed in spring mud season, and for 24 hours after rain or snow events. Closures for wet conditions only apply within the municipal limits of the City of Duluth, not the whole trail. There are no trail campsites within Duluth. Check superiorhiking.org for trail alerts as to closures.

$▲ UMN Bagley Campsites
0.4 mile off trail
46.824095 -92.082997 ///compounds.rushes.maddening
6 hosted tent sites for SHT hikers
primitive, one fire ring, latrine
fee
some are reservable
managed by University of Minnesota
umdrsop.d.umn.edu/campground
218-726-6134

      $HCs
      +0.4 spur
      2.8 miles
      +0.5 road
      $L

✷ city of Duluth
46.786322 -92.097114   ///wakes.hood.crew
services spread over many miles

$ ■ *Motels*

various off trail
several commercial lodging options near Lakewalk
fee

$ ■ *Hostel Du Nord*

0.5 mile off trail
46.785312 -92.102628   ///misty.claps.amuse
commercial hostel
bunks, rooms, other amenities
fee
hosteldunord.com
218-940-0742

$L
+0,5 road
3.6 miles
+0.8 road
$L

$ ■ *Motel 6*

0.8 mile off trail on 27th Ave W
46.760673 -92.128842   ///mental.bulb.secret
commercial lodging
30+ rooms
fee
motel6.com
218-723-1123

$L
+0.8 road
6.2 miles
$L

$ ■ *Allyndale Motel*

46.741704 -92.182123   ///sapping.rectangles.improves
commercial lodging
6 rooms
fee
allyndale-motel.hotelsofminnesota.com
218-628-1061

$L
1.5 miles
+0.7 spur
$L

$ ■ *Willard Munger Inn*

0.7 mile off trail via Kingsbury Creek Trail
46.72383 -92.191435   ///drove.harvesting.recruited
commercial lodging
rooms, suites
fee
mungerinn.com
218-624-4814

$L
+0.7 spur
2.9 miles
+0.7 spur
$CCg

$▲ *Indian Point Campground*
1.2 miles off trail via Kingsbury Creek Trail
46.72154 -92.184251 ///harp.hunched.fragments
commercial campground
76 campsites, vehicular and walk-in
fee
duluthindianpointcampground.com
218-628-4977

$▲ *Spirit Mountain*
0.7 mile off trail via Spirit Mountain Loop
46.71376 -92.222377 ///magnifying.drainage.swanky
commercial campground
73 vehicular and walk-in sites
electric and non-electric
tables, fire rings, bathhouse, laundry
fee
spiritmt.com
218-624-8544

$CCg
+0.7 spur
16.8 miles
+0.3 road
$PCg

↔ city limit Duluth
46.676299 -92.301114 ///prude.perfection.issuing
↔ boundary mixed ownership

$▲ *Fond du Lac Campground*
1.2 miles off trail via SHT spur and 131st Ave W
46.660018 -92.280396 ///taking.myriad.churn
commercial campground
57 sites
vehicular and walk-in, cabins
tables, fire rings, bathhouse
fondduclaccampground.com
218-591-2857

$▲ *Jay Cooke State Park Campground*
0.3 mile off trail
46.656821 -92.371161 ///lowers.frown.call
public campground
79 vehicular sites, cabins
electric and non-electric
tables, fire rings, bathhouse
fee
managed by Jay Cooke SP
dnr.state.mn.us
651-296-6157

$PCg
+0.3 road
2.2 miles
+0.2 spur
$PCs

$△ *High Landing Backpacker Campsite*

0.2 mile off trail
46.642827   -92.350726   ///sheltering.rentals.unionists
public campsite
table, fire ring, latrine, bear box
fee
managed by Jay Cooke SP
dnr.state.mn.us
651-296-6157

$PCs
+0.2 spur
0.2 mile
+0.4 spur
$PCs

$△ *Ash Ridge Backpacker Campsite*

0.4 mile off trail
46.642289   -92.34417   ///helm.whispering.ranges
public campsite
table, fire ring, latrine, bear box
fee
managed by Jay Cooke SP
dnr.state.mn.us
651-296-6157

$PCs
+0.4 spur
5.1 miles
PCs

△ *Red River Valley Campsite*

46.609936   -92.295204   s///grew.dosed.juggles
public land
primitive, benches, fire ring, latrine
maintained by volunteers of the SHTA

PCs
0.3 mile
state/ affiliate boundary

Minnesota/Wisconsin border
46.607724   -92.291985
///earliest.shorten.passageway
Superior Hiking Trail Association
superiorhiking.org
↔ **Affiliate boundary**

Wisconsin

See legend and general info for help in interpreting the listings
Wisconsin remote camping regulations do not state any specific distance you must be off road to camp, but in some cases it is stated that you must be out of sight of the road. Some road walks are bounded by state land where one could go off-road to camp. A good practice is to be at least 200 feet away, and 1/8 mile (660 feet) would be even better.

↔ **Chapter boundary**
Minnesota/ Wisconsin state line
46.607774 -92.291986   ///controller.pancake.discusses
Brule-St. Croix Chapter
northcountrytrail.org/trail/wisconsin/bsc

                    state/ chapter boundary
                    3.3 miles
                    PCs

△ *Clear Creek Campsite*
46.573033 -92.290356   ///legends.wonderfully.contexts
public land
primitive, bench, fire ring, latrine
maintained by Brule-St. Croix Chapter
bsc@northcountrytrail.org

                    PCs
                    3.2 miles
                    PCs

$p△ *Spruce Point Campsite*
46.555772 -92.263705   ///happening.millionaire.earl
public land
primitive, bench, fire ring, latrine
water access +0.2 mile
permit fee
maintained by Brule-St. Croix Chapter
bsc@northcountrytrail.org

                    PCs
                    0.7 mile
                    $pD

↔ boundary mixed ownership
46.559519 -92.260615   ///leisure.amps.grumble
↔ boundary Douglas County Forest

Note: dispersed camping is allowed in Douglas County Forest with a paid permit. Find full link in the Appendix.

                    $p△ *dispersed camping* allowed
                    1.3 miles in Douglas Co. Forest
                    with paid permit
                    full link in Appendix

↔ boundary Douglas County Forest
46.546.558486 -92.241454   ///divorce.amendments.trundle
↔ boundary private land

$pD
7.2 miles
$pD

↔ boundary private land
46.549648 -92.192873   ///tags.taxing.charities
↔ boundary Douglas County Forest

$p△ *dispersed camping* allowed
0.3 mile in Douglas Co. Forest
with paid permit
1/8 mile off road
ONLY on west/north side of Dehdam Road
full link in Appendix

↔ boundary Douglas County Forest
46.547109 -92.197852   ///clinically.tracks.skid
↔ boundary private land

$pD
4.9 miles
$PCg

↔ boundary private land
46.536333 -92.130163   ///recruitment.parrot.furniture
↔ boundary Pattison State Park

Note: camp only in designated places in Pattison State Park

$▲ *Pattison State Park Campground*
0.1 mile minimum off trail
46.536008 -92.116731   ///complicated.beaks.rummage
public campground
59 sites, electric, water, bathhouse
fee
dnr.wisconsin.gov
715-399-3111

$PCg
+0.1 spur
7.1 miles
$pD

$△ *Pattison SP backpacking sites*
1.25 miles minimum off trail (across river)
46.522117   -92.124155 and beyond
///selection.crass.intimately
public campsites
4 primitive sites, table, fire ring, latrine, dry
fee
dnr.wisconsin.gov
715-399-3111

↔ boundary Pattison State Park
46.475796 -92.134326   ///partied.captain.offices
↔ boundary Douglas County Forest

$p△ *dispersed camping* allowed
2.9 miles in Douglas Co. Forest
with paid permit
1/8 mile off road
full link in Appendix

↔ boundary Douglas County Forest
46.475175 -92.082828   ///inspector.schoolyard.hairpin
↔ boundary private land

$pD
2.8 miles
$pD

↔ boundary private land
46.443167 -92.071303   ///divot.leaky.truth
↔ boundary Douglas County Forest (intermittent)

$p△ *dispersed camping* allowed
1.8 miles in Douglas Co. Forest
with paid permit
1/8 mile off road
but note many private parcels along road
full link in Appendix

$p△ *Bear Creek campsite*
0.3 mile off trail
46.417811 -92.077689   ///unintended.butterflies.soliciting
public land
primitive, fire ring, bench, latrine
permit fee
full link in Appendix

$p△ *dispersed camping* allowed
6.8 miles in Douglas Co. Forest
with paid permit
1/8 mile off road
but note many private parcels along road
full link in Appendix

↔ boundary Douglas County Forest (intermittent)
46.370834 -91.997429   ///bystanders.flasks.complain
↔ boundary Douglas County Forest

$p△ *dispersed camping* allowed
0.4 mile in Douglas Co. Forest
with paid permit
1/8 mile off road
full link in Appendix

$p△ *Jackson Box Trail Campsite*
0.3 mile off trail
46.366376 -91.999442   ///moderation.smirks.plasma
primitive, fire ring, bench, latrine
permit fee
full link in Appendix

$p△ *dispersed camping* allowed
6.5 miles in Douglas Co. Forest
with paid permit
1/8 mile off road
full link in Appendix

↔ boundary Douglas County Forest
46.291433   -91.988009   ///splash.disarmed.counterpart
↔ boundary private land

$pD
1.6 miles
$pD

↔ boundary private land
46.284078   -91.967409
///elegant.hugs.doubles
↔ boundary Douglas County Forest

$p△ *dispersed camping* allowed
2.2 miles in Douglas Co. Forest
with paid permit
1/8 mile off road
full link in Appendix

↔ boundary Douglas County Forest
46.258537   -91.984833   ///belt.excited.universally
↔ boundary private land

$pD
1.1 miles
PCs

↔ boundary private land
46.257943   -91.967281   ///fillings.politics.spokeswoman
↔ boundary St. Croix National Scenic Riverway

△ *Scott Rapids Campsite*
46.256311   -91.962603   ///unable.browser.eclipsing
public campsite
primitive, table, fire ring, latrine
managed by NPS
715-483-2274

PCs
1.6 miles
$pD

↔ boundary St. Croix National Scenic Riverway
46.258745   -91.939128   ///speculation.couches.stuttering
↔ boundary Douglas County Forest

$p△ *dispersed camping* allowed
0.8 mile in Douglas Co. Forest
with paid permit
full link in Appendix

$▲ *Gordon Dam County Park*
0.7 mile off trail
46.253218 -91.928273   ///noun.fluent.develop
public campground
tables, fire rings, latrine
fee
managed by Douglas County
douglascountywi.gov

$p△ *dispersed camping* allowed
5.2 miles in Douglas Co. Forest
with paid permit
full link in Appendix

$p△ *Rover's Lake Campsite*
46.284232 -91.851092
///expects.measuring.format
public land
table, fire ring, latrine
permit fee
managed by Douglas County
douglascountywi.gov

$p△ *dispersed camping* allowed
3.6 miles in Douglas Co. Forest
with paid permit
full link in Appendix

$p△ *Leo Creek Campsite*
0.1 mile off trail
46.321485 -91.823836   ///prepares.pharmacies.broadcasts
table, fire ring, latrine
permit fee
managed by Douglas County
douglascountywi.gov

$p△ *dispersed camping* allowed
0.5 mile in Douglas Co. Forest
with paid permit
full link in Appendix

↔ boundary Douglas County Forest
46.324115 -91.824868   ///disrupting.clinking.objecting
↔ boundary private land

$pD
1.3 miles
$CCg

↔ boundary private land
46.349078 -91.819697   ///impress.legends.doodle
↔ boundary Lucius Woods County Park

$ ■ *Swanson's Motel & Campground*
46.337346 -91.820254   ///animated.confessed.citrus
15 cabins (campground is seasonal rentals only)
fee
swansonsmotel.com
715-378-2215

$CCg
1.2 miles
$PCg

$▲ Lucius Woods County Park
46.350988 -91.814686   ///forgetful.fairway.buying
public campground
23 electric sites, 6 non-electric
table, fire ring, bathhouse, water
fee
managed by Douglas County
douglascountywi.gov

$PCg
0.1 mile
+0.1 road
$L

↔ boundary Lucius Woods County Park
46.353669 -91.816124   ///waitresses.signifying.stacked
↔ boundary private land

$ ■ St. Croix Inn
0.1 off trail
46.353156 -91.81300   ///cross.equine.newsprint
commercial lodging
rooms, suites, cabins
fee
stcroixinnmotel.com
715-378-4444

$L
+0.1 road
1.0 mile
$D

↔ boundary private land
46.363429 -91.816663   ///calculator.discount.expendable
↔ boundary Douglas County Wildlife Area

$p△ *dispersed camping* allowed
0.3 mile in Douglas Co. Forest
with paid permit
full link in Appendix

↔ boundary Douglas County Wildlife Area
46.367027 -91.814839   ///rehearsed.cancel.undisputed
↔ boundary state land

D
0.2 mile
PCs

△ Aden Creek Campsite
46.369277 -91.815107   ///baggage.certainty.annual
public land
primitive, table, fire ring, latrine
maintained by Brule-St. Croix Chapter
northcountrytrail.org/wisconsin/bsc

            PCs
            3.1 miles
            pD or pCS

↔ boundary state land
46.395624 -91.789342   /// rushing.shies.snake
↔ boundary Brule River State Forest

Note: There is conflicting information about dispersed camping in Brule River SF. One contact says that dispersed camping is allowed, while the DNR web site says you can camp only in the designated sites along the NCT. The established campsites are in the best locations, so it's probably wise to use these. The text is formatted to camp only at the established sites. Camping, either dispersed or at the designated sites, requires a free permit. Call 715-372-5678 or email matthew.leischer@wisconsin.gov.

p△ *Catlin Creek Campsite*
46.395624 -91.789342   ///rushing.shies.snake
public land
primitive, table, fire ring, latrine
free permit required 715- 372-5678
maintained by Brule-St. Croix Chapter
northcountrytrail.org/wisconsin/bsc

            pPCs
            6.5 miles
            pPCs

p△ *Jersett Creek Campsite*
46.414178 -91.706645   ///wicked.universe.dances
public land
primitive, table, fire ring, latrine
free permit required 715- 372-5678
maintained by Brule-St. Croix Chapter
northcountrytrail.org/wisconsin/bsc

            pPCs
            2.6 miles
            pPCs

p△ *Highland Campsite*
46.424947 -91.666025   ///assumptions.silently.slogged
public land
primitive, table, fire ring, latrine
free permit required 715- 372-5678
maintained by Brule-St. Croix Chapter
northcountrytrail.org/wisconsin/bsc

            pPCs
            6.9miles
            pPCs

↔ boundary Brule River State Forest
46.456834 -91.596978   ///chattering.confirming.pads
↔ boundary private land

↔ boundary private land
46.460382 -91.592729   ///stereotype.phones.physics
↔ boundary Brule River State Forest

p△ *Paul Schoch Campsite*
46.46996 -91.58818   ///blaring.bounty.headlights
public land
primitive, table, fire ring, latrine
free permit required 715- 372-5678
maintained by Brule-St. Croix Chapter
northcountrytrail.org/wisconsin/bsc

>pPCs
>**4.8 miles**
>pPCs

p△ *Winneboujou Bluff Campsite*
46.517053 -91.588137   ///abandons.seekers.supposed
public land
primitive, table, fire ring, latrine
water to filter is 0.3 mile away
free permit required 715- 372-5678
maintained by Brule-St. Croix Chapter
northcountrytrail.org/wisconsin/bsc

>pPCs
>**1.3 miles**
>+1.0 spur
>$PCg

$▲ *Bois Brule Campground*
1.0 mile off trail
46.539286 -91.592257   /// retailers.truthfully.fortune
public campground
18 vehicular, 4 walk-in sites
tables, fire rings, restroom, water, no electric
managed by Brule River State Forest
p.widencdn.net/qwstme/BoisBruleCampground

>$PCg
>+1.0 spur
>**1.5 miles**
>D

↔ boundary Brule River State Forest
46.533412 -91.553548   ///envisaged.hillside.flashed
↔ boundary Bayfield County Forest

Note: dispersed camping is allowed in Bayfield County Forest

>△ *dispersed camping* allowed
>**4.1 miles** in Bayfield County Forest
>bayfieldcounty.wi.gov

△ *Morris Pond Campsite*
46.50896 -91.501406   ///hide.gymnasium.pass
public land
primitive, table, fire ring, latrine
maintained by Brule-St. Croix Chapter
northcountrytrail.org/wisconsin/bsc

△ *dispersed camping* allowed
0.8 mile in Bayfield County Forest
bayfieldcounty.wi.gov

△ *Erick Lake Campsite*
46.513597   -91.490677   ///outperform.birthing.reflector
public land
primitive, table, fire ring, latrine
maintained by Brule-St. Croix Chapter
northcountrytrail.org/wisconsin/bsc

△ *dispersed camping* allowed
3.9 mile in Bayfield County Forest
bayfieldcounty.wi.gov

chapter boundary

Ruth Lake Trailhead
46.494601   -91.43859   ///driftwood.thyroid.created
Brule-St. Croix Chapter
northcountrytrail.org/trail/wisconsin/bsc
↔ **Chapter boundary**

↔ **Chapter Boundary**
46.494607 -91.438534   ///realist.frock.shoppers
Chequamegon Chapter
northcountrytrail.org/trail/wisconsin/che

        chapter boundary
        0.8 mile
        D

↔ boundary Bayfield County Forest   WI 106.2
46.493392 -91.427034   ///format.depends.retaliate
↔ boundary Chequamegon NF

    △ *dispersed camping* allowed
    6.6 miles in Chequamegon NF
    fs.usda.gov

↔ internal boundary Chequamegon NF
46.446802 -91.339456   ///portfolio.superstars.chemistry
↔ boundary Rainbow Lake Wilderness (Cheq NF)

Note: see Appendix for link to Federal Wilderness regulations

    △ *dispersed camping* allowed
    6.7 miles in Rainbow Lake Wilderness
    see notes on Designated Wilderness use
    fs.usda.gov

        $▲ *Perch Lake Campsites*
        1.8 miles off trail
    46.402437   -91.270865   ///increased.insist.matched
        public campsites
        16 vehicular sites
        no reservations
        table, fire ring, restroom, latrine, water
        fee
        fs.usda.gov

↔ boundary Rainbow Lake Wilderness (Cheq NF)
46.3884 -91.283838   ///neon.experienced.circle
↔ internal boundary Chequamegon NF

    △ *dispersed camping* allowed
    13.8 miles in Chequamegon NF
    fs.usda.gov

        $▲ *Drummand Lake Campground*
        1.2 miles off trail
    46.337251   -91.26084   ///enclave.accuse.first
        public campground
        27 electric sites, 3 tent sites
        table, fire ring, restroom, $shower
        fee
        drummondlakecampground.com
        715-580-0016

↔ internal boundary Chequamegon NF
46.301076 -91.179155   ///thyroid.roadshow.purifier
↔ boundary Porcupine Lake Wilderness (Cheq NF)
Note: see Appendix for link to Federal Wilderness regulations

△ *dispersed camping* allowed
0.2 miles in Porcupine Lake Wilderness
see notes on Designated Wilderness use
fs.usda.gov

$▲ Two Lakes Campground
1.0 mile off trail
46.293808 -91.191729   ///whisks.hardback.countries
public campground
94 vehicular sites
table, fire ring, latrine, water
fee
managed by Chequamegon NF
715-739-6334

△ *dispersed camping* allowed
6.8 miles in Porcupine Lake Wilderness
see notes on Designated Wilderness use
fs.usda.gov

↔ boundary Porcupine Lake Wilderness (Cheq NF)
46.303507 -91.092981   ///define.distraction.groomed
↔ internal boundary Chequamegon NF

△ *dispersed camping* allowed
0.4 mile in Chequamegon NF
fs.usda.gov

△ East Davis Lake Campsite
46.303833 -91.090449   ///rocks.relational.charging
public land
primitive, table, fire ring, latrine
maintained by Chequamegon Chapter
che@northcountrytrail.org

△ *dispersed camping* allowed
7.0 miles in Chequamegon NF
fs.usda.gov

∠ Marengo River Shelter
46.307213 -90.991485   ///draw.slings.primaries
public land
open shelter, fire ring, latrine
maintained by Chequamegon Chapter
che@northcountrytrail.org

△ *dispersed camping* allowed
4.8 miles in Chequamegon NF
fs.usda.gov

△ *Whiskey Creek Campsite*
46.3068 -90.915102   ///waterproof.boosted.sunglasses
public land
primitive, table, fire ring, latrine
maintained by Chequamegon Chapter
che@northcountrytrail.org

△ *dispersed camping* allowed
3.9 miles in Chequamegon NF
fs.usda.gov

$▲ *Lake Three Campground*
0.1 mile off trail
46.318539 -90.858453   ///preset.usually.snuck
public campground
16 vehicular sites
8 RV sites, 8 tent sites
tables, fire rings, latrine, water
maintained by Chequamegon NF
fs.usda.gov

△ *dispersed camping* allowed
6.1 miles in Chequamegon NF
fs.usda.gov

△ *Trout Brook Campsite*
46.322028 -90.765005   ///toenail.kettle.launcher
public land
primitive, table, fire ring, latrine
maintained by Chequamegon Chapter
che@northcountrytrail.org

△ *dispersed camping* allowed
1.1 miles in Chequamegon NF
fs.usda.gov

∠ *Penoke Ski Trail Shelter*
46.32028 -90.747474   ///employer.deputy.partnering
public land
open shelter, fire ring, latrine
maintained by Chequamegon Chapter
che@northcountrytrail.org

△ *dispersed camping* allowed
4.2 miles in Chequamegon NF
fs.usda.gov

↔ boundary Chequamegon NF
46.327689 -90.707606   ///jeep.infuses.sheepishly
↔ boundary private land

D
2.4 miles
+0.7 road
$L

✲ city of Mellen
46.326147 -90.660413   ///pennies.blazing.buck
limited services

$ ■ *Mellen Motel*
0.7 mile off trail
46.315656 -90.665506   ///producers.grapefruit.falsely
commercial lodging
5 rooms
fee
mellenwi.com
text 630-235-7504

                $L
                +0.7 road
                1.1 miles
                D

↔ boundary private land
46.336681 -90.652164   /// pollen.unfair.united
↔ boundary state land

            △ *dispersed camping* allowed
            0.5 mile on state land
            fs.usda.gov

↔ boundary state land
46.342384 -90.649332   /// hobbies.bulb.yearly
↔ boundary private land

                D
                1.5 miles
                $PCg

↔ boundary private land
46.346393 -90.644518   /// mergers.whisks.reclaim
↔ boundary Copper Falls State Park

$▲ *Copper Falls South Campground*
0.1 mile off trail
46.359011 -90.646321   ///relatives.album.distinction
public campground
23 non-electric sites
19 vehicular, 4 walk-in sites
table, fire ring, latrine, water
fee
dnr.wisconsin.gov
715-274-5123

                $PCg
                +0.1 road
                0.6 mile
                $PCg

$▲ *Copper Falls North Campground*
46.366119   -90.647351   ///applauding.smiling.loosen
public campground
vehicular sites
29 electric, 4 non-electric sites
table, fire ring, water, latrine
fee
dnr.wisconsin.gov
715-274-5123

      $PCg
      2.1 miles
      +0.3 spur
      $PCs
      chapter boundary

Copper Falls Sandstone Ledges spur
46.385391   -90.632799   ///brilliance.mistaking.glucose
Chequamegon Chapter
northcountrytrail.org/trail/wisconsin/che
↔ **Chapter Boundary**

↔ **Chapter Boundary**
Copper Falls Sandstone Ledges spur
46.385391   -90.632799   ///brilliance.mistaking.glucose
Heritage Chapter
northcountrytrail.org/trail/wisconsin/htg

                    chapter boundary

$△ *Sandstone Ledges Campsite*
0.3 mile off trail
46.384832   -90.638853   ///form.distort.sounds
public campsite
primitive, bench, fire ring, latrine
fee
maintained by Copper Falls SP
dnr.wisconsin.gov
715-274-5123

                    $PCs
                    +0.3 spur
                    9.1 miles
                    D

↔ boundary Copper Falls State Park
46.396613   -90.632673   ///modern.stage.motives
↔ boundary private land

↔ boundary private land WI
46.399691   -90.628811   // charity.desk.cakes
↔ boundary Copper Falls State Park

↔ boundary Copper Falls State Park
46.408628   -90.622202   ///radiators.dreading.fortunate
↔ boundary private land

Y junction new section off road trail, see note
46.407196   -90.569539   ///barefoot.chests.crabby

Note: this guide follows the new off-road trail from WI 169 to the forest road crossing. This section is complete except for the bridge across Tyler Forks Creek, to be built by the WI DNR, proposed for 2025. Without the bridge, this route may be impassible. The water can be 5 feet or more deep in the spring or after rain events. Check waterdata.usgs.gov/monitoring-location/04026561. Stricker Road is about two miles downstream from the crossing, so if the water is 5 feet deep at the gage, it will be about the same or a little less (a tributary flows in between the points) at the crossing. Additionally, there is a depth gauge in the river to help you decide whether to wade if you reach the water's edge.

The alternate route is via WI 169 and County Line Road

↔ boundary private land 185.1
46.409575   -90.548817   ///liberty.hearing.acre
↔ boundary Iron County Forest

△ *dispersed camping* allowed
1.4 miles in Iron County Forest
ironcountyforest.org

Y junction new section off road trail, see note
46.400344 -90.529073   ///handrail.workaholic.cleans

△ *Porcupine Hill East Campsite*
46.392291 -90.519377   ///prying.headboard.flood
public land
primitive, fire ring, latrine
maintained by the Heritage Chapter
htg@northcountrytrail.org

△ *dispersed camping* allowed
1.1 miles in Iron County Forest
ironcountyforest.org

△ *Bill Thomas Campsite*
0.1 mile off trail
46.399787 -90.50823   ///smothered.facing.regulating
public land
primitive, table, fire ring, latrine
maintained by the Heritage Chapter
htg@northcountrytrail.org

△ *dispersed camping* allowed
2.7 miles in Iron County Forest
ironcountyforest.org

△ *Gold Mine West Campsite*
0.15 mile off trail
46.391203 -90.475678   ///gushes.rugs.matches
public land
primitive, table, fire ring, latrine
maintained by the Heritage Chapter
htg@northcountrytrail.org

△ *dispersed camping* allowed
4.1 miles in Iron County Forest
ironcountyforest.org

△ *Tilted Gabbro Campsite*
46.408635 -90.452397   ///relocated.fragrances.fists
public land
primitive, table, fire ring, latrine
maintained by the Heritage Chapter
htg@northcountrytrail.org

△ *dispersed camping* allowed
6.4 miles in Iron County Forest
ironcountyforest.org

↔ boundary Iron County Forest
46.456107 -90.50838   ///stall.resonated.meaningless
↔ boundary private land

Note: the next five miles of trail will begin moving off road, fall 2024

D
5.8 miles
D

↔ boundary private land WI 208.8
46.529372 -90.498007   ///deferring.shouts.emerge
↔ boundary Iron County Forest

△ *dispersed camping* allowed
3.7 miles in Iron County Forest
ironcountyforest.org

↔ boundary Iron County Forest
46.559125 -90.444449   ///piper.entertain.events
↔ boundary private land

D
0.5 mile
$PCg

$▲ *Saxon Harbor Campground & Marina*
46.559243 -90.43887   ///visitor.dunk.foolish
public campground
31 electric sites, 5 tent sites
tables, fire rings, bathhouse
fee
Managed by Iron County
ironcountyforest.org
715-893-2370

$PCg
1.8 miles
state/ chapter boundary

Wisconsin/ Michigan state line
46.557384 -90.414483   ///fiasco.supplier.giving
Heritage Chapter
northcountrytrail.org/trail/wisconsin/htg
↔ **Chapter boundary**

Michigan - Upper Peninsula

See legend and general info for help in interpreting the listings. You must have a free permit, a separate page for each night, to disperse camp in Michigan State Forests.

↔ **Chapter boundary**
Wisconsin/ Michigan state line
46.557384   -90.414483   ///fiasco.supplier.giving
Ni-Miikanaake Chapter
northcountrytrail.org/trail/wisconsin/nmk

                        state/ chapter boundary
                        1.5 miles
                        D

↔ boundary private land
46.550085   -90.402918   ///fact.breathe.matters
↔ boundary Gogebic County land

                    △ *dispersed camping* allowed
                    10.5 miles on Gogebic County land
                    gogebic.gov

↔ boundary Gogebic County land
46.578626   -90.259441   ///chiefs.comprehend.asleep
↔ boundary private land
                        D
                        18.4 miles
                        D

↔ boundary private land
46.609414   -90.083574   ///emulated.pearls.riverbeds
↔ boundary Ottawa National Forest

                    △ *dispersed camping* allowed
                    5.4 miles in Ottawa NF
                    fs.usda.gov/ottawa

$▲ *Black River Harbor Campground*
0.3 mile off trail
46.66266   -90.052396   ///spares.abstraction.mattress
public campground
40 sites, some reservable
tables, fire rings, restroom
fee
fs.usda.gov
906-932-1330

                    △ *dispersed camping* allowed
                    7.0 miles in Ottawa NF
                    fs.usda.gov/ottawa

↔ boundary Ottawa NF
46.656828   -89.952253   ///debut.guitar.burger
↔ boundary private land

                        D
                        5.8 miles
                        +0.3 road
                        $PCg

↔ boundary private land
46.656335 -89.947944   ///victorious.bookcases.misted
↔ boundary Porcupine Mountain Wilderness SP

Notes on PMWSP:
There are extensive rules for staying in the park. All park roads close to vehicles Dec 1-to late spring (earlier or later if snow dictates).
From May 15-Nov 30, you must reserve any camping option whether a backpack site, cabin, yurt, or campground. No dispersed camping is allowed.
Backcountry campsites have no latrine. Dig a six-inch hole 200 feet from the campsite and bury waste.
You can disperse camp from Dec 1- May 14, but must register at the HQ.
You are supposed to check in at the HQ before going to your campsite, but this may be impossible for long-distance hikers with no vehicle. Call 906-885-5275 ext 0. Hikers using backcountry campsites may check in this way, but if you reserve a cabin, you must somehow pick up the key at HQ.
www2.dnr.state.mi.us/parksandtrails/Details.aspx?id=426&type=SPRK

$▲ *Presque Isle Campground*
0.3 mile off trail
46.70724 -89.977598   ///jigsaw.copies.leaders
public campground
50 vehicular campsites
tables, fire rings, latrine. seasonal water
fee
www2.dnr.state.mi.us/parksandtrails
906-885-5275

$PCg
2.0 miles
$PE

$ ◯ *Speaker's Cabin*
46.723291 -89.945541   ///distinctly.bronzes.indulgence
public lodging
four person cabin, table, wood stove, latrine
no dogs
fee
www2.dnr.state.mi.us/parksandtrails
906-885-5275

$PE
0.1 mile
+0.2 spur
$PCs

$△ *Backpacking Campsites LS-1 and LS-2*
0.2 mile off trail
46.725483 -89.941314   ///humiliated.losing.beams
public campsite
primitive, fire ring, no latrine
fee
www2.dnr.state.mi.us/parksandtrails
906-885-5275

$PCs
+0.2 spur
3.5 miles
+0.2 spur
$PCs

$△ Backpacking Campsite LS-3
0.2 mile off trail
46.725483 -89.941314   ///humiliated.losing.beams
public campsite
primitive, fire ring, no latrine
fee
www2.dnr.state.mi.us/parksandtrails
906-885-5275

$PCs
+0.2 spur
0.2 mile
$PE

$⌂ Little Carp Cabin
46.751967 -89.903612   ///extend.insolvent.forgetful
public lodging
four person cabin, wood stove, fire ring, table, latrine
no dogs
fee
www2.dnr.state.mi.us/parksandtrails
906-885-5275

$PE
0.3 mile
$PCs

$△ Backpacking Campsites LC-11- LC-14
all near 46.756642 -89.898634   ///rubble.hang.listens
public campsite
primitive, fire ring, no latrine
fee
www2.dnr.state.mi.us/parksandtrails
906-885-5275

$PCs
0.2 mile
$PCs

$△ Backpacking Campsites LS-4 and LS-5
near 46.75823 -89.896875   ///mile.towards.glass
public campsite
primitive, fire ring, no latrine
fee
www2.dnr.state.mi.us/parksandtrails
906-885-5275

$PCs
0.4 mile
$PCs

$△ Backpacking Campsite LS-6
near 46.762287   -89.891725   ///unexplored.skin.skunks
public campsite
primitive, fire ring, no latrine
fee
www2.dnr.state.mi.us/parksandtrails
906-885-5275

$PCs
0.3 mile
$PCs

$△ *Backpacking Campsites LS-7 – LS-9*
all near 46.766109 -89.88709   ///folders.grooves.repayment
public campsite
primitive, fire ring, no latrine
fee
www2.dnr.state.mi.us/parksandtrails
906-885-5275

$PCs
0.2 mile
$PE

$◻ *Big Carp 4 Cabin*
$◻ *Lake Superior Cabin*
$◻ *Big Carp 6 Cabin*
all near 46.767314 -89.885202   ///tipped.aliens.landmark
public lodging
four person cabins, except Big Carp 6 sleeps 6, wood stove, fire ring, table, latrine
no dogs
fee
www2.dnr.state.mi.us/parksandtrails
906-885-5275

$PE
1.0 mile
$PCs

$△ *Backpacking Campsite BC-8*
46.763992 -89.878485   ///forbidding.tent.moons
public campsite
primitive, fire ring, no latrine
fee
www2.dnr.state.mi.us/parksandtrails
906-885-5275

$PCs
0.2 mile
$PCs

$△ *Backpacking Campsite BC-7*
46.757936 -89.867499   ///intervened.draw.prefer
public campsite
primitive, fire ring, no latrine
fee
www2.dnr.state.mi.us/parksandtrails
906-885-5275

$PCs
2.5 miles
$PCs

$△ *Backpacking Campsites BC-4 – BC-6*
all near 46.768695 -89.827631   ///searing.taxed.promotional
public campsite
primitive, fire ring, no latrine
fee
www2.dnr.state.mi.us/parksandtrails
906-885-5275

$PCs
2.9 miles
$PCs

$△ Backpacking Campsites BC-1 - BC-3
all near 46.792955 -89.789458   ///milked.pricier.studs
public campsite
primitive, fire ring, no latrine
fee
www2.dnr.state.mi.us/parksandtrails
906-885-5275
$PCs
1.8 miles
$PCs

$△ Backpacking Campsite ES-2
near 46.805088 -89.762163   ///sulky.motorbike.interlude
public campsite
primitive, fire ring, no latrine
fee
www2.dnr.state.mi.us/parksandtrails
906-885-5275
$PCs
2.8 miles
$PCs

$△ Backpacking Campsite ES-1
near 46.813313 -89.714012   ///topping.largest.harness
public campsite
primitive, fire ring, no latrine
fee
www2.dnr.state.mi.us/parksandtrails
906-885-5275
$PCs
2.5 miles
$PCs

$△ Backpacking Campsites GP-1, GP-2
near 46.798743 -89.68895   ///burst.ignore.futuristic
public campsite
primitive, fire ring, no latrine
fee
www2.dnr.state.mi.us/parksandtrails
906-885-5275
$PCs
2.5 miles
$PCs

$△ Backpacking Campsite LL-1
46.768122 -89.69101   ///significant.seasons.rent
public campsite
primitive, fire ring, no latrine
fee
www2.dnr.state.mi.us/parksandtrails
906-885-5275
$PCs
1.0 mile
$PE

$⌂ *Lost Creek Yurt*
near 46.763478 -89.678736   ///gulped.undercover.remains
public lodging
four person yurt, wood stove, fire ring, table, latrine
no dogs
fee
www2.dnr.state.mi.us/parksandtrails
906-885-5275

$PE
0.7 mile
$PCs

$△ *Lost Creek Rustic Campsite*
46.754011 -89.678822   ///informer.skateboard.punctured
public campsite
3 vehicular sites
primitive, table, fire ring, latrine
fee
www2.dnr.state.mi.us/parksandtrails
906-885-5275

$PCs
3.0 miles
D

↔ boundary Porcupine Mountain Wilderness SP
46.744248 -89.638567   ///symphony.important.vending
↔ boundary Ottawa National Forest

△ *dispersed camping* allowed
7.0 miles in Ottawa NF
fs.usda.gov/ottawa
chapter boundary

M-64
46.692733 -89.590747   /// chamber.crunches.encoder
Ni-Miikanaake Chapter
northcountrytrail.org/trail/wisconsin/nmk
↔ **Chapter boundary**

↔ **Chapter boundary**
M-64
46.692733 -89.590747   ///chamber.crunches.encoder
Peter Wolfe Chapter
northcountrytrail.org/trail/michigan/pwc

chapter boundary
△ *dispersed camping* allowed
24.1 miles in Ottawa NF
fs.usda.gov/ottawa

↔ boundary Ottawa National Forest
46.668172 -89.360647   ///digesting.fetch.looking
↔ boundary private land

D
3.4 miles
D

↔ boundary private land   MI
46.679538 -89.303141   ///newsletter.tamer.zoom
↔ boundary Ottawa National Forest

△ *dispersed camping* allowed
3.4 miles in Ottawa NF
fs.usda.gov/ottawa

↔ boundary Ottawa National Forest
46.690843 -89.250269   ///boomed.slug.crossed
↔ boundary private land

D
0.8 mile
D

↔ boundary private land
46.693316 -89.239369   ///preferable.modes.inclination
↔ boundary Ottawa National Forest

△ *dispersed camping* allowed
0.3 mile in Ottawa NF
fs.usda.gov/ottawa

↔ boundary Ottawa National Forest
46.694199 -89.235764   ///celery.avoids.topped
↔ boundary private land

D
1.3 miles
HE

△ *Old Victoria Shelter*
46.704353 -89.227524   ///spreading.staying.grand
hosted site
4 bunks, no latrine (bury human waste), no amenities
artesian well 0.5 mile east
no camping except in shelter
maintained by Peter Wolfe Chapter
pwc@northcountrytrail.org

                            HE
                            3.0 miles
                            D

↔ boundary private land
46.688694 -89.209328   ///substitute.saturation.voltage
↔ boundary Ottawa National Forest

                    △ *dispersed camping* allowed
                    10.6 miles in Ottawa NF
                    fs.usda.gov/ottawa

↔ boundary Ottawa National Forest
46.631745 -89.111009   ///allergy.devastated.catcher
↔ boundary private land
                            D
                            0.3 mile
                            D
↔ boundary private land
46.632099 -89.10573   ///sensations.crew.blessing
↔ boundary Ottawa National Forest

                    △ *dispersed camping* allowed
                    13.7 miles in Ottawa NF
                    fs.usda.gov/ottawa
                            $▲ *Bob Lake Campground*
                                        1.1 miles off trail
                            46.661634 -88.913276   ///airborne.lies.comic
                                        public campground
                                        17 vehicular sites
                            tables, fire rings, latrine, seasonal water
                                        fee
                                        fs.usda.gov/ottawa
                                        906-932-1330

                    △ *dispersed camping* allowed
                    7.9 miles in Ottawa NF
                    fs.usda.gov/ottawa

↔ boundary Ottawa National Forest
46.680675 -88.78231   ///original.kick.unbeatable
↔ boundary private land
                            D
                            1.2 miles
                            D
↔ boundary private land
46.679479 -88.761026   ///armrests.stunningly.merits
↔ boundary Ottawa National Forest
                    △ *dispersed camping* allowed
                    13.8 miles in Ottawa NF
                    fs.usda.gov/ottawa

↔ boundary Ottawa National Forest
46.582402 -88.615759   ///framework.compromised.treat
↔ boundary Baraga State Forest

Note: dispersed camping is allowed in Michigan state forests with a free permit that can be found online. You are supposed to fill out and leave one copy of this permit at each campsite. See Appendix for full link.

                      p△ *dispersed camping* allowed
                      1.3 miles in Baraga SF
                      michigan.gov/dnr

⌂△ *Oren Krumm Shelter*
46.580105 -88.600351   ///determines.conclusions.homecoming
public land
4 bunks, two tent sites
fire ring, latrine
maintained by Peter Wolfe Chapter
pwc@northcountrytrail.org

                      p△ *dispersed camping* allowed
                      2.1 miles in Baraga SF
                      michigan.gov/dnr

↔ boundary Baraga State Forest
46.592993 -88.589279   ///submitting.magnitudes.caressing
↔ boundary Baraga Plains State Wildlife Area

Note: dispersed camping is allowed in MI State Wildlife and Game Areas only between Sep 11 and May 14 with permit, and at least one mile away from designated campgrounds/ campsites. See Appendix

                      p△ seasonal *dispersed camping* allowed
                      3.6 miles in Baraga Plains State Wildlife Area
                      michigan.gov/dnr

$▲ *Big Lake State Forest Campground*
0.1 mile off trail
46.611245 -88.570525   ///campus.accomplice.portray
public campground
12 vehicular sites
tables, fire rings, latrine, seasonal water
managed by Baraga State Park
www2.dnr.state.mi.us
906-353-6558

                      p△ seasonal *dispersed camping* allowed
                      4.3 miles in Baraga Plains State Wildlife Area
                      michigan.gov/dnr

↔ boundary Baraga Plains State Wildlife Area
46.635902 -88.542793   ///extensive.heartburn.avoids
↔ boundary private land
Note: a portion of this land may be closed for fall hunting

                      pD seasonal
                      5.5 miles
                      D

↔ boundary private land
46.62547 -88.470309   ///curiosity.textiles.navigation
↔ boundary Lyme Timber property

△ *dispersed camping*   allowed
8.6 miles on Lyme Timber property
no fires

↔ boundary Lyme Timber property
46.640867 -88.368964   ///behaved.dash.behaving
↔ boundary private land

D
1.6 miles
D

↔ boundary private land
46.642782 -88.335104   ///limp.loiter.little
↔ boundary Baraga State Forest

△ *dispersed camping* allowed
2.1 miles in Baraga State Forest
michigan.gov/dnr

↔ boundary Baraga State Forest
46.638333 -88.319654   ///devalued.legion.maternal
↔ boundary private land

D
2.9 miles
+0.1 spur
PE

△ *Manger Lynch Shelter*
0.1 mile off trail
46.623185 -88.290858   ///fixed.whisk.planner
hosted screened shelter
4 bunks, latrine
maintained by Peter Wolfe Chapter
pwc@northcountrytrail.org

HE
+0.1 spur
5.0 miles
chapter boundary

Long Lake Road
46.609744 -88.227755   ///requirement.mostly.pocket
Peter Wolfe Chapter
northcountrytrail.org/trail/wisconsin/pwc
↔ **Chapter boundary**

↔ **Chapter boundary**
Long Lake Road
46.609744 -88.227755   ///requirement.mostly.pocket
Marquette Area Chapter
northcountrytrail.org/trail/michigan/mac

                      chapter boundary
                      1.4 miles
                      +0.1 spur
                      $PCs

↔ boundary private land
46.605675 -88.210435   ///necklaces.whisker.grooves
↔ boundary Craig Lake State Park

Note: Camp only at designated sites. As of 2023, all backcountry campsites in Craig Lake SP are seasonal, open only May 20 through Nov 1, and must be reserved in advance (6 months maximum). MIDNRReservations.com. You are supposed to check in at Van Riper SP before going to your campsite, but this may be impossible for long-distance hikers with no vehicle. Call 906-339-4461. Hikers using backcountry campsites may check in this way.

$△ *Craig Lake SP Campsite 12*
0.1 mile off trail
46.602992 -88.206487   ///smudges.twisty.debates
public campsite
primitive, fire ring, no latrine
MIDNRReservations.com

                      $PCs
                      +0.1 spur
                      1.2 miles
                      $PCs

$△ *Craig Lake SP Campsites 10, 11, 22*
46.599306 -88.186617   ///generations.shampoos.slip
public campsites
primitive, fire ring, no latrine
MIDNRReservations.com

                      $PCs
                      0.6 mile
                      +0.15 spur
                      $PCs

$△ *Craig Lake SP Campsites 6-8*
0.15 mile off trail
46.604761 -88.180609   ///brilliant.specifics.storybook
public campsites
primitive, fire ring, no latrine
MIDNRReservations.com

                      $PCs
                      +0.15 spur
                      0.4 mile
                      +0.3 spur
                      $PCs

$△ *Craig Lake SP Campsites 13, 14*
0.3 mile off trail (east)
46.606795 -88.167133 ///airborne.reception.replying
public campsites
primitive, fire ring, no latrine
MIDNRReservations.com

$△ *Craig Lake SP Campsite 4,5*
0.3 mile off trail (west)
46.608564 -88.177304 ///redundancy.fuel.lotteries
public campsites
primitive, fire ring, no latrine
MIDNRReservations.com

$PCs
+0.3 spur
2.6 miles
$PCs

$△ *Craig Lake SP Campsite 15*
46.625808 -88.157778 ///tripped.chatting.integrating
public campsite
primitive, fire ring, no latrine
MIDNRReservations.com

$PCs
1.5 miles
$PCs

$△ *Craig Lake SP Campsite 16*
46.621152 -88.131342 ///picking.fortnight.plea
public campsite
primitive, fire ring, no latrine
may be defunct
MIDNRReservations.com

$PCs
1.1 miles
D

↔ boundary Craig Lake State Park
46.623775 -88.116493 ///monorail.resorting.surveys
↔ boundary Lyme Timber

△ *dispersed camping* allowed
1.3 miles on Lyme Timber property
no fires

↔ boundary Lyme Timber
46.626575 -88.097696 ///lighthouse.blackberry.head
↔ boundary private land

D
1.5 miles
D

↔ boundary private land MMI 216.1
46.633824 -88.076024   ///copy.fabricated.tarred
↔ boundary Lyme Timber

△ *dispersed camping* allowed
0.9 mile on Lyme Timber property
no fires

↔ boundary Lyme Timber
46.633441 -88.064523   ///floppy.incorrect.handbag
↔ boundary private land

D
0.8 mile
D

↔ boundary private land
46.635357 -88.052807   ///cage.reassuring.union
↔ boundary Ottawa National Forest
McCormick Wilderness

Note: see Appendix for link to Federal Wilderness regulations

△ *dispersed camping* allowed
7.4 mile in Ottawa NF
McCormick Wilderness

↔ boundary Ottawa National Forest
↔ boundary McCormick Wilderness
46.653977 -87.960392   ///widgets.oxidation.frustration
↔ boundary Lyme Timber

△ *dispersed camping* allowed
0.4 mile on Lyme Timber property
no fires

↔ boundary Lyme Timber MI 225.6
46.656658 -87.954684   ///inlets.immune.smiling
↔ boundary private land

D
0.2 mile
D

↔ boundary private land
46.656587 -87.949607   ///externally.booster.captive
↔ boundary Lyme Timber

△ *dispersed camping* allowed
2.1 mile on Lyme Timber property
no fires

↔ boundary Lyme Timber
46.665099 -87.917806   ///readership.display.ordered
↔ boundary private land

D
2.2 miles
D

↔ boundary private land
46.662605 -87.886601   ///heater.flinch.ground
↔ boundary Lyme Timber

△ *dispersed camping* allowed
0.4 mile on Lyme Timber property
no fires

↔ boundary Lyme Timber
46.665337 -87.881343   ///actions.upbringing.mannerisms
↔ boundary private land

D
3.1 miles
D

↔ boundary private land
46.67295 -87.840134   ///grapefruit.recliner.insects
↔ boundary Lyme Timber

△ *dispersed camping* allowed
0.1 mile on Lyme Timber property
no fires

↔ boundary Lyme Timber
46.67292 -87.837902   ///matched.fencing.hoops
↔ boundary private land

D
0.8 mile
D

↔ boundary private land
46.671816 -87.824084   ///states.blackberry.revived
↔ boundary Lyme Timber

△ *dispersed camping* allowed
3.6 miles on Lyme Timber property
no fires

↔ boundary Lyme Timber
46.639532 -87.792047   ///revised.shovels.jockey
↔ boundary Gwinn State Forest

p△ *dispersed camping* allowed
0.1 mile in Gwinn SF with permit
michigan.gov/dnr

↔ boundary Gwinn State Forest
46.639578 -87.78994   ///differ.quite.backer
↔ boundary private land

D
0.2 mile
D

↔ boundary private land MI 238.4
46.639962 -87.786443   ///tangent.wins.potentials
↔ boundary Gwinn State Forest

      p△ *dispersed camping* allowed
      0.2 mile in Gwinn SF with permit
      michigan.gov/dnr

↔ boundary Gwinn State Forest
46.636558 -87.784082   ///tolerable.groceries.measure
↔ boundary private land

      D
      9.6 miles
      D

↔ boundary private land
46.643011 -87.661001   ///unleashing.fondest.overlaid
↔ boundary Lyme Timber

      △ *dispersed camping* allowed
      0.9 mile on Lyme Timber property
      no fires

↔ boundary Lyme Timber
46.643099 -87.644951   ///paddock.chattering.proper
↔ boundary private land

      D
      4.6 miles
      D

↔ boundary private land
46.657476 -87.573025   ///stepfather.emeralds.stylish
↔ boundary Gwinn State Forest

      p△ *dispersed camping* allowed
      0.4 mile in Gwinn SF with permit
      michigan.gov/dnr

△ *Little Garlic Falls Campsite*
0.8 mile off trail
46.66805 -87.577012   ///listeners.swoop.shudder
public land
primitive, fire ring, latrine
maintained by the Marquette Area Chapter
mac@northcountrytrail.org

      p△ *dispersed camping* allowed
      3.5 miles in Gwinn SF with permit
      michigan.gov/dnr

↔ boundary Gwinn State Forest
46.66531 -87.547919   ///inflamed.moving.heartbreak
↔ boundary private land

D
3.1 miles
D

↔ boundary private land
46.643807   -87.507664   ///tunnel.pitching.nuances
↔ boundary Gwinn State Forest

p△ *dispersed camping* allowed
1.1 miles in Gwinn SF
michigan.gov/dnr

↔ boundary Gwinn State Forest
46.639122   -87.492902   ///sheltering.composites.distinction

↔ internal boundary Gwinn State Forest

Note: no dispersed camping in this section

D
4.9 miles
D

$△ *Little Presque Isle Cabins*
2.2 miles off trail
46.627471   -87.494826   ///mocking.transfers.cheerfully
public lodging
rustic cabins
8 bunks, wood stove, table, seasonal water, latrine
fee
managed by Michigan DNR
906-339-4461

↔ internal boundary Gwinn State Forest
46.609855   -87.46977   ///rhino.rebound.towels
↔ boundary Gwinn State Forest MI

p△ *dispersed camping* allowed
0.6 mile in Gwinn SF with permit
michigan.gov/dnr

↔ boundary Gwinn State Forest
46.607482   -87.478525   ///stuttering.preparation.geek
↔ boundary mixed ownership

D
0.3 mile
D

↔ boundary mixed ownership
46.606332   -87.481443   ///cookers.workplaces.renewals
↔ boundary Gwinn State Forest

p△ *dispersed camping* allowed
0.6 mile in Gwinn SF with permit
michigan.gov/dnr

↔ boundary Gwinn State Forest
46.600346 -87.487795   ///cavity.celebrities.antenna
↔ boundary mixed ownership

        D
        0.5 mile
        +0.3 mile road
        $PCs

$△ *Bear Tree Homestead HipCamp*

0.3 mile off trail
46.59919 -87.49076   ///fillers.perhaps.belongings
HipCamp with several tent sites
fee
hipcamp.com

        $PCs
        +0.3 road
        1.0 mile
        $PCg

$▲ *Forestville Campground*

46.584318 -87.479812   ///encounters.secret.confirm
public campground
15 primitive vehicular sites
tables, fire rings, water, latrine
fee
managed by Noquemanon Trail Network
noquetrails.org/forestville
906-235-6861

        $PCg
        4.3 miles
        +0.6 road
        $PCg

$▲ *Tourist Park Campground*

0.6 mile off trail
46.569166 -87.411825   ///luxury.spell.defeat
public campground
100 full hook-up sites, 10 tent sites
table, some grills, bathhouse
fee
managed by City of Marquette
marquettemi.gov
906-228-0460

        $PCg
        +0.6 road
        4.0 miles
        +various road
        $L

✱ city of Marquette
46.540684 -87.392666   ///rudder.redefining.wordy
services

$ ■ *Motels*

0.1 to 2 miles off trail
many near 46.540684 -87.392666   ///rudder.redefining.wordy
commercial lodging
fee

      $L
      +various road
      7.2 miles
      +0.6 road
      $CCg

$▲ *Chocolay River Camping*

0.6 mile off trail
46.478159 -87.281302   ///unleash.headless.sigh
commercial campground
49 vehicular sites, full hook ups
10 tent sites, table, fire ring, water, bathhouse
fee
chocolayrivercamping.com
906-356-3577

      $CCg
      +0.6 road
      2.6 miles
      +0.2 road
      $CCg

$▲ *Gitche Gumee Campground*

0.2 mile off trail
46.486278 -87.230629   ///listeners.swoop.shudder
commercial campground
58 vehicular sites, 2 tent sites
tables, fire rings, bathhouse
fee
gitchegumeepark.com
906-235-6861

      $CCg
      +0.2 road
      0.6 mile
      D

↔ boundary mixed ownership
46.481561 -87.221775   ///doting.flows.smothered
↔ boundary Gwinn State Forest

      p△ *dispersed camping* allowed
      1.7 miles in Gwinn SF with permit
      michigan.gov/dnr

↔ boundary Gwinn State Forest
46.485402 -87.192335   ///corrections.opposites.songs
↔ boundary private land

      D
      0.7 mile
      D

↔ boundary private land
46.489332 -87.179718   ///greet.typewriter.noon
↔ boundary Gwinn State Forest

        p△ *dispersed camping* allowed
        1.0 mile in Gwinn SF with permit
        michigan.gov/dnr

↔ boundary Gwinn State Forest
46.490573 -87.158603   ///investments.rejoined.crunched
↔ boundary private land

        D
        0.4 mile
        HE

⌂ *Lakenenland Shelter*
46.489184 -87.15178   ///defrost.despite.sulky
hosted enclosed shelter
2 bunks, table, fire ring, latrine

        HE
        0.7 mile
        D

↔ boundary private land
46.487264 -87.137746   ///culprit.dinner.overlooked
↔ boundary Gwinn State Forest

        p△ *dispersed camping* allowed
        0.5 mile in Gwinn SF with permit
        michigan.gov/dnr

↔ boundary Gwinn State Forest
46.487323 -87.127189   ///purifying.outpost.eyebrows
↔ boundary private land

        D
        0.4 mile
        D

↔ boundary private land
46.485609 -87.122683   ///begin.consoles.flashbacks
↔ boundary Gwinn State Forest

        p△ *dispersed camping* allowed
        0.7 mile in Gwinn SF with permit
        michigan.gov/dnr

↔ boundary Gwinn State Forest
46.478487 -87.11646   ///habitat.scans.slices
↔ boundary private land

        D
        0.8 mile
        D

↔ boundary private land
46.468557 -87.116675   ///restrict.trains.workplaces
↔ boundary Gwinn State Forest

△ *dispersed camping* allowed
2.4 mile in Gwinn SF with permit
michigan.gov/dnr

↔ boundary Gwinn State Forest
46.442066 -87.106676   ///animated.dealing.drilling
↔ boundary Lyme Timber

△ *dispersed camping* allowed
0.8 mile on Lyme Timber property
no fires

↔ boundary Lyme Timber
46.434525 -87.106933   ///adjustable.major.cheers
↔ boundary private land

D
1.0 mile
D

↔ boundary private land
46.419971 -87.100968   ///counters.spreads.dispute
↔ boundary Lyme Timber

△ *dispersed camping* allowed
3.1 mile on Lyme Timber property
no fires

↔ boundary Lyme Timber
46.405665 -87.056636   ///situation.monument.chatter
↔ boundary Laughing Whitefish Falls SP

Note: no camping at Laughing Whitefish Falls SP

D
1.1 miles
D

↔ boundary Laughing Whitefish Falls SP
46.402943 -87.048761   ///easels.spectators.branched
↔ boundary Lyme Timber

△ *dispersed camping* allowed
0.5 mile on Lyme Timber property
no fires

↔ boundary Lyme Timber
46.402114 -87.04065   ///leasing.multiplied.mountains
↔ boundary mixed ownershp

D
1.7 miles
D

↔ boundary mixed ownership
46.397778 -87.022572   ///jaguar.bossy.golfer
↔ boundary Lyme Timber

△ *dispersed camping* allowed
3.6 miles on Lyme Timber property
no fires

↔ boundary Lyme Timber
46.42821   -86.991137   ///overlooking.labs.reissued
↔ internal boundary Hiawatha National Forest
Rock River Canyon Wilderness

Note: see Appendix for link to Federal Wilderness regulations

△ *dispersed camping* allowed
1/4 mile from roads
4.1 miles in Hiawatha NF
Rock River Canyon Wilderness

↔ boundary Hiawatha National Forest
Rock River Canyon Wilderness
46.400845   -86.934327   ///waxers.safely.nutty
↔ boundary mixed ownership

D
0.8 mile
D

↔ boundary mixed ownership
46.394689   -86.923985   ///digit.quarrel.heavyweight
↔ internal boundary Hiawatha National Forest
Rock River Canyon Wilderness

△ *dispersed camping* allowed
1/4 mile from roads
0.6 mile in Hiawatha NF
Rock River Canyon Wilderness

↔ internal boundary Hiawatha National Forest
Rock River Canyon Wilderness
chapter boundary

Rock River Road
46.389713   -86.91522   ///nominal.streetcar.impaled
Marquette Area Chapter
northcountrytrail.org/trail/michigan/mac
↔ **Chapter boundary**

↔ **Chapter boundary**
Rock River Road
46.389713   -86.91522   ///nominal.streetcar.impaled
Superior Shoreline Chapter
northcountrytrail.org/trail/michigan/ssc

chapter boundary
△ *dispersed camping* allowed
17.0 miles in Hiawatha NF
fs.usda.gov/hiawatha

$▲ *Au Train Lake NF Campground*
1.5 miles via Campground Rd
46.393652   -86.836666   ///gagging.megawatt.proudly
public campground
37 vehicular sites
tables, fire rings, latrine, water
fee
fs.usda.gov
906-428-5800

↔ boundary Hiawatha National Forest
46.382904   -86.683992   ///snacks.uncle.implements
↔ boundary mixed ownership

Note: the section near Wagner Falls is scheduled to come off road 2024

D
3.2 miles
$L

✳ city of Munising
46.409979   -86.64977   ///portray.suave.invents
limited services
$ ■ *Motels*
various on and near trail
commercial lodging
fee
$L
6.8 miles
$PCs

↔ boundary mixed ownership
46.423997   -86.624551   ///product.corners.below
↔ boundary Pictured Rocks National Lakeshore

Notes on Pictured Rocks: No dispersed camping. You must have a permit for overnight stays, and you must reserve campsites and stick to your itinerary. Reserving early is important because these permits fill quickly each year. nps.gov/piro/planyourvisit/permits.htm. Alternately, see the Bonus section of text for a way to day hike through PIRO.

$△ *Cliffs Campsite*

46.473318   -86.570649   ///toothpaste.becomes.curbed
public campsite
primitive, fire ring, latrine, bear box, dry
nps.gov/piro

$PCs
3.7 miles
$PCs

$△ *Potato Patch Campsite*

46.497636 -86.530051   ///mothering.gobbling.realist
public campsite
primitive, fire ring, latrine, bear box, dry
nps.gov/piro

$PCs
3.0 miles
$PCs

$▲ *Mosquito River Group Campsite*

46.524779 -86.493358   ///brewery.dolphins.biter
public campsite
groups of 7-20 only
primitive, no fires, latrine, bear box
nps.gov/piro

$PCs
0.2 mile
$PCs

$△ *Mosquito River Campsite*

46.526905 -86.4922   ///overhead.mortal.transferred
public campsite
primitive, no fires, latrine, bear box
nps.gov/piro

$PCs
4.1 miles
$PCs

$△ *Chapel Campsite*

46.546064 -86.441646   ///booked.ignores.captures
public campsite
primitive, no fires, latrine, bear box
nps.gov/piro

$PCs
2.7 miles
$PCs

$▲ *Coves Group Campsite*

46.561086 -86.396241   ///rates.refused.scared
public campsite
groups of 7-20 only
primitive, fire ring, latrine, bear box
nps.gov/piro

$PCs
1.4 miles
$PCs

$△ Coves Campsite
46.568079 -86.372294   ///woes.mainframe.storing
public campsite
primitive, fire ring, latrine, bear box
nps.gov/piro

$PCs
1.4 miles
$PCs

$△ Beaver Creel Campsite
46.577047 -86.349978   ///mainly.unanswered.hacker
public campsite
primitive, fire ring, latrine, bear box
nps.gov/piro

$PCs
1.3 miles
$PCs

$△ Pine Bluff Campsite
46.58625 -86.32895   ///suggest.fostering.patting
public campsite
primitive, fire ring, latrine, bear box
nps.gov/piro

$PCs
1.4 miles
$PCs

$△ Trappers Lake Campsite
0.4 mile off trail
46.586368 -86.31659   ///helpfully.regain.lands
public campsite
primitive, fire ring, latrine, bear box
nps.gov/piro

$▲ Trappers Lake Group Campsite
0.4 mile off trail
46.58802 -86.315389   ///linen.pillowcase.rescue
public campsite
groups of 7-20 only
primitive, fire ring, latrine, bear box
nps.gov/piro

$PCs
4.1 miles
$PCs

$△ Sevenmile Creek Campsite
46.619244 -86.259127   ///inflation.menu.dressed
public campsite
primitive, fire ring, no latrine, bear box
nps.gov/piro

$PCs
0.1 mile
$PCs

$▲ *Sevenmile Creek Group Campsite*
46.620423   -86.257496   ///coconut.raving.thermal
public campsite
groups of 7-20 only
primitive, fire ring, no latrine, bear box
nps.gov/piro

$PCs
2.9 miles
$PCs

$△ *Twelvemile Creek Campsite*
46.643291   -86.208916   ///fondest.anybody.pushover
public campsite
primitive, fire ring, latrine, bear box
nps.gov/piro

$PCs
0.5 mile
$PCs

$△ *Benchmark Creek Campsite*
46.646826   -86.201148   ///career.fingernail.simulating
public campsite
primitive, fire ring, latrine, bear box
nps.gov/piro

$PCs
2.3 miles
$PCg

$▲ *Lower Hurricane River Campground*
46.666094   -86.166022   ///mixture.rectangles.alarmed
public campsite
12 vehicular sites
tables, fire rings, latrine, seasonal water, no bear boxes
nps.gov/piro

$PCg
1.6 miles
$PCs

$▲ *AuSable Group Campsite*
46.671071   -86.136668   ///darkroom.detain.unfriendly
public campsite
groups of 7-20 only
primitive, fire ring, latrine, bear box
nps.gov/piro

$PCs
0.1 mile
$PCs

$△ AuSable Campsite
46.66929   -86.134994   ///stouts.inferior.sauntered
public campsite
primitive, fire ring, latrine, bear box
nps.gov/piro

$PCs
3.1 miles
$PCs

$▲ Masse Homestead Group Campsite
0.2 mile off trail
46.647964   -86.094493   ///multiply.teaches.opening
public campsite
groups of 7-20 only
primitive, fire ring, no latrine, bear box, dry
nps.gov/piro

$△ Masse Homestead Campsite
46.646918   -86.091274   ///highest.moped.quits
public campsite
primitive, fire ring, no latrine, bear box, dry
nps.gov/piro

$PCs
6.8 miles
$PCg

↔ boundary Pictured Rocks National Lakeshore
46.672794   -85.999714   ///romance.imprint.parents
↔ boundary mixed ownership

$▲ Woodland Park Campground
46.673005   -85.993978   ///pigeons.earlobe.incomplete
public campground
117 vehicular sites, some with electric
tables, fire rings, bathhouse, laundry
some tent sites have no amenities
fee
Managed by Burt Township
burttownship.com
906-494-2381

$PCg
0.6 mile
$L

✳ village of Grand Marais
46.670739   -85.983323   ///period.cattle.radioactive
limited services

$ ■ Motels
several near this location
commercial lodging
fee

$L
2.1 miles
D

↔ boundary mixed ownership
46.669398 -85.941771   ///safari.sapped.bared
↔ boundary Shingleton State Forest

p△ *dispersed camping* allowed
1.0 mile in Shingleton SF with permit
michigan.gov/dnr

↔ boundary Shingleton State Forest
46.660038 -85.927237   ///service.innings.absorbing
↔ boundary mixed ownership

D
3.8 miles
D

↔ boundary mixed ownership MI 389.2
46.678767 -85.894188   ///precursors.ledge.roughness
↔ boundary Shingleton State Forest

p△ *dispersed camping* allowed
2.2 miles in Shingleton SF with permit
michigan.gov/dnr

↔ boundary Shingleton State Forest
46.689277 -85.864491   ///siblings.courtrooms.shepherdess
↔ boundary Newberry State Forest

p△ *dispersed camping* allowed
3.6 miles in Newberry SF with permit
michigan.gov/dnr

↔ boundary Newberry State Forest
46.666723 -85.817155   ///prowling.intrusions.character
↔ boundary Blind Sucker River Flooding State WMA

See note in Appendix on camping in Michigan WMAs and SGAs

p△ seasonal *dispersed camping* allowed
1.7 miles in Blind Sucker RF WMA
with permit
michigan.gov/dnr

↔ boundary Blind Sucker River Flooding State WMA
46.667371 -85.800204   /// corals.purse.reimbursed
↔ boundary Newberry State Forest

p△ *dispersed camping* allowed
2.7 miles in Newberry SF with permit
michigan.gov/dnr

$▲ *Lake Superior State Forest Campground*
46.677538 -85.763243   ///year.consume.helper
public campground
18 vehicular sites
primitive, tables, fire rings, latrine, seasonal water
fee
Managed by Michigan DNR
www2.dnr.state.mi.us/parksandtrails
906-658-3338

p△ *dispersed camping* allowed
5.8 miles in Newberry SF with permit
michigan.gov/dnr

↔ boundary Newberry State Forest
46.675174 -85.650896   ///herself.hacking.disbelief
↔ boundary private land

D
1.7 miles
$PCg

↔ boundary private land
46.676219 -85.645809   ///slick.blip.claimed
↔ boundary Muskallonge Lake State Park

Note: camp only in designated sites in Muskallonge Lake SP

$▲ *Muskallonge Lake State Park Campground*
46.675763 -85.630424   ///blank.comfort.graduating
public campground
159 vehicular sites
tables, fire rings, bathhouse
fee
Managed by Michigan DNR
www2.dnr.state.mi.us/parksandtrails

$PCg
0.9 mile
D

↔ boundary Muskallonge Lake State Park
46.67616 -85.619759   ///beans.shirk.spend
↔ boundary private land

↔ boundary private land MI 407.8
46.674423 -85.614223   ///assumptions.counter.breath
↔ boundary Newberry State Forest

p△ *dispersed camping* allowed
1.0 mile in Newberry SF with permit
michigan.gov/dnr

↔ boundary Newberry State Forest
46.672406 -85.5968   ///steeps.sentimental.winemaker
↔ boundary private land
        D
        0.3 mile
        D

↔ boundary private land
46.671758 -85.594032   ///fantasy.nickname.twilight
↔ boundary Newberry State Forest

        p△ *dispersed camping* allowed
        1.1 miles in Newberry SF with permit
        michigan.gov/dnr

↔ boundary Newberry State Forest
but note forest only on one side in some areas
46.670381 -85.578314   ///declaring.gurgled.data
↔ boundary private land
        D
        0.4 mile
        D

↔ boundary private land
46.672634 -85.573164   ///thumbs.sequences.coconuts
↔ boundary Newberry State Forest

        p△ *dispersed camping* allowed
        0.9 mile in Newberry SF with permit
        michigan.gov/dnr

↔ boundary Newberry State Forest
46.671839 -85.557521   ///anyhow.bakers.long
↔ boundary private land
        D
        0.5 mile
        D

↔ boundary private land
46.66807 -85.5522   ///crops.engaged.named
↔ boundary Newberry State Forest

        p△ *dispersed camping* allowed
        8.8 miles in Newberry SF
        Note: the eastern half mile includes the bridge
        and road to the campground
        in the HSS Chapter section- no camping
        michigan.gov/dnr

Mouth of the Two Hearted River
46.698691 -85.422934   ///structured.sleep.gifts
Superior Shoreline Chapter
northcountrytrail.org/trail/michigan/ssc
↔ **Chapter boundary**

↔ **Chapter boundary**
Mouth of the Two Hearted River MI 420.9
46.698691   -85.422934   ///structured.sleep.gifts
Hiawatha Shore-to-Shore Chapter
northcountrytrail.org/trail/michigan/hss

chapter boundary

$▲ *Mouth of the Two Hearted River SF Campground*
46.698286   -85.421649   ///bungalows.fingernail.matches
public campground
36 vehicular sites
primitive, tables, fire rings, latrine, seasonal water
fee
Managed by Michigan DNR
www2.dnr.state.mi.us/parksandtrails
906-492-3415

p△ *dispersed camping* allowed
4.6 miles in Newberry SF with permit
michigan.gov/dnr

$▲ *Culhane Lake SF Campground*
46.695063   -85.359979   ///undetected.represented.harmlessly
public campground
15 vehicular sites
primitive, table, fire pit, latrine, seasonal water
fee
Managed by Michigan DNR
www2.dnr.state.mi.us/parksandtrails
906-492-3415

p△ *dispersed camping* allowed
9.0 miles in Newberry SF with permit
michigan.gov/dnr

↔ boundary Newberry State Forest
46.608573   -85.349722   // clutching.blamed.backpacks
↔ boundary private land

D
5.2 miles
$PCs

↔ boundary private land
46.601556   -85.323458   ///entitle.fathers.mismatched
↔ boundary Tahquamenon Falls State Park

Note: no dispersed camping in Tahquamenon Falls SP. Backcountry campsites must be reserved in advance, and this is also recommended for the large campgrounds.

$△ *Tahquamenon Wilderness Backcountry Campsite*
46.590056 -85.28008   ///underscore.microwaves.scared
public campsite
primitive, table, fire ring, latrine
fee
reservation required
Managed by Michigan DNR
midnrreservations.com
1-800-447-2757

        $PCs
        6.5 miles
        $PCg

$▲ *Tahquemenon Lower Falls Campground*
46.609101 -85.210385   ///hurried.emphasis.threadbare
public campground
188 vehicular sites
electric, tables, fire rings, bathhouse
fee
Managed by Michigan DNR
midnrreservations.com
1-800-447-2757

        $PCg
        5.5 miles
        +0.1 spur
        $PCs

$△ *Tahquamenon Old Stove Backcountry Campsite*
0.1 mile off trail
46.569404 -85.177512   ///iconic.shocks.screen
public campsite
primitive, table, fire ring, latrine
fee
reservation required
Managed by Michigan DNR
midnrreservations.com
1-800-447-2757

        $PCs
        +0.1 spur
        10 miles
        +0.3 road
        $PCg

$▲ *Tahquamenon River Mouth Campgrounds*
0.3 mile off trail
46.558782 -85.035977   ///putty.consecutive.motivations
public campgrounds
72 vehicular, electric sites in Rivermouth Modern CG
35 rustic sites in Pines Campground
tables, fire rings, bathhouse at Modern CG
fee
Managed by Michigan DNR
midnrreservations.com
800-447-2757

$PCg
4.5 miles
D

↔ boundary Tahquamenon State Park
46.526519 -85.068314   ///cigar.progressed.informer
↔ boundary private land

↔ boundary private land
46.505728 -85.070052   /// walked.enacts.confessed
↔ boundary Hiawatha National Forest

△ *dispersed camping* allowed
7.3 miles in Hiawatha NF
south side of road only between Bark Dock
and the parking area near
Naomikong Overlook
fs.usda.gov/hiawatha

∠ *Naomikong Pond Shelter*
46.467856 -84.956515   ///views.prying.wobbles
public land
open shelter, fire ring, no latrine
maintained by Hiawatha Shore-to-Shore Chapter
hss@northcountrytrail.org

△ *dispersed camping* allowed
11.8 miles in Hiawatha NF
fs.usda.gov/hiawatha

$▲ *Soldier Lake NF Campground*
0.3 mile off trail
46.350383 -84.866093   /// corporation.fish.boater
44 vehicular sites
primitive, tables, fire rings, latrine, seasonal water
fee
Maintained by Hiawatha NF
fs.usda.gov/hiawatha
906-428-5800

△ *dispersed camping* allowed
14.1 miles in Hiawatha NF
fs.usda.gov/hiawatha

△ *Dick Road Campsite*
0.2 mile off trail
46.231099 -84.895277   ///spends.studios.sprinkle
public land- unofficial
primitive, no amenities
hikercentral.com/campgrounds/116468.html

△ *dispersed camping* allowed
1.4 miles in Hiawatha NF
fs.usda.gov/hiawatha

△ *Pine River Campsite*
46.228129 -84.876345   ///sing.unanswered.mooring
public land- unofficial
primitive, fire ring
hikercentral.com/campgrounds/116536.html

△ *dispersed camping* allowed
33.1 miles in Hiawatha NF
fs.usda.gov/hiawatha

$▲ *Brevoort Lake NF Campground*
0.5 mile off trail
46.00759 -84.972301   ///primer.wiring.lakes
public campground
70 vehicular sites, most with hook-ups
some tent sites
tables, fire rings, restroom
fee
Maintained by Hiawatha NF
fs.usda.gov/hiawatha
906-643-7900

△ *dispersed camping* allowed
14.9 miles in Hiawatha NF
fs.usda.gov/hiawatha

△ *Castle Rock Road Campsites*
0.8 mile off trail
45.922312 -84.797911   ///repudiates.digressing.distressingly
public land
several vehicular sites
primitive, no amenities
freecampsites.net

△ *dispersed camping* allowed
1.7 miles in Hiawatha NF
fs.usda.gov/hiawatha

↔ boundary Hiawatha National Forest
45.891667 -84.769312   ///dean.green.kazoo
↔ boundary private land

D
3.4 miles
+various road
$L

✼ city of St. Ignace
45.868967 -84.727962   ///attracting.tailing.skater
services

$ ■ *Motels*
various off trail
several commercial lodging options
fee

$L
+various road
1.8 miles
+0.1 road
$PCg

↔ boundary private land
45.853332   -84.718583   ///lunching.able.warrant
↔ boundary Straits State Park

Note: camp only in designated areas in Straits SP

$▲ *Straits State Park Campground*
0.1 mile off trail
45.853257   -84.720364   ///spelling.pops.classifies
commercial campground
270 vehicular sites
251 electric, 19 non-electric
2 mini-cabins
tables, fire rings, bathhouse, latrine
fee
midnrreservations.com
800-447-2757

$PCg
+0.1 road
5.1 miles
chapter boundary

↔ boundary mixed ownership
45.850462   -84.719999   ///responders.rope.grew
↔ boundary Straits State Park
↔ boundary Mackinac Bridge Authority (state of Michigan)
mackinacbridge.org

Note: the Mackinac Bridge can be crossed on foot only on Labor Day of each year as part of the annual Bridge Walk. If you are on the north side of the bridge, and need transport, go to the Administration Building. If you are on the south side of the bridge, call 906-643-7600. Fee

south end Mackinac Bridge
45.786809   -84.731951   ///strictest.sleeveless.resembling
Hiawatha Shore-to-Shore Chapter
northcountrytrail.org/trail/michigan/hss
↔ **Chapter boundary**

Michigan - Lower Peninsula

See legend and general info for help in interpreting the listings. You must have a free permit, a separate page for each night, to disperse camp in Michigan State Forests.

↔ **Chapter boundary**
South end Mackinac Bridge
45.786809 -84.731951   ///strictest.sleeveless.resembling
Harbor Springs Chapter
northcountrytrail.org/trail/michigan/hbr

Note: the Mackinac Bridge can be crossed on foot only on Labor Day of each year as part of the annual Bridge Walk. If you are on the north side of the bridge, and need transport, go to the Administration Building. If you are on the south side of the bridge, call 906-643-7600. Fee

chapter boundary

✱ village of Mackinaw City
45.784235 -84.731915   ///comprehend.songbook.soups
services

$▲ *Commercial Campgrounds*

$ ■ *Motels*

various distances off trail
commercial campgrounds and lodging
fee

$PCg, $L
+ various road
1.6 miles
+0.2 road
$CCg

$▲ *Mackinaw City KOA*
+0.2 mile off trail
45.767623 -84.740627   ///detachable.steely.thumbnail
commercial campground
94 vehicular sites
11 cabins, some tent sites
tables, fire rings, bathhouse, laundry
koa.com
231-436-5643

$CCg
+0.2 road
0.5 mile
D

↔ boundary private land
45.759939 -84.744948   ///bathtubs.concur.manuals
↔ boundary Mackinac State Forest

p△ *dispersed camping* allowed
0.3 mile in Mackinaw SF
but may be swampy
michigan.gov/dnr

↔ internal boundary Mackinac State Forest
45.759511   -84.751834   ///snacking.ripple.pivots
↔ internal boundary Mackinac State Forest
French Farm Flooding State Wildlife Management Area

Note: camp only at designated sites in French Farm Flooding WMA

>D
>**1.5 miles**
>PCg

p▲ *French Farm Lake Campsites*
all near 45.758074 -84.76694   ///phrases.obstinate.merits
public campsites
8 vehicular sites
primitive, fire rings, no latrine
michigan.gov/dnr

>PCg
>**2.6 miles**
>D

↔ internal boundary Mackinac State Forest
French Farm Flooding State Wildlife Management Area
45.733127   -84.793419   ///doodle.twig.mats
↔ internal boundary Mackinac State Forest

>p△ *dispersed camping* allowed
>**3.4 miles** in Mackinaw SF
>michigan.gov/dnr

↔ boundary Mackinac State Forest
45.736842   -84.853114   ///dangle.radically.sobs
↔ boundary Wilderness State Park

Note: camp only in designated areas in Wilderness State Park

>D
>**0.7 mile**
>$PCs

$△ *Backcountry Campsite Wilderness SP*
45.742502   -84.863714   ///finance.mornings.rock
public campsite
primitive, fire ring, no latrine
www2.dnr.state.mi.us
231-436-5381

>$PCs
>**2.7 miles**
>$PCg

$▲ Wilderness State Park Pines Campground
0.1 mile off trail
45.744015   -84.900636   ///cubic.patient.printer
public campground
99 vehicular campsites
tables, fire rings, bathhouse
fee
midnrreservations.com
800-447-2757

OR

$▲ Wilderness State Park Lakeshore Campgrounds
0.5 mile off trail
45.749585   -84.890165   ///yours.welfare.solidly
public campground
over 300 vehicular campsites
tables, fire rings, bathhouse
fee
midnrreservations.com
800-447-2757

$PCg
14.0 miles
D

↔ boundary Wilderness State Park
45.653251   -84.996198   ///moping.getaway.berries
↔ boundary Mackinaw State Forest

p△ *dispersed camping* allowed
2.5 miles in Mackinaw SF with permit
michigan.gov/dnr

↔ boundary Mackinaw State Forest
45.636694   -84.975545   ///shreds.galloped.baths
↔ boundary private land

D
6.3 miles
D

↔ boundary private land
45.586861   -84.995887   ///frosted.temperature.unsettled
↔ boundary Mackinaw State Forest

p△ *dispersed camping* allowed
8.2 miles in Mackinaw SF with permit
michigan.gov/dnr

↔ boundary Mackinaw State Forest
45.508179   -84.925849   ///hiking.foreground.reminder
↔ boundary private land

                D
                1.0 mile
                D

↔ boundary private land
45.507667   -84.903769   ///heroism.overpaid.crabby
↔ boundary Mackinaw State Forest

              p△ *dispersed camping* allowed
              6.5 miles in Mackinaw SF with permit
              michigan.gov/dnr

↔ boundary Mackinaw State Forest
45.442727   -84.873833   ///wanted.widest.sprinkles
↔ boundary mixed ownership

              chapter boundary

Kipp Road
45.442727   -84.873833   ///wanted.widest.sprinkles
Harbor Springs Chapter   MI 559.4 - 608.5
northcountrytrail.org/trail/michigan/hbr
↔ **Chapter boundary**

↔ **Chapter boundary**
Kipp Road
45.442727   -84.873833   ///wanted.widest.sprinkles
Jordon Valley 45° Chapter
northcountrytrail.org/trail/michigan/j45

                        chapter boundary
                        D
                        4.9 miles
                        +0.8 road
                        $PCg

$▲ *Petoskey State Park Campground*

0.8 mile off trail to check in, actual campsites are closer
45.395796   -84.90499   ///largest.relatives.coordinated
public campground
176 vehicular sites with full hookups
2 mini-cabins that sleep 4
tables, fire rings, bathhouse
fee
www2.dnr.state.mi.us/parksandtrails
231-347-2311

                        $PCg
                        +0.8 road
                        3.2 miles
                        +various road
                        $L

✲ city of Petoskey
45.375541   -84.960265   ///bathrobe.scribble.trams

$ ■ *Motels*
various off trail
commercial lodging
fee

OR

$▲ *Magnus Park Campground*

0.8 mile off trail
45.373092   -84.974474   ///gloriously.cobras.tunnels
public campground
68 vehicular sites
tables, fire rings, bathhouse, laundry
managed by city of Petoskey
petoskey.us/services/parks___recreation/campground.php
231-347-2500

                        $L, $PCg
                        + various
                        9.2 miles
                        +0.1 spur
                        HE

⌂ *Skyline Shelter*
0.1 mile off trail
45.328705 -84.890399   ///broads.operate.gullible
hosted site
fully enclosed shelter with porch, 8 bunks
fire ring, latrine
call number posted on door on arrival
AirBnB units may also be available

      HE
      +0.1 spur
      2.5 miles
      D

↔ mixed ownership
45.313699 -84.858663   ///glimmer.barman.mile
↔ boundary Mackinaw State Forest

     p△ *dispersed camping* allowed
     2.4 miles in Mackinaw SF with permit
     michigan.gov/dnr

↔ boundary Mackinaw State Forest
45.301898 -84.823966   ///clinch.summer.emotionally
↔ boundary private land
      D
      1.1 mile
      D

↔ boundary private land   MI 631.8
45.30389 -84.807915   ///worldwide.soundtrack.haggling
↔ boundary Mackinaw State Forest

     p△ *dispersed camping* allowed
     12..7 miles in Mackinaw SF with permit
     michigan.gov/dnr

↔ boundary Mackinaw State Forest
45.18493 -84.813838   ///equality.pinpoints.talent
↔ boundary private land
      D
      5.1 miles
      D

↔ boundary private land
45.153433 -84.856624   ///refine.sailors.closet
↔ boundary Mackinaw State Forest

     p△ *dispersed camping* allowed
     3.4 miles in Mackinaw SF with permit
     michigan.gov/dnr

↔ boundary Mackinaw State Forest
45.116378 -84.878168   ///combination.prom.spine
↔ boundary private land

                    D
                    2.2 miles
                    D

↔ boundary private land
45.092812 -84.883403   ///reaffirmed.pull.hiker
↔ boundary Mackinaw State Forest

                    p△ *dispersed camping* allowed
                    3.8 miles in Mackinaw SF with permit
                    michigan.gov/dnr

↔ internal boundary Mackinaw State Forest at M-32
Jordan Valley Pathway
45.085201 -84.926332   ///assets.doorframe.warning

Note: dispersed camping prohibited between M-32 and southern SF boundary. Only camping is at Pinney Bridge

                    D
                    12.1 miles
                    $PCg

$▲ *Pinney Bridge SF Campground*
45.017233 -85.028071   ///film.surges.invoked
public campsite
15 primitive sites
primitive, table, fire ring, latrine, seasonal water
fee
www2.dnr.state.mi.us/parksandtrails
231-582-7523

                    $PCg
                    8.0 miles
                    D

↔ boundary Mackinaw State Forest/ Jordan Valley Pathway MI 675.3
44.989407 -84.989833   ///sweeter.quitter.constructs
↔ boundary private land

↔ boundary private land   MI 679.1
44.943522 -84.976887   ///prominently.butlers.humble
↔ boundary Mackinaw State Forest

                    p△ *dispersed camping* allowed
                    8.4 miles in Mackinaw SF
                    michigan.gov/dnr

↔ boundary Mackinaw State Forest
44.858605 -84.928264   ///heights.detective.abandoning
↔ boundary Pere Marquette State Forest

p△ *dispersed camping* allowed
0.5 mile in Pere Marquette SF
michigan.gov/dnr
chapter boundary

Starvation Lake Road
44.851473 -84.932373   ///kettles.volley.noses
Jordan Valley 45° Chapter
northcountrytrail.org/trail/michigan/j45
↔ **Chapter boundary**

↔ **Chapter boundary**
Starvation Lake Road MI 688
44.851473   -84.932373   ///kettles.volley.noses
Grand Traverse Chapter
northcountrytrail.org/trail/michigan/gtc

                              p△ *dispersed camping* allowed
                              6.8 miles in Pere Marquette SF
                              michigan.gov/dnr

$▲ *Pickerel Lake SF Campground*
44.796194   -84.973625   ///appropriate.retailers.advertises
public campground
39 vehicular sites
primitive, fire rings, latrine, seasonal water
fee
managed by Michigan DNR
www2.dnr.state.mi.us/parksandtrails
989-348-7068

↔ boundary Pere Marquette State Forest
44.793468   -84.975428   ///letter.consumption.quite
↔ boundary private land

                              $PCg
                              1.5 miles
                              D

↔ boundary private land
 44.798249   -84.989847   ///conflicted.spin.superstars
↔ boundary Pere Marquette State Forest

                              p△ *dispersed camping* allowed
                              1/4 mile from road
                              0.7 mile in Pere Marquette SF
                              michigan.gov/dnr

↔ boundary Pere Marquette State Forest
44.809485   -84.999933   ///podcast.removals.rallies
↔ boundary private land

                              D
                              5.2 miles
                              D

↔ boundary private land
44.811555   -85.091943   ///matchbox.confessing.urgent
↔ boundary Pere Marquete State Forest

                              p△ *dispersed camping* allowed
                              1/4 mile from road
                              note- SF not always on both sides of road
                              6.3 mile in Pere Marquette SF
                              michigan.gov/dnr

↔ boundary Pere Marquete State Forest
44.757032 -85.143785   ///unlock.severe.huts
↔ boundary mixed ownership

                D
                0.8 mile
                $PCg

$▲ *Log Lake County Campground*

44.749402 -85.150126   ///refresher.surpasses.rowers
public campground
40 vehicular sites
tables, fire rings, restroom, $ shower, seasonal water fee
managed by Kalkaska County
kalkaskacounty.net
231-258-2940

                $PCg
                0.1 mile
                D

↔ boundary mixed ownership
44.749826 -85.153848   ///insurer.kennel.sweeping
↔ boundary Pere Marquette SF

                p△ *dispersed camping* allowed
                1/4 mile from road
                0.6 mile in Pere Marquette SF
                michigan.gov/dnr

↔ boundary Pere Marquette SF
44.746412 -85.163761   ///wakes.converting.synthetic
↔ boundary private land

                D
                1.5 miles
                +various road
                $L

✻ village of Kalkaska
44.737202 -85.17432   ///tarnished.thumbs.wolf
services

$ ■ *Motels*

various on and off trail
commercial lodging
fee

Note: a mile of trail on the south side of Kalkaska is scheduled to come off road soon

                $L
                +various road
                2.4 miles
                D

↔ boundary private land
44.720941 -85.211784   ///undertaken.immaterial.briefs
↔ boundary Pere Marquette SF

          p△ *dispersed camping* allowed
          3.6 miles in Pere Marquette SF
          michigan.gov/dnr

↔ boundary Pere Marquette SF
44.703293 -85.262788   ///shadowing.configured.regain
↔ edge Pere Marquette

          p△ *dispersed camping* allowed
          on north side of trail only
          2.0 mile in Pere Marquette SF
          michigan.gov/dnr

↔ edge Pere Marquette
44.703141 -85.293301   ///multiplied.twinge.berries
↔ boundary Pere Marquette

          p△ *dispersed camping* allowed
          3.2 miles in Pere Marquette SF
          michigan.gov/dnr

$▲ *Guernsey Lake SF Campground*
44.712992 -85.323385   ///surging.apartment.renovating
public campground
27 vehicular sites, 8 walk-in sites
primitive, tables, fire rings, latrine
fee
managed by Michigan DNR
www2.dnr.state.mi.us/parksandtrails
231-922-5270

          p△ *dispersed camping* allowed
          5.5 miles in Pere Marquette SF
          michigan.gov/dnr

↔ boundary Pere Marquette SF
44.688818 -85.368384   ///ripe.resolutely.feared
↔ boundary private land
          D
          0.1 mile
          D

↔ boundary private land
44.688284 -85.368899   ///laces.informers.prices
↔ boundary Pere Marquette SF

          p△ *dispersed camping* allowed
          7.1 miles in Pere Marquette SF
          michigan.gov/dnr

$▲ Scheck's Place SF Campground
44.652378   -85.454579   ///stormed.worldly.merits
public campground
30 vehicular sites
primitive, tables, fire rings, latrine
fee
managed by Michigan DNR
www2.dnr.state.mi.us/parksandtrails
231-922-5270

        p△ *dispersed camping* allowed
        7.4 miles in Pere Marquette SF
        michigan.gov/dnr

↔ boundary Pere Marquette SF
44.598698   -85.393747   ///rationed.westerner.landing
↔ boundary private land

    D
    1.5 miles
    D

↔ boundary private land
44.577273   -85.393647   ///telling.velocities.breeding
↔ boundary Pere Marquette SF

        p△ *dispersed camping* allowed
        4.3 miles in Pere Marquette SF
        michigan.gov/dnr

$▲ Spring Lake SF Campground
44.563763   -85.362801   ///installs.lungs.frosts
public campground
32 vehicular sites
primitive, tables, fire rings, latrine, seasonal water
fee
managed by Michigan DNR
www2.dnr.state.mi.us/parksandtrails
231-922-5270

        p△ *dispersed camping* allowed
        note small private sections
        8.4 miles in Pere Marquette SF
        michigan.gov/dnr

$▲ Old US 131 SF Campground
44.49188   -85.42144   ///temptation.hubcaps.matter
public campground
20 vehicular sites, 5 walk-in sites
primitive, tables, fire rings, latrine
fee
managed by Michigan DNR
www2.dnr.state.mi.us/parksandtrails
231-775-7911

p△ *dispersed camping* allowed
6.7 miles in Pere Marquette SF
michigan.gov/dnr

↔ boundary Pere Marquette SF
44.502483 -85.497083   ///defectors.cheater.cartons
↔ edge Pere Marquette SF

p△ *dispersed camping* allowed
1/4 mile from road, east side only
0.7 mile in Pere Marquette SF
michigan.gov/dnr

↔ edge Pere Marquette SF
44.512215 -85.49674   ///involve.veggies.sharpening
↔ boundary private land

D
2.6 miles
D or
+0.5 road
$PCg

$▲ *Baxter Bridge SF Campground*
0.5 mile off trail
44.491738 -85.524386   ///saddens.tweaked.females
public campground
25 vehicular sites
primitive, tables, fire rings, latrine, seasonal water
fee
managed by Michigan DNR
www2.dnr.state.mi.us/parksandtrails
231-775-7911

↔ boundary private land
44.49682 -85.527262   ///chap.dragging.tending
↔ boundary Pere Marquette SF

p△ *dispersed camping* allowed
11.2 miles in Pere Marquette SF
michigan.gov/dnr

↔ boundary Pere Marquette SF
44.453643 -85.650515   ///lyrics.skateboard.easy
↔ boundary private land

D
0.5 mile
D

↔ boundary private land
44.447332 -85.648068   ///sugary.heartless.rescuer
↔ boundary Pere Marquette SF

                    p△ *dispersed camping* allowed
                    1.5 miles in Pere Marquette SF
                    michigan.gov/dnr

↔ boundary Pere Marquette SF
44.442521   -85.650021   ///miraculous.graciously.baths
↔ boundary private land
                              D
                              0.3 mile
                              D
↔ boundary private land
44.442544   -85.655589   ///acre.paintbrush.engravings
↔ boundary Pere Marquette SF

                    p△ *dispersed camping* allowed
                    2.4 miles in Pere Marquette SF
                    michigan.gov/dnr

↔ boundary Pere Marquette SF
44.439192   -85.688365   ///slipping.covered.syndicate
↔ boundary private land
                              D
                              5.8 miles
                              +0.9 road
                              $L

✷ village of Sherman
44.423281   -85.698772
///bandit.different.springing
no services

✷ village of Mesick
1.0 mile off trail
44.405635   -85.713502   ///tragedy.certainty.overseeing
services

$ ■ *Mushroom Cap Motel*
0.9 mile off trail
44.405941   -85.71789   ///related.enhances.logic
commercial lodging
16 rooms
fee
mcmotel.wordpress.com
231-885-1222
                              D
                              +0.9 road
                              5.8 miles
                              $CCg

$▲ *Fletcher Creek Campground*
44.402658 -85.74878   ///quaking.snowflakes.details
commercial campground
30 vehicular sites
tables, fire rings, latrine
fee
231- 885-1199

     $CCg
     0.5 mile
     HCs

△ *Backpacker Campsite*
44.396373 -85.749982   ///astronauts.environment.mealtime
hosted site
primitive, table
Consumers Energy
maintained by Grand Traverse Chapter
gtc@northcountrytrail.org

     HCs
     2.1 miles
     $CCg

$▲ *Northern Exposure Campground*
44.382511 -85.783885   ///parent.reinstated.nods
commercial campground
260 vehicular sites, full hook-ups
7 cabins
tables, fire rings, bathhouse, (hikers can shower free)
fee
northernexposureinc.com
231- 885-1199

     $CCg
     2.7 miles
     D

    chapter boundary

Hodenpyl Dam at Blueberry Lane
44.372726 -85.825191   ///sliding.honeybees.originates
Grand Traverse Chapter
northcountrytrail.org/michigan/gtc
↔ **Chapter boundary**

↔ **Chapter boundary**
Hodenpyl Dam at Blueberry Lane
44.372726 -85.825191   ///sliding.honeybees.originates
Spirit of the Woods Chapter
northcountrytrail.org/trail/michigan/spw

chapter boundary
↔ boundary Manistee National Forest

Note: dispersed camping is allowed in Manistee NF.

△ *dispersed camping* allowed
11.4 miles in Manistee NF
fs.usda.gov/hmnf

$△ *Red Bridge NF Campground*
1.1 miles off trail
44.283698 -85.86212   ///thumbnail.scattering.misled
public campground
4 vehicular sites
primitive, tables, fire rings, latrine, seasonal water
fee, advance reservation required
maintained by Manistee NF
recreation.gov
800-877-6777

△ *Government Landing NF Campsites*
0.3 and 0.8 mile off trail
44.268086 -85.884902   ///highly.submerge.pressuring
and 44.263092   -85.887134
///unwinding.gather.lodge
public campsites
3 vehicular sites
primitive, table fire ring, latrine
reservation required Memorial Day Friday through Labor Day
maintained by Manistee NF
fs.usda.gov/hmnf
877-444-6777

△ *dispersed camping* allowed
2.4 miles in Manistee NF
fs.usda.gov/hmnf

↔ boundary Manistee NF
44.27562 -85.92607   ///payout.cavity.draining
↔ boundary Little River Band Ottawa Indians

Note: no camping on tribal land.

D
0.5 mile
D

↔ boundary Little River Band Ottawa Indians
44.277863 -85.934868   ///bunny.revert.introduces
↔ boundary Manistee NF

△ *dispersed camping* allowed
1.3 miles in Manistee NF
fs.usda.gov/hmnf

$▲ *Sawdust Hole NF Campground*
0.4 mile off trail
44.26852   -85.951897   ///recruit.publisher.excavate
public campground
8 vehicular sites
primitive, tables, fire rings, latrine
fee
maintained by Manistee NF
fs.usda.gov/hmnf
231-577-8902

△ *dispersed camping* allowed
5.2 miles in Manistee NF
fs.usda.gov/hmnf

↔ boundary Manistee NF
44.268074   -86.01406   ///whistle.dedication.statues
↔ internal boundary river corridor

D
0.2 mile
D

↔ internal boundary river corridor
44.266123   -86.015026   ///itself.sponsoring.rational
↔ boundary Manistee NF

△ *dispersed camping* allowed
0.5 miles in Manistee NF
fs.usda.gov/hmnf

↔ boundary Manistee NF
44.263143   -86.019733   ///ingredients.dupe.purest
↔ boundary Little River Band Ottawa Indians

Note: no camping on tribal land.

D
0.1 mile
D

↔ boundary Little River Band Ottawa Indians 816.9
44.262267   -86.021643   ///summit.looking.incursion
↔ boundary Manistee NF

△ *dispersed camping* allowed
0.8 mile in Manistee NF
fs.usda.gov/hmnf

$▲ Blacksmith Bayou NF Campground
0.4 mile off trail
44.261881 -86.03633   ///broth.works.inclusive
public campground
6 vehicular sites
primitive, tables, fire rings, latrine
maintained by Manistee NF
fee
fs.usda.gov/hmnf
231-577-8902

△ **dispersed camping** allowed
0.3 mile in Manistee NF
fs.usda.gov/hmnf

↔ boundary Manistee NF
44.254658 -86.035174   ///points.knees.partial
↔ boundary private land

D
1.9 miles
HCs

△ Pine Knolls
44.240273 -86.050911   ///petal.decode.movement
hosted site
for NCT hikers only
primitive, table, fire ring, latrine
maintained by owner

HCs
0.9 miles
D

↔ boundary private land
44.240242 -86.060181   ///toured.prospered.disposable
↔ boundary Manistee NF

△ **dispersed camping** allowed
1.4 miles in Manistee NF
fs.usda.gov/hmnf

↔ boundary Manistee NF
44.230272 -86.077527   ///slap.exclude.factored
↔ boundary private land

D
0.2 mile
D

↔ boundary private land
44.226397 -86.077248   ///coolest.nutritious.indexes
↔ boundary Manistee NF

△ **dispersed camping** allowed
5.8 miles in Manistee NF
fs.usda.gov/hmnf

↔ boundary Manistee NF
44.17648 -86.102804   ///copying.durable.repeats
↔ boundary private land

             D
             1.0 mile
             D

↔ boundary private land
44.164321 -86.097654   ///bidder.dusters.unanswered
↔ boundary Manistee NF
             △ *dispersed camping* allowed
             1.9 miles in Manistee NF
             fs.usda.gov/hmnf
↔ boundary Manistee NF
44.145616 -86.082805   ///takeovers.conductor.parcels
↔ boundary private land
             D
             0.3 mile
             D
↔ boundary private land
44.142074 -86.082183   ///haggis.recall.hikers
↔ boundary Manistee NF
             △ *dispersed camping* allowed
             8.9 miles in Manistee NF
             fs.usda.gov/hmnf

                    $▲ *Bear Track NF Campground*
                              1.1 miles off trail
             44.146201 -86.031028   ///packet.applied.shrink
                              20 vehicular sites
                    table, fire ring, latrine, seasonal water
                              fee
                    maintained by Manistee NF
                              fs.usda.gov/hmnf
                              231-775-2421

↔ boundary Manistee NF
44.066385 -86.006957   ///wriggling.makeovers.weightless
↔ boundary private land
             D
             2.7 miles
             D

↔ boundary private land
44.061821 -85.95945   ///besides.rail.armrests
↔ boundary Manistee NF
             △ *dispersed camping* allowed
             4.5 miles in Manistee NF
             fs.usda.gov/hmnf

△ *McCarthy Lake*
0.2 mile off trail
44.021717 -85.950695   ///remotes.transcript.jabs
public land- unofficial
primitive, no amenities
vehicle access

             △ *dispersed camping* allowed
             8.2 miles in Manistee NF
             fs.usda.gov/hmnf

$▲ *Timber Creek NF Campground*
0.15 mile off trail
43.94767   -85.996443   ///others.liberal.returns
public campground
9 vehicular sites
primitive, tables, fire rings, latrine, seasonal water
fee
maintained by Manistee NF
fs.usda.gov/hmnf
231-745-4631

△ *dispersed camping* allowed
1.9 miles in Manistee NF
fs.usda.gov/hmnf

↔ boundary Manistee NF
43.931663   -86.004468   ///napkins.implication.steaming
↔ boundary private land

D
1.2 miles
D

↔ boundary private land
43.927954   -86.01996   ///imitations.gives.ornaments
↔ boundary Manistee NF

no camping- too close to road and river
0.3 mile in Manistee NF
fs.usda.gov/hmnf

▲ *Sulak NF Campground*
0.25 mile off trail
43.924415   -86.013072   ///produce.approve.scrum
public campground
12 vehicular sites
primitive, table, fire ring, latrine
maintained by Manistee NF
fs.usda.gov/hmnf
231-745-4631

△ *dispersed camping* allowed
1.3 miles in Manistee NF
fs.usda.gov/hmnf

↔ boundary Manistee NF
43.916718   -85.998932   ///drumbeat.property.stuffed
↔ boundary private land

D
0.6 mile
D

↔ boundary private land
43.916501   -85.98831   ///salutes.concert.forgetting
↔ boundary Manistee NF

△ *dispersed camping* allowed
2.7 miles in Manistee NF
fs.usda.gov/hmnf

△ **Bowman Lake Campsites**
0.1 mile off trail
43.89362 -85.968269   ///punters.coiled.vows
public campsites
4 walk-in sites
tent pads, tables, fire rings
maintained by Spirit of the Woods Chapter
spw@northcountrytrail.org

△ *dispersed camping* allowed
1.8 miles in Manistee NF
fs.usda.gov/hmnf

$▲ **Bowman Bridge Campground**
0.5 mile off trail
43.888409 -85.943313   ///reacts.toasted.ruthlessly
public campground
16 vehicular sites, 4 walk-in sites
primitive, tables, fire rings, latrine, seasonal water
fee
maintained by Manistee NF
recreation.gov
877-444-6777

△ *dispersed camping* allowed
3.0 miles in Manistee NF
fs.usda.gov/hmnf

↔ boundary Manistee NF
43.861464 -85.91883   ///embedding.people.embellish
↔ boundary private hunt club

Note: trail is fenced. Stay on narrow ROW

D
0.3 mile
D

↔ boundary private hunt club
43.857998 -85.918659   ///surrounding.popping.stole
↔ boundary Manistee NF

△ *dispersed camping* allowed
5.3 miles in Manistee NF
fs.usda.gov/hmnf
chapter boundary

96th Street
43.818779 -85.911148   ///plugs.trembles.circuit
Spirit of the Woods Chapter
northcountrytrail.org/michigan/spw
↔ **Chapter boundary**

↔ **Chapter boundary**
96th Street
43.818779 -85.911148 ///plugs.trembles.circuit
Western Michigan Chapter
northcountrytrail.org/trail/michigan/wmi

                            chapter boundary
                    △ *dispersed camping* allowed
                    5.1 miles in Manistee NF
                    fs.usda.gov/hmnf

$▲ *Highbank Lake NF Campground*
0.5 mile off trail
43.772004 -85.887631 ///capers.warranties.retained
public campground
9 vehicular sites
primitive, tables, fire rings, latrine, seasonal water
fee
managed by Manistee NF
fs.usda.gov/hmnf
231-745-4631

                    △ *dispersed camping* allowed
                    0.6 mile in Manistee NF
                    fs.usda.gov/hmnf

△ *Sawkaw Lake Campsite*
0.15 mile off trail
43.762396 -85.900119 ///decays.enjoyed.leaned
public campsite
1 or 2 vehicular sites
primitive, latrine
managed by Manistee NF
fs.usda.gov/hmnf
231-745-4631

                    △ *dispersed camping* allowed
                    0.2 mile in Manistee NF
                    fs.usda.gov/hmnf

△ *Condon Lake Campsite*
0.2 mile bushwhack
43.758615 -85.899347 ///stag.alleges.entered
public campsite
1 or 2 vehicular sites
primitive, latrine
managed by Manistee NF
fs.usda.gov/hmnf
231-745-4631

                    △ *dispersed camping* allowed
                    3.4 miles in Manistee NF
                    fs.usda.gov/hmnf

$▲ Walkup Lake NF Campground
0.2 mile off trail
43.733456   -85.905999   ///clutching.coincidence.outsmart
public campground
12 vehicular sites
primitive, tables, fire rings, latrine, seasonal water
fee
managed by Manistee NF
fs.usda.gov/hmnf
231-745-4631

△ *dispersed camping* allowed
1.6 miles in Manistee NF
fs.usda.gov/hmnf

$▲ Nichols Lake NF Campground
0.3 mile off trail
43.72285   -85.903981   ///booked.niece.wordy
public campground
29 vehicular sites
primitive, tables, fire rings, bathhouse
fee
managed by Manistee NF
recreation.gov
877-444-6777

△ *dispersed camping* allowed
31.9 miles in Manistee NF
fs.usda.gov/hmnf

$▲ White Cloud Campground
1.8 miles off trail
43.549321   -85.78502   ///gems.shortly.states
public campground
86 vehicular campsites
electric, tables, fire rings, bathhouse
fee
Managed by Newaygo County
newaygocountymi.gov
231- 689-2021

$■ Trailside Motel
0.3 mile off trail
43.48189   -85.773582   ///discarding.incensed.laser
commercial lodging
rooms and other services
fee
trailsideetc.com
231-679-2188

△ *dispersed camping* allowed
0.7 mile in Manistee NF
fs.usda.gov/hmnf

$▲ *Twinwood Lake NF Campground*
0.2 mile off trail
43.476263 -85.768243   ///songwriter.desire.pies
public campground
5 vehicular sites
primitive, tables, fire rings, latrine
fee
Managed by Manistee NF
fs.usda.gov/hmnf
231-745-4631

↔ boundary Manistee NF
43.476263 -85.768243   ///songwriter.desire.pies
↔ boundary private land
$PCg
+0.2 road
1.9 miles
D
↔ boundary private land
43.451001 -85.76217   ///seriously.hope.casting
↔ boundary Manistee NF

△ *dispersed camping* allowed
4.2 miles in Manistee NF
fs.usda.gov/hmnf

↔ boundary Manistee NF
43.464256 -85.70799   ///skirt.between.vinegar
↔ boundary private land
D
0.1 mile
D
↔ boundary private land
43.462403 -85.707582   ///hires.guitars.technically
↔ boundary Manistee NF

△ *dispersed camping* allowed
1.2 miles in Manistee NF
fs.usda.gov/hmnf

↔ boundary Manistee NF
43.453525 -85.687991   ///guide.gliders.pasted
↔ boundary private land
D
0.6 mile
D
↔ boundary private land
43.446047 -85.687905   ///duck.deters.moves
↔ boundary Manistee NF

△ *dispersed camping* allowed
1.1 miles in Manistee NF
fs.usda.gov/hmnf

↔ boundary Manistee NF
43.436886 -85.677563   ///guidebooks.feudal.configured
↔ boundary mixed ownership

        D
        1.0 mile
        +0.1 road
        $CCg

$▲ *Croton Dam Float Trips Campground*
0.1 mile off trail
43.436769 -85.667928   ///eaters.thousands.method
commercial campground
cabins, electric sites, tent sites
tables, fire pits, latrine, seasonal water
fee
crotondamfloattrips.com
231-652-6037

        $CCg
        +0.1 road
        5.8 miles
        D

↔ boundary mixed ownership
43.398981 -85.672241   ///octane.answers.presenter
↔ edge Manistee NF

        △ *dispersed camping* allowed
        1/4 mile from road
        west side only
        0.2 miles in Manistee NF
        fs.usda.gov/hmnf

↔ edge Manistee NF
43.395364 -85.672198   ///shave.appointed.distortion
↔ boundary private land

        D
        9.8 miles
        D

↔ boundary private land
43.293565 -85.701831   ///scarf.chimps.refrain
↔ boundary Rogue River State Game Area
managed by Michigan DNR

Note: dispersed camping is allowed in MI state wildlife and game areas only between Sep 11 and May 14 with permit, and at least one mile away from designated campgrounds/ campsites. See Appendix

        p△ seasonal *dispersed camping* allowed
        7.6 miles in Rogue River SGA
        michigan.gov/dnr

↔ boundary Rogue River SGA
43.237752 -85.650762   ///develop.fingernail.insisting
↔ boundary private land

        pD seasonal
        6.0 miles
        $L

$ ■ *Holiday Inn Express*

43.223207 -85.570274 ///jots.tattoo.dreamy
commercial lodging
rooms, suites
fee
hiexpress.com
616-696-0450

$L
5.1 miles
+0.25 spur
$CCg

↔ boundary private land
43.223619 -85.556177 ///binder.hard.inhabited
↔ boundary White Pine Trail
Managed by the Michigan DNR

✲ city of Cedar Springs
0.2 mile off trail
43.223625 -85.55113 ///quickly.extremes.redefining
services

$▲ *Detach Primitive Campground*

0.25 mile off trail
43.16674 -85.57227 ///blindly.saturation.defeated
commercial campground
10 unique campsites (yurts, cabins, teepees, hobbit hole)
tables, fire pits, latrine, seasonal water
fee
godetach.com
616- 500-3885

$CCg
+0.25 spur
3.9 miles
$L

↔ boundary White Pine Trail
43.119745 -85.561214 ///tulips.overdue.ditched
↔ boundary mixed ownership

✲ city of Rockford
43.119709 -85.558191 ///shocked.ruthlessly.donation
services

$ □ *Grandma 's House AirBnB*

43.116612 -85.555479 ///speculates.cakes.pipes
commercial lodging
4 rooms, shared baths
fee
grandmashousebb.com
616- 866-4111

$L
10.4 miles
pDseasonal

↔ boundary mixed ownership
43.043068 -85.472954   ///slice.seducing.scriptures
↔ edge Cannonsburg State Game Area
Managed by Michigan DNR

Note: dispersed camping is allowed in MI State Wildlife and Game Areas only between Sep 11 and May 14 with permit, and at least one mile away from designated campgrounds/ campsites. See Appendix

p△ seasonal *dispersed camping* allowed
1/4 mile from road
north side of road only
0.9 miles in Canonsburg SGA with permit
michigan.gov/dnr

↔ edge Cannonsburg State Game Area
43.042895 -85.489842   ///palms.spotlights.successor
↔ boundary private land

pD seasonal
0.2 mile
pD seasonal

↔ boundary private land
43.039319 -85.490335   ///listeners.camping.gradually
↔ boundary Cannonsburg State Game Area

p△ seasonal *dispersed camping* allowed
watch for private inholdings
1/4 mile from road
1.6 miles in Canonsburg SGA with permit
michigan.gov/dnr

↔ boundary Cannonsburg State Game Area
43.028351 -85.505271   ///netting.overlaps.exposing
↔ boundary mixed ownership

pD seasonal
19.1 miles
pD seasonal

↔ boundary mixed ownership MI 998.3
42.976708 -85.313501   ///groans.proclaims.motivations
↔ boundary Saranac-Lowell State Game Area
Managed by Michigan DNR

Note: dispersed camping is allowed in MI state wildlife and game areas only between Sep 11 and May 14 with permit, and at least one mile away from designated campgrounds/ campsites. See Appendix

p△ seasonal *dispersed camping* allowed
3.0 miles in Saranac-Lowell SGA w/ permit
michigan.gov/dnr

↔ boundary Saranac-Lowell State Game Area
42.947815   -85.322127   ///magnificent.essence.hugs
↔ boundary mixed ownership

pD seasonal
2.6 miles
+0.15 road or +0.5 road
$L or HCs

✻ city of Lowell
42.934541   -85.337803   ///chairs.paints.will
services
NCTA Headquarters

$ ■ *Main Street Inn*
0.15 mile off trail
42.934149   -85.340348   ///skinny.hats.judges
commercial lodging
7 rooms
fee
mainstreetinnlowell.com
616-897-1171

△ *Kent County Fairgrounds*
0.5 mile off trail
42.929643   -85.339627   ///crisp.inner.drag
camping for NCT hikers with permission
lowellmi.gov
616-897-8457

$L or HCs
+0.15 road or +0.5 road
11.0 miles
but see hostel option off trail
+1 road
$CCg

⌂ *Bin Walkin' Hostel*
2.25 miles off trail
42.843733   -85.3889   ///desirability.capers.floral
private hostel, enclosed shelter
2 bunks, mini-kitchen, latrine, solar shower
owner will provide rides
kevinhough8@gmail.com

$▲ *Tyler Creek Campground*
1.0 mile off trail
42.804723   -85.33529   ///gift.displaying.battled
commercial campground
200 vehicular sites. 2 cabins
159 electric/water, 41 rustic
tables, fire rings, bathhouse
fee
tylercreekgolfandcamp.com
616-868-6751

$CCg
+1.0 road
2.5 miles
chapter boundary

Kent/Barry County line
42.769571   -85.358852   ///fall.rezoning.filmmakers
Western Michigan Chapter
northcountrytrail.org/trail/michigan/wmi
↔ **Chapter boundary**

↔ **Chapter boundary**
Kent/Barry County line
42.769571 -85.358852   ///fall.rezoning.filmmakers
Chief Noonday Chapter
northcountrytrail.org/trail/michigan/cnd

        chapter boundary
        1.5 miles
        pD seasonal

↔ boundary private land
42.769288 -85.388378   ///refuse.shrink.committed
↔ boundary Middleville State Game Area

Note: dispersed camping is allowed in MI State Sildlife and Game Areas only between Sep 11 and May 14 with permit, and at least one mile away from designated campgrounds/ campsites. See Appendix

        p△ seasonal *dispersed camping* allowed
        1/4 mile from road
        0.7 miles in Middleville SGA with permit
        michigan.gov/dnr

↔ boundary Middleville State Game Area   MI 1019.6
42.758134 -85.388249   ///telescopes.sandals.outlines
↔ boundary mixed ownership

        pD seasonal
        2.6 miles
        pD seasonal

↔ boundary mixed ownership MI 1022.2
42.736531 -85.407518   ///crowds.unwanted.chests
↔ boundary Middleville State Game Area

        p△ seasonal *dispersed camping* allowed
        1/4 mile from roads
        2.9 miles in Middleville SGA with permit
        michigan.gov/dnr

↔ boundary Middleville State Game Area
42.725466 -85.446721   ///circulars.fright.fantastic
↔ boundary private land

        pD seasonal
        7.7 miles
        pD seasonal

✲ village of Middleville
42.711296 -85.46512   ///piled.ladders.soaked
limited services

↔ boundary private land
42.667518 -85.427213   ///chills.mouthpiece.notion
↔ boundary Barry State Game Area

Note: dispersed camping is allowed in MI state wildlife and game areas only between Sep 11 and May 14 with permit, and at least one mile away from designated campgrounds/ campsites. See Appendix

                                  p△ seasonal *dispersed camping* allowed
                                  5.2 miles in Barry SGA with permit
                                  michigan.gov/dnr

↔ boundary Barry State Game Area
42.633066 -85.471223   ///holding.touches.ingredients
↔ boundary Yankee Springs State Recreation Area

Note: no dispersed camping allowed in Yankee Springs Recreation Area at any time.

                                  pD seasonal
                                  4.8 miles
                                  pD seasonal

↔ boundary Yankee Springs State Recreation Area
42.604485 -85.463197   ///spouse.innovations.eyeful
↔ boundary Barry State Game Area

Note: dispersed camping is allowed in MI state wildlife and game areas only between Sep 11 and May 14 with permit, and at least one mile away from designated campgrounds/ campsites. See Appendix

                                  p△ seasonal *dispersed camping* allowed
                                  2.2 miles in Barry SGA with permit
                                  michigan.gov/dnr

↔ boundary Barry State Game Area
42.581201 -85.456202   ///gobblers.speculative.inches
↔ boundary private land

                                  pD seasonal
                                  0.2 mile
                                  HCs

△ *Circle Pines Campsite*

42.578897 -85.45637   ///broadcasts.glorious.parades
hosted site
primitive, no amenities
circlepinescenter.org
269-623-5555

                                  HCs
                                  3.8 miles
                                  pD seasonal

↔ boundary private land
42.555698 -85.507139   ///prodigy.quoted.piper
↔ boundary Barry State Game Area

                                  p△ seasonal *dispersed camping* allowed
                                  1/4 mile from road
                                  0.3 mile in Barry SGA with permit
                                  michigan.gov/dnr

↔ boundary Barry State Game Area
42.551984 -85.507997   ///blackouts.parents.shutting
↔ boundary private land

    pD seasonal
    0.5 mile
    pD seasonal

↔ boundary private land
42.544838 -85.50834   ///folding.depths.echo
↔ boundary Barry State Game Area

    p△ seasonal *dispersed camping* allowed
    1/4 mile from road
    0.3 miles in Barry SGA with permit
    michigan.gov/dnr

↔ boundary Barry State Game Area
42.541107 -85.504049   ///signatures.attention.infects
↔ boundary mixed ownership

    pD seasonal
    34.7 miles
    +various road
    $L

    $▲ *Fort Custer Recreation Area*
    1.6 miles off trail
    42.319266 -85.349146   ///reddish.sometime.unusual
    219 vehicular sites, some electric
    3 cabins
    tables, fire rings, bathhouse, latrines
    fee
    managed by Michigan DNR
    midnrreservations.com
    800-447-2757

✱ city of Battle Creek
various off trail near McCamily St.
42.321799 -85.182575   ///stir.rice.brains
services

$ ■ $ ▢ *Motels, AirBnBs*
fee

    $L
    +various road
    7.0 miles
    $L

$ ■ *Kimball Pines Motel*
42.31085 -85.127471   ///majority.pitied.swallowing
commercial lodging
13 rooms
fee
269-968-6339

    $L
    +various
    3.7 miles
    $PCg

$ ■ *Quality Inn*
0.5 mile off trail
42.297204 -85.080823   ///winced.guarded.swigs
commercial lodging
fee
rooms, laundry
choicehotels.com
269-789-7890

$L
+0.5 road
9.5 miles
$PCg

✲ city of Marshall
0.5 mile off trail
42.272109 -84.964213   ///gazed.lecturers.mosaic
services

$▲ *Calhoun County Fairgrounds*
0.2 mile off trail
42.265446 -84.947849   ///factored.lance.scares
primitive, no fire rings, electric, water
fee
calhouncountyfairgrounds.com
269-781-8161

$PCg
11.7 miles
+0.1 road
$L

✲ city of Albion
1.0 mile off trail
42.261151 -84.756379   ///dynasties.lunging.seekers
services

$ ■ $ ☐ *Motels, AirBnBs*
0.1 mile off trail
42.244155 -84.753023   ///educations.magnificent.trim
several commercial lodging options
fee

$L
+0.1 road
17.5 miles
chapter boundary

✲ village of Homer MI
42.146737 -84.805101   ///puzzle.bowls.bought
limited services

Calhoun/Hillsdale County Line
42.071849 -84.782842   ///puzzle.bowls.bought
Chief Noonday Chapter
northcountrytrail.org/trail/michigan/cnd
↔ **Chapter boundary**

295

↔ **Chapter boundary**
Calhoun/Hillsdale County Line
42.071849   -84.782842   ///puzzle.bowls.bought
Chief Baw Beese Chapter
northcountrytrail.org/trail/michigan/baw

        chapter boundary
        mixed ownership
        5.0 miles
        PCs

✲ village of Litchfield
42.043857   -84.758424   ///resisting.worldly.jugs
limited services

△ *Litchfield Nature Trail Campground*
42.032192   -84.737395   ///impaled.congestion.backed
campsite for NCT hikers
primitive, 2 tent pads, table, fire ring
managed by city of Litchfield
cityoflitchfield.org
517-542-2921

        PCs
        2.0 miles
        +0.1 spur
        HE HCs

△ ⌂ *NCT Kayak Camp*
0.1 mile off trail
42.014743   -84.720062   ///wires.radiators.item
hosted site
tent sites, small enclosed sleeping shelters
primitive, table, fire ring, latrine
reservation required
nctkayakcamp.com
419-266-5885

        HE HCs
        +0.1 spur
        4.0 miles
        +0.8 road
        $CCg

$▲ *Way Back In Campground*
0.8 mile off trail
41.995088   -84.685002   ///tennis.superb.foods
commercial campsite
43 vehicular sites
electric, tables, fire rings, bathhouse
facebook.com/waybackcampground
517-849-0082

        $CCg
        +0.8 road
        1.0 mile
        $L

✽ city of Jonesville
41.983925 -84.661558   ///magnifying.withdraw.countries
services

$ ■ $ ☐ *Motels, AirBnB*
various off trail
east and west near US 12
commercial lodging
fee

       $L
       3.2 miles
       $L

$ ■ *Days Inn*
41.944264 -84.650505   ///fury.cones.speedboat
commercial lodging
fee
wyndhamhotels.com
517-439-3297

       $L
       2.4 miles
       +0.1 road
       $L

✽ city of Hillsdale
0.25 mile off trail
41.920206 -84.631967   ///buttons.shop.charms
services

$ ☐ *Heart of Hillsdale AirBnB*
0.1 mile off trail
41.922416 -84.630999   ///vowels.slouched.observer
commercial lodging
1 apartment
fee
airbnb.com
872-985-9339

       $L
       +0.1 road
       6.5 miles
       D

✽ village of Osseo
41.886786 -84.544156   ///bumper.spokes.devise
no services

↔ boundary mixed ownership
41.879374 -84.529908   ///porch.rational.outfitters
↔ boundary Lost Nation State Game Area

Note: dispersed camping is allowed in MI state wildlife and game areas only between Sep 11 and May 14 with permit, and at least one mile away from designated campgrounds/ campsites. See Appendix

      p△ seasonal *dispersed camping* allowed
      2.4 miles in Lost Nation SGA
      michigan.gov/dnr

↔ boundary Lost Nation State Game Area
41.86167   -84.514416   ///breath.rearranged.prosecuted
↔ boundary private land

    pD seasonal
    0.5 mile
    pD seasonal

↔ boundary private land
41.854574   -84.514995   ///catcher.purifying.preset
↔ boundary Lost Nation SGA

    p△ seasonal *dispersed camping* allowed
    1.0 mile in Lost Nation SGA
    michigan.gov/dnr

↔ boundary Lost Nation SGA
41.854446   -84.495705   ///mile.piled.productions
↔ boundary private land

    pD seasonal
    0.7 mile
    pD seasonal

↔ boundary private land
41.84639   -84.495791   ///upsetting.opens.resize
↔ boundary Lost Nation SGA

    p△ seasonal *dispersed camping* allowed
    3.1 mile in Lost Nation SGA
    michigan.gov/dnr

↔ boundary Lost Nation SGA
41.823784   -84.475191   ///encryption.benefit.cafe
↔ boundary private land

    pD seasonal
    10.6 miles
    state/ chapter boundary

Michigan/Ohio state line
41.704987   -84.428315   ///cheaply.neuter.summaries
Baw Beese Chapter
northcountrytrail.org/trail/michigan/baw
↔ **Chapter boundary**

Ohio

See legend and general info for help in interpreting the listings. There is no dispersed camping in Ohio State Forests.

↔ **Affiliate boundary**
Michigan/Ohio state line
41.704987 -84.428315 ///cheaply.neuter.summaries
NORTA- Northwest Ohio Rails to Trails Association
facebook.com/nortaofnwohio

state line/ chapter/affiliate boundary
13.7 miles
HCs

✲ village of Alvordton
41.666086 -84.437714 ///personality.ponies.zoos
no services

✲ village of West Unity
41.58653 -84.434109 ///certain.decided.chum
limited services

△ ***Bates Run Campsite***
41.582966 -84.350596 ///rented.intruding.searing
hosted site
primitive, table, no latrine
maintained by NORTA
mbduvendack@gmail.com

HCs
11.5 miles
HCs

△ ***Wauseon Rotary Park***
41.556015 -84.137527 ///boats.digit.slowly
hosted site
primitive, no amenities
hosted by city of Wauseon
call police to reserve site
419-335-3821

HCs
4.3 miles
HCs

✲ city of Wauseon OH 25.3
41.555252 -84.13438 ///leans.cargo.voice
services, motels are 2.5 miles N at OH Turnpike

△ ***Wye Campsite***
41.555808 -84.061362 ///bookmark.secrets.unfortunate
hosted site
primitive, table, no latrine, dry
maintained by NORTA
mbduvendack@gmail.com

HCs
3.2 miles
HCs

△ *Delta Campsite*
41.556057 -84.000015   ///december.powered.underscore
hosted in grassy area by NORTA HQ
primitive, table, latrine, seasonal water
maintained by NORTA
mbduvendack@gmail.com

HCs
6.8 miles
+0.25 spur
$PCg

↔ boundary mixed ownership
41.556309 -83.882683   ///reflectors.downswing.each
↔ boundary Oak Openings Metropark

Note: camp only at designated sites in Oak Openings

$▲ *Springbrook Campsite*
0.25 mile off trail
41.558524 -83.868542   ///brightness.rental.enhancement
public campground
12 equestrian campsites
primitive, table, fire ring, latrine, seasonal water
fee
reservation required
metroparkstoledo.com
419-407-9700

$PCg
1.4 miles
HE HCs

△ ⌂ *Buzzard Crest*
41.54632 -83.864164   ///filed.liquid.mastermind
private host
tenting, indoor accommodations
mbduvendack@gmail.com

HE HCs
2.5 miles
+0.6 road
$PE

$⌂ *Caretaker's Cottage*
0.6 mile off trail
41.543845 -83.839613   ///splinters.situation.evaporated
public lodging
sleeps 6, electric, full kitchen
fee
reservation required
managed by Toledo Metroparks
metroparkstoledo.com
419-407-9700

$PE
+0.6 road
0.6 mile
+0.5 road
$CCg

$▲ *Twin Acres Campground*
0.5 mile off trail
41.526572 -83.830989   ///spinach.posting.innocence
commercial campground
200 vehicular sites
electric, tables, fire rings, bathhouse
fee
twinacrescampground.com
419-877-2684

↔ boundary Oak Openings Metropark
41.530371 -83.836483
↔ boundary Maumee State Forest

Note: Ohio State Forests do not allow dispersed camping

↔ boundary Maumee State
41.51625 -83.836912   ///conclude.repeat.unleash
↔ boundary mixed ownership

✣ city of Whitehouse
41.518026 -83.802815   ///watery.rags.updated
services

$PCg
9.5 miles
junction Buckeye Trail

✣ city of Waterville
41.500275 -83.725103   ///implanted.dispensing.stitching
services

Y junction of NCT and Buckeye Trail. BT loop continues east.
41.486882 -83.73576   ///hypnotist.donations.alcove

affiliate boundary

Buckeye Trail junction
41.486882 -83.73576   ///hypnotist.donations.alcove
NORTA- Northwest Ohio Rails to Trails Association
facebook.com/nortaofnwohio
↔ **Affiliate boundary**

↔ **Affiliate boundary**
Buckeye Trail junction at Defiance Pt 20
41.486882 -83.73576   ///hypnotist.donations.alcove
Defiance Section
defiance@buckeyetrail.org

Y junction of NCT and Buckeye Trail. BT loop continues east.
41.486882 -83.73576   ///hypnotist.donations.alcove

                    affiliate boundary
                    1.0 mile
                    $PCs

$△ ◌ *Farnsworth Campsites*
41.477222 -83.749128   ///feuds.sandals.chemist
public campsite
2 primitive sites for tent only
shelter, table, fire ring, latrine
fee
reservation required
metroparkstoledo.com
419-407-9700
sent form email about shelters April 27, 2024

                    $PCs
                    0.5 mile
                    $L

$ ■ *Riverwood Log Cabins*
41.472123 -83.754847   ///tempting.flourishes.brightest
commercial lodging
12 cabins and cottages
fee
riverwoodlogcabins.com
419-654-3323

                    $L
                    3.5 miles
                    $L

$ ☐ *Uncle Chuck's Cabin Rental*
41.443385 -83.803812   ///notched.balloon.lemons
commercial lodging
rustic cabin sleeps 5
fire pit, latrine, generator
achydraulics@aol.com
419-250-1163

                    $L
                    3.9 miles
                    +0.25 road
                    $L

�֍ city of Grand Rapids
41.411521 -83.861211   ///defines.uniformity.alienated
services

$ ☐ *Mill House BnB*
0.25 mile off trail
41.412871 -83.865712   ///resisting.hamstrings.pharmacies
commercial lodging
fee
themillhouse.com
419-832-6455

                                      $L
                                      +0.25 road
                                      8.3 miles
                                      HE

✷ village of Texas
41.42359 -83.9533   ///hello.independent.presides
no services

∠ *Henry County Shelter*
41.411154 -84.009032   ///since.pestle.gathering
hosted site
open shelter, no amenities, no water access
managed by the Buckeye Trail Association
defiance@buckeyetrail.org

                                        HE
                                      1.3 miles
                                      HCS

△ *Rotary Riverside Preserve Campsite*
41.414283 -84.032186   ///forgets.observation.truth
hosted by Black Swamp Conservancy
primitive, no amenities
reserve 48 hours in advance
419-833-1025

                                      HCs
                                      13.5 miles
                                      $PCg

✷ city of Napoleon
41.391982 -84.125398   ///stereotype.overthrown.exporters
services, motel 1.5 mile north

✷ village of Florida
41.322425 -84.200663   ///owners.rivalry.assess
limited services

$▲ *Independence Dam State Park*

41.293396 -84.241411 ///workforce.stew.grouped
public campground
primitive, tables, fire rings, latrine
fee
reservation required
ohiodnr.gov
419-237-2593

$PCg
14.1 miles
HCs

⁂ city of Defiance
41.286579 -84.362031 ///lung.middle.calm
services, motels are 1.2 miles north

△ *Defiance Reservoir*

41.267978 -84.399904 ///whiplash.lawfully.melody
hosted by city of Defiance
primitive, no amenities
call police before arrival
419-784-5050

HCs
6.8 miles
section boundary

⁂ village of Junction
41.194722 -84.456909 ///intelligent.slopes.awestruck
no services

village of Junction/ Defiance Pt 1
41.194722 -84.456909 ///intelligent.slopes.awestruck
Defiance Section
defiance@buckeyetrail.org
↔ **Affiliate Section boundary**

↔ **Affiliate Section boundary**
village of Junction/ Delphos Pt 24
41.194722 -84.456909   ///intelligent.slopes.awestruck
Delphos Section
delphos@buckeyetrail.org

       section boundary
       2.9 miles
       HCs

△ *Viall's Lock Campsite*
41.154505 -84.449356   ///fidgeted.guide.constrain
public land
primitive, fire ring, no latrine
maintained by BTA
delphos@buckeyetrail.org

       HCs
       9.6 miles
       HCs

△ *Hipp's Lock Campsite*
41.046359 -84.379704   ///sleeps.manicured.laundry
public land
primitive, no amenities
maintained by BTA
delphos@buckeyetrail.org

       HCs
       18.9 miles
       +0.1 spur
       HCs

✣ village of Mandale
41.019687 -84.359256   ///workbench.cheesy.commodities
no services

✣ village of Ottoville
40.932214 -84.339327   ///placidly.preset.scanning
limited services

✣ village of Fort Jennings
40.905331 -84.295961   ///reference.messengers.pouting
limited services

△ *Jennnings Creek Aquaduct Campsite*
0.1 mile off trail
40.861329 -84.341232   ///domains.loving.stutter
public land
primitive, no amenities
maintained by BTA
delphos@buckeyetrail.org

       HCs
       +0.1 spur
       1.1 mile
       +0.25 road
       $L

$ ☐ *Victorian Guesthouse*

0.25 mile off trail
40.844773 -84.336136 ///approaching.thud.printing
commercial lodging
5 guest rooms
fee
facebook.com/thevictorianguesthousedelphos
954-724-7253

$L
+0.25 road
4.8 miles
HE

✲ city of Delphos
40.83979 - 84.340518 ///speculative.blocks.foster
services

∠ *Lock 18 Shelter*

40.769452 -84.339856 ///launch.loners.everybody
public land
open shelter on opposite side of canal
access may be tricky
no amenities
maintained by BTA
delphos@buckeyetrail.org

HE
3.9 miles
HCs

△ *Old Acadia Park*

40.715038 -84.35126 ///fully.vortex.habitat
public land
primitive, no amenities, seasonal water
maintained by Village of Spencerville
spencervilleoh.com
call police at 419-647-4141 for permission

HCs
4.6 miles
boundary Delphos Section

✲ village of Spencerville
40.708963 -84.354063 ///ringside.late.progressive
limited services

✲ village of Kossuth
0.1 mile east
40.659583 -84.348162 ///panics.players.edgier
no services

village of Kossuth/ Delphos Pt 1
40.658777 -84.349788 ///sandwich.clogging.stomach
Delphos Section
delphos@buckeyetrail.org

↔ **Affiliate Section boundary**

↔ **Affiliate Section boundary**
village of Kossuth/ St Marys Pt 29
40.658777 -84.349788 ///sandwich.clogging.stomach
St. Marys Section
stmarys@buckeyetrail.org

section boundary
4.4 miles
HCs

△ *Lock 14 Park*

40.600446 -84.369224 ///ambition.retraced.pogo
public land
primitive, no amenities
notify info@htparks.org 24 hours in advance
hosted by Heritage Trails Park District

HCs
4.4 miles
HCs

△ *City of St. Marys*

40.551585 -84.391587 ///experiments.stitching.chest
hosted by city of St. Marys
primitive, no amenities
cityofstmarys.net
419-394-2325 (police)

HCs
0.5 mile
+1.0 road
$L

$▲ *America 's Best Value Inn*

1.0 mile off trail
40.543673 -84.403824 ///whites.timely.informed
commercial lodging
rooms, laundry
fee
sonesta.com
419-394-2341

$L
7.1 miles
HE

✲ city of St. Marys
40.543406 -84.387397 ///marketable.doted.sensibly
services

∠ *Kuenning-Dicke Natural Area Shelter*

40.44898 -84.371269 ///clients.amuses.vets
hosted site
open shelter
4 bunks, table, latrine and water nearby
managed by New Bremen Foundation
newbremenfoundation.org

HE
0.9 mile
+0.15 road
$L

$▲ *Iron & Rind Guest House*
0.15 mile off trail
40.438605 -84.382386 ///reborn.newlyweds.flop
commercial lodging
8 rooms
fee
ironandrind.com
937-726-4882

$L
+0.15 road
3.2 miles
+0.15 road
$L

✲ village of New Breman
40.436743 -84.38049 ///muffled.transmits.upbringing
services

✲ village of Minster
40.393058 -84.376714 ///frog.hopper.luminosity
services

$ ☐ *The Crescent Motel*
0.15 mile off trail
40.392055 -84.38066 ///spoiler.cashew.ambulances
commercial lodging
5 rooms
fee
thecrescentmotel.com
419-501-2611

$L
+0.15 road
3.7 miles
$PCg

$▲ *Lake Loramie State Park*
40.358252 -84.356215 ///nominations.present.causes
public campground
163 vehicular sites, 14 non-electric walk-in sites
tables, fire rings, bathhouse
fee
ohiodnr.gov
937-295-3900

$PCg
5.1 miles
+0.5 road
$PCg

✱ village of Fort Loramie
40.350816 -84.375039   ///liquid.minimal.tickle
services

$▲ White Oak Campground
0.5 mile off trail
40.314225 -84.377271   ///sharpening.progress.trapped
commercial campground
8 tent sites, tables, fire rings, restroom
937-295-2018

                $PCg
                +0.5 road
                6.1 miles
                HE

✱ village of Newport
40.295865 -84.369675   ///shies.sharper.proceeds
limited services

∠ Eagle Scout Cole Shelter
40.26376 -84.330117   ///intercepts.decreased.guarantees
hosted site
open shelter, fireplace
maintained by the Buckeye Trail Association
stmarys@buckeyetrail.org

                HE
                8.5 miles
                HCs

△ Lockington Reserve Campsite
0.2 mile off trail
40.217607 -84.242275   ///punky.sawdust.rushes
public land
2 small shelters, no amenities
managed by Miami Conservancy District

                HCs
                4.0 miles
                section boundary

✱ village of Lckington
40.208337 -84.233692   ///blatant.sprinkling.rice
no services

County Road 110/ St. Marys Pt 1
40.184116 -84.259565   ///meanest.eaters.shortly
St. Marys Section
stmarys@buckeyetrail.org
↔ **Affiliate Section boundary**

↔ **Affiliate Section boundary**
County Road 110/ Troy Section Pt 15
40.184116 -84.259565   ///meanest.eaters.shortly
Troy Section
troy@buckeyetrail.org

        section boundary
        11.4 miles
        +0.9 road
        $L

✲ city of Piqua
40.146684 -84.239571   ///expand.shops.habit
motels are 1 mile east, no easy access on foot
possible AirBnB
services

$ ■ *Hampton Inn*
0.9 mile off trail
40.052922 -84.237473   ///contracting.bamboozled.fault
commercial lodging
rooms, suites
fee
hilton.com
937-339-7801

        $L
        +0.9 road
        15.4 miles
        $PCs

✲ city of Troy
40.038393 -84.20032   ///collects.breakdowns.wounds
services

✲ city of Tipp City
39.961204 -84.173727   ///golf.sheriff.redouble
motel is 1.4 miles west at interstate
possible AirBnB
services

$△ *Taylorsville Trailside Campsite*
39.872786 -84.169829   ///warping.preserves.sequel
public campsite
primitive, no fires, latrine, dry
fee
managed by Five Rivers Metropark
metroparks.org
reserve in advance using link in appendix

        $PCs
        9.3 miles
        $PCs

$△ *Island A Trailside Campsite*
39.781953 -84.198776   ///buddy.store.stage
public campsite
primitive, no fires, latrine, water
fee
managed by Five Rivers Metropark
metroparks.org
reserve in advance using link in appendix

$PCs
1.3 miles
+0.5 road
$L

✻ city center Dayton
0.7 mile off trail
39.759896 -84.190139   ///lasted.comic.deputy
center of the largest city on the NCT
services

$ ■ *AC Hotel*
0.5 mile off trail
39.761462 -84.184969   ///gave.skinny.washed
commercial lodging
rooms, suites
fee
marriott.com
937-965-7500

$L
+0.5 road
3.8 miles
$PCs

$△ *Eastwood A Trailside Campsite*
39.787049 -84.124917   ///sobs.clean.glow
primitive, no fires, latrine, dry
fee
managed by Five Rivers Metropark
metroparks.org
reserve in advance using link in appendix

$PCs
0.6 mile
$L

$ ■ *Comfort Suites Dayton Wright-Patterson*
39.784663 -84.118381   ///humans.cubs.fired
commercial lodging
rooms, suites
fee
choicehotels.com
937-425-6498

$L
6.8 miles
section boundary

✽ city of Fairborn
39.819188   -84.021128   ///admire.spout.neon
services

East Dayton Dr at Central Ave/ Troy Section Pt 1
39.819188   -84.021128   ///admire.spout.neon
Troy Section
troy@buckeyetrail.org
↔ **Affiliate Section boundary**

↔ **Affiliate Section boundary**
Caesar Creek Section Pt 25
39.819188 -84.021128   ///admire.spout.neon
Caesar Creek Section
caesarcreek@buckeyetrail.org

                                      section boundary
                                      0.8 mile
                                      +0.1 road
                                      $L

$ ■ *Comfort Inn*
0.1 off trail
39.819056 -84.006794   ///leaned.light.eggs
commercial lodging
rooms, suites, laundry
fee
choicehotels.com
937-754-9109

                                      $L
                                    +0.1 road
                                    9.5 miles
                                    + various road
                                    $L

$ ■ *Motels*
various
39.807401 -83.88907   ///upon.crumbs.become
commercial lodging
fee

✻ city of Yellow Springs
39.807401 -83.88907   ///upon.crumbs.become
services

                                    $L
                                  + various road
                                  7.0 miles
                                  $PCs

                                                              $▲ *John Bryan State Park*
                                                                     1.6 miles off trail
                                     39.788026 -83.867345   ///dipped.caps.brigade
                                                              public campground
                                                                     vehicular sites
                                                  16 electric, 40 non electric
                                               tables, fire rings, bathhouse
                                                                          fee
                                                             ohiodnr.gov
                                                             866-644-6727.

$△ *Old Town Reserve Campsite*

39.723046 -83.934835 ///truckload.equine.accuse
public campsite
primitive, table, grill, latrine, water
reservation required
managed by Green County Parks and Trails
gcparkstrails.com
937-562-6440
after hours 937-376-5111

$PCs
1.4 miles
+0.5 road
$PCg

$▲ *Green County Fairgrounds*

0.5 mile off trail
39.699288 -83.939915 ///shade.offers.libraries
public campground
no camping during Fair Week
100 vehicular sites
some electric, tables, fire rings, bathhouse
fee
managed by Green County
greenecoexpocenter.com/camping

$PCg
+0,5 road
1.3 miles
+0.2 road
$L

$ ■ *Guest Houses*

0.2 mile E and W
39.683848 -83.929147 ///ropes.zoom.smile
commercial lodging
fee

$L
+0.2 road
7.1 miles
$PCs

✲ city of Xenia
39.684812 -83.929549 ///gained.career.frosted
services

✲ village of Spring Valley
39.608705 -84.009195 ///rice.horizon.headset
limited services

Y Buckeye Trail and NCT separate/join here. BT is east along Caesar Creek Reservoir. NCT remains on the multi-use trail. BT 71.4
39.608705 -84.009195 ///rice.horizon.headset

$△ *Constitution Park*
39.60663 -84.012102   ///firelight.hood.screenplay
public campsite
0.2 mile off trail
primitive, table, no latrine
fee, reservation required
managed by Green County Parks and Trails
gcparkstrails.com
937-562-6440
after hours 937-376-5111

$PCs
7.8 miles
+0.5 road
$L

$ ■ *Motels*
0.5 mile off trail
2 motels in Waynesville near
39.526794 -84.08979   ///employs.elders.carnation
commercial lodging
fee

$L
+0,5 road
3.2 miles
section boundary

Y *Buckeye Trail and NCT separate/join here. BT is east along Caesar Creek Reservoir. NCT remains on the multi-use trail* BT 46.3
39.482605 -84.107084   ///proud.luminaries.campfires

Corwin Road at Elbon Road/ Caesar Creek Section Pt 1
39.482605 -84.107084   ///proud.luminaries.campfires
Caesar Creek Section
caesarcreek@buckeyetrail.org
↔ **Affiliate Section boundary**

↔ **Affiliate Section boundary**
Corwin Road at Elbon Road/ Loveland Section Pt 27
39.482605 -84.107084 ///proud.luminaries.campfires
Loveland Section
loveland@buckeyetrail.org

section boundary
3.7 miles
$HCs

⁂ village of Oregonia
39.45476 -84.09725 ///forgetful.panther.effortless
limited services

$△ ***Little Miami Canoe Rental***
39.43225 -84.101719 ///seamlessly.embedding.mondays
commercial campsite
primitive, table, latrine, restroom during business hours
hosted site for hikers/cyclists
fee
advance reservation required
littlemiamicanoerental@hotmail.com
513-899-3616

$HCs
4.2 miles
$CCg

$▲ ***Morgan 's Riverside Campground***
0.15 mile off trail
39.379515 -84.093174 ///economical.samples.successes
commercial campground
74 vehicular sites
4 cabins
primitive, tables, fire rings, latrine
fee
morganscanoe.com/riverside
513-899-2166

$PCg
16.1 miles
PCs

⁂ village of Morrow
39.354872 -84.134511 ///stumble.adjustable.clay
services

△ ***City of Loveland Campsite***
39.274163 -84.256461 ///deny.stage.milk
public land
primitive, fire ring, restroom
reserve in advance
lovelandoh.gov
dkennedy@lovelandoh.gov

PCs
22.3 miles
PE

✲ city of Loveland
39.267934 -84.258533 ///rank.remit.bronze
services

✲ village of Miamiville
39.212492 -84.299941 ///blossoming.submitting.resettle
limited services

$∠ *Jim Terrell Park Shelter*

0.15 mile off trail
39.170084 -84.298654 ///pipeline.carried.visitors
public land
open shelter, table, grill, latrine
reserve in advance, may be difficult for thru-hikers
link to permit in Appendix
513-831-4192

Y junction with Buckeye Trail spur to Cincinnati
Y junction- American Discovery Trail follows BT to Cincinnati and is concurrent with BT/NCT eastward
Y NCT bends east/north on main BT loop
39.171324 -84.299706 ///dentistry.gifted.camels

section boundary

Little Miami Scenic Trail at US 50/ Loveland Section Pt 9
"The Junction" in Milford
39.171324 -84.299706 ///dentistry.gifted.camels
Loveland Section
loveland@buckeyetrail.org
↔ **Affiliate Section boundary**

↔ **Affiliate Section boundary**
Little Miami Scenic Trail at US 50/ Williamsburg Section Pt 29
"The Junction" in Milford
39.171324 -84.299706   ///dentistry.gifted.camels
Williamsburg Section
williamsburg@buckeyetrail.org

Y junction with Buckeye Trail spur to Cincinnati
Y junction- American Discovery Trail follows BT to Cincinnati and is concurrent with BT/NCT eastward
Y NCT bends north/east on main BT loop

        section boundary
        0.4 mile
        +0.25 road
        $PCs

✲ city of Milford
39.172865 -84.296172   ///galaxy.suggested.whimpering
services

$△ *Riverside Park*
0.25 mile off trail
39.176509 -84.295787   ///docking.curiosity.dispenses
hosted by City of Milford
tables, grills, restroom
fee
reserve in advance, may be difficult for thru-hikers
link to permit in Appendix
513-831-4192

        $PCs
        +0.25 road
        1.2 miles
        HE HCs

↔ boundary private land
39.165412 -84.291515   ///managers.firming.triumph
↔ boundary Valley View Foundation

Note: camp only at designated area within Valley View property

∠ △ *Valley View Shelter*
39.161153 -84.287438   ///frowns.assist.weeping
hosted by Valley View Foundation
open shelter, space for tents
table, fire ring, water is 0.3 mile west
valleyviewcampus.org
info@valleyviewcampus.org
513-218-1098

        HE HCs
        2.2 miles
        + various
        $L

↔ boundary Valley View Foundation
39.164938 -84.282267   ///working.crumples.earthworms
↔ boundary mixed ownership

$ ■ *Motels*
various off trail near this point
39.158133 -84.272536   ///treats.poem.unduly
commercial lodging
fee

                        $L
                        + various
                        16.7 miles
                        PCs

✻ village of Batavia
39.077928 -84.178682   ///older.glorified.proudly
motels are 2 miles east along Rt 32
services

↔ boundary mixed ownership
39.044372 -84.153061   ///mattress.communicate.toddler
↔ boundary East Fork State Park

Note: Camp only at designated sites in East Fork SP, free, but permit is required. See link in Appendix.

△ *East Fork SP Backpack Camp #5*
39.020054 -84.162017   ///acting.bats.courtrooms
public campsite
primitive, fire ring
managed by East Fork SP
ohiodnr.gov

                        PCs
                        6.7 miles
                        +0.3 spur
                        PE

∠ *East Fork SP Backpack Shelter #1*
0.3 mile off trail if approached from east on Cedar Trail
39.007333 -84.133942   ///elimination.tumble.genuinely
public campsite
open shelter
fire ring
managed by East Fork SP
ohiodnr.gov

                        PE
                        +0.3 spur
                        4.0 miles
                        PE

∠ *East Fork SP Backpack Shelter #2*
38.992558 -84.105897   ///engaged.december.defining
public campsite
open shelter
fire ring, may be dry
managed by East Fork SP
ohiodnr.gov

                    PE
                    5.2 miles
                    PCs

△ *East Fork SP Backpack Shelter #3*
38.998128 -84.074612   ///attracting.infants.bunch
public campsite
primitive, fire ring, benches
managed by East Fork SP
ohiodnr.gov

                    PCs
                    16.8 miles
                    section boundary

↔ boundary East Fork State Park
39.033873 -84.053025   ///cluster.acting.exchanging
↔ boundary private land

✻ village of Williamsburg
0.9 mile off trail
39.054871 -84.05442   ///baggage.concern.flute
services

Junction OH 774 and Co 208/ West Union section pt 1
38.994317 -83.93383   ///limes.roosters.resign
Williamsburg Section
williamsburg@buckeyetrail.org
↔ **Affiliate Section boundary**

↔ **Affiliate Section boundary**
Junction OH 774 and Co 208/ West Union Section Pt 29
38.994317 -83.93383 ///limes.roosters.resign
West Union Section
westunion@buckeyetrail.org

                  section boundary
                  11.4 miles
                  HE

✲ village of Russellville BT 1283.2
38.866799 -83.787143 ///greet.debates.necklace
limited services

∠ *Vogel Shelter*
38.928655 -83.853748 ///approaching.groans.repeat
privately hosted open shelter
fire ring, latrine, water cache
please notify owner per instructions in shelter

                  PE
                  25.5 miles
                  0.1 road
                  $L

$ ■ *Hopewell Croft Cabin*
0.1 mile off trail
38.753623 -83.661871 ///audit.avoided.fluency
large cabin, sleeps 9
fee
hopewellcroft.com

                  $L
                  +0.1 road
                  21.6 miles
                  but see hostel option off trail at 13.1 miles
                  section boundary

✲ village of Bentonville
38.749371 -83.61323 ///divergence.dupe.advertises
no services

                        $○ $△ *Moon Doggie LIVER-ee*
                        1.5 miles off trail
            38.733686 -83.473753 ///mushroom.mutate.teller
                        private hostel, enclosed shelter sleeps 3
                        electric, microwave, TV, water
                        tent sties, latrine
                        fee
                        owner will provide rides
                        MoonDoggieLIVERee2020@gmail.com

↔ boundary private land
38.745676 -83.464594 ///indoor.vortex.magazines
↔ boundary Edge of Appalachia Nature Preserve

Note: Camp only at designated location in Edge of Appalachia; please do not stray from trail

section boundary

West Fork Rd/ West Union Section Pt 1
38.727633 -83.421442   ///bookmarks.recover.tricky
West Union Section
westunion@buckeyetrail.org
↔ **Affiliate Section boundary**

↔ **Affiliate Section boundary**
West Fork Rd/ Shawnee Section Pt 25
38.727633   -83.421442   ///bookmarks.recover.tricky
Shawnee Section
shawnee@buckeyetrail.org

Note: Camp only at designated location in Edge of Appalachia; please stay on trail

section boundary
6.0 miles
pHCs

△ *Moon Hollow Campsite*
38.733931   -83.35728   ///imparts.lease.decode
primitive, no amenities
hosted site, must have permit
ohio@tnc.org.
937-544-2880

pHCs
16.4 miles
PCs

↔ boundary Edge of Appalachia Nature Preserve
38.716287   -83.332132   ///padded.destroyer.vocab
↔ boundary private land

↔ boundary private land
38.717493   -83.314708   ///inspire.exulted.sensitive
↔ boundary Shawnee State Forest

Note: Ohio State Forests do not allow dispersed camping. Camp only at designated sites. You must have a free permit that can be obtained at the TH on Route 125 at Shawnee State Park.

△ *Shawnee State Forest Camp #7*
38.724112   -83.251947   ///gull.unexplored.composers
primivite
fire ring, latrine, water
permit required
maintained by Ohio DNR
ohiodnr.gov
740-858-6685

PCs
10.4 miles
$CCg

Permit Kiosk
obtain free permit at State Rt 125 TH
38.741894   -83.19733   ///cleanser.adjusts.pedestrian

$▲ *Shawnee State Park Campground*
1.5 miles off trail
38.729216 -83.179269   ///item.lotteries.matchup
public campground
107 vehicular sites,2 cabins
86 are electric, 21 non-electric
tables, fire rings, bathhouse, laundry
fee
reserveohio.com
866-644-6727

↔ boundary Shawnee State Forest
38.784929   -83.193899   ///flab.enacted.caravan
↔ boundary private land

△ $ ☐ *Ben's Happy Trails Stable and Campground*
38.791088   -83.200017   ///testy.spurred.secures
commercial lodging friendly to hikers
cabins, bunkhouse, tent sites
hikers may be able to tent free
western-style lodge for relaxation
fee
benshappytrails.org
740-372-2702

                        $CCg
                        8.9 miles
                        HE

◌ △ *Ballinger Shelter*
38.811084   -83.269773   ///puzzled.chum.periods
hosted site
enclosed shelter
space for tents
latrine
maintenance uncertain

                        HE
                        11.7 miles
                        +0.8 road
                        $L

$ ☐ *Mineral Springs Lake Resort*
0.8 mile off trail
38.916358   -83.373201   ///likes.surgery.began
commercial lodging
3 large cabins, no tenting
fee
mineralspringslakeresort.com
740- 637-1151

                        $L
                        +0.8 road
                        2.4 miles
                        section boundary

↔ boundary private land
38.930837   -83.365193   ///unreadable.muzzle.briefed
↔ boundary Davis Memorial State Nature Preserve

Note: no camping in Nature Preserve; please stay on trail

↔ boundary Davis Memorial State Nature Preserve
38.94015   -83.352275   ///subway.shouts.crucially
↔ boundary private land

Beaver Pond Road at Davis Memorial entrance/ Shawnee Section Pt 1
38.940111   -83.353395   ///ripe.pearls.unjust
Shawnee Section
shawnee@buckeyetrail.org
↔ **Affiliate Section boundary**

↔ **Affiliate Section boundary**
Beaver Pond Road at Davis Memorial entrance/ Sinking Spring Section Pt 27
38.940111   -83.353395   ///ripe.pearls.unjust
Sinking Spring Section
sinkingspring@buckeyetrail.org

                      section boundary
                      10.8 miles
                      +0.5 road
                      HCs

✲ village of Peebles
38.945773   -83.426599   ///creeps.traitor.ruining
limited services

△ *Goodseed Farm Campsite*
0.5 mile off trail
38.976721   -83.442129   ///clench.mountain.shatter
hosted site
fire ring, no latrine
contact owner 24 hours in advance
steve@goodseedfarm.com
937-587-7021   HCs
                      +0.5 road
                      7.7 miles
                      HE

↔ boundary private land
39.023142   -83.435799   ///arching.folding.placid
↔ boundary Serpent Mound State Memorial

Note: No camping in Serpent Mound; be respectful.

↔ boundary Serpent Mound State Memorial
39.023609   -83.427559   ///paces.applauding.seated
↔ boundary private land

∠ *Andy Jones Shelter*
39.023284   -83.426712   ///minimalist.tempting.foolish
open shelter
contact owner 24 hours in advance
937-587-3953
                      HE
                      14.7 miles
                      +0.2 road
                      HCs

↔ boundary private land BT
39.057016   -83.391242   ///lobster.booming.shielding
↔ boundary Strait Creek Prairie Bluffs Nature Preserve

Note: no camping in Nature Preserve

↔ boundary Strait Creek Prairie Bluffs Nature Preserve
39.06668   -83.376136   ///elbow.philosopher.coasts
↔ boundary private land

✱ village of Sinking Spring
39.072783 -83.386702   ///agents.hard.variation
limited services

↔ boundary private land BT 1162.9
39.101663 -83.404791   ///scratches.dices.reaffirmed
↔ boundary Fort Hill Memorial Nature Preserve

Note: No camping in Nature Preserve

↔ boundary Fort Hill Memorial Nature Preserve
39.119312 -83.391487   ///richly.press.chronicles
↔ boundary Pike Lake State Forest

Note: Ohio State Forests do not allow dispersed camping.

△ *Butler Springs Christian Camp*
0.2 mile off trail
39.11331 -83.378473   ///cartoon.forwarded.barks
hosted site
primitive, bathhouse
check in at office or call ahead
937-588-2205

                 HCs
                +0.2 road
               11.4 miles
                 HCs

↔ boundary Pike Lake State Forest
39.115953 -83.364241   ///legends.darts.upholds
↔ boundary mixed ownership

$▲ *Cave Lake Park*
1.3 miles off trail
39.091042 -83.337362   ///saturate.match.recipes
private campground
300 vehicular sites
200 electric, 100 non-electric
tables, fire rings, bathhouse, laundry
fee
ylaleads.org/cave-lake
937-588-3252

↔ boundary mixed ownership
39.111793 -83.295871   ///somebody.corporate.loomed
↔ boundary Pike Lake State Forest

Note: Ohio State Forests do not allow dispersed camping.

↔ boundary Pike Lake State Forest
39.101136 -83.259994   ///occupations.bowling.begin
↔ boundary mixed ownership

✴ village of Latham
0.5 mile off trail
39.098805 -83.246325   ///writing.goalkeeper.universal
limited services

△ Western School District Campsite
39.103834 -83.25464   ///strictest.condition.simplified
hosted site near ball field
primitive
740-493-2881

            HCs
            7.5 miles
            +0.5 road
            $CCg

↔ boundary mixed ownership
39.110798 -83.255654
↔ boundary Pike Lake State Forest

Note: Ohio State Forests do not allow dispersed camping.

$▲ LB Campground
0.5 mile off trail
39.149265 -83.233231   ///unhappy.multiplied.somewhere
commercial campground
60 vehicular sites
tables, fire rings, electric, bathhouse
fee
ohiocamper.com/lbcamping.html
740-493-4614

            $CCg
            +0.5 road
            1.9 miles
            $PCg

$▲ Pike Lake State Park Campground
39.156735 -83.218576   ///pledge.aged.wells
public campground
79 vehicular sites, cabins
electric, tables, fire rings, bathhouse
fee
reservations required
reserveohio.com
866- 644-6727

            $PCg
            0.1 mile
            section boundary

Pike Lake Dam/ Sinking Spring Section Pt 1
39.159181 -83.221365   ///vibrations.looms.bedrooms
Sinking Spring Section
sinkingspring@buckeyetrail.org
↔ **Affiliate Section boundary**

↔ **Affiliate Section boundary**
Pike Lake Dam/ Scioto Trail Section Pt 34
39.159181   -83.221365   ///vibrations.looms.bedrooms
Scioto Trail Section
sciototrail@buckeyetrail.org

                          section boundary
                          13.7 miles
                          HCs

↔ boundary Pike Lake State Forest
39.176416   -83.173021   ///beans.inflicting.weaned
↔ boundary mixed ownership

✲ village of Nipgen
39.191182   -83.149432   ///springs.chicken.eggshell
limited services

△ *Mapleberry Farm Campsite*
39.191182   -83.149432   ///springs.chicken.eggshell
hosted site
primitive, water
call in advance
740-947-2331   HCs
                          3.1 miles
                          HCs

△ *BTA Schmidt Campsite*
39.187371   -83.03792   ///shillings.duplicity.fetch
hosted site
primitive, no amenities
maintained by BTA
sciototrail@buckeyetrail.org
call BTA Office in advance
740-394-2008   HCs
                          10.9 miles
                          $PCg

↔ boundary mixed ownership
39.193681   -82.96379   ///objects.daylight.gems
↔ boundary Scioto Trail State Forest

Note: Ohio State Forests do not allow dispersed camping.

▲ *Scioto Trail State Park Stewart Lake*
0.5 mile off trail
39.217707   -82.961409   ///imagine.unstated.examine
public campsites
18 walk-in campsites
primitive, tables, fire rings, latrine
non-reservable
740-887-4818

```
              PCg
              +0.5 road and spur
              **0.9 mile**
              +0.9 road
              $PCg
```

$▲ *Scioto Trail State Park Caldwell Lake*

0.9 mile off trail
39.23054   -82.955755   ///walnuts.partial.comment
public campground
55 vehicular sites, 2 cabins
15 electric, 40 non-electric
tables, fire rings, latrine
fee
reservation required
reserveohio.com
866-644-6727

```
              $PCg
              +0.9 road
              **27.1 miles**
              +0.2 spur
              $PCs
```

↔ boundary Scioto Trail State Forest
39.21099   -82.866105   ///digestion.ruthlessly.revive
↔ boundary private land

✽ village of Londonderry
0.6 mile off trail
39.26665   -82.790285   ///roadblocks.winter.global
limited services

↔ boundary private land
39.304049   -82.80033   ///heave.pools.loosely
↔ boundary Tar Hollow State Forest

Note: Ohio State Forests do not allow dispersed camping.

$△ *Tar Hollow State Forest Backpacker Campsite*

0.2 mile off trail
39.372685   -82.762509   ///bravery.explanation.jobs
public campsites
5 primitive sites
no amenities, dry
fee
permit form at trailhead kiosk near fire tower
call in advance
740-887-4818

↔ boundary Tar Hollow State Forest
39.344141   -82.724732   ///kilts.ketchup.antiseptic
↔ boundary private land

$PCs
+0.2 spur
4.6 miles
section boundary

State Route 327 at Clark Hollow Road/ Scioto Trail Section Pt 1
39.343921   -82.724375   ///eradicate.parachutes.unloaded
Scioto Trail Section
sciototrail@buckeyetrail.org
↔ **Affiliate Section boundary**

↔ **Affiliate Section boundary**
State Route 327 at Clark Hollow Road/ Old Man's Cave Section Pt 29
39.343921   -82.724375   ///eradicate.parachutes.unloaded
Old Man's Cave Section
oldmanscave@buckeyetrail.org

      section boundary
      8.4 miles
      +0.1 spur
      HCs

△ *Pretty Run Campsite*
0.1 mile off trail
39.350222   -82.624053   ///totally.vital.surrounding
hosted site
primitive, bench, fire ring, latrine, dry
maintained by BTA
oldmanscave@buckeyetrail.org

↔ boundary private land
39.395945   -82.545528   ///whisk.mouth.compete
↔ boundary Hocking Hills State Park

Note: Camp only in at designated areas in Hocking Hills State Park.

      HCs
      +0.1 spur
      14.2 miles
      +0.3 spur
      $PCg

$▲ *Hocking Hills SP Old Man's Cave Campground*
0.3 mile off trail
39.433128   -82.537932   ///indications.diversions.cultivation
public campground
137 vehicular sites, 14 non-electric walk-in sites
3 cabins
tables, fire rings, bathhouse
fee
reserve in advance
reserveohio.com
866-644-6727

      $PCg
      +0.3 spur
      10.3 miles
      $L

$ ■ *Lodges / Guesthouses*
39.503082   -82.534864   ///records.accentuate.rosier
4 commercial options along Rocky Fork Road
fee

$L
13.4 miles
HCs or +0.1 road $CCs

△ *Boesel Campsite*
39.592848 -82.451094   ///logical.entrusted.wicket
hosted campsite
primitive, no amenities, no fires

$△ *Lazy Ferret Glamping*
0.1 mile off trail
39.592692 -82.44867   ///advertises.silver.diagonally
commercial campsite
2 large canvas platform tents
tables, fire rings, latrine
fee
hipcamp.com

HCs
6.6 miles
section boundary

Boch Hollow West Trailhead/ Old Man's Cave Section Pt 1
39.627546 -82.431887   ///printed.draining.pave
Old Man's Cave Section
oldmanscave@buckeyetrail.org
↔ **Affiliate Section boundary**

↔ **Affiliate Section boundary**
Boch Hollow West Trailhead/ New Straitsville Section Pt 34
39.627546 -82.431887   ///printed.draining.pave
New Straitsville Section
newstraitsville@buckeyetrail.org

        section boundary
        11.6 miles
        but see hosted option off trail at 4.2 miles
        HE

↔ boundary private land
39.627546 -82.431887   ///printed.draining.pave
↔ boundary Boch Hollow Nature Preserve

Note: no camping in Nature Preserve. Please stay on the trail.

↔ boundary Boch Hollow Nature Preserve
39.617156 -82.398074   ///enjoyed.prop.defines
↔ boundary private land

        △ *Crisler Family*
        3.1 miles off trail
        39.572201 -82.392448   ///refresher.traitor.lunged
        private host
        will pick up hikers if available
        free tenting, use of bathroom
        contact in advance if possible
        jkcrisler@hockingcounty.com

↔ boundary private land
39.607537 -82.312644   ///sugar.blockbuster.fees
↔ boundary Wayne National Forest

Note: dispersed camping is allowed in Wayne National Forest

        △ *dispersed camping* allowed
        1.2 miles in Wayne NF
        fs.usda.gov/wayne

↔ boundary Wayne National Forest
39.599588 -82.30037   ///hint.females.inclusive
↔ boundary private land
        D
        0.2 mile
        HE

∟ *100 Acre Shelter*
39.600767 -82.299107   ///danced.suggested.commended
hosted open shelter
no fires
owner contact in shelter
        HE
        0.2 mile
        D

↔ boundary private land
39.601374 -82.293418   ///learnt.soothing.owns
↔ boundary Wayne National Forest

△ *dispersed camping* allowed
6.1 miles in Wayne NF
fs.usda.gov/wayne

△ *Stone Church Trailhead Camp*
39.608536 -82.248196   ///roofs.sentimental.truth
equestrian camp
primitive
maintained by Wayne National Forest
fs.usda.gov/wayne

△ *dispersed camping* allowed
4.0 miles in Wayne NF
fs.usda.gov/wayne

△ *Tecumseh Lake*
39.59942 -82.212146   ///brain.unhelpful.sufferings
primitive camping with advance permission
tables in picnic area, no latrine
shawneetrailtowncoordinator@gmail.com
740-580-2065

△ *dispersed camping* allowed
7.0 miles in Wayne NF
fs.usda.gov/wayne

✽ village of Shawnee
0.4 mile off trail from Tecumseh Lake
39.603848 -82.211944   ///menu.beans.humiliated
limited services
BTA Headquarters

↔ boundary Wayne National Forest
39.554712 -82.176877   ///rock.glimmers.patriotism
↔ boundary private land

D
1.7 mile
D

↔ boundary private land
39.534447 -82.165928   ///crabby.accelerate.view
↔ boundary Wayne National Forest

△ *dispersed camping* allowed
0.6 mile in Wayne NF
fs.usda.gov/wayne

↔ boundary Wayne National Forest
39.526586 -82.164919   ///weaving.qualify.splendid
↔ boundary mixed ownership

D
2.8 miles
+0.1 road
HCs

✲ village of Murray City
39.512984 -82.164386 ///logbook.wavelength.decode
no services

△ *Smoke Rise Ranch*

0.1 mile off trail
39.531175 -82.146769 ///thyroid.basic.spenders
hosted campsite
primitive, bathhouse
first tent night free for hikers
also has cabins for fee
smokeriseranch.com
740-767-2624

HCs
+0.1 road
5.4 miles
D

↔ boundary mixed ownership
39.525283 -82.136813 ///author.headings.caretakers
↔ boundary Wallace H. O'Dowd Wildlife Area

Note: no camping in Wildlife Area

↔ boundary Wallace H. O'Dowd Wildlife Area
39.537331 -82.105012 ///disturbance.grandest.merits
↔ boundary private land

↔ boundary private land
39.538026 -82.087138 ///constants.basis.inhibition
↔ boundary Wayne National Forest

Note: dispersed camping allowed in Wayne National Forest

△ ***dispersed camping*** allowed
3.5 miles in Wayne NF
fs.usda.gov/wayne

↔ boundary Wayne National Forest
39.54479 -82.061834 ///chatters.moping.autumn
↔ boundary Burr Oak State Park

Note: camp only in designated sites in Burr Oak SP

$▲ *Burr Oak Cove FS Campground*
0.5 mile off trail
39.549058 -82.059133   ///gull.participate.deranged
public campground
19 primitive sites
tables, fire pits, latrine, water
fee
managed by the Wayne National Forest
fs.usda.gov/wayne

                      D or +0.5 to Cove
                      4.1 miles
                      $PCg

$▲ *Burr Oak Sp Dock 2 Campground*
39.5234 -82.041127   ///pavilions.spindles.admitting
public campground
81 vehicular sites, 45 non-electric, 4 cabins
tables, fire rings, bathhouse
fee
reserveohio.com
866-644-6727

                      $PCg
                      1.6 miles
                      $L

$ ■ *Burr Oak Lodge and Conference Center*
0.4 mile off trail
39.53073 -82.03513   ///fallen.botch.alternative
commercial lodging
rooms, suites, cabins
fee
reserveohio.com
866-644-6727

                      $L
                      +0.4 road
                      5.1 miles
                      $PCg

$▲ *Burr Oak SP Dock 3 Campground*
39.551095 -82.023594   ///noodle.incomplete.troll
public campground
8 primitive sites
tables, fire rings, latrine
fee
reserveohio.com
866-644-6727

                      $PCg
                      3.8 miles
                      D

↔ boundary Burr Oak State Park
39.580307 -82.018176   ///rightfully.avid.delved
↔ boundary Wayne National Forest

△ *dispersed camping* allowed
1.9 miles in Wayne BF
fs.usda.gov/wayne

↔ boundary Wayne National Forest
39.577727   -82.00455   ///fries.surgical.reassuring
↔ boundary private land

D
0.5 mile
section boundary

State Route 78 at East Branch Church Rd./ New Straitsville Section Pt 1
39.577744   -81.99719   ///treatable.runner.refreshing
New Straitsville Section
newstraitsville@buckeyetrail.org
↔ **Affiliate Section boundary**

↔ **Affiliate Section boundary**
State Route 78 at East Branch Church Rd/ Stockport Section Pt 31
39.577744 -81.99719   ///treatable.runner.refreshing
Stockport Section
stockport@buckeyetrail.org

        section boundary
        5.5 mile
        HCs

△ $⌂ *Shew 's Orchard*
39.54642 -81.939699   ///elsewhere.scandalous.hiking
hosted site
free tent site in pasture if available, no amenities
cabin has fee, no electric, latrine, showers
shewpm@gmail.com
740-557-3032

        HCs
        21.2 miles
        $L

✲ village of Chesterhill
39.490505 -81.865369   ///horizon.lavished.impressions
limited services

Y Junction with American Discovery Trail which follows roads from Layman, OH, and is concurrent with BT/NCT to Milford

✲ village of Stockport
39.548522 -81.791832   ///oversaw.sofa.headphones
limited services

$ ■ *Stockport Mill Inn*
39.547992 -81.79033   ///certain.bureaucrats.gave
commercial lodging
14 rooms/suites
stockportmill.com
740-559-2822

        $L
        12.0 miles
        +0.8 road
        HE
        Pt 7 Stockport Section

Y Junction with main loop of Buckeye Trail, NCT takes Whipple and Road Fork Sections through Wayne NF. The Main Loop of the BT cuts across the mouth of what is sometimes called the "Wilderness Loop." (Not to be confused with designated wilderness.)
39.620001 -81.701128   ///ballooned.calibrate.largest

∟ Onion Run Shelter
0.8 mile off trail
39.630297   -81.698917   ///falsely.flashed.dreamy
hosted site
open shelter, no amenities
call 24 hours in advance
740-535-3204

Onion Run Rd at McMannis-Riggs Rd/ Stockport Section Pt 7
39.620001   -81.701128   ///ballooned.calibrate.largest
Stockport Section
stockport@buckeyetrail.org
↔ **Affiliate Section boundary**

↔ **Affiliate Section boundary**
Jct Onion Run Rd and McMannis-Riggs Rd/ Whipple Section Pt 25
39.620001 -81.701128 ///ballooned.calibrate.largest
Whipple Section
whipple@buckeyetrail.org

section boundary
32.1 miles
+0.8 road
HCs

⁂ village of Macksburg
0.3 mile off trail
39.631801 -81.455952 ///wings.invite.concept
no services

⁂ village of Warner
39.562192 -81.416813 ///apply.horizon.astronomer
no services

⁂ village of Whipple
39.521164 -81.415016 ///brightness.meadows.fulfilled
limited services

△ ***Halfhill Campsite***
0.8 mile off trail
39.508839 -81.393396 ///firms.tolerating.anticipated
hosted campsite
no amenities
notify owner in advance
halfhill757@gmail.com

HCs
+0.8 road
11.1 miles
D

⁂ village of Stanleyville
39.471987 -81.410788 ///blames.internet.venue
no services

$△ ***Lane Farm NF Campground***
1.5 miles off trail
39.435551 -81.358596 ///performance.cloudy.important
public campsite
5 primitive sites
tables, fire rings, latrine
fee
often has flooding problems
managed by Wayne National Forest
fs.usda.gov/wayne

↔ boundary mixed ownership
39.451473 -81.320606 ///stream.compacted.sorters
↔ boundary Wayne National Forest

Note: dispersed camping is allowed in the Wayne NF

△ *dispersed camping* allowed
2.5 miles in Wayne NF
fs.usda.gov/wayne

↔ boundary Wayne National Forest
39.462714 -81.301626   ///primaries.quadruple.outboard
↔ boundary private land

D
0.1 mile
D

↔ boundary private land
39.461862 -81.299856   ///short.scavengers.behaved
↔ boundary Wayne National Forest

△ *dispersed camping* allowed
6.7 miles in Wayne NF
fs.usda.gov/wayne

↔ boundary Wayne National Forest
39.465606 -81.222522   ///backers.handshakes.groove
↔ boundary private land

D
0.3 mile
D

↔ boundary private land
39.463452 -81.218445   ///sounded.amounts.bulk
↔ boundary Wayne National Forest

△ *dispersed camping* allowed
0.4 mile in Wayne NF
fs.usda.gov/wayne

↔ boundary Wayne National Forest
39.460189 -81.213767   ///fetching.analogy.unassuming
↔ boundary private land

D
0.7 mile
D

↔ boundary private land
39.46386 -81.204575   ///challenger.central.sues
↔ boundary Wayne National Forest

△ *dispersed camping* allowed
4.1 miles in Wayne NF
fs.usda.gov/wayne
section boundary

Jct County Rd 9 and T 356/ Whipple Section Pt 1
39.475473 -81.176835   ///wiser.interesting.panning
Whipple Section
whipple@buckeyetrail.org
↔ **Affiliate Section boundary**

↔ **Affiliate Section boundary**
Jct County Rd 9 and T 356/ Road Fork Section Pt 31
39.475473 -81.176835   ///wiser.interesting.panning
Road Fork Section
roadfork@buckeyetrail.org

      section boundary

     △ *dispersed camping* allowed
     16.7 miles in Wayne NF
     fs.usda.gov/wayne

↔ boundary Wayne National Forest
39.564972 -81.139968   ///doghouse.hazy.exclude
↔ boundary private land

     D
     1.2 miles
     D

↔ boundary private land
39.576286 -81.137393   ///swung.important.achieve
↔ boundary Wayne National Forest

     △ *dispersed camping* allowed
     2.6 miles in Wayne NF
     fs.usda.gov/wayne

↔ boundary Wayne National Forest
39.597089 -81.141513   ///ooze.debating.tactile
↔ boundary private land

     D
     0.5 mile
     D

↔ boundary private land
39.600991 -81.13675   ///backer.sweeper.fairness
↔ boundary Wayne National Forest

     △ *dispersed camping* allowed
     1.7 miles in Wayne NF
     fs.usda.gov/wayne

$△ *Ring Mill NF Campground*
39.608149 -81.122126   ///incomplete.goodbye.rattler
public campground
3 primitive sites
tables, fire rings, latrine
fee
managed by Wayne National Forest
fs.usda.gov/wayne

     △ *dispersed camping* allowed
     1/4 mile from road
     1.0 mile in Wayne NF
     fs.usda.gov/wayne

↔ boundary Wayne National Forest
39.606347 -81.130892   ///mistaking.mulled.segregation
↔ boundary private land

                              D
                         4.5 miles
                              D

↔ boundary private land
39.609722 -81.18497   ///excavating.loved.homeward
↔ boundary Wayne National Forest

$△ *Lamping Homestead NF Campground*

39.630445 -81.188918   ///eyeliner.innocently.scan
public campground
6 primitive campsites
table, fire ring, latrine
fee
managed by Wayne National Forest
fs.usda.gov/wayne

↔ boundary Wayne National Forest
39.630445 -81.188918   ///eyeliner.innocently.scan
↔ boundary mixed ownership

                            $PCs
                         7.6 miles
                              D

↔ boundary mixed ownership
39.680516 -81.26195   ///personal.precise.marzipan
↔ boundary Wayne National Forest

                    △ *dispersed camping* allowed
                    1/4 mile from road, south side only
                    0.3 mile in Wayne NF
                    fs.usda.gov/wayne

↔ boundary Wayne National Forest
39.682438 -81.26681   ///hunks.village.summertime
↔ boundary private land

                              D
                         6.2 miles
                              HE

∠ *Hulls Shelter*

39.661826 -81.341569   ///wobbles.baseballs.tingly
hosted site
open shelter, bench, no latrine
maintained by BTA
roadfork@buckeyetrail.org

                              HE
                         2.6 miles
                              $L

$ ☐ *The Barn/ Hayloft AirBnB*
39.685535 -81.373004   ///beware.overjoyed.papers
commercial lodging
sleeps 4
kitchen, bath
fee
airbnb.com
search Barn at Caldwell, OH

$L
17.3 miles
section boundary

✱ village of Belle Valley
0.25 mile off trail
39.790098 -81.554917   ///connectors.parcels.drifters
services

Y Junction with main loop of Buckeye Trail, NCT takes Road Fork and Whipple Sections through Wayne NF. The Main Loop of the BT cuts across the mouth of what is sometimes called the "Wilderness Loop." (Not to be confused with designated wilderness.)
39.786801 -81.548265   ///array.geological.wages

Belle Valley- Main St and Lake Dr/ Road Fork Section Pt 1
39.786801 -81.548265   ///array.geological.wages
Road Fork Section
roadfork@buckeyetrail.org
↔ **Affiliate Section boundary**

↔ **Affiliate Section boundary**
Belle Valley- Main St and Lake Dr/ Belle Valley Section Pt 25
39.786801 -81.548265 ///array.geological.wages
Belle Valley Section
bellevalley@buckeyetrail.org

Y Junction with main loop of Buckeye Trail, NCT takes Road Fork and Whipple Sections through Wayne NF. The Main Loop of the BT cuts across the mouth of what is sometimes called the "Wilderness Loop." (Not to be confused with designated wilderness.)

section boundary
0.2 mile
+0.6 road
$PCg

↔ boundary private land
39.788548 -81.547053 ///waitresses.originals.straying
↔ boundary Wolf Run State Park

Note: camp only in designated campgrounds in Wolf Run SP

$▲ ***Wolf Run State Park Campground***
0.6 mile off trail
39.791871 -81.539124 ///cooled.bristle.liberal
public campground
137 vehicular sites, cabin
72 electric, 65 non-electric
tables, fire rings, bathhouse, laundry
fee
reservation required
managed by Ohio DNR
reserveohio.com
866-644-6727

$PCg
+0.6 road
15.1 miles
+0.2 road
$L

✲ village of Belle Valley
39.786363 -81.551649 ///massaged.navigation.dates
limited services

↔ boundary Wolf Run State Park
39.812243 -81.543385 ///looking.blatantly.taker
↔ boundary private land

$ ☐ *Seneca Lake Cabins*
0.2 mile off trail
39.899842 -81.418587   ///culprit.mime.mainland
public lodging
two cabins
mini kitchen, electric, private bath
fee
info@senecalakecabins.com
740-685-2896

$L
+0.2 road
2.3 miles
+0.3 road
$CCg

↔ boundary private land
39.908427 -81.425123   ///fantasy.embodied.dodgy
↔ boundary Seneca Lake Area
managed by Muskingum Watershed Conservancy District

Note: camp only in designated campgrounds in Seneca Lake Area

$▲ *Seneca Marina Point Campground*
0.3 mile off trail
Seneca Park has multiple sections, tent camping on the point
39.928197 -81.43025   ///readers.solidly.bikes
commercial campground
321 vehicular sites
table, fire ring, bathhouse
fee
camplife.com/797/reservation/step1
740-685-6013

$CCg
+0.3 road
15.9 miles
+0.8 road
$CCg

↔ boundary Seneca Lake Area
39.937784 -81.425509   ///pouted.wrestle.answer
↔ boundary private land

✻ village of Old Washington
0.6 mile off trail
40.037774 -81.444931   ///borderline.enormous.vipers
limited services

↔ boundary private land
40.053689 -81.415819   ///defended.pivots.basically
↔ boundary Salt Fork State Park
managed by Ohio DNR

Note: camp only in designated campground in Salt Fork State Park

$▲ *Barn Yard Camping*
0.8 mile off trail
40.085688 -81.424692   ///clay.prettiest.vibrant
commercial campground
24 vehicular sites
tables, fire rings, electric, latrine, shower
fee
740-825-4594

$CCg
+0.8 road
13.5 miles
section boundary

$▲ *Salt Fork State Park Campground*
2.0 miles minimum off trail to park office, and then even farther to the campsites
40.096339 -81.476117   ///assess.spilt.proceed
215 campsites
electric, tables, fire rings, bathhouse, laundry
fee
managed by Ohio DNR
reserveohio.com
866-644-6727

↔ boundary Salt Fork State Park
40.131563 -81.447147   ///counts.successes.requirement
↔ boundary private land

Lodge Rd at Half Penny Lane/ Belle Valley Section Pt 1
40.132582 -81.358358   ///submitting.only.instant
Belle Valley Section
bellevalley@buckeyetrail.org
↔ **Affiliate Section boundary**

↔ **Affiliate Section boundary**
Lodge Rd at Half Penny Lane/ Bowerston Section Pt 32
40.132582 -81.358358 ///submitting.only.instant
Bowerston Section
bowerston@buckeyetrail.org

section boundary
11.5 miles
+0.25 spur
$CCg

↔ boundary private land
40.163416 -81.230929 ///closing.march.monarch
↔ boundary Piedmont Lake Area
managed by US Army Corps of Engineers

Note: camp only in designated campground in Piedmont Lake Area

$▲ *Piedmont Lake Marina and Campground*

0.25 mile off trail
40.168165 -81.228955 ///boom.crossroads.telephone
public campground
71 vehicular campsites, 6 cabins
electric, tables, fire rings, bathhouse, laundry
fee
managed by Muskingum Watershed Conservancy District
mwcd.org/places/piedmont-lake
740-658-1029

$PCg
+0.25 road
19.6 miles
+0.1 road
$CCg

↔ boundary Piedmont Lake Area
40.192926 -81.212142 ///giant.paused.steely
↔ boundary private land

✲ village of Piedmont
0.3 mile off trail
40.191352 -81.20313 ///fascination.reshape.title
limited services

↔ boundary private land BT 732.1
40.242577 -81.202727 ///litter.remake.shrugging
↔ boundary Clendening Lake Area
managed by Muskingum Watershed Conservancy District

Note: camp only in designated campground in Clendening Lake Area

$▲ *Clendening Lake Marina and Campground*
1.5 miles off trail
40.241415   -81.224056   ///spurred.dugouts.denoting
80 vehicular sites, cabins
some electric, some primitive
tables, fire rings, restroom
fee
managed by Muskingum Watershed Conservancy District
mwcd.org/places/clendening-lake
740-433-4858

$▲ *Hillbilly Hideaway Campground*
0.1 mile off trail
40.259553   -81.184721   ///pancake.period.barged
commercial campground
100 electric and primitive sites
tables, fire rings, latrine
fee
text in advance
740-582-5809

$CCg
+0.1 road
21.0 miles
$PCg

↔ boundary Clendening Lake Area
40.276122   -81.189099   ///opportunity.restores.winded
↔ boundary private land

✲ village of Deersville
0.4 mile off trail
40.307822   -81.188219   ///risky.planets.armpit
limited services

↔ boundary private land
40.308836   -81.197317   ///composes.shelters.differently
↔ boundary Tappan Lake Area

$▲ *Tappan Lake Park*
1.5 miles off trail
40.31884   -81.186107   ///duplicity.shop.detectable
public campground
500 campsites, electric and primitive, 11 cabins
tables, fire rings, bathhouse
fee
managed by Muskingum Watershed Conservancy District
mwcd.org/places/tappan-lake
740-922-3649

↔ boundary Tappan Lake Area
40.375031   -81.213608   ///mountain.pylon.punky
↔ boundary private land

✴︎ village of Bowerston
40.425321   -81.187808   ///kilt.belonging.balloon
limited services

↔ boundary private land
40.455044   -81.178924   ///villa.impact.interesting
↔ boundary Leesville Lake Area
managed by Muskingum Watershed Conservancy District

Note: camp only in designated campground in Leesville Lake Area

$▲ *Leesville Lake South Fork Marina*
40.465115   -81.190037   ///detonator.repeated.slimy
100 vehicular sites, some electric
tables, fire rings, restroom
fee
managed by Muskingum Watershed Conservancy District
mwcd.org/places/leesville-lake
330-343-6780

$PCg
11.8 miles
section boundary

↔ boundary Leesville Lake Area
40.468279   -81.202967   ///decreasing.evaporated.aviation
↔ boundary private land

Henderson School Rd at Tabor Ridge Rd/ Bowerston Section Pt 1
40.544211   -81.314537   ///ranches.brick.probed
Bowerston Section
bowerston@buckeyetrail.org
↔ **Affiliate Section boundary**

↔ **Affiliate Section boundary**
Henderson School Rd at Tabor Ridge Rd/ Massillon Section Pt 28
40.544211 -81.314537   ///ranches.brick.probed
Massillon Section
massillon@buckeyetrail.org

        section boundary
        6.7 miles
        $HCs

$p△ *Camp Tuscazoar Boy Scout Camp*
40.564166 -81.396289   ///gearbox.crumbs.seamstress
hosted site
hikers allowed to camp with permit
primitive, latrine
contact several weeks in advance
fee
tuscazoar.org
330-859-2288

        $HCs
        4.5 miles
        junction BT/ NCT

Y Junction with the main loop of the Buckeye Trail which continues north (counter-clockwise) from here. NCT south of here is concurrent with the BT. To the east, the NCT heads toward Pennsylvania.
40.608362 -81.428531   ///fetch.elite.sitcom

Iron Bridge at Zoar/ Massillon Section Pt 23
40.608362 -81.428531   ///fetch.elite.sitcom
Massillon Section
massillon@buckeyetrail.org
↔ **Affiliate /Chapter boundary**

↔ **Affiliate/ Chapter boundary**
Iron Bridge at Zoar
40.608362 -81.428531 ///fetch.elite.sitcom
Wampum Chapter
northcountrytrail.org/pennsylvania/wam

junction BT/NCT
0.6 mile
HCs

✲ historic village of Zoar
40.613416 -81.422354 ///listens.feasts.mining
limited services

$ ☐ ***Zoar Guest House***
40.611778 -81.423854 ///curable.atoms.sideways
commercial lodging
2 rooms/suites
fee
zoarguesthouse.com
330-323-1529

$L
0.4 mile
HCs

△ ***Zoar Campsite***
40.615892 -81.418342 ///brightly.pausing.requirement
hosted site
primitive, no amenities, dry
no fires
property managed by village of Zoar
and Muskingum Watershed Conservancy District
call on arrival 330-874-2113

HCs
31.3 miles
$L

✲ village of Magnolia
40.651624 -81.298618 ///grazed.slogans.waging
limited services

✲ village of Waynesburg
40.667775 -81.257257 ///rice.impeccably.deranged
limited services

✲ village of Malvern
40.689711 -81.180267 ///constructed.teaches.fiesta
limited services

$ ☐ ***Breezewood Cabin***
40.729713 -81.028773 ///funnels.diet.primer
commercial lodging
cabin for 3 guests
fee
reserve through AirBnB
airbnb.com/rooms/32333305

$L
7.7 miles
$L

✲ village of Hanoverton
40.753063 -80.936698 ///counted.rant.robots
limited services

$ ☐ *Spread Eagle Tavern and Inn*

40.753623 -80.934874 ///harp.distort.plums
commercial lodging
6 rooms/suites
fee
spreadeagletavern.com
330-223-1583

$L
3.3 miles
HCs

△ *Church of St. Philip Neri*

40.735969 -80.883579 ///struck.furnace.straps
hosted site
tenting behind the church
space for small trailer
table, restroom in building, electric
contact in advance
firekernaljoe@yahoo.com
330–424-7648

HCs
12.0 miles
+0.5 road
$L

✲ village of Lisbon
40.772156 -80.76806 ///pencil.ready.ankle
services

$ ■ *Motels*

0.5 mile off trail
40.765566 -80.750765 ///defeat.sprint.locked
commercial lodging
two small motels south on US 30
fee

$L
+0.5 road
1.7 miles
$L

$ ■ *Days Inn*

40.765591 -80.729661 ///suggestions.driveway.suffer
commercial lodging
fee
wyndhamhotels.com
330-420-0111

$L
1.3 miles
HCs

△ Shortest Covered Bridge Campsite
40.762127 -80.703738   ///purchasers.immune.swallowing
hosted site
primitive, bench, no latrine
owned by
Elk Run Township Tourism
elkruntownshiptourismbureau.org

HCs
4.0 miles
+0.3 road
$L

↔ boundary private land
40.75548 -80.679535   ///limited.sleepy.rear
↔ boundary Beaver Creek State Park
managed by Ohio DNR

Note: camp only in designated areas in Beaver Creek SP

↔ boundary Beaver Creek State Park
40.746182 -80.670179   ///ranch.tonics.online
↔ boundary private land

$ ■ Getaway Beaver Creek
0.3 mile off trail
40.741217 -80.648766   ///clocks.stylish.realist
commercial lodging
38 tiny cabins, mini-kitchen
no tents
fee
getaway.house/pittsburgh-cleveland

$L
+0.3 road
2.1 miles
$PCg

↔ boundary private land
40.732567 -80.626493   ///functions.bulges.recipes
↔ boundary Beaver Creek State Park

Note: camp only at designated areas in Beaver Creek SP

$▲ Beaver Creek SP Family Campground
40.731467 -80.622667 ///milked.hears.uses
public campground
45 vehicular sites
6 electric, 39 non-electric
2 rustic cabins
tables, fire rings, latrine
reservation required
fee
managed by Ohio DNR
reserveohio.com
866-644-6727

                $PCg
                3.8 miles
                $PCg

$▲ Beaver Creek SP Group Campsites
40.706178 -80.58223 ///mats.wires.saints
public campsites
primitive group campsite
tables, fire rings, latrine
reservation required
fee
managed by Ohio DNR
reserveohio.com
866-644-6727

                $PCg
                1.5 miles
                +0.2 spur
                $PCg

$▲ Beaver Creek SP Equestrian Campground
0.2 mile off trail
40.713469 -80.581828 ///nudged.swing.gasp
public campground
59 primitive sites, dry
tables, fire rings, latrine
reservation required
fee
managed by Ohio DNR
reserveohio.com
866-644-6727

                $PCg
                +0.2 spur
                7.1 miles
                HE HCs

↔ boundary Beaver Creek State Park
40.71694 -80.589428 ///basin.suggestive.ranks
↔ boundary private land

∠ △ *Pappy Z's Shelter*
40.740681   -80.559452   ///strings.rankings.gifted
hosted site
open shelter, tents allowed
primitive, fire ring, dry
water spigot is 0.5 trail mile west at
40.738535   -80.565546
///encounters.scrambles.songbook

HE HCs
5.7 miles
state line

↔ boundary private land
40.741055   -80.547564   ///grafted.lightly.drills
↔ boundary Sheepskin Hollow Nature Preserve

Note: no camping in Sheepskin Hollow

↔ boundary Sheepskin Hollow Nature Preserve
40.747947   -80.54044   ///physical.chainsaw.easiest
↔ boundary private land

↔ boundary private land
40.753572   -80.538938   ///apart.whizzed.expiration
↔ boundary Sheepskin Hollow Nature Preserve

Note: no camping in Sheepskin Hollow

↔ boundary Sheepskin Hollow Nature Preserve
40.769516   -80.537587   ///noteworthy.fiction.claw
↔ boundary private land

Ohio/Pennsylvania state line
40.774862   -80.519197   ///likely.chatted.shaping
Wampum Chapter
northcountrytrail.org/pennsylvania/wam
↔ **Chapter Internal boundary**

Pennsylvania

See legend and general info for help in interpreting the listings. There is no camping in Pennsylvania State Game Areas which host many miles of the NCT.

↔ **Chapter Internal boundary**
Wampum Chapter
Ohio/Pennsylvania state line
40.774862   -80.519197   ///likely.chatted.shaping
northcountrytrail.org/pennsylvania/wam

        state line
        4.0 miles
        HE HCs

↔ boundary private land
40.774862   -80.519197   ///likely.chatted.shaping
↔ boundary State Game Lands #285
managed by Pennsylvania State Fish and Wildlife

Note: no camping in Pennsylvania SGAs.

∠ △ *Watt 's Mill Shelter*
40.791934   -80.491217   ///tolerance.rebounds.newsprint
hosted site
open shelter, space for tents
table, fire ring, no latrine
maintained by Wampum Chapter
wam@northcountrytrail.org

        HE
        2.5 miles
        +0.3 road
        $CCg

↔ boundary State Game Lands #285
40.792343   -80.469167   ///expensive.rungs.innovators
↔ boundary private land

$▲ *Crawford 's Camping Park*
0.3 mile off trail
40.787809   -80.458332   ///curvy.surgically.proposes
commercial campground
109 vehicular sites
tables, fire rings, bathhouse
fee
cash or check only
crawfordscampground.com
724-846-5964

        $CCg
        +0.3 road
        11.4 miles
        HE HCs

✱ village of Darlington PA 10.6
40.809397 -80.42312   ///arrows.lower.bonfire
limited services

∠ △ *Enon Valley Picnic Shelter*
40.863602 -80.400793   ///consoled.turtle.helpfully
hosted site
open shelter, space for tents
table, fire ring, no latrine

HE HCs
2.9 miles
HCs

△ *Edwards Farm*
40.860148 -80.367973   ///manly.havens.buttons
hosted site
camp in farmhouse lawn or woods on south side of road
no amenities, dry
contact in advance
wam@northcountrytrail.org

HCs
2.7 miles
$CCg

↔ boundary private land
40.859588 -80.363227   ///camels.mount.email
↔ boundary State Game Lands #148

Note: no camping in Pennsylvania SGAs.

↔ boundary State Game Lands #148
40.873609 -80.34825   ///advise.mend.advance
↔ boundary private land

$▲ *Mines & Meadows ATV Camp*
40.876901 -80.344614   ///threadbare.irritable.hiked
commercial campground
focus is ATVs but they do have tent sites
tables, fire rings, restroom
minesandmeadows.com
724-535-6026

$CCg
0.4 mile
HE

∠ *Shelter at Wampum Underground*
40.87668   -80.337193   ///inventions.riddle.officials
hosted site
table, fire ring, water and restroom at Mines & Meadows
maintained by Wampum Chapter
wam@northcountrytrail.org

                        HE
                        6.8 miles
                        HE HCs

✷ village of Wampum
40.8882   -80.337866   ///silly.salvage.pump
limited services

∠ △ *Sankey Hill Eagle's Nest Shelter*
40.931352   -80.316634   ///longest.poker.assess
hosted site
open shelter, space for tents
bench, fire ring, no latrine, dry
maintained by Wampum Chapter
wam@northcountrytrail.org
                        HE HCs
                        11.0 miles
                        +0.8 road
                        $CCg

✷ village of Energy
0.1 mile off trail
40.924812   -80.263181   ///pony.snore.invited
limited services

↔ boundary private land
40.929747   -80.241167   ///bumper.glue.discoveries
↔ boundary McConnell's Mill State Park
managed by the Pennsylvania DCNR

Note: no camping in McConnell's Mill SP

$▲ *Breakneck Campground*
0.8 mile off trail
40.936932   -80.168426   ///crockery.boiled.sawdust
commercial campground
vehicular sites, tent sites, cabins
tables, fire rings, bathhouse
fee
cheesemanfarm.com/breakneckcampground
724-368-3405
                        $CCg
                        +0.8 road
                        1.8 miles
                        chapter boundary

↔ boundary McConnell's Mill State Park
40.958938   -80.16831   ///request.bargained.reluctantly
↔ boundary private land

Wampum Chapter
Lawrence/Butler county line
40.957958   -80.163425   ///statues.resumes.undergoing
northcountrytrail.org/pennsylvania/wam
↔ **Chapter boundary**

↔ **Chapter boundary**
Butler Chapter
Lawrence/Butler county line
40.957958   -80.163425   ///statues.resumes.undergoing
northcountrytrail.org/pennsylvania/but

                                    chapter boundary
                                    7.7 miles
                                    $PE

↔ boundary private land
40.957447   -80.131797   ///graph.campers.retailers
↔ boundary Moraine State Park

Note: camp only at designated sites in Moraine SP

∠ *Link Road Shelter*
40.972545   -80.09648   ///apartment.scornful.spooks
open shelter
table, fire ring, latrine
fee
reservation required
managed by Pennsylvania DCNR
dcnr.pa.gov
888-727-2757 $PE
                    2.6 miles
                    +0.5 spur
                    $PE

$⌂ *Davis Hollow Outdoor Center*
0.5 mile off trail
40.961341   -80.068671   ///graver.remake.nightmares
historic cabin with bunks
currently closed, but it may reopen for hiker lodging in the future
contact Diane Winston
dianeswinston@yahoo.com
724-575-0471.
                    $PE
                    +0.5 spur
                    21.8 miles
                    HE

↔ boundary Moraine State Park
41.007797   -80.000629   ///inputs.harp.gatekeeper
↔ boundary private land

✷ village of West Sunbury
0.5 mile off trail
41.005935   -79.896516   ///scanty.prevented.potentially
limited services

↔ boundary private land
41.038863   -79.89613   ///resorting.buzzing.matches
↔ boundary State Game Land #95

Note: No camping in Pennsylvania SGAs

↔ boundary State Game Land #95
41.068118 -79.892654   ///kick.slang.derivative
↔ boundary private land

∠ John Stehle Memorial Shelter
41.07433 -79.886646   ///corrosive.gems.speculative
hosted site
open shelter
table, fire pit, no latrine
maintained by Butler Chapter
but@northcountrytrail.org

                HE
                18.7 miles
                $L

↔ boundary private land
41.075948 -79.88141   ///salute.surpassing.patch
↔ boundary State Game Land #95

Note: No camping in Pennsylvania SGAs

↔ boundary State Game Land #95
41.093701 -79.826309   ///cubist.wand.casually
↔ boundary private land

↔ boundary private land
41.097873 -79.718978   ///avoids.mashing.facelift
↔ boundary State Game Land #95

Note: No camping in Pennsylvania SGAs

↔ boundary State Game Land #95
41.079533 -79.69016   ///famed.bleary.configured
↔ boundary private land

✻ city of Parker
41.091847 -79.682057   ///conjunction.speech.unloads
services

$ ■ Parker House Hotel
41.096957 -79.680838   ///mobbed.hamburgers.financial
historic hotel under renovation
call for information
fee
724-399-9911 $L
                0.7 miles
                chapter boundary

Butler Chapter
Allegheny River at Parker
41.102069 -79.677643   ///dentures.sunrise.kinks
northcountrytrail.org/pennsylvania/but
↔ **Chapter boundary**

↔ **Chapter boundary**
Clarion Chapter
Allegheny River at Parker
41.102069 -79.677643   ///dentures.sunrise.kinks
northcountrytrail.org/pennsylvania/cla

                           chapter boundary
                           2.7 miles
                           $L

↔ boundary private land
41.102069 -79.677643   ///dentures.sunrise.kinks
↔ boundary Allegheny Valley Trail System
managed by avta-trails.org

Note: no dispersed camping in Allegheny Valley Trail corridor

$ ■ *Foxburg Inn and Hotel*
41.140207 -79.679245   ///compliant.equine.moment
commercial lodging
24 rooms/suites
fee
foxburginn.com
724-659-3116

                           $L
                           3.5 miles
                           $L

$ ■ *Barnard House BnB*
41.176641 -79.703884   ///complies.glove.adulthood
commercial lodging
6 rooms/suites
fee
thebarnardhouse.com
724-867-2261

                           $L
                           11.2 miles
                           HE

✲ borough of Emlenton
41.1764 -79.708306   ///developer.shreds.objection
services

∠ *AVTA Shelter*
41.268138 -79.795081   ///terms.lodges.anthem
hosted site
open shelter
table, fire ring, no latrine
maintained by Allegheny Valley Trail Association
avta-trails.org

                           HE
                           18.7 miles
                           HE

∠ Sandy Creek Shelter
41.308064   -79.661732   ///sitcom.loser.ants
hosted site
open shelter
fire ring, no latrine
maintained by Clarion Chapter
cla@northcountrytrail.org

                 HE
                 17.2 miles
                 +0.7 road
                 $CCg

↔ boundary Allegheny Valley Trail System
41.314446   -79.658556   ///edgy.fasts.refresher
↔ boundary private land

↔ boundary private land
41.317757   -79.636896   ///bathtubs.minimum.sparks
↔ boundary State Game Lands #45

Note: No dispersed camping in Pennsylvania SGAs

↔ boundary State Game Land #45
41.29993   -79.588917   ///concur.toast.stickler
↔ boundary private land

↔ boundary private land
41.293175   -79.569348   ///kettle.jiggle.layers
↔ boundary Allegheny Valley Trail System
managed by avta-trails.org

Note: no dispersed camping in Allegheny Valley Trail corridor

Allegheny Valley Trail System continues.
41.280825   -79.487648   ///toxic.little.golfer
↔ boundary State Game Lands #63
Clarion Highlands Trail continues through SGA

Note: no dispersed camping in Allegheny Valley Trail corridor
Note: no dispersed camping in Pennsylvania SGAs

↔ boundary Allegheny Valley Trail System
41.260762   -79.476189   ///bunker.indoors.shocked
↔ boundary State Game Land #63

↔ boundary State Game Land #63
41.24994   -79.47495   ///misled.prickly.insulated
↔ boundary private land

✶ borough of Shippenville
0.8 mile off trail
41.251328   -79.463578   ///sporty.craving.respectful
no services

↔ boundary private land
41.243745   -79.473062   ///sweated.farming.motivates
↔ boundary State Game Land #63

Note: no dispersed camping in Pennsylvania SGAs

$▲ Rustic Acres
0.7 mile off trail
41.235379   -79.439291   ///forgetting.soprano.apple
commercial campground
95 vehicular sites
full hookups to rustic, tables, fire rings, bathhouse
fee
camprustic.com
814-226-9850

      $CCg
      +0.7 road
      4.0 miles
      HE

↔ boundary State Game Land #63
41.221121   -79.441133   ///complicate.tremor.snapping
↔ boundary private land

∠ Doe Run Shelter
41.22271   -79.419822   ///doodle.development.swings
hosted site
open shelter
bench, fire ring, no latrine
maintained by Clarion Chapter
cla@northcountrytrail.org

      HE
      14.3 miles
      +0.3 road
      $CCg

↔ boundary private land PA 155.8
41.242189   -79.39084   ///gull.placed.roundabout
↔ boundary State Game Land #72

Note: no dispersed camping in Pennsylvania SGAs

↔ boundaryState Game Land #72 PA 159.4
41.260321   -79.36346   ///farmed.swaying.promise
↔ boundary private land

$▲ Kalyumet Camping and Cabins
0.3 mile off trail
41.309661 -79.289731   ///shocks.millionaire.fidelity
commercial campground
143 vehicular sites, luxury cabin
125 electric,18 non-electric
tables, fire rings, bathhouse, laundry
fee
kalyumet.com
814-744-9622

$CCg
+0.3 road
1.2 miles
HE

↔ boundary private land
41.300505 -79.282908   ///rips.fumble.boring
↔ boundary State Game Land #283

Note: no dispersed camping in Pennsylvania SGAs

∠ Highland Shelter
41.298997 -79.276209   ///corrugated.cartridges.upshot
hosted site
open shelter
bench, fire ring, no latrine
maintained by Clarion Chapter
cla@northcountrytrail.org

HE
3.3 miles
HCs

$△ Clarion River Campsites
41.306703 -79.252434   ///stag.technical.reality
public campsites
3 legal campsites along Clarion River
table, fire ring, latrine
fee
reservation required
maintained by Cook Forest State Park
reserveamerica.com (complete link in Appendix)
814-744-8407

PCs
9.2 miles
+0.8 road
$CCg

↔ boundary State Game Land #283
41.319815 -79.22231   ///playfully.citrus.makes
↔ boundary Cook Forest State Park

Note: no dispersed camping in Cook Forest State Park

$▲ Deer Meadow Campground
0.8 mile off trail
41.369483   -79.21771   ///forklift.royally.inaccurate
commercial campground
over 500 vehicular sites
mostly an RV park, but will accommodate tents
tables, fire rings, bathhouse, laundry
fee
deermeadow.com
814-927-8125

$CCg
+0.8 road
3.3 miles
D

↔ boundary Cook Forest State Park
41.394258   -79.219134   ///willow.informal.realist
↔ boundary private land

↔ boundary private land
41.398991   -79.200037   ///looking.tricky.refurbish
↔ boundary Clear Creek State Forest

Note: primitive camping in Pennsylvania State Forests (defined as not having a motor vehicle) is allowed for one night at a location. To stay more than one night, you must acquire a permit.

△ *dispersed camping* allowed
1.3 miles in Clear Creek State Forest
dcnr.pa.gov

∠ Maple Creek Shelter
41.411351   -79.199222   ///lifts.overall.deciding
hosted site
open shelter
bench, fire ring, no latrine
maintained by Clarion Chapter
cla@northcountrytrail.org

△ *dispersed camping* allowed
0.3 miles in Clear Creek State Forest
dcnr.pa.gov

↔ boundary Clear Creek State Forest
41.41115   -79.203706   ///recovery.supreme.beneath
↔ boundary private land

D
3.8 miles
boundary Clarion Chapter

↔ boundary private land
41.421062   -79.212204   ///finance.enlarge.collage
↔ boundary State Game Land #24

Note: No dispersed camping in Pennsylvania SGAs

↔ boundary State Game Land #24
41.443746 -79.21083   ///icons.spilt.pumps
↔ boundary Allegheny National Forest

Clarion Chapter PA 189
south boundary Allegheny National Forest
41.443746 -79.21083   ///icons.spilt.pumps
northcountrytrail.org/pennsylvania/cla
↔ **Chapter boundary**

↔ **Chapter boundary**
Allegheny National Forest Chapter
south boundary Allegheny National Forest
41.443746   -79.21083   ///icons.spilt.pumps
northcountrytrail.org/pennsylvania/anf

Note: dispersed camping is allowed in the Allegheny NF

△ *dispersed camping* allowed
0.6 mile in Allegheny NF
fs.usda.gov/allegheny

△ *Cicely Campsite*
41.449021   -79.212976   ///reveals.tailors.boots
public land
primitive, fire ring, no latrine
maintained by Allegheny NF Chapter
anf@northcountrytrail.org

△ *dispersed camping* allowed
2.2 miles in Allegheny NF
fs.usda.gov/allegheny

∠ *Amsler Spring Shelter*
41.469891   -79.199687   ///shuddering.catcher.rubble
public land
open shelter
table, fire ring, no latrine
maintained by Allegheny NF Chapter
anf@northcountrytrail.org

△ *dispersed camping* allowed
3.2 miles in Allegheny NF
fs.usda.gov/allegheny

△ *Little Salmon Creek Campsite*
41.495964   -79.191962   ///pounding.barrage.musts
public land
primitive, fire ring, no latrine
maintained by Allegheny NF Chapter
anf@northcountrytrail.org

△ *dispersed camping* allowed
4.7 miles in Allegheny NF
fs.usda.gov/allegheny

△ *Four Mile Run Campsite*
41.519811   -79.215137   ///ringleader.rural.peanut
public land
primitive, fire ring, no latrine
maintained by Allegheny NF Chapter
anf@northcountrytrail.org

△ *dispersed camping* allowed
2.0 miles in Allegheny NF
fs.usda.gov/allegheny

∠ *Big Boulder Shelter*
41.539119 -79.223677   ///shortages.waltz.storybook
public land
open shelter
table, fire ring, no latrine
maintained by Allegheny NF Chapter
anf@northcountrytrail.org

△ *dispersed camping* allowed
1.3 miles in Allegheny NF
fs.usda.gov/allegheny

△ *Branch Road FS Campsites*
41.542685 -79.241444   ///everyone.futures.threadbare
public land
primitive, fire ring, no latrine
maintained by Allegheny NF
fs.usda.gov/allegheny

PCs
1.1 mile
$PCg

↔ boundary Allegheny National Forest
41.542267 -79.243761   ///household.ejects.extract
↔ boundary private land

$▲ *Kellettville Campground*
41.544483 -79.256335   ///reshape.scribbling.removes
public campground
19 vehicular sites, yurt
tables, fire rings, restroom
fee
reservation required
managed by USACE
recreation.gov/camping/campgrounds/251959

$PCg
0.9 mile
D

↔ boundary private land
41.54519 -79.264403   ///wanted.importantly.taping
↔ boundary Allegheny NF

Note: dispersed camping allowed in Allegheny NF

△ *dispersed camping* allowed
1.6 miles in Allegheny NF
fs.usda.gov/allegheny

△ **East Fork Campsite**
41.563145 -79.273738   ///migrations.prices.persuades
public land
primitive, fire ring, no latrine
maintained by Allegheny NF Chapter
anf@northcountrytrail.org

△ *dispersed camping* allowed
3.1 miles in Allegheny NF
fs.usda.gov/allegheny

△ **Spring Campsite**
41.593739 -79.259147   ///botch.detriment.again
public land
primitive, fire ring, no latrine
maintained by Allegheny NF Chapter
anf@northcountrytrail.org

△ *dispersed camping* allowed
0.1 mile in Allegheny NF
fs.usda.gov/allegheny

△ **Spring Road Campsite**
41.595087 -79.260907   ///carrots.lyrical.pitchers
public land
primitive, fire ring, no latrine
maintained by Allegheny NF Chapter
anf@northcountrytrail.org

△ *dispersed camping* allowed
1.6 miles in Allegheny NF
fs.usda.gov/allegheny

△ **Beaver Run Campsite**
41.611902 -79.272065   ///guided.blank.smoking
public land
primitive, fire ring, no latrine
maintained by Allegheny NF Chapter
anf@northcountrytrail.org

△ *dispersed camping* allowed
2.7 miles in Allegheny NF
fs.usda.gov/allegheny

△ **Coalbed Run Campsite**
41.637983 -79.243655   ///private.tokens.spuds
public land
primitive, fire ring, no latrine
maintained by Allegheny NF Chapter
anf@northcountrytrail.org

△ *dispersed camping* allowed
1.5 miles in Allegheny NF
fs.usda.gov/allegheny

∠ **Queen Creek Shelter**
41.654531   -79.23902   ///caller.vandalism.payment
public land
open shelter
table, fire ring, no latrine
maintained by Allegheny NF Chapter
anf@northcountrytrail.org

△ *dispersed camping* allowed
4.4 miles in Allegheny NF
fs.usda.gov/allegheny

△ **Across West Fork Campsite**
41.657638   -79.184518   ///forum.genuinely.candy
public land
primitive, fire ring, no latrine
maintained by Allegheny NF Chapter
anf@northcountrytrail.org

△ *dispersed camping* allowed
1.0 mile in Allegheny NF
fs.usda.gov/allegheny

△ **Triple West Fork Campsites**
41.648499   -79.171815   ///independent.autographs.before
public land
2 primitive sites, fire ring, no latrine
maintained by Allegheny NF Chapter
anf@northcountrytrail.org

△ *dispersed camping* allowed
2.1 miles in Allegheny NF
fs.usda.gov/allegheny

△ **Fool's Creek Campsite**
41.651225   -79.147139   ///defers.cone.insults
public land
primitive, fire ring, no latrine
maintained by Allegheny NF Chapter
anf@northcountrytrail.org

△ *dispersed camping* allowed
1.1 miles in Allegheny NF
fs.usda.gov/allegheny

△ **Lower Sheriff Campsite**
41.653982   -79.129501   ///procures.hugged.defend
public land
primitive, fire ring, no latrine
maintained by Allegheny NF Chapter
anf@northcountrytrail.org

△ *dispersed camping* allowed
2.1 miles in Allegheny NF
fs.usda.gov/allegheny

△ *Upper Sheriff Campsite*
41.660074   -79.109803   ///money.curricula.book
public land
primitive, fire ring, no latrine
maintained by Allegheny NF Chapter
anf@northcountrytrail.org

△ *dispersed camping* allowed
0.9 mile in Allegheny NF
fs.usda.gov/allegheny

∠ *Hunter Station Shelter*
41.649947   -79.102282   ///marking.noodle.robed
public land
open shelter
table, fire ring, no latrine
maintained by Allegheny NF Chapter
anf@northcountrytrail.org

△ *dispersed camping* allowed
2.2 miles in Allegheny NF
fs.usda.gov/allegheny

△ *Pell Run Campsite*
41.654271   -79.080492   ///prancing.sights.terribly
public land
primitive, fire ring, no latrine
maintained by Allegheny NF Chapter
anf@northcountrytrail.org

△ *dispersed camping* allowed
1.8 miles in Allegheny NF
fs.usda.gov/allegheny

△ *Messenger Run Campsite*
41.636132   -79.064498   ///undercover.deflect.grudges
public land
primitive, fire ring, no latrine
maintained by Allegheny NF Chapter
anf@northcountrytrail.org

△ *dispersed camping* allowed
4.3 miles in Allegheny NF
fs.usda.gov/allegheny

△ *Caterpillar Tree Campsite*
41.644695   -79.023428   ///queens.plunger.comparisons
public land
primitive, fire ring, no latrine
maintained by Allegheny NF Chapter
anf@northcountrytrail.org

△ *dispersed camping* allowed
1.5 miles in Allegheny NF
fs.usda.gov/allegheny

△ *Tionesta South FS Campsites*
41.634644 -78.996764   ///ears.plotted.searing
public land
primitive, fire ring, no latrine
maintained by Allegheny National Forest
fs.usda.gov/allegheny

△ *dispersed camping* allowed
0.2 mile in Allegheny NF
fs.usda.gov/allegheny

△ *Cherry Run FS Campsites*
41.633778 -78.995262   ///lace.perfected.iconic
public land
primitive, fire ring, no latrine
maintained by Allegheny National Forest
fs.usda.gov/allegheny

△ *dispersed camping* allowed
1.0 mile in Allegheny NF
fs.usda.gov/allegheny

∠ *Cherry Run Shelter*
41.639022 -78.979683   ///downloaded.mint.colder
public land
open shelter
table, fire ring, no latrine
maintained by Allegheny NF Chapter
anf@northcountrytrail.org

△ *dispersed camping* allowed
1.3 miles in Allegheny NF
fs.usda.gov/allegheny

△ *Rock City Campsite*
41.648355 -78.961123   ///triangular.dimension.compensate
public land
primitive, fire ring, no latrine, dry
maintained by Allegheny NF Chapter
anf@northcountrytrail.org

△ *dispersed camping* allowed
5.6 miles in Allegheny NF
fs.usda.gov/allegheny

△ *Fox 's Dam Campsite*
41.701341 -78.939515   ///veggies.icons.resounding
public land
primitive, fire ring, no latrine
maintained by Allegheny NF Chapter
anf@northcountrytrail.org

△ *dispersed camping* allowed
2.5 miles in Allegheny NF
fs.usda.gov/allegheny

△ *Two Mile Campsite*
41.710072   -78.909431   ///tattoo.aimlessly.blesses
public land
primitive, fire ring, no latrine
maintained by Allegheny NF Chapter
anf@northcountrytrail.org

△ *dispersed camping* allowed
1.0 mile in Allegheny NF
fs.usda.gov/allegheny

∠ *Gibb Spring Shelter*
41.719426   -78.896041   ///utter.flipping.alarms
public land
open shelter
table, fire ring, no latrine
maintained by Allegheny NF Chapter
anf@northcountrytrail.org

△ *dispersed camping* allowed
4.6 miles in Allegheny NF
fs.usda.gov/allegheny

△ *Bliss Hill Campsite*
41.750074   -78.885441   ///engendered.cocktail.radioactive
public land
primitive, fire ring, no latrine
maintained by Allegheny NF Chapter
anf@northcountrytrail.org

△ *dispersed camping* allowed
2.6 miles in Allegheny NF
fs.usda.gov/allegheny

$▲ *Red Bridge Recreation Area*
0.2 mile off trail
41.778404   -78.886817   ///snipped.noise.filler
public campground
55 vehicular sites (electric), 10 walk-in sites, cabins
tables, fire rings, bathhouse
managed by Allegheny NF
recreation.gov
814-362-4613

△ *dispersed camping* allowed
1.7 miles in Allegheny NF
fs.usda.gov/allegheny

△ **Root Run Campsite**
41.790139 -78.870383   ///landlords.witness.hindering
public land
primitive, fire ring, no latrine
maintained by Allegheny NF Chapter
anf@northcountrytrail.org

△ *dispersed camping* allowed
2.0 miles in Allegheny NF
fs.usda.gov/allegheny

∠ *Chappel Fork Shelter*
41.803001 -78.876585   ///mouthpiece.scarcely.skaters
public land
open shelter
table, fire ring, no latrine
maintained by Allegheny NF Chapter
anf@northcountrytrail.org

△ *dispersed camping* allowed
2.0 miles in Allegheny NF
fs.usda.gov/allegheny

△ *Briggs Run Campsite*
41.810278 -78.886155   ///recounting.pollution.description
public land
primitive, fire ring, no latrine
maintained by Allegheny NF Chapter
anf@northcountrytrail.org

△ *dispersed camping* allowed
1.0 mile in Allegheny NF
fs.usda.gov/allegheny

△ *Chappel Bay Campsite*
41.81055 -78.904244   ///decode.instant.shadowed
public land
primitive, fire ring, no latrine
maintained by Allegheny NF Chapter
anf@northcountrytrail.org

△ *dispersed camping* allowed
2.7 miles in Allegheny NF
fs.usda.gov/allegheny

△ *Hemlock Run Campsite*
41.841474 -78.884438   ///wordy.duck.exchanges
public land
primitive, fire ring, no latrine
maintained by Allegheny NF Chapter
anf@northcountrytrail.org

△ *dispersed camping* allowed
4.6 miles in Allegheny NF
fs.usda.gov/allegheny

△ *Hammond Run Campsite*
41.87331   -78.860728   ///grills.unfolds.submitting
public land
primitive, fire ring, no latrine
maintained by Allegheny NF Chapter
anf@northcountrytrail.org

△ *dispersed camping* allowed
0.3 mile in Allegheny NF
fs.usda.gov/allegheny

∠ *Hammond Run Shelter*
41.874684   -78.864783   ///squeaking.blamed.jigsaw
public land
open shelter
table, fire ring, no latrine
maintained by Allegheny NF Chapter
anf@northcountrytrail.org

△ *dispersed camping* allowed
0.1 mile in Allegheny NF
fs.usda.gov/allegheny

△ *Hammond Run Waterfall Campsite*
41.875563   -78.865727   ///lend.fridge.modern
public land
primitive, fire ring, no latrine
maintained by Allegheny NF Chapter
anf@northcountrytrail.org

△ *dispersed camping* allowed
1.1 miles in Allegheny NF
fs.usda.gov/allegheny

△ *Sugar Run Campsites*
41.882864   -78.879052   ///saturation.drifter.spurted
public land
2 primitive sites, fire ring, no latrine
maintained by Allegheny NF Chapter
anf@northcountrytrail.org

△ *dispersed camping* allowed
0.3 mile in Allegheny NF
fs.usda.gov/allegheny

△ **Fishing Hole Campsite**
41.884973   -78.880694   ///nurture.nurse.disdain
public land
primitive, fire ring, no latrine
maintained by Allegheny NF Chapter
anf@northcountrytrail.org

△ *dispersed camping* allowed
1.7 miles in Allegheny NF
fs.usda.gov/allegheny

△ **Nelse Run Campsite**
41.899612   -78.900038   ///awaiting.foremost.buzzed
public land
primitive, fire ring, no latrine
maintained by Allegheny NF Chapter
anf@northcountrytrail.org

△ *dispersed camping* allowed
3.7 miles in Allegheny NF
fs.usda.gov/allegheny

△ **Johnnycake Run Campsite**
41.928741   -78.921512   ///divisional.drift.login
public land
primitive, fire ring, no latrine
maintained by Allegheny NF Chapter
anf@northcountrytrail.org

△ *dispersed camping* allowed
2.3 miles in Allegheny NF
fs.usda.gov/allegheny

∠ **Tracy Ridge Shelter**
0.8 mile off trail
41.965934   -78.919576   ///unimpeded.cool.pulpit
public land
open shelter
table, fire ring, no latrine
maintained by Allegheny NF Chapter
anf@northcountrytrail.org

△ *dispersed camping* allowed
0.3 mile in Allegheny NF
fs.usda.gov/allegheny

△ **Tracy Run North and South Campsites**
41.959723   -78.921613   ///recollect.apron.sideburns
public land
2 primitive sites, fire ring, no latrine
maintained by Allegheny NF Chapter
anf@northcountrytrail.org

△ *dispersed camping* allowed
0.2 mile in Allegheny NF
fs.usda.gov/allegheny

∠ *Tracy Run North Shelter*
41.961764 -78.918774   ///stub.unsettled.underwrite
public land
open shelter
table, fire ring, no latrine
maintained by Allegheny NF Chapter
anf@northcountrytrail.org

△ *dispersed camping* allowed
4.5 miles in Allegheny NF
fs.usda.gov/allegheny

$▲ *Willow Bay Recreation Area*
1.2 miles off trail to tent sites
41.98874 -78.923309   ///stole.reinstated.referee
public campground
101 vehicular sites: 38 electric, 63 non-electric
11 cabins
tables, fire rings, bathhouse
fee
managed by Allegheny NF
recreation.gov
814-368-4158

△ *Schoolhouse Hollow Campsite*
41.993357 -78.897399   ///rulings.finely.amuses
public land
primitive, fire ring, no latrine
maintained by Allegheny NF Chapter
anf@northcountrytrail.org

△ *dispersed camping* allowed
0.4 mile in Allegheny NF
fs.usda.gov/allegheny

↔ boundary Allegheny National Forest
41.997918 -78.897948   ///hairspray.heads.reggae
↔ boundary Allegany State Park

Allegheny National Forest Chapter
Pennsylvania/New York state line
41.997918 -78.897948   ///hairspray.heads.reggae
northcountrytrail.org/pennsylvania/anf
↔ **Chapter boundary**

New York

See legend and general info for help in interpreting the listings. New York has many small state forests which make possible most of the off-road miles across the state. Dispersed camping is allowed in almost all of these, and no permit is required.

↔ **Chapter/ Affiliate boundary**
Pennsylvania/New York state line
41.997918   -78.897948   ///hairspray.heads.reggae
Finger Lakes Trail Conference
fingerlakestrail.org
The FLT section of the NCT has been arbitrarily divided into 4 segments
Maps M1-M4 1 maintained by Foothills Trail Club
585-658-9320

↔ boundary Allegheny National Forest
41.997918   -78.897948   ///hairspray.heads.reggae
↔ boundary Allegany State Park

state line
7.2 miles
PE

Note: dispersed camping not allowed in State Park

∠ *Willis Creek Shelter*
42.004469   -78.838759   ///parrot.squeak.overpower
public land
open shelter, space for tent
table, fire ring, latrine
maintained by FLTC and Foothills Trail Club
fingerlakestrail.org

PE
6.4 miles
PE

∠ *Stony Brook Shelter*
42.035252   -78.767234   ///surveys.powering.sticks
public land
open shelter, space for tent
table, fire ring, latrine
maintained by FLTC and Foothills Trail Club
fingerlakestrail.org

PE
5.6 miles
PE

∠ *Beck Hollow Shelter*
42.086172   -78.776354   ///grain.hooking.benefit
public land
open shelter, space for tent
table, fire ring, latrine
maintained by FLTC and Foothills Trail Club
fingerlakestrail.org

PE
7.6 miles
$L

↔ boundary Allegany State Park
42.107818 -78.770644 ///bonkers.tactic.grazes
↔ boundary Seneca Indian Reservation

Note: no camping on Seneca Nation land

$ ■ *Seneca Casino*

42.158739 -78.74335 ///temperament.shortage.storyline
commercial hotel and casino
413 rooms
fee
senecacasinos.com

$L
0.8 mile
$L

$ □ *White Pine Lodge*

42.156993 -78.74898 ///baked.catching.drills
commercial inn
8 rooms/suites
fee
whitepine716.com
716-945-7600

⁂ village of Salamanca
1.4 miles off trail to center of town
42.15526 -78.716292 ///documents.geology.misfit
limited services
one additional BnB

$L
6.0 miles
D

Note: The Bucktooth SF Shelter and the Bucktooth Bivouac Area are not accessible on foot during the hunting closures, May 1-31 and October 1-December 22. The Bucktooth Shelter can be reached by vehicle on W. Branch Bucktooth Run Road and a 0.2 mile walk. Be sure to consult Finger Lakes Trail Maps.

↔ boundary Seneca Indian Reservation
42.156014 -78.79206 ///velocities.golfer.upwardly
↔ boundary private land

↔ boundary private land
42.175036 -78.818582 ///harmless.scanning.stepped
↔ boundary Bucktooth State Forest

Note: dispersed camping is allowed in NY state forests

△ *dispersed camping* allowed
2.3 miles in Bucktooth SF
dec.ny.gov

∠ *Bucktooth SF Shelter*
42.198093   -78.815857   ///grinders.kitten.backer
public land
open shelter
table, benches, fire ring, latrine
maintained by FLTC and Foothills Trail Club
fingerlakestrail.org

△ *dispersed camping* allowed
0.5 mile in Bucktooth SF
dec.ny.gov

↔ boundary Bucktooth State Forest
42.203575   -78.812044   ///waters.broadcasts.value
↔ boundary private land

D
0.4 mile
PCs

↔ boundary private land
42.204592   -78.805177   ///miles.flunk.slender
↔ boundary Bucktooth State Forest

△ *Bucktooth Bivouac Area*
42.205135   -78.805193   ///bouquet.deep.supplied
public land
primitive
fire ring, no latrine, dry
maintained by FLTC and Foothills Trail Club
fingerlakestrail.org

△ *dispersed camping* allowed
0.5 mile in Bucktooth SF
dec.ny.gov

↔ boundary Bucktooth State Forest
42.201477   -78.797474   ///sensitive.rectangles.calibrated
↔ boundary private land

D
2.0 miles
D

↔ boundary private land
42.226359   -78.798568   ///docking.fences.pitchers
↔ boundary Elkdale State Forest

Note: dispersed camping is allowed in NY state forests

△ *dispersed camping* allowed
1.9 miles in Elkdale SF
dec.ny.gov

↔ boundary Elkdale State Forest
42.22871 -78.768098   ///defectors.cost.lapses
↔ boundary private land

D
3.0 miles
D

↔ boundary private land
42.2043 -78.735225   ///friction.elegant.amplifier
↔ boundary Rock City State Forest

Note: dispersed camping is allowed in NY state forests

△ *dispersed camping* allowed
1.8 miles in Rock City SF
dec.ny.gov

∠ *Little Rock City Shelter*

42.20827 -78.715895   ///guideline.boardroom.experiments
public land
open shelter
table, benches, fire ring, latrine, dry
maintained by NY DEC
dec.ny.gov

△ *dispersed camping* allowed
0.4 mile in Rock City SF
dec.ny.gov

△ *Little Rock City Day Use Area Campsite*

0.2 mile off trail
42.207702 -78.706869   ///indecision.ditches.motivating
public land
tables, dry
maintained by NY DEC
dec.ny.gov

△ *dispersed camping* allowed
2.5 miles in Rock City SF
dec.ny.gov

△ *Seneca CCC Camp Campsite*

42.223308 -78.700893   ///accumulate.bubble.purchaser
public land
primitive, table
maintained by NY DEC
dec.ny.gov

△ *dispersed camping* allowed
1.6 miles in Rock City SF
dec.ny.gov

↔ boundary Rock City State Forest
42.238116 -78.696859   ///dent.headphones.passwords
↔ boundary McCarty Hill SF

Note: dispersed camping is allowed in NY state forests

△ *dispersed camping* allowed
1.5 miles in McCarty Hill SF
dec.ny.gov

↔ boundary McCarty Hill SF
42.256998 -78.695514   ///pint.magazines.procession
↔ boundary private land

△ *Radio Tower Bivouac Area*
42.256998 -78.695514   ///pint.magazines.procession
hosted site
primitive, no amenities, dry
please call in advance
managed by Holiday Valley Ski Area
716-699-2345

∠ *Gravel Floor Shelter*
0.3 mile off trail
42.256998 -78.695514   ///pint.magazines.procession
hosted
open shelter with gravel floor
table, dry
please call in advance
managed by Holiday Valley Ski Area
716-699-2345

HCs and HE
+0.3 spur to shelter
0.9 mile
HCs

△ *Holiday Valley Bivouac Area*
42.26497 -78.69354   ///reborn.speeded.detection
primitive
table
please call in advance
managed by Holiday Valley Ski Area
716-699-2345

HCs
7.1 miles
HCs

✳ village of Ellicottville
0.75 mile off trail
42.275783 -78.671139   ///compiled.diggers.garbage
services
additional commercial lodging

Note: Poverty Hill Bivouac Area is not accessible during the hunting closures, May 1-31 and October 1-December 22. Be sure to consult the Finger Lakes Trail maps.

△ *Poverty Hill Bivouac Area*
42.309116 -78.672813   ///lists.retire.logistical
hosted site
primitive, fire ring, no latrine, dry
maintained by FLTC
fingerlakestrail.org

                        HCs
                        6.4 miles
                        $HE

$ △ *Teach Bunkhouse*
42.342652 -78.613116   ///promotes.woke.awarded
private rustic cabin
sleeps 3, mini kitchen, bottled water provided, no shower
fee
contact 24 hours in advance
716-930-5434
716-335-6625

                        $HE
                        3.7 miles
                        HCs

Y junction with Conservation Trail Branch (branch goes north) of the FLT system
42.348503 -78.584179   ///installing.deserve.application

△ *Cobb Campsite*
0.25 off trail
42.337863 -78.577756   ///isolated.gushed.adamant
hosted site
primitive, table, fire ring, grill, stream at NY 242
maintained by FLTC
fingerlakestrail.org

                        HCs
                        1.8 miles
                        D

↔ boundary private land
42.337704 -78.554968   ///formula.ventilation.executive
↔ boundary Boyce Hill State Forest

Note: dispersed camping is allowed in NY state forests

                 △ *dispersed camping* allowed
                 1.4 miles in Boyce Hill SF
                 dec.ny.gov

∠ *Boyce Hill Shelter*
42.334278 -78.533252   ///extension.passage.uneducated
public land
open shelter,
table, bench, fire ring, latrine
maintained by FLTC
fingerlakestrail.org

△ *dispersed camping* allowed
0.7 mile in Boyce Hill SF
dec.ny.gov

△ *Boyce Hill Bivouac Area*
42.332565 -78.52115   ///emptiness.help.known
public land
primitive, no amenities
maintained by FLTC
fingerlakestrail.org

△ *dispersed camping* allowed
0.5 mile in Boyce Hill SF
dec.ny.gov

↔ boundary Boyce Hill State Forest
42.337387   -78.51703
///iconic.owners.salmon
↔ boundary private land

D
1.9 miles
D $▲ *Triple R Campground*
                                               1.3 miles off trail
42.335314 -78.492317   ///deprives.sketchbook.noble
                                           commercial campground
                                             over 700 sites, cabins
                                  electric, tables, fire rings, bathhouse
                                                               fee
                                                     triplercamp.com
                                                        716-676-3856

↔ boundary private land
42.349282 -78.495229   ///lottery.further.margins
↔ boundary Bear Creek State Forest

Note: dispersed camping is allowed in NY state forests

△ *dispersed camping* allowed
1.8 miles in Bear Creek SF
dec.ny.gov

↔ boundary Bear Creek State Forest
42.360635 -78.477977   ///soliciting.handrail.dislodge
↔ boundary private land

D
4.8 miles
boundary M4, M5

Finger Lakes Trail
Kingsbury Hill Road
42.362356 -78.417076   ///blush.spirits.instructed
Finger Lakes Trail Conference
fingerlakestrail.org
Maps M1-M4 maintained by Foothills Trail Club
585-658-9320
↔ **Affiliate internal boundary**

↔ **Affiliate internal boundary**
Kingsbury Hill Road
42.362356 -78.417076   ///blush.spirits.instructed
Finger Lakes Trail Conference
fingerlakestrail.org
Maps M5-M9 maintained FLTC volunteers

                      boundary M4, M5
                      1.5 miles
                      $CCg

$▲ *Harwood Haven Campground*
42.37758 -78.393072   ///sandbags.extras.unsure
commercial campground
114 vehicular sites, cabins
electric and non-electric
tables, fire rings, bathhouse, laundry
fee
harwoodhaven.com
716-676-4747

                      $CCg
                      1.7 miles
                      D

↔ boundary mixed ownership M5 3.2
42.372634 -78.381442   ///cabins.protrude.dress
↔ boundary Bush Hill State Forest

Note: dispersed camping is allowed in NY state forests

                  △ *dispersed camping* allowed
                  0.6 mile in Bush Hill SF
                  dec.ny.gov

△ *Peet Hill Bivouac Area*
42.37517 -78.372001   ///custom.decorating.scatter
public campsite
no amenities
maintained by FLTC
fingerlakestrail.org

                  △ *dispersed camping* allowed
                  2.5 miles in Bush Hill SF
                  dec.ny.gov

↔ boundary Bush Hill State Forest
42.380116 -78.338226   ///pedestrian.regal.regular
↔ boundary private land
                      D
                      1.8 miles
                      D

↔ boundary private land
42.39083 -78.324965   ///earl.documents.overall
↔ boundary Farmersville State Forest

Note: dispersed camping is allowed in NY state forests

△ *dispersed camping* allowed
0.4 mile in Bush Hill SF
dec.ny.gov

△ *Farmersville Bivouac Area*
42.396535   -78.322734   ///seasonings.comforting.earpiece
public campsite
fire ring, dry
maintained by FLTC
fingerlakestrail.org

△ *dispersed camping* allowed
3.2 miles in Bush Hill SF
dec.ny.gov

↔ boundary Farmersville State Forest
42.42388   -78.324708   ///unsure.pedicure.rigorously
↔ boundary private land

D
3.0 miles
$CCg

$▲ *Windy Hills Campground*
0.3 mile off trail
42.442986   -78.265195   ///catches.quiet.insist
commercial campground
60 vehicular, electric sites
tables, fire rings, bathhouse
fee
windyhillscampgrounds.com
585-567-2779

$CCg
1.5 miles
D

↔ boundary private land
42.458185   -78.249832   ///fathers.blizzards.attractions
↔ boundary Swift Hill State Forest

Note: dispersed camping is allowed in NY state forests

△ *dispersed camping* allowed
1.6 miles in Swift Hill SF
dec.ny.gov

↔ boundary Swift Hill State Forest
42.469013   -78.226486   ///stepfather.rubbing.panicking
↔ boundary private land

                    D
                    2.4 miles
                    +0.3 spur
                    HCs

△ *Sixtown Creek Campsite*
0.3 mile off trail
42.466512   -78.197904   ///marketing.hothouse.oozing
hosted site
primitive, table
maintained by FLTC
fingerlakestrail.org
                    HCs
                    +0.3 spur
                    8.5 miles
                    HCs

Note: The Camp Sam Wood Shelter is not accessible during the hunting closures, May 1-31 and October 1-December 22. Be sure to consult Finger Lakes Trail Maps.

∠ *Camp Sam Wood Shelter*
42.524798   -78.121172   ///appreciated.nights.nitrate
hosted open shelter
table, latrine, unreliable pond water
owned by Camp Sam Wood
wnyscouting.org
                    HCs
                    2.3 miles
                    +0.1 road
                    $CCg

$▲ *Four Winds Campground*
1.0 mile off trail
42.549663   -78.089186   ///formally.shame.mistreated
commercial campground
about 200 sites
most electric, 20 tent sites
tables, fire rings, bathhouse, laundry
fee
abcamping.com/abfourwinds/campsites.php
585-493-2794
                    $CCg
                    +0.1 road
                    7.4 miles
                    HE

Y   junction with Letchworth Branch of the FLT system
42.554753   -78.053008   ///demand.prompting.feudal

✲   hamlet of Portageville
0.5 mile off trail
42.567428   -78.04532   ///attracting.drain.scrapped
limited services

$ ■ *Genesee Falls Inn*
42.57002 -78.039705
1.1 miles off trail
///thickened.options.arrows
historic commercial hotel
12 rooms/suites
fee
thegeneseefallsinn.com
631-882-3328

∠ *Hesse Shelter*
42.535558 -78.031172 ///ants.hospitality.crowned
private open shelter
fire ring
hikers may use if family is not using
maintained by Hesse family

HE
7.6 miles
+0.3 spur or 0.1 road
HCs or $L

✻ hamlet of Dalton
42.540902 -77.952423 ///prodigy.work.doubt
limited services

↔ boundary private land
42.502124 -77.878608 ///loaded.scriptures.medical
↔ boundary Rattlesnake Hill Wildlife Management Area

Note: camping is prohibited in NY State WMAs

↔ boundary Rattlesnake Hill Wildlife Management Area
42.500289 -77.859425 ///unionists.crocodiles.attainable
↔ boundary mixed ownership

✻ hamlet of Swain
42.477915 -77.853546 ///guru.doodle.champions
limited services

$ ■ *Swain Resort*
0.1 mile off trail
42.479625 -77.85818 ///alligators.betraying.lifts
commercial lodging
rooms/suites/condos
fee
swain.com/lodging/
607-545-6511

△ *Swain Hill Campsite*
0.3 mile off trail
42.479625 -77.85818 ///alligators.betraying.lifts
hosted site
primitive
water at owner's outside faucet

HCs or $L
+0.3 spur or 0.1 road
13.2 miles
+0.1 spur
HE

△ *Bossard's Cabin*
0.1 mile off trail
42.443395 -77.823304   ///ladders.loudness.created
hosted cabin
latrine, dry

Note: Bossard's Cabin is not accessible during the hunting closures, May 1-31 and October 1-December 22. Be sure to consult the Finger Lakes Trail maps.

HE
+0.1 spur
2.0 miles
D

↔ boundary private land M9 1.0
42.426609 -77.822617   ///communicate.unloads.kennel
↔ boundary Slader Creek State Forest

Note: dispersed camping is allowed in NY state forests

△ *dispersed camping* allowed
0.1 mile in Slader Creek SF
dec.ny.gov

△ *Slader Creek SF Bivouac Area*
42.420273 -77.824591   ///cure.chairlift.balanced
public site
latrine, dry
maintained by FLTC
fingerlakestrail.org

△ *dispersed camping* allowed
1.9 miles in Slader Creek and Klipnocky SF
dec.ny.gov

↔ boundary Slader Creek State Forest
42.415394 -77.82236   ///intro.clicker.booming
↔ boundary Klipnocky State Forest

△ *Klipnocky SF Bivouac Area*
42.397775 -77.81442   ///hack.orientation.watercress
public land
no amenities
maintained by FLTC
fingerlakestrail.org

△ *dispersed camping* allowed
2.3 miles in Klipnocky SF
dec.ny.gov

↔ boundary Klipnocky Forest
42.368929 -77.824033   ///dodgy.placidly.group
↔ boundary private land

D
1.3 miles
D

↔ boundary private land
42.358909 -77.820085   ///streaking.structured.squirted
↔ boundary Bully Hill State Forest

Note: dispersed camping is allowed in NY state forests

△ *dispersed camping* allowed
0.7 mile in Bully Hill SF
dec.ny.gov

∠ *Bully Hill Shelter*
42.356062 -77.810429   ///relaxation.mixes.reliving
public open shelter
fire ring, latrine
maintained by FLTC
fingerlakestrail.org

△ *dispersed camping* allowed
4.8 miles in Bully Hill SF
dec.ny.gov

↔ boundary Bully Hill State Forest
42.338475 -77.749253   ///captive.petrified.possibility
↔ boundary mixed ownership

D
2.1 miles
HE

∠ *Old Kanakadea Shelter*
42.345549 -77.73316   ///darker.clapped.winters
hosted shelter, poor condition
latrine
maintained by FLTC
fingerlakestrail.org

HE
0.2 mile
HE

∠ *Kanakadea Shelter*
0.1 mile off trail
42.348181 -77.729512   ///distortion.immaterial.cycle
hosted shelter
fire ring
maintained by FLTC
fingerlakestrail.org

HE
0.6 mile
$PCg

$▲ *Steuben County Kanakadea Park and Campground*
42.350333   -77.7130   //parents.revise.bends
public campground
70 vehicular sites
40 electric, 30 non-electric, 2 cabins
tables, fire rings, bathhouse
fee
managed by Steuben County
steubencountyny.gov/307/Parks
607-590-0535

                                         $PCg
                                         4.9 miles
                                         boundary M9, M10

Finger Lakes Trail
Webbs Crossing Road
42.366089   -77.68185   ///overlooked.atoms.possible
Finger Lakes Trail Conference
fingerlakestrail.org
Maps M5-M9 maintained FLTC volunteers
↔ **Affiliate internal boundary**

↔ **Affiliate internal boundary**
Webbs Crossing Road
42.366089 -77.68185   ///overlooked.atoms.possible
Finger Lakes Trail Conference
fingerlakestrail.org
Maps M10-M13 maintained FLTC volunteers

        boundary M9, M10
        0.3 mile
        $L

$ ■ *Days Inn*
42.367191 -77.675702   ///suggestive.golfer.disputes
commercial lodging
fee
wyndhamhotels.com/days-inn/

        $L
        10.7 miles
        D

↔ boundary private land
42.313503 -77.576042   ///enhances.unofficial.maximum
↔ boundary Burt Hill State Forest

Note: dispersed camping is allowed in NY state forests

        △ *dispersed camping* allowed
        0.6 mile in Burt Hill SF
        dec.ny.gov

∠ *Burt Hill Shelter*
42.312956 -77.565646   ///centuries.bottles.sharpens
public land
open shelter
table, fire ring, latrine
maintained by FLTC
fingerlakestrail.org

        △ *dispersed camping* allowed
        0.2 mile in Burt Hill SF
        dec.ny.gov

↔ boundary Burt Hill State Forest
42.313075 -77.563168   ///holding.dude.smudge
↔ boundary private land

        D
        7.1 miles
        +0.6 road
        $CCg

$▲ Lake Demmon Recreation Area
0.6 mile off trail
42.350022   -77.475586   ///swam.rare.shatter
commercial campground
68 vehicular sites. cabins
50 electric, 18 non-electric
tables, fire rings, bathhouse, laundry
fee
607-566-3511

$CCg
+0.6 road
20.8 miles
+0.7 spur
$CCg

✸ city of Bath M11 11.2
2.1 miles off trail (some motels closer)
42.336954   -77.318215   ///performance.daylight.settle
services

$▲ Hickory Hill Campground
0.7 mile off trail
42.365972   -77.31009   ///voters.consuming.buzzer
commercial campground
300 vehicular sites, cabins
electric, tables, fire rings, bathhouse, laundry
fee
hickoryhillcampingresort.com
800-760-0947

$CCg
+0.7 spur
0.2 mile
HE

∠ Hickory Hill Shelter M12 1.7
42.371647   -77.321855   ///imaginative.dishwasher.perkily
hosted site
open shelter
table, latrine
maintained by Hickory Hill Campground

HE
8.4 miles
$L

Y junction with Bristol Hills Branch of the FLT system (BH Branch turns north)
42.401837   -77.31563   ///tapes.enhanced.calculates

$ ■ Vinehurst Inn and Suites
42.388514   -77.259151   ///discarding.brochure.spinach
commercial lodging
25 rooms/suites
fee
vinehurstinn.com
607-569-2300

$L
3.2 miles
HCs

△ *June Bug Bivouac Area*
42.386232 -77.229099   ///reaffirmed.silly.massage
hosted site
primitive, fire ring, dry
maintained by FLTC
fingerlakestrail.org

HCs
4.9 miles
HE

∠ *Bob Muller Shelter*
42.396263 -77.177215   ///expressions.thickening.plucky
hosted site
open shelter
table, bench, latrine, may be dry
maintained by FLTC
fingerlakestrail.org

HE
0.7 mile
D

↔ boundary private land
42.395946 -77.1661   ///young.showcasing.grow
↔ boundary Birdseye Hollow State Forest

Note: dispersed camping is allowed in NY state forests

△ *dispersed camping* allowed
7.5 miles in Birdseye Hollow SF
dec.ny.gov

↔ boundary Birdseye Hollow State Forest M13 6.3
42.345724 -77.149749   ///immense.bookcases.kitchen
↔ boundary private land

D
0.4 mile
D

↔ boundary private land M13 6.7
42.341601 -77.152324   ///translated.villa.concealing
↔ boundary Birdseye Hollow State Forest

△ *dispersed camping* allowed
1.1 miles in Birdseye Hollow SF
dec.ny.gov

↔ boundary Birdseye Hollow State Forest M13 7.4
42.33716 -77.141423   ///travel.chunks.ferried
↔ boundary private land

                    D
                    2.6 miles
                    D

↔ boundary private land
42.30454 -77.127862   ///straps.soup.procured
↔ boundary South Bradford State Forest

Note: dispersed camping is allowed in NY state forests

                    △ *dispersed camping* allowed
                    1.3 miles in South Bradford SF
                    dec.ny.gov

Y junction with Crystal Hills Branch of the FLT system/ Great Eastern Trail (CH Branch turns south)
42.28924 -77.118764   ///overlooked.braves.channel

∠ *Moss Hill Shelter*
42.28924 -77.118764   ///overlooked.braves.channel
public land
open shelter
table, fire ring, latrine
maintained by FLTC
fingerlakestrail.org
                    △ *dispersed camping* allowed
                    2.9 miles in South Bradford SF
                    dec.ny.gov

↔ boundary South Bradford State Forest
42.311613 -77.101624   ///satisfy.montage.ready
↔ boundary Goundry Hill State Forest

                    △ *dispersed camping* allowed
                    1.7 miles in Goundry Hill SF
                    dec.ny.gov

△ *Corbett Hollow Bivouac Area*
42.31203 -77.092757   ///serving.points.driven
public land
primitive, fire ring
maintained by FLTC
fingerlakestrail.org
                    △ *dispersed camping* allowed
                    2.4 miles in Goundry Hill SF
                    dec.ny.gov

△ *Witch Hazel Camp*
0.5 mile off trail
42.327325 -77.070785   ///sprinkling.gone.mountain
hosted site
primitive, latrine
maintained by owner

△ *dispersed camping* allowed
0.5 mile in Goundry Hill SF
dec.ny.gov

△ *Pine Creek Bivouac Area*
42.327388 -77.057824   ///intrigues.spiral.insect
public land
primitive, fire ring
maintained by FLTC
fingerlakestrail.org

△ *dispersed camping* allowed
0.2 miles in Goundry Hill SF
dec.ny.gov

↔ boundary Goundry Hill State Forest
42.327293 -77.054091   ///segregation.still.monarch
↔ boundary private land

D
0.5 mile
D

↔ boundary private land
42.33459 -77.053361   ///relaxing.investors.motherhood
↔ boundary Sugar Hill State Forest

Note: dispersed camping is allowed in NY state forests

△ *dispersed camping* allowed
2.2 miles in Sugar Hill SF
dec.ny.gov

↔ boundary Sugar Hill State Forest
42.360834 -77.059946   ///hygiene.balance.tuition
↔ boundary private land

D
1.7 miles
D

↔ boundary private land
42.368698 -77.046299   ///fountain.grossly.porridge
↔ boundary Sugar Hill State Forest

△ *dispersed camping* allowed
1.5 miles in South Bradford SF
dec.ny.gov
boundary M13, M14

Finger Lakes Trail
Maple Lane
42.369364 -77.02261   ///beep.leotard.regain
Finger Lakes Trail Conference
fingerlakestrail.org
Maps M10-M13 maintained FLTC volunteers
↔ **Affiliate internal boundary**

↔ **Affiliate internal boundary**
Finger Lakes Trail
Maple Lane
42.369364 -77.02261   ///beep.leotard.regain
Finger Lakes Trail Conference
fingerlakestrail.org
Maps M14-M17 maintained FLTC and Cayuga Trails Club volunteers

boundary M13, M14

△ *dispersed camping* allowed
0.4 mile in Sugar Hill SF
dec.ny.gov

∠ *Parks Hollow Shelter*
0.25 mile off trail
42.369054 -77.012891   ///applauding.fluid.alligators
public shelter
no amenities
maintained by FLTC
fingerlakestrail.org

△ *dispersed camping* allowed
1.5 miles in Sugar Hill SF
dec.ny.gov

▲ *Sugar Hill Fire Tower Campground*
0.5 mile off trail
42.386871 -77.002484   ///suspecting.sofas.cycle
public campground
26 primitive sites
tables, fire rings, seasonal restroom
maintained by the NY DEC
dec.ny.gov

△ *dispersed camping* allowed
0.1 mile in Sugar Hill SF
dec.ny.gov

∠ *Sugar Hill Shelters*
42.382068 -77.002526   ///guests.animator.disappeared
public land
2 open shelters
table, latrine
maintained by FLTC
fingerlakestrail.org

△ *dispersed camping* allowed
3.4 mile in Sugar Hill SF
but watch for private property signs as trail often wanders over boundaries
dec.ny.gov

∠ Buck Settlement Shelter
42.372939 -76.955551   ///squint.blunders.language
public land
open shelter
table, fire ring, latrine
maintained by FLTC
fingerlakestrail.org

△ *dispersed camping* allowed
0.7 mile in Sugar Hill SF
dec.ny.gov

△ Ebenezer Crossing Bivouac Area
42.368754 -76.958721   ///depict.retain.pave
public land
primitive, no amenities
maintained by FLTC
fingerlakestrail.org

△ *dispersed camping* allowed
0.3 mile in Sugar Hill SF
dec.ny.gov

↔ boundary Sugar Hill State Forest
42.367758 -76.951678   ///correctly.studies.qualifier
↔ boundary private land

D
5.1 miles
+0.8 spur
$PCg

↔ boundary private land
42.361368 -76.930284   ///ultrasound.slicing.nickname
↔ boundary Watkins Glen State Park

Note: camp only in designated campground in Watkins Glen SP

$▲ Watkins Glen SP Campground
0.8 mile off trail
42.367809 -76.886291   ///crossroads.leading.divergence
public campground
276 vehicular sites, 9 cabins
electric, tables, fire rings, bathhouse
managed by the NY DEC
dec.ny.gov

$PCg
+0.8 spur
0.4 mile
+ various road
$L

↔ boundary Watkins Glen State Park
42.374555 -76.871141   ///reaches.directly.hurried
↔ boundary mixed ownership

✵ village of Watkins Glen
42.38107 -76.871506 ///supposed.optimal.cabinet
services

$ ■ *Motels*

various distances off or along trail
42.38107 -76.871506 ///supposed.optimal.cabinet
multiple commercial lodging options in
fee

                    $L
                    + various
                    5.1 miles
                    +0.1 road
                    $L

$ ☐ *Burdett House BnB*

0.1 mile off trail
42.417244 -76.849845 ///official.grounded.explode
commercial lodging
4 rooms
fee
burdetthousebandb.com
617-835-4492

                    $L
                    +0.1 road
                    1.6 miles
                    D

↔ boundary private land
42.441386 -76.848134 ///sharpen.margins.disbelief
↔ boundary Finger Lakes National Forest
managed by the USDA Forest Service
fs.usda.gov/gmfl

Note: dispersed camping is allowed in the Finger Lakes National Forest except in pastures from May 15-October 31 (due to cattle grazing).

            △ *dispersed camping* allowed
            1.9 miles in Finger Lakes NF
            watch boundaries near trail
            fs.usda.gov/gmfl

↔ boundary Finger Lakes National Forest
42.438377 -76.836075 ///expectancy.hard.occupiers
↔ boundary private land
                    D
                  0.6 mile
                  D

↔ boundary private land M15 9.2
42.442257 -76.830003 ///bodyguards.special.lyricism
↔ boundary Finger Lakes National Forest

            △ *dispersed camping* allowed
            1.5 miles in Finger Lakes NF
            watch boundaries near trail
            fs.usda.gov/gmfl

Y junction with Interlochen Branch of the FLT system (Interlochen Branch turns north)
42.442399 -76.811141   ///pile.despite.timely

∠ *Dunham Shelter*
42.440665 -76.810852   ///circulars.specifying.detonator
public land
open shelter
table, fire ring, latrine, dry
maintained by FLTC
fingerlakestrail.org

△ *dispersed camping* allowed
0.9 mile in Finger Lakes NF
watch boundaries near trail
fs.usda.gov/gmfl

↔ boundary Finger Lakes National Forest
42.431813 -76.815175   ///smacked.visited.chips
↔ boundary private land

D
2.8 miles
D

↔ boundary private land
42.415149 -76.794318   ///herself.resurface.paddocks
↔ boundary Texas Hollow State Forest

Note: dispersed camping is allowed in NY state forests

△ *dispersed camping* allowed
3.1 miles in Texas Hollow SF
watch boundaries near trail
dec.ny.gov

↔ boundary Texas Hollow State Forest
42.392111 -76.763849   ///cheesecake.colder.goodbye
↔ boundary private land

D
1.4 miles
HE

∠ *Rogers Hill Shelter*
42.38052 -76.756671   ///dame.changed.bathes
hosted site
open shelter
latrine
maintained by owner

HE
16.7 miles
HCs

↔ boundary private land
42.343579 -76.730321   ///imparting.research.mashed
↔ boundary Connecticut Hill Wildlife Management Area
managed by NY DEC
dec.ny.gov

Note: No camping in New York State WMAs.

↔ boundary Connecticut Hill Wildlife Management Area
42.383533   -76.660927   ///disagrees.gravel.overnight
↔ boundary mixed ownership

↔ boundary mixed ownership
42.407176   -76.640413   ///orchestras.sizzle.guests
↔ boundary Stevenson Nature Preserve
managed by Finger Lakes Land Trust
fllt.org

Note: no camping in Stevenson Nature Preserve

↔ boundary Stevenson Nature Preserve
42.390062   -76.664102   ///lads.bundle.concealing
↔ boundary mixed ownership

△ *Reiman Woods Bivouac Area*
42.406241   -76.633117   ///harnessing.however.spine
owned by FLTC
primitive, fire ring
maintained by FLTC
fingerlakestrail.org

        HCs
        0.5 mile
        HE

∠ *Locust Shelter*
42.402938   -76.625425   ///changed.supervision.imprinted
owned by FLTC
open shelter
table, fire ring, latrine
maintained by FLTC
fingerlakestrail.org

        HE
        1.1 miles
        +0.1 road
        $CCg

$▲ *Pinecreek Campground*
0.1 mile off trail
42.408935   -76.61152   ///actual.blunt.unassuming
191 vehicular sites, cabins
electric, tables, fire rings, bathhouse, laundry
pinecreekcampground.com
607-273-1974

        $CCg
        +0.1 road
        4.5 miles
        PE

↔ boundary mixed ownership
42.40453   -76.605341   ///discusses.seagulls.backer
↔ boundary Robert Treman State Park
managed by the NY DEC
dec.ny.gov

Note: camp only at designated places in Robert Treman SP.

△ *Sierra Shelter*

42.394397 -76.560258 ///proclaimed.torso.keyboard
public land
open shelter
hikers only may stay one night
one tent allowed outside shelter
latrine
managed by the NY DEC
dec.ny.gov

PE
0.3 mile
+0.2 spur
PCg

$▲ *Robert Treman State Park Campground*

0.2 mile off trail
42.396409 -76.555376 ///frill.slushy.confirm
public campground
70 vehicular sites, 14 cabins
tables, fire rings, bathhouse
fee
reservation required
newyorkstateparks.reserveamerica.com
607-273-3440

$PCg
+0.2 spur
8.3 miles
D

✲ city of Ithaca
2+ miles to services
location given is for Wegman's grocery
downtown is an additional mile
42.43565 -76.510497 ///laying.barn.stable
services

↔ boundary Robert Treman State Park
42.397377 -76.543021 ///sheltering.sweeter.jolly
↔ boundary mixed ownership

↔ boundary mixed ownership
42.400102 -76.539931 ///dispute.dreamers.strictest
↔ boundary Sweedler Nature Preserve
owned by Finger Lakes Land Trust
fllt.org

↔ boundary Sweedler Nature Preserve
42.395575 -76.533376 ///snippets.astonishing.plotted
↔ boundary private land

↔ boundary private land
42.329333 -76.503679 ///extract.imparting.breezes
↔ boundary Danby State Forest

Note: dispersed camping is allowed in NY state forests

△ *dispersed camping* allowed
0.9 mile in Danby SF
dec.ny.gov

∠ *Chestnut Shelter*
42.327572 -76.488197   ///grasped.writers.calculate
public land
open shelter
table, fire ring, latrine
maintained by FLTC
fingerlakestrail.org

△ *dispersed camping* allowed
6.2 miles in Danby SF
dec.ny.gov

∠ *Tamarack Shelter*
42.317006 -76.42296   ///skirting.gourmet.dislodged
public land
open shelter
table, fire ring, latrine
maintained by FLTC
fingerlakestrail.org

△ *dispersed camping* allowed
0.1 mile in Danby SF
dec.ny.gov

↔ boundary Danby State Forest
42.318073 -76.42196   ///statue.linking.class
↔ boundary mixed ownership

D
2.4 miles
boundary M17, M18

Eastman Hill Road
42.327784 -76.401816   ///fingernail.traffic.goodbyes
Finger Lakes Trail Conference
fingerlakestrail.org
Maps M14-M17 maintained FLTC and Cayuga Trails Club volunteers
↔ **Affiliate internal boundary**

↔ **Affiliate internal boundary**
Eastman Hill Road
42.327784 -76.401816   ///fingernail.traffic.goodbyes
Finger Lakes Trail Conference
fingerlakestrail.org
Maps M18-M21 maintained FLTC

boundary M17,M18
4.2 miles
D

↔ boundary private land
42.331861 -76.363063   ///editorials.antlers.farmhouses
↔ boundary Shindagin Hollow State Forest
managed by NY DEC
dec.ny.gov

Note: dispersed camping is allowed in NY state forests

△ *dispersed camping* allowed
0.9 mile in Shindagin Hollow SF
dec.ny.gov

△ *Shindagin Bivouac Area*
42.33202 -76.348322   ///character.befriended.clip
public land
primitive, no amenities
maintained by FLTC
fingerlakestrail.org

△ *dispersed camping* allowed
2.2 miles in Shindagin Hollow SF
dec.ny.gov

∠ *Shindagin Shelter*
42.327585 -76.328711   ///refrain.clap.overpriced
public land
open shelter, space for tents
table, fire ring, latrine
maintained by FLTC
fingerlakestrail.org

△ *dispersed camping* allowed
2.3 miles in Shindagin Hollow SF
dec.ny.gov

↔ boundary Shindagin Hollow State Forest
42.330184 -76.296176   ///meatball.cloudy.chicken
↔ boundary private land

D
1.2 miles
D

↔ boundary private land
42.335593 -76.276457   ///attainable.sliders.orders
↔ boundary Potato Hill State Forest

Note: dispersed camping is allowed in NY state forests

△ *dispersed camping* allowed
2.2 miles in Potato Hill SF
dec.ny.gov

↔ boundary Potato Hill State Forest
42.356813 -76.261586   ///resold.simply.winced
↔ boundary mixed ownership
D
2.9 miles
D
↔ boundary mixed ownership
42.383446 -76.272229   ///iconic.truckload.apron
↔ boundary Robinson Hollow State Forest

Note: dispersed camping is allowed in NY state forests

△ *dispersed camping* allowed
0.9 mile in Robinson Hollow SF
dec.ny.gov

∠ *Kimmie Shelter*
0.1 mile off trail
42.391877 -76.271757   ///redundancy.eggshells.shallower
public land
open shelter
table, fire ring, latrine
maintained by FLTC
fingerlakestrail.org

△ *Kimmie Bivouac Area*
42.390578 -76.272358   ///blaming.organs.crowds
public land
primitive, table, fire ring, latrine
maintained by FLTC
fingerlakestrail.org

△ *dispersed camping* allowed
1.7 miles in Robinson Hollow SF
dec.ny.gov

↔ boundary Robinson Hollow State Forest
42.410717 -76.26381   ///miracle.justifying.digesting
↔ boundary Hammond Hill State Forest

△ *dispersed camping* allowed
3.7 miles in Hammond Hill SF
dec.ny.gov

↔ boundary Hammond Hill State Forest
42.441825 -76.28519   ///defects.bagels.bounce
↔ boundary mixed ownership

D
6.0 miles
HCs

△ *Eric's Path Bivouac Area*
0.3 mile off trail
42.460422 -76.230023   ///invaluable.cherubs.tomorrow
hosted site
primitive, bench, fire ring, no latrine
maintained by owner

HCs
0.5 mile
D

↔ boundary mixed ownership
42.4706 -76.231418   ///fridge.replicated.brothers
↔ boundary James Kennedy State Forest

Note: dispersed camping is allowed in NY state forests

△ *dispersed camping* allowed
0.9 mile in James Kennedy SF
dec.ny.gov

△ *Swedish Loop Bivouac Area*
42.473951 -76.215909   ///extent.burns.parcel
public land
primitive, fire ring, no latrine
maintained by FLTC
fingerlakestrail.org

△ *dispersed camping* allowed
3.9 miles in James Kennedy SF
*but watch for private property signs as
trail often wanders over boundaries*
dec.ny.gov

△ *Kells Tent Site*
42.472591 -76.182653   ///accomplice.idea.factually
public land
primitive, fire ring, no latrine
maintained by FLTC
fingerlakestrail.org

△ *dispersed camping* allowed
0.2 mile in James Kennedy SF
*but watch for private property signs as
trail often wanders over boundaries*
dec.ny.gov

∠ *Foxfire Shelter*
42.472922 -76.178825   ///incurring.orchestras.pledged
public land
open shelter
table, fire ring, latrine
maintained by FLTC
fingerlakestrail.org

△ *dispersed camping* allowed
3.3 miles in James Kennedy SF
*but watch for private property signs as
trail often wanders over boundaries*
dec.ny.gov

↔ boundary James Kennedy State Forest
42.496559 -76.151724   ///relied.fridge.tenure
↔ boundary private land

D
1.0 mile
D

↔ boundary private land
42.489851 -76.137605   ///embers.lawyer.prominently
↔ boundary James Kennedy State Forest

△ *dispersed camping* allowed
0.8 mile in James Kennedy SF
dec.ny.gov

↔ boundary James Kennedy State Forest
42.489756 -76.126705   ///simulation.roaming.hunched
↔ boundary private land

D
2.6 miles
D

↔ boundary private land
42.503362 -76.112371   ///adamant.gurgle.sunflowers
↔ boundary Tuller Hill State Forest

Note: dispersed camping is allowed in NY state forests

△ *dispersed camping* allowed
1.4 miles in Tuller Hill SF
dec.ny.gov

∠ *Woodchuck Hollow Shelter*
42.51241 -76.121029   ///harmless.pigeons.average
public land
open shelter
fire ring, latrine
maintained by FLTC
fingerlakestrail.org

△ *dispersed camping* allowed
2.8 miles in Tuller Hill SF
watch boundaries near trail
dec.ny.gov

↔ boundary Tuller Hill State Forest
42.53403 -76.106417   ///sugary.organs.spires
↔ boundary private land

D
6.9 miles
D

↔ boundary private land
42.496419 -76.057793   ///bridge.dales.simulations
↔ boundary Hoxie Gorge State Forest

Note: dispersed camping is allowed in NY state forests

△ *dispersed camping* allowed
0.4 mile in Hoxie Gorge SF
dec.ny.gov

△ *Hoxie Gorge Bivouac Area*
42.499235 -76.064799   ///looms.viewpoints.socialite
public land
primitive, fire ring, no latrine
maintained by FLTC
fingerlakestrail.org

△ *dispersed camping* allowed
5.9 miles in Hoxie Gorge SF
dec.ny.gov

∠ *Hoxie Gorge Shelter*
42.544708 -76.065629   ///liquids.separating.shadowing
public land
open shelter
table, bench, fire ring, latrine
maintained by FLTC
fingerlakestrail.org

↔ boundary Hoxie Gorge State Forest
42.544874 -76.064985   ///stews.payment.homes
↔ boundary private land

D
4.4 miles
D

↔ boundary private land
42.568219 -76.02957   ///backward.outraged.entitlement
↔ boundary Baker Schoolhouse State Forest

Note: dispersed camping is allowed in NY state forests

△ *dispersed camping* allowed
2.1 miles in Baker Schoolhouse SF
dec.ny.gov

↔ boundary Baker Schoolhouse State Forest
42.587448 -76.012275   ///elite.insulating.recoup
↔ boundary private land

D
2.5 miles
D

↔ boundary private land
42.600228 -75.989789   ///rise.tribes.charismatic
↔ boundary Taylor Valley State Forest

Note: dispersed camping is allowed in NY state forests

△ *dispersed camping* allowed
2.9 miles in Taylor Valley SF
watch boundaries near trail
dec.ny.gov

△ *Hill Top Pond Bivouac Area*
42.628534 -75.968127   ///carpenters.resolutely.pinches
public land
primitive, no amenities
maintained by FLTC
fingerlakestrail.org

△ *dispersed camping* allowed
2.2 miles in Taylor Valley SF
watch boundaries near trail
dec.ny.gov

△ *Cheningo Campground*
42.637848 -75.967789   ///relinquish.excavated.massage
public land
6 vehicular campsites
primitive, tables
maintained by NY DEC
dec.ny.gov

△ *dispersed camping* allowed
0.7 mile in Taylor Valley SF
watch boundaries near trail
dec.ny.gov

∠ *Taylor Valley Shelter*
42.638214 -75.961911   ///cultivated.strongman.examiner
public land
open shelter
table, fire ring, latrine, dry
maintained by FLTC
fingerlakestrail.org

△ *dispersed camping* allowed
1.6 miles in Taylor Valley SF
watch boundaries near trail
dec.ny.gov

↔ boundary Taylor Valley State Forest
42.646801 -75.940153   ///herbs.sedative.spaced
↔ boundary private land

D
0.9 miles
D

↔ boundary private land
42.653413 -75.929446   ///guidebooks.sapped.pockets
↔ boundary Cuyler Hill State Forest

Note: dispersed camping is allowed in NY state forests

△ *dispersed camping* allowed
3.3 miles in Cuyler Hill SF
dec.ny.gov

△ *Wiltsey Glen Bivouac Area*
42.679368 -75.909072   ///decking.partied.stamps
public land
bench, fire ring, no latrine
maintained by FLTC
fingerlakestrail.org

△ *dispersed camping* allowed
0.6 mile in Cuyler Hill SF
dec.ny.gov

△ *Rose Hollow Bivouac Area*
0.2 mile off trail
42.687269 -75.91228   ///subscribed.cavalier.safety
public land
bench, no latrine
maintained by FLTC
fingerlakestrail.org

△ *dispersed camping* allowed
2.5 miles in Cuyler Hill SF
dec.ny.gov

boundary M19, O1

↔ boundary Cuyler Hill State Forest
42.707749 -75.91099   ///swear.anthems.offset
↔ boundary mixed ownership

Stoney Brook Road
42.707749 -75.91099   ///swear.anthems.offset
Finger Lakes Trail Conference
fingerlakestrail.org
Maps M18-M21 maintained FLTC
↔ **Affiliate internal boundary**

↔ **Affiliate internal boundary**
Onondaga Branch Finger Lakes Trail at Stoney Brook Road
42.707749   -75.91099   ///swear.anthems.offset
Onondaga Chapter, Adirondack Mountain Club
adk-on.org
Maps O1-O2 maintained by ADK-ON

boundary M19, O1

△ *dispersed camping* allowed
0.2 mile in Cuyler Hill SF
dec.ny.gov

Y junction- NCT follows Onondaga Branch of the FLT system north, while main FLT continues east.
42.708258   -75.911266   ///rescuer.obvious.bandit

↔ boundary Cuyler Hill State Forest O1 0.25
42.707233   -75.914753   ///evoked.elbow.allowances
↔ boundary private land

D
2.2 miles
D

↔ boundary private land
42.724631   -75.934085   ///interns.dictation.removing
↔ boundary Maxon Creek State Forest

Note: dispersed camping is allowed in NY state forests

△ *dispersed camping* allowed
1.1 miles in Maxon Creek SF
dec.ny.gov

↔ boundary Maxon Creek State Forest
42.723294   -75.942689   ///allows.radial.removable
↔ boundary private land

D
4.2 miles
D

↔ boundary private land
42.736755   -75.992036   ///hobble.pigs.serving
↔ boundary Morgan Hill State Forest

Note: dispersed camping is allowed in NY state forests

△ *dispersed camping* allowed
2.6 miles in Morgan Hill SF
dec.ny.gov

△ **Morgan Hill Bivouac Area**
42.767228 -75.997529   ///warmed.local.commuted
public land
primitive, no amenities, dry
maintained by ADK-ON
adk-on.org

△ *dispersed camping* allowed
0.9 mile in Morgan Hill SF
dec.ny.gov

∠ **Hemlock Glen Shelter**
42.767566 -76.009867   ///blasted.percussion.fingertips
public land
open shelter, latrine
maintained by ADK-ON
adk-on.org

△ *dispersed camping* allowed
0.8 mile in Morgan Hill SF
dec.ny.gov

△ **Hemlock Glen Bivouac Area**
42.769307 -76.018155   ///study.calculating.taxing
public land
primitive, no amenities

△ *dispersed camping* allowed
1.3 miles in Morgan Hill SF
dec.ny.gov

↔ internal boundary Morgan Hill State Forest
42.780921 -76.02907   ///inform.loose.oyster
↔ boundary Labrador Hollow State Unique Area

Note: no camping or fires in Labrador Hollow SUA, or Onondaga County Forest through which the trail also wanders

↔ boundary Labrador Hollow State Unique Area
↔ boundary Morgan Hill State Forest
42.791252 -76.041344   ///contain.monumental.whips
↔ boundary private land

D
2.6 miles
D

↔ boundary private land
42.797204 -76.030873   ///reclusive.reduced.fully
↔ boundary Morgan Hill State Forest

△ *dispersed camping* allowed
0.3 mile in Morgan Hill SF
dec.ny.gov

p▲ *Spruce Pond Campsite*
0.1 mile off trail
42.800998 -76.026302   ///juggled.challenger.tanned
public campsite
10 primitive sites, fire rings, seasonal latrine
managed by NY DEC
permit required May 1- Sep 30
call 607-674-4036 ext. 600 during business hours

△ *dispersed camping* allowed
4.3 miles in Morgan Hill SF
dec.ny.gov

↔ boundary Morgan Hill State Forest
42.809216 -75.988043   ///weds.charity.giggled
↔ boundary private land

D
10.1 miles
D

↔ boundary private land
42.811577 -75.941866   ///bunker.collision.amaze
↔ boundary Highland Forest County Park

Note: no camping in Highland Forest County Park, open dawn to dusk

↔ boundary Highland Forest County Park
42.830047 -75.908671   ///straying.moguls.baggage
↔ boundary private land

↔ boundary private land
42.820164 -75.876721   ///unarmed.terms.basis
↔ boundary DeRuyter State Forest

Note: dispersed camping is allowed in NY state forests

△ *dispersed camping* allowed
1.1 miles in DeRuyter SF
watch boundaries near trail
dec.ny.gov

△ *Tromp Road Bivouac Area*
0.2 mile off trail
42.818983 -75.863546   ///congregate.punky.headphones
public land
primitive, no amenities
maintained by ADK-ON
adk-on.org

△ *dispersed camping* allowed
0.6 mile in DeRuyter SF
watch boundaries near trail
dec.ny.gov

↔ boundary DeRuyter State Forest
42.821974 -75.855778   ///lawns.lettuce.weeds
↔ boundary private land

D
6.9 miles
boundary Onondaga Branch

↔ boundary private land
42.856649 -75.824951   ///extensively.clocking.rescue
↔ boundary Tioughnioga Wildlife Management Area
managed by NY DEC
dec.ny.gov

Note: camping is prohibited in NY State WMAs

Onondaga Branch Finger Lakes Trail
Holmes Road
42.866086 -75.809673   ///greased.contestant.reframe
Onondaga Chapter, Adirondack Mountain Club
adk-on.org
Maps O1-O2 maintained by ADK-ON
↔ **Affiliate/ Chapter boundary**

↔ **Affiliate/ Chapter boundary**
Central New York Chapter
Holmes Road
42.866086 -75.809673   ///greased.contestant.reframe
northcountrytrail.org/new-york/cny

                        affiliate/ chapter boundary
                        8.0 miles
                        +various road
                        $L

Note: camping is prohibited in NY State WMAs

↔ boundary Tioghnioga Wildlife Management Area
42.870362 -75.803182   ///fattening.yell.fingernail
↔ boundary mixed ownership

Note: trail passes through several disconnected segments of Nelson Swamp Unique Area. No camping is allowed in State Unique Areas

✻ village of Cazenovia
42.92989 -75.852936   ///origin.lost.shakes
services

$ ■ *Motels*
+ various off trail
42.92989 -75.852936   ///origin.lost.shakes
commercial lodging options
fee

                        $L
                        +various road
                        16.7 miles
                        PCs

✻ village of Canastota
43.07942 -75.75144
///claimed.buzzed.snored
limited services

$ ■ *Days Inn*
0.7 mile off trail
43.089821 -75.751663   ///hotel.lolly.output
commercial lodging
rooms, laundry
wyndhamhotels.com
315-288-6358

                        $L
                        +0.7 road
                        13.2 miles
                        PCs

✻ village of Durhamville
43.118027 -75.669786   ///tactical.compensate.lucky
limited services

△ Lock 21 State Campsite
43.20831   -75.619115   ///lecture.finishes.holdings
public camptiste
primitive, no fires, no amenities, latrine, dry
call in advance
canals.ny.gov/trails/camping.html
315-336-8229

>PCg
>**8.9 miles**
>+various road
>$L

✲ city of Rome
43.210586   -75.457381   ///snack.polite.toward
large city
services

$ ■ Motels
various off trail
several within walking distance of this location
43.210586   -75.457381   ///snack.polite.toward
commercial lodging
fee

>$L
>+various road
>**8.0 miles**
>$PCg

$▲ Delta Lake State Park
43.290334   -75.416885   ///correct.rods.consecutive
public campground
101 vehicular, electric sites
tables, fire rings, restroom
fee
newyorkstateparks.reserveamerica.com
315-337-4670

>$PCg
>**11.2 miles**
>D

Note: within a few years the trail will be rerouted through Clark Hill State Forest. This trail is under construction.

↔ boundary private land
43.401946   -75.355896   ///cleared.tactical.poem
↔ boundary Buck Hill State Forest

Note: dispersed camping is allowed in NY state forests

>### △ dispersed camping allowed
>**0.4 mile** in Buck Hill SF
>dec.ny.gov

↔ boundary Buck Hill State Forest
43.401213 -75.347506   ///shed.dine.toothbrush
↔ boundary Pixley Falls State Park

Note: In general there is no camping in Pixley Falls State Park, however, see below

        D
        0.3 miles
        +0.2 spur
        HCs

△ *Pixley Falls Backpacker Site*
43.40456 -75.34386   ///urban.remains.peculiarly
special arrangement, only NCT long-distance hikers may camp no more than 2 nights
primitive, no fires, food must be hung or in a canister, restroom
call Delta Lake SP 315-337-4670 to request the free permit.
Printed or electronic permit must be available to display to authorities

        HCs
        +0.2 spur
        6.8 mile
        $L

↔ boundary Pixley Falls State Park
43.412587 -75.34013   ///improvise.counter.roughly
↔ boundary private land

✲ village of Boonville
43.482842 -75.328751   ///diagram.galaxies.partial
services

$ ■ *Motels*
various off trail
several within walking distance of this location
43.482842 -75.328751   ///diagram.galaxies.partial
commercial lodging
fee

        $L
        1.5 miles
        $CCg

$▲ *Stysh 's Brown Barn Campground*
0.4 mile off trail
43.507 -75.3093   ///adjustable.screamed.occurs
commercial campground
vehicular sites, electric & non-electric
tables fire rings, bathhouse
fee
brownbarncampground.com
315-942-4749

        $PCg
        14.8 miles
        D

$ ☐ *Adirondack Sport Center*
1.1 miles off trail
43.501122 -75.250693   ///spending.ambulances.skips
commercial lodging
3 large cabins
fee
adirondacksportcenter.com
315-942-2431

✲ village of Forestport
43.442043 -75.206942   ///cityscape.dentist.learns
limited services

↔ boundary private land NY 91
43.453252 -75.06696   ///helicopters.potentially.illustrates
↔ boundary Black River Wild Forest, Adirondack Park

Central New York Chapter
Oneida/Herkimer county line
43.444095 -75.090085   ///code.nagged.creamed
northcountrytrail.org/new-york/cny
↔ **Chapter/ Affiliate boundary**

↔ **Chapter/Affiliate boundary**
Adirondack Mountains
Herkimer/Oneida county line
43.444095   -75.090085   ///code.nagged.creamed
Adirondack Mountain Club, coordinated by Onondaga Chapter
adk-on.org

chapter/ affiliate boundary
1.6 miles
D

Note: The route of the NCT through the Adirondacks is mostly determined. However, at this time, passage across one piece of private land is still being negotiated between Black River Wild Forest and West Canada Lakes Wilderness. Therefore, there is currently a long road walk through Old Forge. This list will include the information for that section. When the actual trail goes through, the camping options will increase since it will be largely in Adirondack Forest Preserve land where dispersed camping is allowed.

The trail on the eastern side of the park will eventually continue from Jones Hill through Hammond Pond Wild Forest, but that is further in the future.

As mentioned in the text of this book, you need National Geographic maps 743, 744, and 745. The NCT Adirondack maps are not very accurate. It is hoped this will be corrected within two years. Trail mileages for this section have been taken from the Nat Geo Maps.

Another Note: At time of publication, the bridge on Stone Dam Trail is out, which connects with Chub Pond and Gull Lake Trails to Bear Lake Trail. Little Woodhull Creek can probably be crossed on rocks. However, a suggested alternative is Little Woodhull Lake and Sand Lake Trails to connect to Bear Lake Trail. Both options are covered below

Option 1- Stone Dam Trail and Chub Pond Trail

↔ boundary Black River Wild Forest, Adirondack Park
managed by the NY DEC and Adirondack Park Agency

Note: dispersed camping allowed in Black River Wild Forest

△ dispersed camping allowed
3.5 miles in Black River Wild Forest
dec.ny.gov

∠ *Chub Pond Shelter #1*
0.3 mile off trail
43.522325   -75.044681   ///forcing.wrist.drips
public land
large shelter with deck, bunks, fire ring, latrine
maintained by volunteers

△ dispersed camping allowed
0.9 mile in Black River Wild Forest
dec.ny.gov

∠ *Chub Pond Shelter #2*
0.2 mile off trail
43.529917 -75.042535   ///indulgence.slushy.albums
public land
open shelter
table, fire ring, latrine
maintained by volunteers

△ *dispersed camping* allowed
4.6 miles in Black River Wild Forest
dec.ny.gov

∠ *Gull Lake Shelter*
0.7 mile off trail
43.553761 -75.059186   ///portfolio.hectic.milkshake
public land
open shelter
table, fire ring, latrine
maintained by volunteers

△ *dispersed camping* allowed
2.1 miles in Black River Wild Forest
dec.ny.gov

Y junction with Bear Lake Trail, turn north
43.567509 -75.050408   ///snored.offered.plays
Note: there is a small private inholding on this corner.

Option 2- Little Woodhull Lake Trail and Sand Lake Falls Trail

↔ boundary Black River Wild Forest, Adirondack Park
managed by the NY DEC and Adirondack Park Agency

△ *dispersed camping* allowed
6.5 miles in Black River Wild Forest
dec.ny.gov

continue on North Lake Rd to Little Woodhull Lake Trail at
43.504841 -74.966358   ///coveted.dispenses.saddens
Turn north on trail. North Lake Road is in Black River Wild Forest, but you need to be 0.25 mile off the road to camp and there are some private holdings. Suggest not camping until you are on the Little Woodhull Lake Trail.

△ *dispersed camping* allowed
9.2 miles in Black River Wild Forest
dec.ny.gov

∠ *Sand Lake Shelter*
43.560097 -75.007935   ///calls.comforted.entries
public land
open shelter
benches, fire ring, latrine
maintained by volunteers

△ *dispersed camping* allowed
3.8 miles in Black River Wild Forest
dec.ny.gov

Y junction with Bear Lake Trail, turn north.
43.567509 -75.050408   ///snored.offered.plays
Note: there is a small private inholding on this corner.

The two options join where Bear Lake Trail turns north off Bear Creek Road

△ *dispersed camping* allowed
2.6 miles in Black River Wild Forest
dec.ny.gov

△ *Bear Lake Campsite*
43.599281 -75.053114   ///javelin.backer.nitrate
public land
primitive, fire ring, latrine is 0.1 mile north near shelter
maintained by volunteers

△ *dispersed camping* allowed
0.1 mile in Black River Wild Forest
dec.ny.gov

∠ *Bryan Farley Shelter*
43.600301   -75.052179   ///requiring.functioning.dentures
public land
open shelter
table, fire ring, latrine
maintained by volunteers

△ *dispersed camping* allowed
2.5 miles in Black River Wild Forest
dec.ny.gov

↔ boundary Black River Wild Forest, Adirondack Park NY 107.5
43.612569 -75.090554   ///housework.warped.banners
↔ boundary private land

D
6.3 miles
+0.2 spur
D

△ *Ha-De-Ron-Dah Wilderness*
0.2 mile off trail
43.676974 -75.051901   ///reflections.trail.signs
dispersed camping allowed in Ha-De-Ron-Dah Wilderness-
potential campsite if you follow Scusa Trail at least 150 feet off road beyond location given
watch boundaries near trail.

D
+0.2 spur
2.5 miles
+0.3 road and spur
D

△ *Ha-De-Ron-Dah Wilderness*

0.3 mile off trail
43.696944 -75.017558 ///fidelity.axed.better
dispersed camping allowed in Ha-De-Ron-Dah Wilderness-
potential campsite if you follow Brown's Tract Trail at least 150 feet off road beyond location given
watch boundaries near trail

D
+0.3 road and spur
2.2 miles
$L

⁜ hamlet of Old Forge
43.706953 -74.978979 ///guiding.blesses.pigeons
services

$ ■ *Motels*

various near trail
43.706953 -74.978979 ///guiding.blesses.pigeons
commercial lodging
fee

$L
5.9 miles
+0.1 spur
D

$▲ *Old Forge Camping Resort*

1.0 mile off trail
43.71821 -74.958158 ///inflatable.fairness.disengage
commercial campground
vehicle needed to store food- backpackers must leave food in camp store due to serious bear problems
many vehicular sites, cabins
tables, fire rings, bathhouse, laundry
fee
oldforgecamping.com
315-369-6011

△ *Fulton Chain Wild Forest*

0.1 mile off trail
43.726407 -74.886811 ///blemishes.mimed.tanned
dispersed camping allowed in Fulton Chain Wild Forest-
potential campsite if you follow Limekiln Creek-Third Lake Trail at least 150 feet off road beyond location given, trail reputed to be overgrown
watch boundaries near trail

D
+0.1 spur
5.7 miles
+various road
$L

⁜ hamlet of Inlet
43.750964 -74.79435 ///insulating.backpacker.develops
services

$ ■ *Motels*
various near trail
43.750964 -74.79435   ///insulating.backpacker.develops
commercial lodging
fee

> $L
> +various road
> **2.5 miles**
> +0.5 road
> $PCg

$▲ *Limekiln Lake State Campground*
0.5 mile off trail
43.721357 -74.795249   ///clap.systems.wrists
public campground
271 vehicular sites
tables, fire rings, bathhouse
fee
managed by NY DEC
newyorkstateparks.reserveamerica.com
315-357-4401

↔ boundary private land
43.721974 -74.792057   ///activates.follow.captivated
↔ boundary Moose River Plains Wild Forest

Note: dispersed camping allowed in Moose River Plains Wild Forest

> △ *dispersed camping* allowed
> **4.0 miles** in Moose River Plains Wild Forest
> 150 feet off road
> dec.ny.gov

△ *Red River Campsites*
43.690113 -74.751244   ///ultraviolet.portray.icicles
between here and where the Brooktrout Lake Trail leaves Indian River Road there are over 100 vehicular campsites along the road. They are all supposed to have a table, fire ring, latrine. Most have one of these, some have two. Additionally, dispersed camping is allowed, but you must be 150 feet off road.

> △ *dispersed camping* allowed
> **7.7 miles** in Moose River Plains Wild Forest
> 150 feet off road
> dec.ny.gov

↔ boundary Moose River Plains Wild Forest
43.645535 -74.689532   ///ashes.remedy.divergence
↔ boundary West Canada Lake Wilderness

Note: dispersed camping allowed in West Canada Lake Wilderness

> △ *dispersed camping* allowed
> **5.6 miles** in West Canada Lake Wilderness
> 150 feet off road
> dec.ny.gov

∠ Brooktrout Lake Shelter

43.602789 -74.658376   ///unlicensed.alarmed.nagged
public land
open shelter
fire ring, latrine
maintained by volunteers

△ *dispersed camping* allowed
2.5 miles in West Canada Lake Wilderness
dec.ny.gov

∠ West Lake Shelter #2

43.597008 -74.623271   ///regenerate.entry.intruding
public land
open shelter
fire ring, latrine
maintained by volunteers

△ *dispersed camping* allowed
0.2 mile in West Canada Lake Wilderness
dec.ny.gov

Y junction with Northville-Placid Trail which goes north from this point. NCT is concurrent with NPT for 0.7 mile between here and West Canada Creek
43.593868 -74.625127   ///signal.notable.functioning

∠ West Lake Shelter #1

43.59303 -74.626704   ///evident.reclined.oils
public land
open shelter
fire ring, latrine
maintained by volunteers

△ *dispersed camping* allowed
0.5 mile in West Canada Lake Wilderness
dec.ny.gov

∠ West Canada Creek Shelter

43.586938 -74.613937   ///preach.ripe.fizzled
public land
open shelter
fire ring, latrine
maintained by volunteers

Y junction with Northville-Placid Trail which goes south from this point. NCT is concurrent with NPT for 0.7 mile between here and West Lake
43.586828 -74.613448   ///scariest.bleat.matters

△ *dispersed camping* allowed
2.5 miles in West Canada Lake Wilderness
dec.ny.gov

∠ **Sampson Lake Shelter**
0.1 mile off trail
43.58072   -74.5766   ///gifted.crated.nuptials
public land
open shelter
fire ring, latrine
maintained by volunteers

△ *dispersed camping* allowed
2.7 miles in West Canada Lake Wilderness
dec.ny.gov

∠ **Pillsbury Lake Shelter**
43.596822   -74.531668   ///comfortable.crass.softly
public land
open shelter
table, fire ring, latrine
maintained by volunteers

△ *dispersed camping* allowed
3.2 miles in West Canada Lake Wilderness
dec.ny.gov

↔ boundary West Canada Lake Wilderness
43.586906   -74.485277   ///crouching.allowances.elimination
↔ boundary Perkins Clearing Easement

Note: Camp only at numbered vehicular sites in Perkins Clearing Easement which is owned by Lyme Timber.

D
1.7 miles
PCs

△ **Perkins Clearing Campsites #10, 11**
43.567195   -74.467123   ///imaginable.hinted.lifts
hosted vehicular site
primitive, fire ring, no latrine

PCs
2.5 miles
PCs

△ **Hardwood Hill Campsites #13, 14**
43.55289   -74.414295   ///pepper.superstars.covertly
hosted vehicular site
primitive, fire ring, no latrine

PCs
0.5 mile
PCs

△ **Perkins Clearing Campsite #14a**
43.54471   -74.406741   ///zoos.retailers.straws
hosted vehicular site
primitive, fire ring, no latrine

     PCs
     4.3 miles
     $L

↔ boundary Perkins Clearing Easement
43.53445 -74.384468 ///genuine.employs.foster
↔ boundary mixed ownership

✻ hamlet of Speculator
0.6 mile off trail
43.501938 -74.364341 ///interfaces.positive.unsecured
services

$ ■ *Motels*

various off trail in Speculator
43.501938 -74.364341 ///interfaces.positive.unsecured
commercial lodging
fee
     $L
     0.1 mile
     D

↔ boundary mixed ownership
43.509447 -74.355801 ///appearances.matter.frustrating
↔ boundary Jessup River Wild Forest

Note: dispersed camping allowed in Jessup River Wild Forest

    △ *dispersed camping* allowed
    0.6 mile in Jessup River Wild Forest
    east side of road only
    150 feet off road
    dec.ny.gov

↔ boundary Jessup River Wild Forest
43.516636 -74.350329 ///articulate.comprehend.roving
↔ boundary private land
     D
     0.2 mile
     D
↔ boundary private land
43.519172 -74.348634 ///stops.stylish.frugal
↔ boundary Jessup River Wild Forest

    △ *dispersed camping* allowed
    0.2 mile in Jessup River Wild Forest
    east side of road only
    150 feet off road
    dec.ny.gov

↔ boundary Jessup River Wild Forest
43.521475 -74.34696 ///fiasco.woes.evoke
↔ boundary private land
     D
     1.0 mile
     D

↔ boundary private land
43.53417 -74.346875   ///kinks.betrayal.legions
↔ boundary Jessup River Wild Forest

△ *dispersed camping* allowed
0.2 mile in Jessup River Wild Forest
east side of road only
150 feet off road
dec.ny.gov

↔ boundary Jessup River Wild Forest
43.536784 -74.345673   ///waterfront.calms.typed
↔ boundary private land

D
5.4 miles
D

↔ boundary private land
43.605182 -74.311268   ///combination.call.spearing
↔ boundary Siamese Ponds Wilderness

Note: dispersed camping allowed in Siamese Ponds Wilderness

△ *dispersed camping* allowed
10.2 miles in Siamese Ponds Wilderness
dec.ny.gov

∠ *West Puffer Pond Shelter*
43.676714 -74.196451   ///wordy.functioning.interacts
public land
open shelter
fire ring, latrine
maintained by volunteers

△ *dispersed camping* allowed
0.2 miles in Siamese Ponds Wilderness
dec.ny.gov

∠ *East Puffer Pond Shelter*
43.677703 -74.192109   ///results.enormously.kidney
public land
open shelter
fire ring, latrine
maintained by volunteers

△ *dispersed camping* allowed
9.0 miles in Siamese Ponds Wilderness
dec.ny.gov

↔ boundary Siamese Ponds Wilderness
43.696263 -74.061603   ///returns.rips.swigs
↔ boundary Vanderwhacker Mountain Wild Forest

Note: dispersed camping allowed in Vanderwhacker Mountain Wild Forest

△ *dispersed camping* allowed
3.8 miles in Vanderwhacker Mt. WF
dec.ny.gov

↔ boundary Vanderwhacker Mountain Wild Forest
43.711651 -74.004697   ///simplistic.best.villager
↔ boundary mixed ownership
D
1.1 mile
$L

✱ hamlet of North Creek
43.702268 -73.989277   ///simplistic.best.villager
services

$ ☐ *BnBs*
+various along and off trail
43.702268 -73.989277   ///simplistic.best.villager
commercial lodging- most are small
fee

$L
+various
11.0 miles
D

✱ hamlet of Olmsteadville
43.771609 -73.931405   ///novice.tips.decimal
limited services

↔ boundary mixed ownership
43.803365 -73.939302   ///leotard.functions.indicative
↔ boundary Vanderwhacker Mountain Wild Forest

Note: dispersed camping allowed in Vanderwhacker Mountain Wild Forest

△ *dispersed camping* allowed
0.4 mile in Vanderwhacker Mt. WF
150 feet from road
dec.ny.gov

↔ boundary Vanderwhacker Mountain Wild Forest
43.809342 -73.937885   ///warms.blames.photo
↔ boundary mixed ownership
D
1.2 miles
D

↔ boundary mixed ownership
43.822998 -73.92544   ///haggling.surging.glassy
↔ boundary Vanderwhacker Mountain Wild Forest

△ *dispersed camping* allowed
1.0 mile in Vanderwhacker Mt. WF
watch boundaries near trail
150 feet from road
dec.ny.gov

↔ boundary Vanderwhacker Mountain Wild Forest
43.825568   -73.906429   ///scares.refrain.groups
↔ boundary mixed ownership

D
1.2 miles
D

↔ boundary mixed ownership
43.835537   -73.891494   ///superb.screenings.elastic
↔ boundary Vanderwhacker Mountain Wild Forest

△ *dispersed camping*   allowed
0.7 mile in Vanderwhacker Mt. WF
watch boundaries near trail
150 feet from road
dec.ny.gov

↔ boundary Vanderwhacker Mountain Wild Forest
43.83676   -73.879478   ///skillet.intervened.interesting
↔ boundary mixed ownership

D
2.5 miles
D

↔ boundary mixed ownership
43.867862   -73.889649   ///heckler.escapades.snowflakes
↔ boundary Hoffman Notch Wilderness

Note: dispersed camping allowed in Hoffman Notch Wilderness

△ *dispersed camping*   allowed
5.7 miles in Hoffman Notch Wilderness
dec.ny.gov

Y junction of Jones Hill Trail and Big Pond Trail with choices. The NCT map is still marked as going through Schroon Lake. However, the trail over Jones Hill with spectacular views can be hiked. It needs a bridge over Platt Brook (currently a ford) and final DEC approval to be put on the maps. Both options will be covered here.
43.85847   -73.811353   ///guarantees.spun.treble

Option 1- Through Schroon Lake to Alder Meadow Road

Big Pond Trail between Jones Hill Trail and Hoffman Road

△ *dispersed camping*   allowed
1.0 mile in Hoffman Notch Wilderness
dec.ny.gov

↔ boundary Hoffman Notch Wilderness
43.845569   -73.804412   ///milkshake.point.cleanest
↔ boundary private land

D
2.6 miles
+various road
$L

✲ hamlet of Schroon Lake
43.836809 -73.761669   ///once.crabby.submitted
limited services

$ ☐ *Inns*
+various along and off trail
43.836809 -73.761669   ///once.crabby.submitted
commercial lodging- most are small
fee

        $L
        +various road
        1.4 miles
        $L

$ ■ *Maple Leaf Lodge*
43.856715 -73.755489   ///hunched.forgives.hugged
commercial lodging
rooms, cabins, suites
fee
mapleleafadk.com
518-532-7474

        $L
        0.4 mile
        junction

Y junction with Alder Meadow Road. The trail is on Alder Meadow Road, currently with two options west of there- north over Jones Hill, or south through Schroon Lake.
43.862632 -73.7547   ///luckily.ground.devotion

Option 2- Over Jones Hill to Alder Meadow Road

Y junction of Jones Hill Trail and Big Pond Trail
43.85847 -73.811353   ///guarantees.spun.treble

        △ *dispersed camping* allowed
        6.0 miles in Hoffman Notch Wilderness
        dec.ny.gov

↔ boundary Hoffman Notch Wilderness
43.897626 -73.754609   ///gains.tonics.prelude
↔ boundary private land

        D
        2.3 miles
        $L

$ ☐ *Schroon Lake BnB*
43.866926 -73.753901   ///held.modems.vintages
commercial lodging
4 rooms/suites
fee
schroonbb.com
518-532-7042

        $L
        0.3 mile
        junction

Y junction with Alder Meadow Road. The trail is on Alder Meadow Road, currently with two options west of there- north and over Jones Hill, or south through Schroon Lake.
43.862632 -73.7547   ///luckily.ground.devotion

The two options join where Alder Meadow Road turns east from US 9

                      junction
                      3.5 miles
                      D

↔ boundary private land
43.859105 -73.688713   ///grunted.banter.novice
↔ boundary Pharaoh Lake Wilderness

Note: dispersed camping allowed in Pharaoh Lake Wilderness

               △ *dispersed camping* allowed
               4.5 miles in Pharaoh Lake Wilderness
               dec.ny.gov

↔ boundary Pharaoh Lake Wilderness
43.879518 -73.678757   ///fascinate.dentures.tattoo
↔ boundary mixed ownership
                      D
                      0.2 mile
                      +0.3 road
                      $PCg

$▲ *Paradox Lake Campground*

0.3 mile off trail
43.884428 -73.679186   ///underworld.fluctuate.shook
public campground
58 vehicular sites
tables, fire rings, bathhouse
managed by NY DEC
reserveamerica.com
518-532-7451

                      $PCg
                      +0.3 road
                      2.1 miles
                      D

↔ boundary mixed ownership
43.895655 -73.642654   ///otters.fateful.hospitality
↔ boundary Hammond Pond Wild Forest

Note: dispersed camping allowed in Hammond Pond Wild Forest

               △ *dispersed camping* allowed
               0.1 miles in Hammond Pond Wild Forest
               possible to 150 feet off Letsonville road
               watch boundaries near trail
               dec.ny.gov

↔ boundary Hammond Pond Wild Forest
43.896061   -73.642509   ///club.earthworms.income
↔ boundary private land

                        D
                        1.8 miles
                        D

↔ boundary private land
43.896328   -73.621347   ///bench.cleared.forgetful
↔ boundary Hammond Pond Wild Forest

             △ *dispersed camping*   allowed
             0.2 miles in Hammond Pond Wild Forest
             150 feet off road
             watch boundaries near trail
             dec.ny.gov

↔ boundary Hammond Pond Wild Forest
43.894155   -73.620661   ///signatures.bead.enrolling
↔ boundary private land

                        D
                        17.7 miles
                        +0.25 road
                        $PCg

$▲ *Crown Point Campground*

0.25 mile off trail
44.026895   -73.422038   ///found.celebrated.explorer
public campground
66 vehicular sites
tables, fire rings, bathhouse
fee
managed by NY DEC
reserveamerica.com
518-597-3603

                        $PCg
                        +0.25 road
                        2.0 miles
                        state line

New York/Vermont state line
44.036198   -73.418396   ///speculation.loomed.consoled
Adirondack Mountain Club, coordinated by Onondaga Chapter
adk-on.org
↔ **Affiliate boundary**

↔ **Affiliate boundary**
New York/ Vermont border
44.036198 -73.418396   ///speculation.loomed.consoled
Middlebury Area Land Trust and Green Mountain Club
maltvt.org

         state line
         0.5 mile
         $CCg

$▲ *10 Acres Campground*
44.033468 -73.408772   ///headliner.dock.chamber
commercial campground
19 vehicular sites, 2 rustic cabins
electric, tables, fire rings, bathhouse, laundry
fee
10acrescampground.com
802-759-2662

         $CCg
         20.9 miles
         $L

$ ■ *Swift House Inn*
44.017886 -73.166389   ///thickly.pound.fuss
commercial lodging
20 rooms
swifthouseinn.com
802-388-9925

         $L
         0.2 mile
         +0.25 road
         $L

✳ city of Middlebury
0.25 mile off trail
44.014741 -73.166872   ///loafer.awake.marines
services

$ ■ *Middlebury Inn*
0.25 mile off trail
44.014412 -73.1662   ///hotel.shower.orientation
commercial lodging
71 rooms
fee
middleburyinn.com
802-388-4961

         $L
         +0.25 road
         4.4 miles
         +0.1 road for $L
         HCs or $L

△ *Court Street Camping*
44.002556 -73.150403   ///rewriting.burn.addictions
hosted site
no amenities, no latrine
maintained by MALT
matlvt.org

$ ■ Courtyard Middlebury
0.1 mile off trail
44.002947 -73.153002   ///verdict.cooling.magic
commercial lodging
many rooms
fee
marriott.com
802-388-7600

                HCs or $L
                +0.1 road for $L
                2.3 miles
                +0.3 road
                $L

$ ■ Middlebury Sweets Motel
0.3 mile off trail
43.991454 -73.139494   ///quaint.clips.relegate
commercial lodging
9 rooms, Vermont's largest candy store
fee
middmotel.com
802-388-4935

                $L
                +0.3 road
                4.8 miles
                D

✻ village of East Middlebury
43.973369 -73.106152   ///raving.outlines.excellent

↔ boundary mixed ownership
↔ boundary of MALT and Green Mountain Club responsibilities is not clearly defined
43.97006 -73.081945   ///induced.free.minority
↔ boundary Green Mountain National Forest
↔ internal boundary Moosalamoo Recreation Area
managed by Green Mountain National Forest
fs.usda.gov/gmfl

Note: dispersed camping is allowed in Moosalamoo Recreation Area

            △ *dispersed camping* allowed
            8.4 miles in Moosalamoo Rec Area
            watch boundaries near trail
            fs.usda.gov/gmfl

$▲ Moosalamoo Campground
43.91896 -73.027031   ///infinite.scared.shrill
public campground
19 vehicular sites
tables, fire rings, latrine
fee
managed by Green Mountain NF
fs.usda.gov/greenmountain
802-747-6700

△ *dispersed camping* allowed
4.2 miles in Moosalamoo Rec Area
watch boundaries near trail
no camping near Goshen Dam
fs.usda.gov/gmfl

↔ internal boundary Moosalamoo Recreation Area VT
43.897882   -72.982968   ///prosecuted.florists.deep
↔ internal boundary Green Mountain National Forest

△ *dispersed camping* allowed
0.7 mile in Green Mountain NF
fs.usda.gov/gmfl

Y junction with the Long Trail which runs N/S the entire length of Vermont. The NCT is concurrent with it between Sucker Brook and Maine Junction.
43.892927   -72.971036   ///luckily.unwanted.wiggly

∠ *Sucker Brook Shelter*
43.892927   -72.971036   ///luckily.unwanted.wiggly
public land
open shelter
fire ring, latrine
maintained by Green Mountain Club
greenmountainclub.org

△ *dispersed camping* allowed
6.0 miles in Green Mountain NF
fs.usda.gov/gmfl

∠ *Sunrise Shelter*
43.831359   -72.960566   ///freezer.cloak.shrimp
public land
open shelter, no tenting at this location
fire ring, latrine
maintained by Green Mountain Club
greenmountainclub.org

△ *dispersed camping* allowed
5.7 miles in Green Mountain NF
fs.usda.gov/gmfl

↔ boundary Green Mountain NF
43.774802   -72.925976   ///powerful.differently.freezers
↔ boundary Mt. Carmel State Forest

Note: Vermont State Forests do not allow dispersed camping above 2500 feet elevation. Camp only at the shelter in Mt. Carmel State Forest

D
0.5 mile
PE

∠ *David Logan Shelter*
43.768418   -72.921596   ///areas.budding.translates
public land
open shelter, fire ring, latrine
maintained by Green Mountain Club
greenmountainclub.org

       PE
      0.6 miles
       D

↔ boundary Mt. Carmel State Forest
43.768697   -72.912369   ///dealing.instead.martini
↔ boundary Green Mountain National Forest

    △ *dispersed camping* allowed
    6.9 miles in Green Mountain NF
    fs.usda.gov/gmfl

∠ *Rolston Rest Shelter*
43.71267   -72.861343   ///dare.extends.firepower
hosted site
open shelter, fire ring, latrine
maintained by Green Mountain Club
greenmountainclub.org

    △ *dispersed camping* allowed
    3.4 miles in Green Mountain NF
    fs.usda.gov/gmfl

∠ *Tucker Johnson Shelter*
43.679563   -72.841902   ///taping.decreased.ministries
public land
open shelter, fire ring, latrine
maintained by Green Mountain Club
greenmountainclub.org

    △ *dispersed camping* allowed
    0.4 mile in Green Mountain NF
    fs.usda.gov/gmfl

Eastern Terminus of the NCT
Maine Junction
43.674722   -72.839352   ///cables.enable.timidly
Green Mountain Club
greenmountainclub.org
↔ **Partner boundary**

Y junction with the Appalachian Trail which goes south and east from this point. The Long Trail continues south and is concurrent with the AT. The NCT is concurrent with the Long Trail between Maine Junction and Sucker Brook.

Note: you must hike one more mile out to VT 4 and parking
43.666231   -72.849342   ///disagrees.generates.button

Appendix

National Recreational Trails database
nrtdatabase.org/trailDetail.php

Website to convert coordinates to and from W3W
https://www.dcode.fr/what3words-coordinates

Regulations for dispersed camping in National Forests
https://www.fs.usda.gov/Internet/FSE_DOCUMENTS/fseprd908212.pdf

Interactive Map of all National Forests
https://www.fs.usda.gov/ivm/
dispersed camping is allowed in all national forests

Federal Wilderness regulations
https://www.fs.usda.gov/Internet/FSE_DOCUMENTS/stelprdb5270137.pdf

Long Distance Hiker application and info
http://explorenct.info/NoCoLo/

North Dakota

Lake Sakakwea State Park map
https://www.parkrec.nd.gov/sites/www/files/documents/Destinations/Lake%20Sakakawea/lssp_main_map.pdf

Chain of Lakes maps
https://www.usbr.gov/gp/dkao/col/

Fort Ransom State Park map
https://www.parkrec.nd.gov/sites/www/files/documents/Destinations/Fort%20Ransom/FRSP_main_map.pdf

Sheyenne National Grasslands map
https://www.fs.usda.gov/Internet/FSE_DOCUMENTS/fseprd902400.pdf

Minnesota

Dispersed camping on MN state land
https://www.dnr.state.mn.us/state_forests/dispersed-camping.html

Tax-forfeit land
http://www.revisor.mn.gov/rules/6100.1350

Maplewood State Park map
https://gdrs.dnr.state.mn.us/gdrs/apps/pub/us_mn_state_dnr/mndnr_geopdf_download/State_Parks/Maplewood%20Summer%20GEO.pdf

Itasca State Park maps
https://www.dnr.state.mn.us/state_parks/park.html?id=spk00181#maps

Mesabi Trail maps
https://mesabitrail.com/trail-maps/

Lake Vermillion- Soudan Underground Mine SP map
https://files.dnr.state.mn.us/maps/state_parks/spk00285.pdf

Judge Magney State Park map
https://files.dnr.state.mn.us/maps/state_parks/spk00193.pdf

Cascade River State Park map
https://files.dnr.state.mn.us/maps/state_parks/spk00133.pdf

Temperance River State Park map
https://files.dnr.state.mn.us/maps/state_parks/spk00268.pdf

George H. Crosby Manitou State Park map
https://files.dnr.state.mn.us/maps/state_parks/spk00163.pdf

Tettegouche State Park map
https://gdrs.dnr.state.mn.us/gdrs/apps/pub/us_mn_state_dnr/mndnr_geopdf_download/State_Parks/Tettegouche%20GEO.pdf

Split Rock Lighthouse State Park map
https://files.dnr.state.mn.us/maps/state_parks/spk00266_summer.pdf

Gooseberry Falls State Park map
https://files.dnr.state.mn.us/maps/state_parks/spk00172_summer.pdf

Jay Cooke State Park map
https://files.dnr.state.mn.us/maps/state_parks/spk00187_summer.pdf

Wisconsin

Wisconsin use of state lands regulations
https://docs.legis.wisconsin.gov/code/admin_code/nr/001/45

Douglas County dispersed camping permit
https://douglascountywi.gov/DocumentCenter/View/14431/DCF_Special_Camping_Permit_Application_012624_CURRENT?bidId=

DNR page that says no dispersed in BRSF
https://dnr.wisconsin.gov/topic/parks/camping/backpack

Pattison State Park map
https://embed.widencdn.net/pdf/download/widnr/zlqq0qifpu/Pattison_Area-Map.pdf?u=lk8nsc&showinbrowser=true

Copper Falls State Park maps
https://dnr.wisconsin.gov/topic/parks/copperfalls/maps

Stricker Road Flow Gage for Tyler Forks
waterdata.usgs.gov/monitoring-location/04026561

Michigan

Dispersed camping allowed in state forests with free permit
https://www.michigan.gov/-/media/Project/Websites/dnr/Documents/Forms/folder2/PR4134_CampRegCard.pdf?

State Game Areas and State Wildlife Areas allow dispersed camping only from

Sep 11 - May 14 with the same free permit. Note additional regulations on page 2.
https://www.michigan.gov/-/media/Project/Websites/dnr/Documents/Forms/folder2/PR4134_CampRegCard.pdf?

List of all State Parks
https://www2.dnr.state.mi.us/parksandtrails/Default.aspx#list

List of State Game Areas with links to maps
https://www.michigan.gov/dnr/things-to-do/hunting/where/state-wildlife-game-areas-list

Porcupine Mountain Wilderness State Park map
https://www.michigandnr.com/Publications/PDFS/RecreationCamping/Porkies_Unit.pdf

Victoria Dam Flow Levels
https://www.uppco.com/hydro-water-levels/

Craig Lake State Park map
https://www.michigandnr.com/Publications/PDFS/RecreationCamping/craig_lake_map.pdf

Pictured Rocks Planner
https://www.nps.gov/piro/planyourvisit/upload/Backcountry_Travel_Planner_2021_508.pdf

Muskallonge State Park map
https://www.michigandnr.com/Publications/PDFS/RecreationCamping/muskallonge_lake_map.pdf

Tahquamenon Falls State Park map
https://www2.dnr.state.mi.us/Publications/PDFS/RecreationCamping/tahquamenon_backcountry_map.pdf

Straits State Park map
https://www.michigandnr.com/Publications/PDFS/RecreationCamping/straits_map.pdf

Wilderness State Park map
https://www.michigandnr.com/Publications/PDFS/RecreationCamping/wilderness_map.pdf

Petoskey State Park map
https://www.michigandnr.com/Publications/PDFS/RecreationCamping/petoskey_map.pdf

Jordan Valley Pathway Loop map
https://www2.dnr.state.mi.us/Publications/PDFS/RecreationCamping/Jordan_Valley_Pathway_Map.pdf

Fife Lake Loop Trail map
https://s26514.pcdn.co/wp-content/uploads/2018/09/CAVB-Trailmaps_2019-fifelakeloop-update.pdf

Manistee River Trail Loop map
https://www.fs.usda.gov/Internet/FSE_DOCUMENTS/fseprd493793.pdf

Barry SGA map
https://www2.dnr.state.mi.us/publications/pdfs/huntingwildlifehabitat/sga/Barry_SGA_map.pdf

Lost Nation State Game Area map
https://www2.dnr.state.mi.us/publications/pdfs/huntingwildlifehabitat/sga/Lost_Nation_SGA_map.pdf

Ohio

Mary Jane Thurston State Park map
https://dam.assets.ohio.gov/image/upload/ohiodnr.gov/documents/parks/parkmaps/maryjthurstonparkmap.pdf

Independence Dam State Park map
https://dam.assets.ohio.gov/image/upload/ohiodnr.gov/documents/parks/parkmaps/independenceparkmap.pdf

Lake Loramie State Park map
https://dam.assets.ohio.gov/image/upload/ohiodnr.gov/documents/parks/parkmaps/lakeloramieparkmap.pdf

Reserve Five Rivers Metroparks Campsites:
Taylorsville, Island A, Eastwood A
https://www.metroparks.org/rentals-permits/reserve-a-campsite/

Greene County, Ohio
https://www.gcparkstrails.com/wp-content/uploads/2021/02/Trail-Camping-090222.pdf

John Bryan State Park map
https://dam.assets.ohio.gov/image/upload/ohiodnr.gov/documents/parks/parkmaps/johnbryancampmap.pdf

Jim Terrell Shelter and Riverside Park Campsites at Milford permit
http://cms6.revize.com/revize/milfordoh/Park%20Camping%20Permit%20UPDATED.pdf

East Fork State Park map
https://dam.assets.ohio.gov/image/upload/ohiodnr.gov/documents/parks/parkmaps/eastforkparkmap.pdf

East Fork State Park trail map
https://dam.assets.ohio.gov/image/upload/ohiodnr.gov/documents/parks/parkmaps/eastforktrailmap.pdf

Shawnee State Forest Backpacking Trail brochure
https://dam.assets.ohio.gov/image/upload/ohiodnr.gov/documents/forestry/maps/shawnee_backpack.pdf

Guide to Shawnee SF Backpacking Trail and map (may be out of date)
https://www.backpackohio.com/etrails/bpo_shawnee.pdf

Pike Lake State Park map
https://dam.assets.ohio.gov/image/upload/ohiodnr.gov/documents/parks/parkmaps/pikelakeparkmap.pdf

Scioto Trail State Park map
https://dam.assets.ohio.gov/image/upload/ohiodnr.gov/documents/parks/parkmaps/sciototrailparkmap.pdf

Tar Hollow State Forest Backpacking Trail map
https://dam.assets.ohio.gov/image/upload/ohiodnr.gov/documents/forestry/maps/tarhollow_backpack.pdf

Hocking Hills State Park map
https://dam.assets.ohio.gov/image/upload/ohiodnr.gov/documents/parks/parkmaps/hockinghillsparkmap.pdf

Hocking Hills Campground map
https://dam.assets.ohio.gov/image/upload/ohiodnr.gov/documents/parks/parkmaps/hockinghillscampmap.pdf

Lake Logan State Park map
https://dam.assets.ohio.gov/image/upload/ohiodnr.gov/documents/parks/parkmaps/lakeloganparkmap.pdf

Burr Oak State Park map
https://dam.assets.ohio.gov/image/upload/ohiodnr.gov/documents/parks/parkmaps/burroakparkmap.pdf

Wolf Run State Park map
https://dam.assets.ohio.gov/image/upload/ohiodnr.gov/documents/parks/parkmaps/wolfrunparkmap.pdf

Salt Fork State Park map
https://dam.assets.ohio.gov/image/upload/ohiodnr.gov/documents/parks/parkmaps/saltforkparkmap.pdf

Beaver Creek State Park map
https://dam.assets.ohio.gov/image/upload/ohiodnr.gov/documents/parks/parkmaps/beavercreekparkmap.pdf

Pennsylvania

Pennsylvania State Game Lands mapping center
https://www.pgc.pa.gov/HuntTrap/StateGameLands/Pages/default.aspx

McConnells Mill State Park map
https://elibrary.dcnr.pa.gov/GetDocument?docId=1737472&DocName=MCMI_ParkMap.pdf

Moraine State Park map
https://elibrary.dcnr.pa.gov/GetDocument?docId=1753227&DocName=MORA_ParkMap.pdf

Cook Forest State Park maps
https://www.dcnr.pa.gov/StateParks/FindAPark/CookForestStatePark/Pages/Maps.aspx

Allegheny Valley River Trail maps
https://www.avta-trails.org/maps.php

Complete Rules for Pennsylvania State Forests
https://elibrary.dcnr.pa.gov/GetDocument?docId=1738468&DocName=StateForestRules.pdf

Link to Reserve River Campsites
pennsylvaniastateparks.reserveamerica.com/permits/cook-forest-state-park/r/wildernessAreaDetails.do?contractCode=PA&parkId=880202

Allegheny National Forest map
https://www.fs.usda.gov/Internet/FSE_DOCUMENTS/fseprd506988.pdf

New York

NY State Forest Camping rules
https://dec.ny.gov/things-to-do/camping/state-land-rules

Rock City and McCarty Hill State Forest maps
https://extapps.dec.ny.gov/docs/lands_forests_pdf/maprockcitymccarty.pdf

Allegany State Park maps
https://parks.ny.gov/parks/1/details.aspx

Watkins Glen State Park map
https://parks.ny.gov/documents/parks/WatkinsGlenWatkinsGlenTrailMap.pdf

Robert H. Treman State Park map
https://parks.ny.gov/documents/parks/RobertHTremanParkMap.pdf

Baker Schoolhouse State Forest map
https://extapps.dec.ny.gov/docs/regions_pdf/bakerschoolhouse.pdf

Taylor Valley State Forest map
https://extapps.dec.ny.gov/docs/regions_pdf/taylorvalleysf.pdf

Morgan Hill State Forest map
https://extapps.dec.ny.gov/docs/regions_pdf/morganhillsf.pdf

Labrodor Hollow Unique Area map
https://extapps.dec.ny.gov/docs/regions_pdf/labhollowgeo.pdf

Pixley Falls State Park maps
https://parks.ny.gov/parks/pixleyfalls

Black River Wild Forest south map
https://extapps.dec.ny.gov/docs/lands_forests_pdf/mapblackriversouth.pdf

Black River Wild Forest north map
https://dec.ny.gov/sites/default/files/mapblackrivernorth.pdf

Moose River Plains Wild Forest north map
https://dec.ny.gov/sites/default/files/mapmooserivernorth.pdf

Moose River Plains Wild Forest south map
https://extapps.dec.ny.gov/docs/lands_forests_pdf/mapmooseriversouth.pdf

Perkins Clearing Easement map
https://dec.ny.gov/sites/default/files/mappcstfcel.pdf

Siamese Ponds Wilderness map
https://dec.ny.gov/sites/default/files/mapsiameseponds.pdf

Hoffman Notch Wilderness map
https://dec.ny.gov/sites/default/files/maphoffmannotch.pdf

Pharaoh Lake Wilderness map
https://dec.ny.gov/sites/default/files/mappharaohlk.pdf

Vermont

Vermont Dispersed Camping
https://fpr.vermont.gov/recreation/activities/camping/primitive-camping

Moosalamoo info
https://www.fs.usda.gov/Internet/FSE_MEDIA/stelprdb5315858.pdf

Green Mountain Club info on overnighting
https://www.greenmountainclub.org/the-long-trail/overnight-accommodations/

Published Works by Joan H. Young

Non-Fiction:
    North Country Cache: Adventures on a National Scenic Trail (2005 Independent Publishers, third place Regional Non-fiction)
    North Country Quest: Completing my National Scenic Trail Adventure
    How to Hike the North Country Trail: not quite a Guide
    Would You Dare?
    Devotions for Hikers
    Get Off the Couch with Joan
    Fall Off the Couch Laughing

Fiction:
Anastasia Raven Mysteries
    News from Dead Mule Swamp
    The Hollow Tree at Dead Mule Swamp
    Paddy Plays in Dead Mule Swamp
    Bury the Hatchet in Dead Mule Swamp
    Dead Mule Swamp Druggist
    Dead Mule Swamp Mistletoe
    Dead Mule Swamp Singer

Dubois Files Mysteries for Children
    The Secret Cellar
    The Hitchhiker
    The ABZ Affair
    The Bigg Boss
    The Lonely Donkey

Other
    Accidentally Yours- a chaotic collection of short works

About the Author

Joan H. Young has enjoyed the out-of-doors her entire life. Highlights of her outdoor adventures include Girl Scouting, which provided yearly training in camp skills, the opportunity to engage in a ten-day canoe trip, and numerous short backpacking excursions. She was selected to attend the 1965 Senior Scout Roundup in Coeur d'Alene, Idaho, an international event to which 10,000 girls were invited. She rode a bicycle from the Pacific to the Atlantic Ocean in 1986, and on August 3, 2010 became the first woman to complete the North Country National Scenic Trail on foot. Not content with one epic hike, she set off at the age of 73, in December 2021, to hike the NCT again, completing the adventure in June 2023. Her mileage total for this hike was 4815 miles. She often writes and gives media programs about her outdoor experiences.

In 2010 she began writing more fiction, including several award-winning short stories. *How to Hike the North Country Trail: not quite a Guide* is intended to help long-distance hikers of the NCT understand the history and various regulations along the trail.

Visit booksleavingfootprints.com for more information.

www.ingramcontent.com/pod-product-compliance
Lightning Source LLC
Chambersburg PA
CBHW070042080526
44586CB00013B/887